How To Get The Degree You Want

BEAR'S GUIDE
to Non-Traditional College Degrees

How To Get The Degree You Want

by John Bear, Ph.D.

Ten Speed Press

For Marina

TEN SPEED PRESS
P O Box 7123
Berkeley, California 94707

You may order single copies prepaid direct from the publisher
for $9.95 + $.75 for postage and handling (California residents
add 6% state sales tax; Bay Area residents add 6½%).

Library of Congress Catalog Number: 82-050905
ISBN: 0-89815-080-9

Book Design by Hal Hershey
Cover Design by Brenton Beck

Illustrations reproduced courtesy of
The Associated Students of The University of California, Berkeley
from the Blue and Gold Yearbook

10   9   8   7   6   5   4   3

Printed in the United States of America.

Contents

About the Author: His Life, His Biases, and a Request for Help

LIFE

I attended school at a time when non-traditional education virtually did not exist in the United States. I did my best to create my own alternative program within the traditional framework. From my junior year at Reed College through my Master's at Berkeley to my Ph.D. from Michigan State University, I always had at least one demanding off-campus job. I kept trying to relate my work as a newspaper reporter, prison psychologist, advertisement writer, and researcher at a school for the deaf, to what I was doing in school, generally with little support from the school or faculty.

I have taught at major universities (Iowa, Berkeley, Michigan State); worked as a business executive (Research Director for Bell & Howell's Education division); as Director of San Francisco's Center for the Gifted Child; and as consultant to organizations as diverse as General Motors, Xerox, Encyclopaedia Britannica, and The Grateful Dead.

Since 1974, I have devoted most of my time to investigating and writing about non-traditional education.

BIAS

As you read this book, you will learn that I am heavily biased. I have very strong opinions about which schools and programs are good, and which are not, and I don't hesitate to say so.

It is also the case that from time to time, I do consulting or advisory work for various schools. Over the years, several dozen schools have hired me, and paid me for my work, either in money, goods, or stock. This has absolutely no bearing on the opinions expressed in this book. Hundreds of excellent schools have never even taken me out to lunch, yet I recommend them highly, and will continue to do so. (I will also accept, if they do offer me lunch.) On the other side of the ledger, there is no way I can be persuaded to say good things about schools I don't like. My biases and opinions are my own, and not subject to outside influence from any direction.

HELP

This edition of my book is based, in part, on information and opinions sent to me by more than two thousand readers of earlier editions. I don't have a staff of researchers and investigators. I depend heavily on feedback from readers. If you are aware of schools or programs I have overlooked, good or bad, please let me know. If you disagree with my evaluation of a school, based on your own experience, don't hesitate to tell me. I may be biased, but I'm also relatively open-minded, and have changed my opinions on many schools (up or down) over the years.

You can reach me at this address:

Dr. John Bear
Ten Speed Press
PO Box 7123
Berkeley, CA 94707

Thank you.

Part One
Important Issues in Alternative Education

Chapter 1

Introduction: What Non-Traditional Education Is All About

The man on the telephone was so distraught, he was almost in tears. For more than twenty years, he had been in charge of sawing off dead tree branches for a large midwestern city. A new law in that city decreed that henceforth, all department heads would have to have a Bachelor's degree. If this man could not earn a degree within two years, he would no longer be permitted to continue in the job he had been performing satisfactorily for two decades.

It is an unfortunate but very real aspect of life today that a college or university degree is often more important than a good education, or substantial knowledge in your field, whether that field is nuclear physics or sawing off branches. It doesn't matter if you've been reading and studying and learning all your life. If you don't have a piece of imitation parchment that certifies you as a Bachelor, Master, or a Doctor, you are somehow perceived as less worthy, and are often denied the better jobs and higher salaries that go to degree holders.

In fact, as more and more degree-holders, from space scientists to historians, are unable to find employment in their specific fields, and move elsewhere in the job market, degrees have become more important than ever. If you were hiring an English teacher and had five applicants with comparable skills, but one had a Doctorate while the other four had Bachelor's degrees, who would probably get the job?

Never mind that a Ph.D. is no more necessary to teach high school English than a B.A. is needed to chop down trees. The fact is that degrees are extremely valuable commodities.

Happily, as the need for degrees has grown, so has their availability. Since the mid-1970's, there has been a virtual explosion in what is now commonly called "alternative education" or "non-traditional education" — ways of getting an education, or a degree (or both, if you wish) without sitting in classrooms day after day, year after year.

The rallying cry was, in fact, sounded in 1973 by Ewald B. Nyquist, then President of the wonderfully innovative University of the State of New York. He said:

"There are thousands of people . . . who contribute in important ways to the life of the communities in which they live, even though they do not have a college degree. Through native intelligence, hard work and sacrifice, many have gained in knowledge and understanding. And yet, the social and economic advancement of these people has been thwarted in part by the emphasis that is put on the possession of credentials. . . . As long as we remain a strongly credentialed society . . . employers will not be disposed to hire people on the basis of what they know, rather than on what degrees and diplomas they hold.

"If attendance at a college is the only road to these credentials, those who cannot or have not availed themselves of this route but have acquired knowledge and skills through other sources, will be denied the recognition and advancement to which they are entitled. Such inequity should not be tolerated."

Alternative education takes many forms: credit (and degrees) for life experience learning; for passing examinations; for independent study; for intensive study (e.g., ten hours a day for a month instead of one hour a day for a year); weekend schools, night schools, summer schools, correspondence study; study by tape or videocassettes; and much more.

This book endeavors to cover all these areas as completely as possible. Yet this is truly an impossible task. New programs are introduced literally every day. In recent years, an average of one new college or university has opened for business every week, while old, established universities are disappearing at the rate of two or three each month.

So, although the book is as current and correct as I can possibly make it, there are bound to be recent changes not covered, as well as, inevitably, errors and omissions. For all of these, I apologize now, and invite your suggestions and criticisms for the next edition. Thank you.

Perhaps the best way to make clear, in a short space, the differences between the traditional approaches to education and degrees, and the non-traditional or alternative approach, is to offer the following dozen comparisons.

Traditional education awards degrees on the basis of time served and credit earned.

Non-traditional education awards degrees on the basis of competencies and performance skills.

Traditional education bases degree requirements on the mediaeval formula of some generalized education and some specialized education.

Non-traditional education bases degree requirements on an agreement between the student and the faculty, aimed at helping the student achieve his or her career, personal, and professional goals.

Traditional education awards the degree when the student meets certain numerical requirements.

Non-traditional education awards the degree when the student's actual work and learning reach agreed-upon levels.

Traditional education considers the years from age 18 to age 22 as the period when a first degree should be earned.

Non-traditional education assumes learning is desirable at any age, and that degrees should be available to people of all ages.

Traditional education considers the classroom as the primary source of instruction and the campus as the center of learning.

Non-traditional education sees any part of the world as appropriate for some learning.

Traditional education believes in printed text materials as the principal learning resource.

Non-traditional education believes the range of learning resources is limitless, from the daily newspaper to personal interviews; from videocassettes to world travel.

Traditional faculty must have appropriate credentials and degrees.

Non-traditional faculty are judged on competency and personal qualities, in addition to credentials and degrees.

Traditional credits and degrees are based primarily on mastery of course content.

Non-traditional credits and degrees also take into consideration learning how to learn and integration of diverse fields of knowledge.

Traditional education cultivates dependence on authority through prescribed curricula, required campus residence, and required classes.

Non-traditional education cultivates self-direction and independence through planned independent study, both on and off campus.

Traditional curricula are generally oriented toward traditional disciplines and well-established professions.

Non-traditional curricula reflect the student's individual needs and goals and are likely to be problem-oriented, issue-oriented, and world-oriented.

Traditional education aims at producing ''finished products'' — students who are done with their education and ready for the job market.

Non-traditional education aims at producing lifelong learners, capable of responding through life to their own evolving needs and those of society.

Traditional education, to adapt the old Chinese saying, gives you a fish and feeds you for a day.

Non-traditional education teaches you how to fish, and feeds you for life.

Traditional education had nothing to offer the dead-tree-limb expert.

Non-traditional education made it possible for him to complete a good Bachelor's degree in less than a year, entirely by correspondence and at modest cost. His job is now secure.

Chapter 2

What Are Colleges and Universities and How Do They Work?

The question may sound trivial or inconsequential, but it turns out to be quite a complex issue, for which there is no simple answer at all.

Many state legislatures, mulling over laws that would govern the awarding of degrees, have fought with the problem of producing precise definitions of words like "college," and "university." (One school even tried to sue its state Department of Education to force them to define "educational process." The state managed to evade the suit.)

Some states have simply given the problem up as unsolvable, which is why they have virtually no laws governing higher education. Needless to say, this encourages the establishing and proliferation of degree mills and other bad schools in those states.

Other states have, from time to time, produced rather ingenious definitions, such as Ohio's (later repealed), stating that a "university" was anything that (a) said it was a university, and (b) had an endowment or facilities worth one million dollars. The assumption, of course, is that no degree mill could be so well endowed. (California had a similar law but the sum was only $50,000. That law is still on the books, although a few other requirements have been added. Still, there are hundreds of unaccredited "$50,000 schools" in California — a few very good, and some quite awful.) Indeed, at the time California Pacifica University was exposed as a flagrant diploma mill on CBS's *60 Minutes*, it was a legal school in California. The owner had bought a truckload of used books, declared them to have a value of $50,000, and consequently was licensed by the state.

The problem of definition is made even more complicated by the inconsistent way in which the words "college" and "university" are used.

In the United States, the two words are used almost interchangeably. Before long, they will probably mean exactly the same thing. Historically, a college has been a subdivision of a university. For instance, the University of California has, within its structure, a College of Liberal Arts, a College of Education, a College of Law, and so on.

But there are many degree-granting colleges that are not a part of any university, and there are universities that have no colleges in their structure. Also, there is an ever-growing trend for colleges to rename themselves as universities, either to reflect their growth, to enhance their image, or both. In the last few years, dozens of colleges, from Antioch in Ohio to San Francisco State in California have turned themselves into universities.

To make the situation even more complex, outside the United States, the word "college" rarely refers to a degree-granting institution, and often is used for what Americans call a high school. Many American personnel managers and admissions officers have been fooled by this fact. An Englishman, for instance, who states on his job application, "Graduate of Eton College," means, simply, that he has completed the high school of that name.

Many readers have told me that they simply will not go to a "college," no matter how good it may be, because the word just doesn't sound real enough to them.

Finally, there are degree-granting institutions that have chosen a name other than ''college'' or ''university.'' The most common words used are ''school'' (e.g., the Union Graduate School) and ''institute'' (e.g., the International Institute for Advanced Studies).

HOW COLLEGES AND UNIVERSITIES WORK

The Calendar

There is no uniform pattern to the calendar, or scheduling of classes, from one school to the next. However, most schools tend to follow one of four basic patterns:

1. The Semester Plan

A semester is 16 to 18 weeks long and there are usually two semesters per year, plus a shorter summer session. Many classes are one semester long, while others will last two semesters or longer (e.g., Algebra I in the fall semester and Algebra II in the spring).

A class that meets three hours a week for one semester is likely to be worth three semester hours of credit. Depending on the amount of homework, additional reading, laboratory time, etc., the *actual* amount of credit could be anywhere from two to six semester hours for such a class.)

2. The Quarter Plan

Many universities divide the year into four quarters of equal length, usually 11 or 12 weeks. Many courses require two or more quarters to complete. A course that meets three hours a week for a quarter will probably be worth three ''quarter hours'' or ''quarter units,'' with a range of two to six. One ''semester unit'' is equal to one and a half ''quarter units.''

3. The Trimester Plan

A small minority of schools divide the year into three equal trimesters of 15 or 16 weeks each. A ''trimester unit'' is usually equal to one and one quarter semester units.

4. Other Alternatives

A model popularized by National University, the University of Phoenix, and other relatively new schools, is that of one course per month. Students can start on the first of any month, and the school offers one complete course, intensively, each month.

Many non-resident programs have no calendar at all. Students can begin work on their independent study program as soon as they have been admitted.

How Credit Is Earned

In a traditional school, most credit is earned by taking classes. Non-traditional units may be earned in many other ways. The most common methods are these four:

1. Life Experience Learning

Credit is given for what you have learned, regardless of how or where it was learned. For example, a given university might offer six courses in German worth four semester units each. If you can show them that you speak and write German just as well as someone who has taken and passed those six courses, then they will give you 24 semester units of German, no matter how you learned the language. The same philosophy is applied to business experience, flying an airplane, military training, and dozens of other non-classroom learning experiences.

2. Equivalency Examinations

Many schools say that if you can pass an examination in a subject, then you should get credit for knowing that subject, without having to sit in a classroom month after month to ''learn'' what you already know. More than 100 standard equivalency exams are offered, worth anywhere from two to 39 semester units each. In general, each hour of examination is worth anywhere from two to six semester units. But different schools may award significantly different amounts of credit for the same examinations. Some schools will design examinations in fields in which there are no standard exams.

3. *Correspondence Courses*

More than 60 universities offer thousands of home study courses, most of which may be taken by people living anywhere in the world. These courses are generally worth anywhere from two to six semester units each, and require anywhere from a month or two to a year or more to complete.

4. *Learning Contracts*

Quite a few schools will negotiate a learning contract with a student. A learning contract is a formal, negotiated agreement between the student and the school, stating that if the student does certain things (for instance, reads these books, writes a paper of this length, does the following laboratory experiments, etc.), then, on their successful completion, the school will award so many units of credit.

Learning contracts can be written for anywhere from a few units up to and including an entire degree program.

Each of these four methods of earning credit by alternative means will be discussed in some detail in later chapters.

Grading and Evaluation Systems

Most schools, traditional and non-traditional, make use of one of four common grading systems. Grades are generally given for each separate course taken. Some schools assign grades to equivalency examinations, learning contract work, and correspondence courses. Life experience credit is rarely graded, but rather is assigned a certain number of units, without further evaluation.

The four common systems are these:

1. *Letter Grades*

An "A" is the highest grade; "B" means "good," "C" means "average," "D" stands for "barely passing" (or, in some cases, "failing"). Some schools will use pluses and minuses, so that a "B+" is better than a "B," but not quite as good as an "A−."

2. *Number Grades*

Many schools use a system in which students are graded on a scale of zero (worst grade) to four (highest grade). The best students will get a 3.9 or 4.0. Other outstanding students might get a 3.7 or 3.8. Often, a 1.0 (or a 1.5) is the lowest passing score; anything lower is a failing score.

3. *Percentage Grades*

A smaller number of schools follow the European system, and grade each student in each class on a percentage score, from 0% to 100%. In most (but not all) schools, a grade of 90% to 100% is considered excellent, 80% to 90% is good, 70% to 80% is fair, 60% to 70% is either failure or barely passing, and below 60% is failing.

4. *Pass/Fail System*

Quite a few universities have inaugurated a pass/fail option, either for some classes or, more rarely, for all classes. In such a system, there is no specific evaluation of a student's performance — only the statement by the teacher that the student has either passed or failed the course. At many schools using this system, students are given the chance to choose a pass/fail option for one or two out of the four or five courses they might be taking during a given semester or quarter.

Grade Point Average

Most schools report a student's overall performance in terms of the "G.P.A." or Grade Point Average. This is the average of all grades received, weighted by the number of semester or quarter units each course is worth.

For example, if a student gets a 4.0 (or an "A") in a course worth 3 semester units, and a 3.0 (or a "B") in a course worth two semester units, his or her G.P.A. would be calculated like this: $3 \times 4 = 12$. And $2 \times 3.0 = 6$. Then $12 + 6 = 18$, divided by a total of five semester units = a G.P.A. of 3.6.

Pass/Fail courses are generally not taken into account in calculating a grade point average.

G.P.A.'s can be very important. Often it is necessary to maintain a certain average in order to earn a degree—typically a 2.0 for a Bachelor's degree, and a 3.0 for a Master's and a Doctorate. Honors degrees, scholarships, even permission to play on the football team, are dependent on the G.P.A. (No, non-resident schools do not have football teams. I keep waiting for a chess-by-mail league to spring up, however.)

Chapter 3

Degrees, Degree Requirements and Transcripts

A degree is a title conferred by a school to show that a certain course of study has been successfully completed. A diploma is the actual document or certificate that is given to the student as evidence of the awarding of the degree.

Diplomas are also awarded for courses of study that do not result in a degree, as, for example, on completion of a program in real estate management, air conditioning repair, or military leadership. This can lead to confusion, often intentional, as in the case of someone who says, "I earned my diploma at Harvard," meaning that he or she attended a weekend seminar there, at the end of which a Diploma of Completion was awarded.

The following six kinds of degrees are awarded by colleges and universities in the United States.

1. The Associate's Degree

The Associate's degree is a fairly recent development, reflecting the tremendous growth of two-year Community Colleges (which is the new and presumably more respectable name for what used to be known as Junior Colleges).

Since many students attend these schools for two years, but do not continue on to another school for the Bachelor's degree, a need was felt for a degree to be awarded at the end of these two years of full-time study (or their equivalent by non-traditional means). More than 2,000 two-year schools now award the Associate's degree, and a small but growing number of four-year schools also award them to students who leave after two years.

The two most common Associate's degrees are the A.A. (Associate of Arts) and the A.S. (Associate of Science). But more than 100 other titles have been devised, ranging from the A.M.E. (Associate of Mechanical Engineering) to the A.D.T. (Associate of Dance Therapy).

An Associate's degree typically requires 60 to 64 semester hours of credit (90 to 96 quarter hours), which, in a traditional program, normally takes four semesters, or six quarters, to complete.

2. The Bachelor's Degree

The Bachelor's degree has been around for hundreds of years. In virtually every nation of the world, it is the first university degree earned. (The Associate's is very little used outside the United States.) The traditional Bachelor's degree requires four years of full-time study (120 to 128 semester units, or 180 to 192 quarter units). In most of the rest of the world, it is three years. But through non-traditional approaches, people have earned Bachelor's degrees in as short a time as two or three months.

The Bachelor's degree is supposed to signify that the holder has accumulated a "batch" of knowledge; that he or she has learned a considerable amount in a particular field of study (the "major"), and some broad general knowledge of the world as well (history, literature, art, social science, science, mathematics). This broad approach to the degree is peculiar to traditional American programs. In many non-traditional programs, as well as in most other countries, Bachelor's degree studies are much more intense in a given field. When an Englishman says, "I read history at Oxford," he is saying that for the better part of three years he did, in fact, read history and not much else. This is one reason traditional American degrees take longer than most foreign ones.

More than 300 different Bachelor's degree titles have been used in the last hundred years, but the great majority of the million-plus Bachelor's degrees awarded in the United States each year are either the B.A. (Bachelor of Arts) or the B.S. (Bachelor of Science), sometimes with additional letters to indicate the field (e.g., B.S.E.E. for electrical engineering, B.A.B.A. for business administration, and so on). Other common Bachelor's degree titles include the B.B.A. (business administration), B.Mus. (music), B.Ed. (education), and B.Eng. (engineering). Some non-traditional schools or programs award the B.G.S. (general studies), B.I.S. (independent studies), and similar titles.

In the late 19th century, educators felt that the title of "Bachelor" was inappropriate for young ladies, so female graduates were often awarded titles such as Mistress of Arts or Maid of Science.

3. The Master's Degree

Until the 20th century, the Master's and the Doctor's titles were used somewhat interchangeably, as an appropriate title for anyone who had completed work of significance beyond the Bachelor's degree. But now a Master's is always the first degree earned after the Bachelor's, and is always considered inferior to the Doctorate.

The traditional Master's degree requires from one to two years of on-campus work after the Bachelor's. Some non-traditional Master's degrees may be earned entirely through non-resident study, while others require anywhere from a few days to a few weeks on campus.

There are several philosophical approaches to the Master's degree. Some schools (or departments within schools) regard it as a sort of advanced Bachelor's, requiring only the completion of one to two years of advanced-level studies and courses. Other schools or departments see it as a junior Doctorate, requiring a moderate amount of creative, original research, culminating in the writing of a thesis, or original research paper. Some programs give the student the option of choosing either approach: they may choose either to take, for example, ten courses and write a thesis, or thirteen courses with no thesis, to earn the degree.

And in a few world-famous schools, including Oxford and Cambridge, the Master's degree is an almost meaningless award, given automatically to all holders of their Bachelor's degree if they have managed, as the saying goes, to stay out of jail for four years, and are able to afford the small fee. (Most American schools had a similar practice at one time, but Harvard abolished it more than a century ago, and the rest followed suit soon after.)

Master's degree titles tend to follow closely those of Bachelor's degrees. The M.A. (Master of Arts) and M.S. (Master of Science) are by far the most common, along with the standby of American business, the M.B.A. (Master of Business Administration). Other common Master's degrees include the M.Ed. (education), M.Eng. (engineering), M.L.S. (library science), and M.J. (either journalism or jurisprudence).

4. The Doctorate

The term "Doctor" has been a title of respect for a learned person since Biblical times. Moses, in *Deuteronomy* 31:28 (Douay version) says, "Gather unto me all the ancients of your tribes and your doctors, and I will speak these words in their hearing."

But it was not until about 800 years ago that the first academic title was used, when outstanding scholars at the University of Bologna and the University of Paris were called either "Doctor" or "Professor" in the mid-12th century.

The first use of the title in America came in the late 17th century, under, as tradition has it, rather amusing circumstances. There had long been a tradition (and, to a large extent, there still is) that "it takes a Doctor to make a Doctor." In other words, only a person with a Doctorate can confer a Doctorate on someone else.

But in all of America, no one had a Doctorate, least of all Harvard's president, Increase Mather who, as a Dissenter, was ineligible for a Doctorate from any English university, all of which were controlled by the Church.

Still, Harvard was eager to get into the Doctorate business, so their entire faculty (that is to say, a Mr. Leverett and a Mr. Brattle) got together and unanimously agreed to award an honorary Doctorate to Mr. Mather, whereupon Dr. Mather was able to confer Doctorates upon his faculty and students.

This, in essence, was the start of graduate education in America, and there are those who say things have gone downhill ever since!

America's second doctorate, incidentally, was rather odd, too. It was the case that a British physician named Daniel Turner was eager to get into the Royal Society of Physicians and Surgeons, for which an M.D. was required. In England, then as now, most doctors have a Bachelor of Medicine; the Doctor of Medicine is an advanced medical degree. English universities would not give Turner a Doctorate because he did not belong to the Church. Scottish universities turned him down because he had published some unkind remarks about the quality of Scottish education. And of course no European university would give a degree to an Englishman. So Mr. Turner made a deal with Yale University.

Yale agreed to award Turner the Doctorate in absentia (he never set foot in America), and he, in turn, gave Yale a gift of 50 valuable medical books. Wags at the time remarked that the M.D. he got must stand for the Latin *multum donavit*, or, "he gave a lot."

Nowadays the academic title of "Doctor" (as distinguished from the professional and honorary titles, to be discussed shortly) has come to be awarded for completion of an advanced course of study, culminating in a piece of original research in one's field, known as the Doctoral thesis, or dissertation.

Traditional Doctorates generally require two years of on-campus study after the Master's degree, followed by the necessary research for the writing of the dissertation. The total elapsed time can be three to five years.

Many non-traditional Doctoral programs waive the necessity for on-campus study, on the assumption that the mature candidate already knows a great deal about his or her field. Such programs require only the writing of the dissertation, to demonstrate creativity.

Some non-traditional doctoral programs permit the use of work already done (books written, symphonies composed, business plans created, etc.) as partial (or, in a few cases, full) satisfaction of the dissertation requirement. But many schools insist on all, or almost all, new work.

The most frequently awarded (and, many people feel, the most prestigious) Doctorate is the Doctorate of Philosophy (known as the Ph.D. in North America, and the D.Phil. in many other countries). The Doctor of Philosophy need have nothing to do with the study of philosophy. It is awarded for studies in dozens of fields, ranging from chemistry to communication, from agriculture to aviation management.

> Until a few decades ago, the Ph.D. was also given as an honorary degree. But in the late 1930's, Gonzaga University in Spokane, Washington, spoiled the whole thing by handing out an honorary Ph.D. to one Harry Lillis "Bing" Crosby, to thank him for donating some equipment to the football team. Dr. Crosby made great sport about being a Doctor on his popular radio program that week. The academic world rose in distressed anger and that, effectively, was the end of the honorary Ph.D.

More than 500 other Doctorate titles have been identified in the English Language alone. After the Ph.D., the most common include the Ed.D. (education), D.B.A. (business administration), D.P.A. (public administration), D.A. (art or administration), Eng.D. (engineering), D.Sc. (science), and D.Hum. (humanities). The latter two often, but not always, are honorary in the U.S. and earned elsewhere.

A Bachelor's degree is almost always required for admission to a Doctoral program, and most traditional schools require a Master's as well. Many non-traditional programs will accept equivalent career experience in lieu of a Master's, and, in rare instances, in lieu of a Bachelor's as well.

5. Professional Degrees

Professional degrees are earned by people who intend to enter what are often called "the professions"—medicine, dentistry, law, the ministry, and so forth. In the United States, these degrees are almost always earned after completing a Bachelor's degree, and almost always carry the title of "Doctor" (e.g., Doctor of Medicine, Doctor of Divinity).

In many other countries, it is common to enter professional school directly from high school; then the first degree earned is a Bachelor's. (For instance, there is the British Bachelor of Medicine, whose holders are invariably called "Doctor," unless they have earned the advanced degree of "Doctor of Medicine," in which case they insist on being called "Mister." No one ever said the British were easy to understand.)

One exception in the United States is the D.C. (Doctor of Chiropractic), a program that students used to be able to enter right from high school, but which now requires two years of college, but no Bachelor's degree. This may be one reason so many medical doctors look down their noses at chiropractors.

Another exception used to be the law degree which, until the mid-1960's, was an LL.B., or Bachelor of Laws. Many lawyers objected to working three or four years beyond their Bachelor's degree simply to end up with another Bachelor's degree, while optometrists, podiatrists, and others were becoming doctors in the same length of time.

And so now it is the case that virtually every American law school awards a Doctorate as the first law degree. This degree is usually the J.D., which stands either for Doctor of Jurisprudence, or Juris Doctor.

All law schools offered their graduates with Bachelor of Law degrees the option of turning in their old LL.B. diplomas and, in effect, being retroactively Doctored with a J.D. The vast majority of lawyers accepted this unprecedented offer.

The LL.D., known both as Doctor of Law and Doctor of Laws, is used almost exclusively as an honorary title in the U.S., but is an earned advanced law degree elsewhere in the world.

The traditional law degree requires three years of study beyond the Bachelor's degree. Some non-traditional approaches will be discussed in chapter 21.

The only widely-accepted medical degree in America is the M.D. (Doctor of Medicine), which requires four years of study beyond the Bachelor's degree, although there are some shorter approaches, and some alternative ones, which will be discussed in chapter 22.

There are other medical or health specialties that have their own respectable professional Doctorate. These include, for instance, D.O. (osteopathy), D.P. (podiatry), and O.D. (optometry).

There are no accelerated approaches to the dental degree, and I'm not sure I'd want to go to any dentist who had taken shortcuts. The traditional dental degree for many years has been the D.D.S. (Doctor of Dental Surgery), although there has been a strong recent trend toward the D.M.D. (Doctor of Medical Dentistry). Either program requires four years of study beyond the Bachelor's degree.

More than 100 different professional degree titles have been identified in the area of religion. None can be said to be the standard one. There are the S.T.D. (sacred theology), D.Min. (ministry), Th.D. (theology), D.D. (divinity), D.Rel. (religion), D.S.R. (science of religion), and so forth, as well as the Ph.D. in religion. (The Canadian mathematician and humorist Stephen Leacock writes that shortly after he received his Ph.D., he was on board a cruise ship. When a lovely young lady fainted, the call went out, "Is there a doctor on board?" Leacock says he rushed to the Captain's cabin, but he was too late. Two D.D.'s and an S.T.D. had gotten there before him.)

There are quite a few other degrees that are regarded as honest professional titles by those who hold them, and are regarded with vigorously-raised eyebrows by many others. These include, for example, the N.D. (either naturopathy or naprapathy), D.Hyp. (hypnotism), H.M.D. or M.D.(H.) (homeopathic medicine), D.M.S. (military science), Met.D. (metaphysics), Graph.D. (graphoanalysis) and so forth.

> A young theologian named Fiddle
> Refused to accept his degree
> For said he, "Tis enough being Fiddle
> Without being Fiddle, D.D."
>
> — Traditional

6. Honorary Degrees

The honorary degree is indeed a stepchild of the academic world, and a most curious one at that. In fact, it has no more relationship or connection with academia than the basketball ace, "Doctor J," has with the world of medicine. It is, purely and simply, a title that some institutions (and some scoundrels) have chosen to bestow, from time to time, and for a wide variety of reasons, upon certain people. These reasons often have to do with the donation of money, or with attracting celebrities to a commencement ceremony.

The honorary Doctorate has no academic standing whatsoever, and yet, because it carries with it the same title, "Doctor," that is used for the earned degree, it has become an extremely desirable commodity for those who covet titles and the prestige they bring. For respectable universities to award the title of "Doctor" via an honorary Doctorate is as peculiar as if the Army were to award civilians the honorary title of "General" — a title the civilians could then use in their everyday life.

More than 1,000 traditional colleges and universities award the honorary Doctorate (anywhere from one to 50 per year, each), and a great many Bible schools, spurious schools, and degree mills hand them out with wild abandon to almost anyone willing to pay the price. The subject will be discussed in detail in Chapter 25.

TRANSCRIPTS

A transcript is, quite simply, the official record of all the work one has done at a given university. While the diploma is the piece of paper (or parchment) that shows that a given degree has been earned, the transcript is the detailed description of all the work done to earn that degree.

Typically, a transcript will be a typewritten (or, more typically nowadays, a computer-printed) sheet of paper listing in columns all the courses taken, when taken, and the grade received. The overall G.P.A. (grade point average) is calculated as of the end of each semester or quarter.

Nearly all non-traditional schools and programs issue transcripts as well. Sometimes they try to make the transcripts look as traditional as possible, listing, for instance, aviation experience as "Aviation 100, 4 units," "Aviation 101, 3 units," etc. Other programs offer a narrative transcript, in which the procedures used by the school in evaluating the experience are described.

The original copy of a transcript is always kept by the university. Official copies, bearing the raised seal of the university, can be made for the student, other schools, or employers, at the student's request.

Unfortunately, there is a great deal of traffic in forged transcripts. Sometimes students will change a few grades to improve the G.P.A., or add entire classes. Of course such changes would be on the copy only. For this reason, most schools and many employers will only accept transcripts that are sent directly from the Office of the Registrar of the university.

Chapter 4

Is a Degree Worth the Effort?

The simple answer, I believe, is this: *Yes* for non-traditional degrees; quite possibly *No* for traditional degrees.

Let me first elaborate on why I think the non-traditional degree is worth the effort, and then offer arguments on why the old-fashioned way may not be worth it.

WHY THE NON-TRADITIONAL DEGREE MAKES SENSE

Much depends on the degree itself, and on the reasons for wanting it. If, for instance, a Bachelor's degree is required for a job, a promotion, or a salary increase, then the accredited degree of the University of the State of New York, earned 100% by correspondence courses, is exactly as good as any Bachelor's degree earned by sitting in classrooms for four years at a state university.

As another example, a non-resident Doctorate, earned by a combination of life experience credit and new work, from one of the better unaccredited, state-licensed universities, such as Columbia Pacific University, may be of minimal value in getting a faculty position at Harvard. But such degrees have proved useful in many cases for advancement in business, government, and industry, not to mention doing wonders for self-image and the respect of others.

Finally a Doctorate purchased for a hundred bucks from a no-questions-asked degree mill may ultimately bring shame, public embarrassment, loss of job, and even a fine and imprisonment.

This covers the full range of possible outcomes. Many non-traditional degrees are good for most people in most situations. But there can be major exceptions, which is why it pays to check out the school in advance (this book is a good place to start), and to make as sure as you can that the degree you seek will satisfy any gatekeepers who may appear on your path.

Let's look at the six main reasons why people choose to pursue non-traditional degrees, and the kinds of degrees that may be most appropriate:

1. Job or salary advancement in business. Many job descriptions in business and industry specify that a certain degree is required, or that additional salary will be paid, if a certain degree is held. In the large majority of these situations, a good, unaccredited degree will suffice. One survey, for instance, asked the top personnel officers of more than 80 large corporations if a non-traditional degree would be acceptable to them, and 100% said yes.

But it is crucial to find out in advance. I have heard from dozens of people who spent many thousands of dollars on degree programs, only to find that the degree they earned was not acceptable to their employer or potential employer.

2. Job or salary advancement in education. The academic world has been more reluctant to accept unaccredited degrees than has the world of business or government. Even some excellent, accredited, non-traditional degrees have occasionally caused problems. However, the situation remains extremely variable. It is almost impossible to draw general rules or conclusions. Many universities refuse to consider hiring a faculty member with an unaccredited degree, or to admit people with such degrees into their graduate programs. Others welcome them. And the most enlightened schools consider each case on its own merits.

Once I surveyed a group of school board presidents, to determine their boards' policies on paying salary increments to district teachers who completed Master's or Doctorates. The results were evenly divided into four categories. About one fourth said the degrees had to be accredited. Another quarter said they could be unaccredited. Twenty-five percent said they judge each case individually. And the remainder either didn't understand the difference between accredited and unaccredited degrees, or said that no one had ever asked the question so there was no policy.

Once again, the watchword is to check in advance before spending any money with any school.

3. Job or salary advancement in the professions. When a profession must be licensed by the state or trade organization, that body often has certain degree requirements. Depending on the state, this may apply to psychologists, marriage counselors, engineers, accountants, real estate brokers, social workers, hypnotists, masseurs, and others. There is absolutely no pattern here in the acceptability of non-traditional degrees, other than a clear trend in favor of their increased acceptance.

Nonetheless, in one state, a psychologist must have a traditionally accredited Doctorate while a civil engineer with sufficient career experience may have an unaccredited degree or no degree at all. In another state, it may be just the opposite. Many regulations are exceedingly unclear on this subject, so a judgment is made in each individual case. Once again, it is crucial to determine in advance if a given degree will meet a given need.

4. Admission to traditional graduate schools. The trend is strongly in the direction of increased acceptance of alternative degrees, including the better unaccredited degrees, for admission to Master's and Doctoral programs at traditional universities. For example, one highly regarded, unaccredited program (International College) reports that its students have transferred to more than thirty traditional universities, getting credit for their work at International. Another unaccredited school (Columbia Pacific University) has letters from Harvard, Yale and Princeton, among others, indicating a willingness to consider their students for admission to graduate school.

5. Self-satisfaction. This is a perfectly good reason for wanting a degree, and no one should ever feel embarrassed for so wanting. Many of my counseling clients seek a degree (generally a Doctorate) for self-satisfaction, to gain respect from others, to feel more comfortable with colleagues, or to "validate" a long and worthwhile career. Such people are generally well satisfied with a degree from one of the better, more respectable unaccredited schools. One of the main criteria to consider here is avoidance of potential embarrassment. More than one holder of a degree from a legitimate, but not especially good, non-traditional school has suffered extreme discomfort or embarrassment when newspaper articles or television stories on the school made big local waves.

6. Fooling people. An alarming number of people want fake degrees for all manner of devious purposes. After CBS broadcast a splendid segment on degree mills on *60 Minutes,* they received a huge number of telephone calls from people wanting to know the address and phone numbers of the fake schools they had just exposed!

Almost every week I hear from people who would like "a Doctorate from Harvard University, please, with no work required, and can it be back-dated to 1974?" The best I can do is warn these people that they are endangering their reputations (and possibly their freedom) by considering such a course. Then I usually suggest that if they must have a degree by next Tuesday, they consider a degree from a far-less-dangerous, second-rate Bible college. Nothing to be especially proud of, but less hazardous to one's health.

WHY THE TRADITIONAL DEGREE
MAKES LESS SENSE THAN THE NON-TRADITIONAL

People attend traditional colleges for a great many different reasons, as Caroline Bird writes in her fascinating book, *The Case Against College*:

> "A great majority of our nine million post-secondary students who are 'in college' are there because it has become the thing to do, or because college is a pleasant place to be . . . because it's the only way they can get parents or taxpayers to support them without working at a job they don't like; because Mother wanted them to go; or for some reasons utterly irrelevant to the course of studies for which the college is supposedly organized."

Basically, I think, there are two main reasons people go to college: either to get an education or to get a degree. The two can be quite independent. There are those who only care about the training; there are those who only want the degree; and there are those who want or need both.

Sadly, there is a strong trend in America toward what David Hapgood calls *"Diplomaism"* in his book of that title. He writes:

> "We are well on our way to repealing the American dream of individual accomplishment and replacing it with a system in which the diploma is the measure of a man, a diploma which bears no relation to performance. The career market is closing its doors to those without degrees. . . . Diplomaism zones people into a set of categories that tends to eliminate the variety and surprise of human experience.
>
> "In a system run by diplomas, all avenues to personal advancement are blocked except one: the school that gives the diploma. . . . when we leave the institution, like carcasses coming off a packing plant's assembly line, an anonymous hand affixes an indelible stamp . . . which thereafter determines what we can do, and how we shall be rewarded. And that stamp, unlike the imprint on a side of beef, reflects neither our personal value to the society, nor the needs of the economic system."

There are, in fact, three major problem areas with traditional schools and traditional degree programs:

1. There may be liitle connection between degrees earned traditionally, and on-the-job performance.

2. There is much evidence that vast numbers of students are spending huge amounts of time being trained for jobs that simply do not exist.

3. It may well be that the cash investment in a traditional college education is an extremely poor investment indeed.

Let us consider each of these three problem areas.

Traditional College Training Versus On-The-Job Performance

Many studies have found little or no relationship between these two factors, and some have even found a negative relationship. One extensive study, by Ivar Berg of Columbia University, published under the delightful title, *Education and Jobs: The Great Training Robbery,* looked at various jobs in which people with degrees and people without were doing identical work. In many situations, there was no difference in performance by the degreed and non-degreed people, and in a few jobs (including air traffic controllers and pants makers), the people without degrees were doing a better job!

Sadly, Berg also found that many bosses either ignored or refused to believe the evidence that had been collected in their own offices and factories. For instance, in one big chemical firm where the laboratory workers without traditional degrees were out-performing those with degrees, the management steadfastly maintained its policy of promoting only those employees with degrees.

Hapgood believes that personnel practices at such firms are not likely to be changed in the forseeable future, because "employers made it clear they were demanding diplomas for reasons that had little to do with job performance." The real reasons, he thinks, had to do with conformity to the dominant culture and with the "ability" to stay in school for four or more years. "It proves that he was docile enough (or good or patient or stupid enough; choose your own adjective) to stay out of trouble for 13 or 17 or 20 years in a series of institutions that demand a high degree of unthinking conformity."

I was given similar responses when I surveyed the personnel managers of major airlines. Almost all require an accredited Bachelor's degree, but they don't care whether the degree is in aviation or Chinese history. The important thing, they say, is the discipline of being able to complete a degree program.

Whatever the reasons, the system is a confused and disarrayed one, with the one strongly positive note being the increasing acceptance of non-traditional degrees, whose holders often have far more practical knowledge and experience through on-the-job training than those who learned about the subject in the college classroom.

There are ever-growing numbers of employers who will say, for instance, that you learn more about practical journalism in your first two weeks working on a daily newspaper than in four years of journalism school. (The same goes for law, advertising, and dozens of other fields.) And the person who has both the experience and the non-traditional degree based, at least in part, on that experience, may be in the best situation of all.

It used to be the case that many employers denied jobs to people without degrees, even if the degree had nothing to do with the ability to peform the job. Now, following a key decision by the Supreme Court (*Griggs vs. Duke Power Company, 1971*), employers must prove that a degree is required to do a certain job or they cannot discriminate against those without them. This is equally true for high school diplomas, Doctorates, and everything in between.

Is a Traditional College Degree Useful in Today's Marketplace?

Once I worked as an assistant to the psychologist in a state prison. The prison was very proud of its vocational training program. It operated a large cotton mill, where the inmates learned how to run the equipment and, in fact, made their own prison uniforms. But when they got out of prison, they learned that not only was the equipment they had learned to operate hopelessly out of date, but the nearest large cotton mill was 2,000 miles away! No wonder many of them returned to a life of crime.

Much the same sort of thing goes on in traditional colleges and universities. As an example, through the 1960's, hundreds of thousands of students were told about the great teacher shortages that were coming, so they graduated with degrees in education. But, as Alexander Mood wrote in a report for the Carnegie Commission:

"It has been evident for some time to professors of education that they were training far more teachers than would ever find jobs teaching school, but few of them bothered to mention that fact to their students. That is understandable, of course, since their incomes depend on having students."

And so, by the 1980's, we find thousands of people with Doctorates teaching in high school; people with Master's degrees teaching first grade; and an awful lot of people with Bachelor's degrees in education waiting on tables and doing office work.

The business world is not exempt. A survey by the *Wall Street Journal* found copious numbers of highly disillusioned M.B.A. students and recent graduates. "I wouldn't have come here and spent all that money if I had known it would be this tight," said one jobless M.B.A. "Graduate school was a waste of time," said another, after ten months of fruitless searching for a business job. But cheer up. The president of the Association of MBA Executives Inc. says things will be much better by 1990.

These problems are by no means confined to education and business. In virtually any field you look at, from space science to civil engineering, you find lots of well-trained and unemployed practitioners. In one recent year, for instance, there were over 100,000 graduates in the field of communications, and about 14,000 new jobs in the communications industries. Five thousand anthropology graduates are finding about 400 job openings in their field. And so it goes.

According to Bird, "Law Schools are already graduating twice as many new lawyers every year as the Department of Labor thinks will be needed. . . ." Mood says that "in the past, the investment in higher education did at least pay off for most students; that is, they did get access to higher-status jobs; now for the first time in history, a college degree is being judged by many parents and students as not worth the price. They see too many of last year's graduates unable to find work, or taking jobs ordinarily regarded as suitable for high school graduates. . . . Moreover, this is not a temporary phenomenon."

The Bureau of Labor Statistics says that about 25% of college graduates entering the labor market are getting jobs previously held by people without degrees. That doesn't mean the degrees are needed to perform those jobs, of course, but only that there are millions of job-seekers with degrees who cannot find jobs requiring their degrees.

So the outlook for the traditional degree is rather bleak. People will continue to pursue them for the wrong reasons, and industry will continue to require them for the wrong reasons. And enlightened people of all ages will, more and more, come to realize that a non-traditional degree can do just about anything a traditional one can — with a much smaller expenditure of time, effort, and money.

Is Pursuing a Traditional Degree Worth the Cost?

Just what is the cost? Anything I write today will be out of date tomorrow, because traditional college costs are escalating so fast. In 1980, the average cost of attending a private college for four years in the United States was in excess of $37,000, including tuition, room and board, books, etc. At public colleges, the average cost was "only" around $21,000.

Based on a highly conservative rate of academic inflation of 6% (most schools do try to hold the line, but there are limits to how much they can do), here is how things look in years to come:

YEAR	4 YRS. PRIVATE COLLEGE	4 YRS. PUBLIC COLLEGE
1980	$37,000	$21,000
1985	$48,000	$28,000
1990	$65,000	$38,000
1995	$87,000	$50,851

The time will come when many people will not be able to afford to pursue a traditional college degree. And yet the value of the degree, in terms of higher salary, increased likelihood of getting better jobs, and personal satisfaction, is well demonstrated. The gap, however, is narrowing. In the early 1970's, the average Bachelor's degree holder was earning about 53% more than the average high school graduate. By the early 1980's, this was down to a 35% advantage. It is not, however, that the degree holders are earning less. Rather, the non-degreed people are earning more.

But even the 35% is indeed substantial. And the gap grows much larger when you take into account Master's, Doctorates, and professional degrees. From the most recent census data, here are the average lifetime earnings for males, based on levels of education. The amount shown is total lifetime earnings, from age eighteen to retirement or death:

Less than 8 years of school: $336,000

Finished 8th grade: $414,000

Attended high school, did not graduate: $468,000

High school graduate, did not go to college: $576,000

Attended college for 1 to 3 years: $654,000

Bachelor's degree: $852,000

Master's degree: $1,140,000

Doctorate: $1,380,000

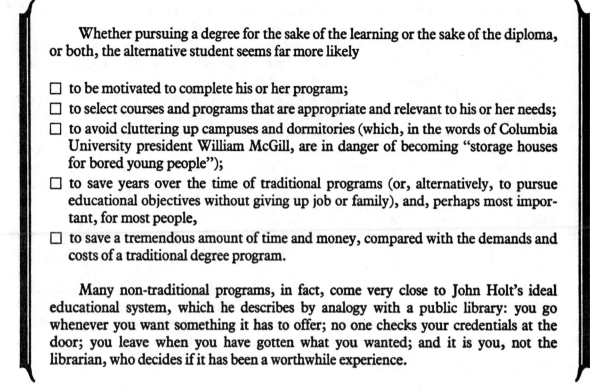

Whether pursuing a degree for the sake of the learning or the sake of the diploma, or both, the alternative student seems far more likely

☐ to be motivated to complete his or her program;

☐ to select courses and programs that are appropriate and relevant to his or her needs;

☐ to avoid cluttering up campuses and dormitories (which, in the words of Columbia University president William McGill, are in danger of becoming "storage houses for bored young people");

☐ to save years over the time of traditional programs (or, alternatively, to pursue educational objectives without giving up job or family), and, perhaps most important, for most people,

☐ to save a tremendous amount of time and money, compared with the demands and costs of a traditional degree program.

Many non-traditional programs, in fact, come very close to John Holt's ideal educational system, which he describes by analogy with a public library: you go whenever you want something it has to offer; no one checks your credentials at the door; you leave when you have gotten what you wanted; and it is you, not the librarian, who decides if it has been a worthwhile experience.

Another way of looking at this is that the average 40-year-old man who finished high school is earning about $17,000 a year, while the average 40-year-old man with a Bachelor's degree is earning about $27,000 a year.

So it may look, to an 18-year-old on the brink of either college or a job, as if taking four years off to earn a Bachelor's degree is going to be worth more than $250,000 in the long run. However, Caroline Bird thinks that if the only reason people go to college is to make more money, then higher education is a truly dumb financial investment.

She argues this way (I have adapted her 1976 figures to the reality of the vastly higher interest rates of the 1980's): The average Princeton graduate will have spent about $50,000 to get a degree, including tuition, room and board, books, travel, etc. If that sum of money were put, instead, into money market accounts earning 13% interest, by the age of 65, never having done a day's work, that person would have over twelve million dollars! That, needless to say, is about fifty times more than the "mere" $250,000 additional that the average Bachelor's degree holder makes in a lifetime.

Of course most people wouldn't have the $50,000 to invest at age 18. But Bird argues that if one enters the job market at 18, the earnings over the next four years, plus, presumably, some advance from parents on what they would otherwise have spent on college tuition, wisely invested, would produce a similar result.

A recent study by Drs. J. H. Hollomon of the Massachusetts Institute of Technology and Richard Freeman of Harvard University concludes that "in the brief span of about five years, the college job market has gone from a major boom to a major bust. Large numbers of young people, for the first time, are likely to obtain less schooling and potentially lower occupational status than their parents."

All well and good, I suppose. But none of these people takes non-traditional education and degrees into account. Bird and others have produced some powerful reasons not to pursue a traditional degree. But it is now possible, and will become increasingly easier, to earn degrees at low cost while remaining fully employed, thereby having the best of both worlds.

WHERE, THEN, ARE THINGS GOING?

One message of Charles Reich's fascinating book, *The Greening of America,* is that things are happening now that have never happened before; that for the first time, the standards and lessons of the past may have no relevance for the future.

Things are indeed changing almost amazingly fast in higher education. The direction in which they are changing is away from traditional education and degrees toward alternative higher education and non-traditional degrees.

It is always difficult—and challenging—to live in a time of great change. On one hand, we have some universities, today, that cannot or will not invite people like Buckminster Fuller, Andrew Wyeth, or Eric Hoffer to lecture, because they have never earned a college degree. And on the other hand, we have people earning higher degrees entirely by correspondence, entering prestigious doctoral programs without even a high school diploma, and earning law degrees without ever seeing the inside of a law school.

A quarter of a century ago, if you wanted to earn a degree without sitting in classrooms for three or four years, and wanted to remain in North America, you had exactly two legal alternatives: the University of London and the University of South Africa, both of which have offered non-resident external degree programs for many years. Today you have a choice of hundreds of alternative degree programs, from the Bachelor's level through the Doctorate and professional degrees—and there are many, many more on the drawing boards all over the world.

At the same time, predictably, traditional universities and colleges are really hurting financially, due to decreased enrollments and rising costs. Unprecedented numbers of traditional schools are simply going out of business, and many others are almost frantically implementing non-traditional programs as a last resort to stay afloat financially. Things can only grow worse for traditional schools, as the declining birth rate of the late 1960's and 1970's starts showing up at college age level during the 1980's.

Alternative education and the non-traditional degree seem, indeed, to be the wave of the educational future.

Chapter 5

Using Titles

There is a question that arises regularly in my degree counseling practice: "If I earn a degree, especially an alternative or non-traditional degree, in what way am I entitled to use the degree, and the title that comes with it (in the case of Doctorates), in my life and career?"

There is no simple answer to this question, since rules and regulations vary from state to state, and from profession to profession. But the basic philosophy of whatever laws there are regulating degrees is essentially the same: You can probably do almost anything you want in the way of titles, as long as you do not do it with the intent of deceiving anyone.

No one ever had Colonel Sanders arrested for pretending to be a military officer, nor is Doc Severinsen in danger of prosecution for impersonating a physician. However, when a man gets a job (as in a recent, well-publicized case) as a meteorologist for a television station, using the title of "Doctor," and that is a degree he never earned, then there is a major problem, because it can be reasonably assumed that the title helped him get the job—even if he was performing his duties satisfactorily without benefit of doctoral training.

In general, as long as the degree comes from an unquestionably legal and legitimate school, there is usually no problem in using that degree in public life, as long as all local and licensing requirements are met.

In some states, a "quickie" Doctorate from a one-room Bible School is sufficient to set up practice as a marriage counselor and psychotherapist. In other states, with stiffer licensing requirements, this same behavior could result in major legal problems.

The use of degree titles varies considerably from profession to profession, and from nation to nation. Most people in the United States do not append a Bachelor's degree notation to their letterhead or signature, while in most of the rest of the world, it is quite common to see, for instance, "John Martinson, B.A.." The name or abbreviation of the school is often appended, as well: "John Martinson, B.A. (Oxon)" or "B.A. (Cantab)" indicating that the degree is from Oxford or Cambridge.

Master's degrees are commonly used in print in the United States, especially the M.B.A. (e.g., "Richard Jaulus, M.B.A.").

Holders of a Doctorate almost always use it in their public or professional lives—with the curious exception of politicians. (Most prominent politicians with earned Doctorates, from Woodrow Wilson to George McGovern, seem to have gone to great lengths to avoid public disclosure of the degree. Perhaps there is merit to columnist Herb Caen's belief that people will never vote for anyone they think is more intelligent than they are!)

There are, and probably always will be, educational conservatives who decry the use of non-traditional (and particularly unaccredited non-traditional) titles. A typical situation has occurred in the field of electrical engineering, where a gentleman in New York formed the "Committee of Concerned E.E.'s" for the purpose of carrying on a vigorous campaign against the right of electrical engineers with unaccredited Doctorates to use the title of "Doctor." The journals in this field often carry articles and letters from people on various sides of this issue.

Despite the complaints of Thomas Carlyle regarding the "peculiar ambition of Americans to hobble down to posterity on crutches of capital letters," Americans are far less likely than Europeans and Asians to use all the letters at their command. Whereas a typical Englishman will list all his degrees, and perhaps a few fellowships besides (e.g., Kenneth Matheson, B.A., M.A., Ph.D. F.R.S., L.C.P.), most Americans would use only their highest degree (e.g., Donald Kirkpatrick, Ph.D.), unless they have more than one Doctorate, in which case both would be listed (e.g., Carole Raye, M.D., Ph.D.).

Not everyone agrees with this. The President of California Christian University, for instance, regularly uses all nine of his claimed Doctorates, with his Civil Service rank (G.S.9) thrown in between Doctorates number four and five, for good measure. And then there was the chap who wrote to me from Massachusetts, using these letters after his name: L.R.A., M.N.G.S., B.S.A. When I asked, he replied that the letters stood for Licensed Real Estate Agent, Member of the National Geographic Society, and Boy Scouts of America.

Holders of honorary Doctorates are treading on far more dangerous ground when they use their degrees in public, especially if such degrees were purchased "over the counter," no matter how legally. Still, public figures from Dr. Billy Graham to Dr. Edward Land, founder of Polaroid, regularly use the title "Doctor" based on honorary degrees from major universities.

Nonetheless, if an insurance agent makes a sale, if a clergyman makes a convert, or if a teacher makes a salary increase that can be attributed, even in part, to the prestige of being called "Doctor," and if that Doctorate is unearned, then the claim can always be made that that person is acting, at least in part, on false pretenses.

Another category of title abusers are those people who use degrees they never earned. What surprises me is how many of them there are. When the head of a major motion picture studio got into legal troubles a few years back, a sidelight of the case was that the degree he said he had from Yale University turned out to be non-existent. At the time, Yale revealed that they keep files on all cases of publicly-claimed Yale degrees that are lies, and that to date they had logged more than 7,000 such claims!

It seems reasonable to hypothesize that these 7,000 are just the tip of the iceberg. Untold thousands of others are going about free, only because so few people ever bother to check up on other people's degrees. Most exposures happen in connection with other events, such as the case of the young woman whose 1981 Pulitzer Prize was taken away when it turned out she had falsified her story on a young drug addict. It also turned out that she had listed two degrees she had never earned on her *Washington Post* job application.

People rarely check up on other people's degrees. Do you know, for instance, where your own doctor, lawyer, and accountant earned their degrees? Have you checked with the schools just to be sure? A diploma on the wall is not sufficient evidence. I know of three different places where people can buy fake diplomas from any school, printed to order for a modest sum. A Doctorate from Harvard, for instance, would cost about $50. What if your family doctor knows the same place? (No, I am not going to give out their names and addresses; they do enough damage in the world as it is.)

This topic moves very rapidly from the abstract to the concrete when something happens nearby. It was clearly brought home to me a few years ago when a locally prominent "certified public accountant," living just down the road from us hurriedly packed his shingle and left town. One of his clients had decided to check, and found out that he simply did not have the credentials he said he had.

So then, in your own situation, common sense should be sufficient to make your decision on how to use a degree in almost any situation. Where there is any doubt at all about using a given degree or title, it may be wise to seek legal advice, or at the very least to check with the relevant state agencies—generally the state education department (see Chapter 6), or the appropriate licensing agencies.

And in general, it isn't a bad idea to worry just a little about other people's degrees and titles. A lot of fakes and frauds are out there right now, practicing medicine, teaching classes, practicing law, counseling troubled families, building bridges, pulling teeth, and keeping books, without benefit of a degree, a license, or proper training. If more people would ask a few more questions about the title before the name, or the document on the wall, these dangerous phonies would be stopped before they do more harm to us all. Almost all schools will confirm, either by mail or by telephone, whether or not a given person has indeed earned a degree from them. This is not an invasion of privacy, since the facts are known as "directory information" available to the public through printed directories or publicly accessible university information files.

(Glad you asked. My own Ph.D. was awarded by Michigan State University, East Lansing, Michigan, on March 19, 1966, and you are most welcome to check it out with them.)

Chapter 6

How to Evaluate a School

Once, I was walking down a city street with an investigative reporter for a large newspaper. "You know," he said, "I could go into any building on this block — that office, that hospital, that laundromat, that factory — and given enough time and money, I would find a story there that would probably make page one."

The same is very likely true of virtually every school in this book, from Harvard on down. Some simply have a lot more skeletons in a lot more closets than others.

There are many times, indeed, when I wish I had an army of trained investigators and detectives at my disposal. With very limited resources and manpower, I cannot do a detailed and intensive investigation of every single school. Happily, I have received a great deal of assistance from readers of this book, who have followed my advice on checking out a school and have reported their findings to me.

Here, then, is the four-step procedure I recommend for investigating schools that are not covered in this book, or further looking into those that are. And please, if you do this, share your research with me. The address appears on page 1. (Thank you.)

STEP ONE: CHECK IT OUT IN THIS BOOK

If it isn't here, it may be because the school is very new, or because I didn't consider it sufficiently non-traditional for inclusion — or quite possibly because I simply missed it. And even if it is listed here, don't take my opinions as the Gospel Truth. Hardly a day passes that I don't get a letter challenging my opinions. Sometimes they begin, "You idiot, don't you know that . . ." and sometimes they begin, "I beg to differ with you in regard to. . . ." Whatever the tone, I am always glad to have these opinions. There have been quite a few instances where such a letter spurred me to look more closely at a school, resulting in a revised opinion, either upward or downward.

STEP TWO: CHECK IT OUT WITH FRIENDS, COLLEAGUES, OR EMPLOYERS

If the degree is needed for a new job, a salary increase, or a state license, be sure to find out specifically if this degree will suffice before you invest any money in any school. Many schools will gladly enter into correspondence with employers, state agencies, or others you may designate, to explain their programs and establish their credentials.

In my counseling practice, I regularly hear from people who have lost thousands of dollars, and wasted incredible amounts of time, in completing a degree that was useless to them. "But the school said it was accredited," they lament.

STEP THREE: CHECK IT OUT WITH THE STATE AGENCY

Every state has an agency which oversees higher education. Check the school out with the agency in your state or in the state in which the school is located. A list of these agencies is given at the end of the chapter. Some correspondence schools are well-known (positively or negatively) to the Better Business Bureau as well.

STEP FOUR: CHECK OUT THE SCHOOL ITSELF

Visit the campus or the offices if at all possible, or if you have any doubts. If the school's literature does not make clear the precise accreditation status, and if you still have any questions, check with the appropriate accrediting agency. They are all listed in Chapter 7. If the accreditor is not listed in Chapter 7, be careful. There are a lot of phony accrediting agencies in operation.

These are some of the questions you may wish to ask:

☐ How many students are currently enrolled? (Curiously, quite a few schools seem reluctant to reveal these numbers. Sometimes it is because they are embarrassed about how large they are, as, for instance, in the case of one alternative school that at one time had more than 3,000 students and a faculty of five! Sometimes it is because they are embarrassed about how small they are, as is the case with one heavily-advertised school, with impressive literature, extremely high tuition, and fewer than 50 students.)

☐ How many degrees have been awarded in the last year?

☐ What is the size of the faculty? How many of these are full-time and how many are part-time? From which schools did the faculty earn their degrees?

☐ From which school(s) did the president, the dean, and other administrators earn their own degrees? (There is nothing inherently wrong with staff members earning degrees from their own school, but when the percentage doing so approaches 100%, as it does at some institutions, it starts sounding a little suspicious to me.)

☐ May I have the names and addresses of some recent graduates in my field of study, and/or in my geographical area?

☐ May I look at the work done by students? (Inspection of some of the Master's theses and Doctoral dissertations can often give a good idea of the quality of work expected, and of the caliber of the students.)

☐ Will your degree be acceptable for my intended needs (state licensing, certification, graduate school admission, salary advance, new job, whatever)?

☐ What exactly is your legal status, with regard to state agencies and to accrediting associations? If accreditation (or candidacy for accreditation) is claimed, is it with an agency that is approved either by the U.S. Department of Education or the Council on Postsecondary Accreditation? If not accredited, are there any plans to seek accreditation?

No legitimate school should refuse to answer questions like these. Remember, you are shopping for something that may cost you several thousand dollars, or more. It is definitely a buyers' market, and the schools all know this. If they see that you are an informed customer, they will know that they must satisfy you or you will take your business elsewhere.

Remember, too, that alternative education does not require all the trappings of a traditional school. Don't expect to find a big campus with spacious lawns, an extensive library, or a football team. Some outstanding non-traditional schools are run from relatively small suites of rented offices.

Another thing I've learned is that you cannot go by the catalogue or other school literature alone. Some really poor schools and some outrageous degree mills have hired good writers and designers, and have produced very attractive catalogues, albeit ones that are full of lies and misleading statements. A common trick, for instance, is to show a photograph of a large and impressive building, which may or may not be the building in which the school rents a room or two, but the implication is that "This is our world headquarters." Another common occurrence is to list a large number of names of faculty and staff, sometimes with photographs of their smiling faces. My files are full of certified, deliver-to-addressee-only letters sent to these people, that have been returned as undeliverable.

On the other side of the ledger, it is also the case that some good, sincere, legitimate schools have issued typewritten and mimeographed catalogues, either to save money or to go along with their low-key images.

STATE AGENCIES FOR HIGHER EDUCATION

These are the agencies in each state, and the District of Columbia, that oversee higher education. If you have any concerns about the legality of an institution, or its right to award degrees, these are the places to ask.

ALABAMA
Commission on Higher Education, 1 Court Square, Montgomery 36104, 205/832-6555.

ALASKA
Commission on Postsecondary Education, Pouch F State Office Building, Juneau 99811, 907/465-2854

ARIZONA
Board of Regents, 1535 West Jefferson, Suite 121, Phoenix 85007, 602/255-4082

ARKANSAS
Department of Higher Education, 1301 West 7th St., Little Rock 72201, 501/371-1441

CALIFORNIA
Postsecondary Education Commission, 1020 12th St., Sacramento 95814, 916/445-7933

COLORADO
Commission on Higher Education, 1550 Lincoln St., Denver 80203, 303/839-2723

CONNECTICUT
State Board of Higher Education, 340 Capitol Ave., Hartford 06115, 203/566-3913

DELAWARE
Postsecondary Education Commisson, 1228 N. Scott St., Suite 1, Wilmington 19806, 302/571-3240

DISTRICT OF COLUMBIA
Commission on Postsecondary Education, 1329 E St. N.W., Washington 20004, 202/727-3685

FLORIDA
State schools: Board of Regents, 107 W. Gaines St., Tallahassee 32301, 904/488-4234
Private schools: State Board of Independent Colleges and Universities, Department of Education, Tallahassee 32301, 904/488-8695

GEORGIA
Board of Regents, 244 Washington St. S.W., Atlanta 30334, 404/656-2202

HAWAII
Postsecondary Education Commission, 2444 Dole St., Honolulu 96822, 808/948-6862

IDAHO
Board of Education, 650 W. State St., Boise 83720, 208/384-2270

ILLINOIS
Board of Higher Education, 4 W. Old Capitol Square, Springfield 62701, 217/782-2551

INDIANA
Commission for Higher Education, 143 W. Market St., Indianapolis 46204, 317/633-6474

IOWA
Board of Regents, Lucas State Office Building, Des Moines 50319, 515/281-3934

KANSAS
Board of Regents, Merchants National Bank Tower, Topeka 66612, 913/296-3421

KENTUCKY
Council on Higher Education, West Frankfort Office Complex, Frankfort 40601, 502/564-3553

LOUISIANA
Louisiana Proprietary School Commission, P.O. Box 44064, Baton Rouge 70804, 504/342-3543

MAINE
Board of Trustees, 107 Maine Ave., Bangor 04401, 207/947-0336

MARYLAND
State Board for Higher Education, 16 Francis St., Annapolis 21401, 301/269-2971

MASSACHUSETTS
Board of Higher Education, 31 St. James Ave., Boston 02118, 617/727-5360

MICHIGAN
State Board of Education, P.O. Box 30008, Lansing 48909, 517/373-3354

MINNESOTA
Higher Education Coordinating Board, 400 Capitol Square, St. Paul 55101, 612/296-3974

MISSISSIPPI
Board of Trustees of State Institutions of Higher Learning, P.O. Box 2336, Jackson 39205, 601/982-6611

MISSOURI
Coordinating Board for Higher Education, 600 Monroe Ave., Jefferson City 65101, 314/751-2361

MONTANA
Board of Regents of Higher Education, 33 S. Last Chance Gulch, Helena 59601 (isn't this a wonderful address!), 406/449-3024

NEBRASKA
Coordinating Commission for Postsecondary Education, 301 Centennial Mall South, Box 95005, Lincoln 68509, 402/471-2847

NEVADA
Board of Regents, 405 Marsh Ave., Reno 89509, 702/784-4901

NEW HAMPSHIRE
Postsecondary Education Commission, 61 S. Spring St., Concord 03301, 603/271-2555

NEW JERSEY
Board of Higher Education, 225 W. State St., Trenton 08625, 609/292-4310

NEW MEXICO
Board of Educational Finance, 1068 Cerillos Rd., Santa Fe 87503, 505/827-2115

NEW YORK
Regents of the University of the State of New York, Department of Education, Albany 12234, 518/474-5844

NORTH CAROLINA
Board of Governors of the University of North Carolina, Box 2688, Chapel Hill 27514, 919/933-6981

NORTH DAKOTA
State Board of Higher Education, State Capitol Building, Bismarck 58505, 701/224-2960

OHIO
Board of Regents, 30 E. Broad St., Columbus 43215, 614/466-6000

OKLAHOMA
State Regents for Higher Education, 500 Education Building, State Capitol Complex, Oklahoma City 73105, 405/521-2444

OREGON
Education Coordinating Commission, 495 State St., Salem 97310, 503/378-3921

PENNSYLVANIA
State Board of Education, Box 911, Harrisburg 17126, 717/787-5041

RHODE ISLAND
Board of Regents for Education, 199 Promenade St., Providence 02908, 401/277-2088

SOUTH CAROLINA
Commission on Higher Education, 1429 Senate St., Columbia 29201, 803/758-2407

SOUTH DAKOTA
State Department of Education, Board of Regents, Pierre 57501, 605/773-3455

TENNESSEE
Higher Education Commission, 501 Union Building, Suite 300, Nashville 37219, 615/741-3605

TEXAS
Coordinating Board, Texas College and University System, P.O. Box 12788, Capitol Station, Austin 78711, 512/475-4361

UTAH
State Board of Regents, 807 East South Temple St., Salt Lake City 84102, 801/533-5617

VERMONT
State College Board of Trustees, P.O. Box 349, Waterbury 05676, 802/244-7871

VIRGINIA
State Council of Higher Education, 700 Fidelity Building, 9th and Main Streets, Richmond 23219, 804/786-2143

WASHINGTON
Council for Postsecondary Education, 908 E. Fifth Ave., Olympia 98504, 206/753-3241

WEST VIRGINIA
Board of Regents, 950 Kanawha Blvd. East., Charleston 25301, 304/348-2101

WISCONSIN
Board of Regents, 1860 Van Hise Hall, 1220 Linden Drive, Madison 53706, 608/262-2324

WYOMING
Board of Trustees, P.O. Box 3434, University Station, Laramie 82071, 307/766-4121

Chapter 7 Accreditation

Accreditation is perhaps the most complex, confusing, and important issue in higher education. It is surely the most misunderstood and the most misused concept—both intentionally and unintentionally.

In selecting a school, there are three important things to know about accreditation: what it is, why it may be important for certain situations, and what are the different kinds of accrediting associations?

WHAT IS ACCREDITATION?

Quite simply, it is a validation—a statement by a group of persons who are, theoretically, impartial experts in higher education—that a given school, or department within a school, has been throughly investigated and found worthy of approval.

Accreditation is a peculiarly American concept. In every other country in the world, all colleges and universities either are operated by the government, or gain the right to grant degrees directly from the government. In the United States, accreditation is an entirely voluntary process, done by private, non-governmental agencies. As a result of this lack of central control or authority, there have evolved good accrediting agencies and bad ones, recognized ones and unrecognized ones, legitimate ones and phony ones.

So when a school says "We are accredited," that statement alone means nothing. The question must always be asked, "Accredited by whom?" Unfortunately, many consumer-oriented articles and bulletins simply say that one is much safer dealing only with accredited schools—but do not attempt to unravel the complex situation. I hear regularly from distressed people who say, about the degrees they have just learned are worthless, "But the school was accredited; I even checked with the accrediting agency." The agency, needless to say, turned out to be as phony as the school.

The wrong kind of accreditation can be a lot worse than none at all.

Normally a school wishing to be accredited will make application to the appropriate accrediting agency. After a substantial preliminary investigation to determine that the school is probably operating legally and is run legitimately, it may be granted correspondent status. Typically this step will take anywhere from several months to several years or more, and when completed does not imply any kind of endorsement or recommendation, but merely an indication that the first steps on a long path have been taken.

Next, teams from the accrediting agency, often composed of faculty of already-accredited institutions, will visit the school. These "visitations," conducted at regular intervals throughout the year, are to observe the school in action, and to study the copious amounts of information that the school must prepare, relating to its legal and academic structure, educational philosophy, curriculum, financial status, planning, and so forth.

After these investigations and, normally, at least two years of successful operation (sometimes a great deal more) the school may be advanced to the status of "candidate for accreditation." Being a candidate means, in effect, "Yes, you are probably worthy of accreditation, but we want to watch your operation for a while longer." This "while" can range from a year or two to six years or more. The great majority of schools that reach candidacy status eventually achieve full accreditation. (The terms "accredited" and "fully accredited" are used interchangeably.)

Once a school is accredited, it is visited by inspection teams at infrequent intervals (five to ten years is common) to see if it is still worthy of its accreditation. The status is always subject to review at any time, should new programs be developed or should there be any significant developments, positive or negative, in the life of the school.

THE IMPORTANCE OF ACCREDITATION

Although accreditation is undeniably important to both schools and students or would-be students, this importance is undermined and confused by three factors:

1. There are no national standards for accreditation. What is accreditable in New York may not be accreditable in California. The demands of the groups that accredit schools of chemistry may be very different from the people who accredit schools of forestry. And so on.

2. Many very good schools (or departments within schools) are not accredited, either by their own choice (since accreditation is a totally voluntary procedure), or because they are too new (all schools were unaccredited at one time in their lives), or too experimental (many would say too innovative) for the generally conservative accreditors.

3. Many very bad schools claim to be accredited—but it is always by unrecognized, often non-existent accrediting associations, often of their own creation.

Still, accreditation is the only widespread system of school evaluation that we have. A school's accreditation status can be helpful to the potential student in this way: While many good schools are not accredited, it is very unlikely that any very bad or illegal school is authentically accredited. (There have been exceptions, but they are quite rare.)

In other words, authentic accreditation is a pretty good sign that a given school or program is legitimate. But it is important to remember that lack of accreditation need not mean that a school is either inferior or illegal.

I stress the term *authentic* accreditation, since there are very few laws or regulations anywhere governing the establishment of an accrediting association. Anyone can start a degree mill, then turn around and open an accrediting agency next door, give his school its blessing, and begin advertising "fully accredited degrees."

The crucial question, then, is this: Who accredits the accreditors?

WHO ACCREDITS THE ACCREDITORS?

There are two agencies, one private and one governmental, that have responsibility for evaluating and approving or recognizing accrediting agencies.

The Council on Postsecondary Accreditation (known as COPA), is a nationwide non-profit corporation, formed in 1975, to evaluate accrediting associations and award recognition to those found worthy.

Within the Department of Education is the Eligibility and Agency Evaluation Staff (EAES), which is required by law to "publish a list of nationally recognized accrediting agencies which [are determined] to be reliable . . . as to the quality of training offered." This is done as one measure of eligibility for federal financial aid programs for students.

EAES has the job of deciding whether unaccredited schools can qualify for federal aid programs, or their students for veterans' benefits. This is done primarily by determining whether credits from any given unaccredited school have been accepted by at least three accredited schools. If they have, then the unaccredited school is recognized by the Department of Education for that purpose.

An already complex situation is confused almost beyond belief by several other factors. One is the Reagan administration's announced plan to dissolve the Department of Education entirely. No one can say what effect this will have, although one probable outcome is that each of the fifty states may end up going into the accreditation business and/or the accrediting agency recognition business. Another is a proposal being entertained by the Department of Education that it get entirely out of the evaluation process, and leave it up to each state. A third is rather frequent in-fighting between COPA and EAES as to who has jurisdiction in various situations.

ACCREDITATION AND NON-TRADITIONAL EDUCATION

One of the frequent complaints levied against the recognized accrediting agencies is that they have, in general, been slow to acknowledge the major trend to alternative or non-traditional education.

A few years ago, the Carnegie Commission on Higher Education conducted research on the relationship between accreditation and non-traditional approaches. Their report, written by Alexander Mood, confirmed that a serious disadvantage of accreditation is "in the suppression of innovation. Schools cannot get far out of line without risking loss of their accreditation — a penalty which they cannot afford."

Also, the report continues, "loss of accreditation implies that the curriculum is somewhat inferior and hence that the degree is inferior. Such a large penalty . . . tends to prevent colleges from striking out in new directions. . . . As we look toward the future, it appears likely that accrediting organizatons will lose their usefulness and slowly disappear. Colleges will be judged not by what some educational bureaucracy declares but by what they can do for their students. Of much greater relevance would be statistics on student satisfaction, career advancement of graduates, and data like that."

Faced with high-powered criticism of this sort, some accrediting agencies sponsored (with a major grant from the Kellogg Foundation) a large-scale study of how the agencies should deal with non-traditional education.

The four-volume report of the findings of this investigation said, in summary, very much what the Carnegie report had to say. The accreditors were advised, in effect, not to look at the easy quantitative factors (percentage of Doctorate-holders on the faculty, books in the library, student-faculty ratio, acres of campus, etc.), but rather to evaluate the far more elusive qualitative factors, of which student satisfaction and student performance are the most crucial.

In other words, if the students at a non-traditional, non-resident university regularly produce research and dissertations that are as good as those of traditional schools or if graduates of non-traditional schools are as likely to gain admission to graduate school or high-level employment and perform satisfactorily there — then the non-traditional school may be just as worthy of accreditation as the traditional school.

Accrediting agencies move slowly. Various committees and commissions are studying this Kellogg report, and others like it, and perhaps some of its recommendations will one day be implemented. Most non-traditional schools are not holding their collective breaths awaiting any such action, although eventually either it must come, or, as the Carnegie report predicts, the traditional accreditors will fade away.

THE APPROVED ACCREDITING AGENCIES

There are six Regional Associations, each with responsibility for schools in one region of the United States and its territories. Each one has the authority to accredit an entire college or university. There are also about eighty Professional Associations, each with authority to accredit either specialized schools or specific departments or programs within a school.

Thus it may be the case, for instance, that the North Central Association (one of the six Regional

Associations) will accredit Dolas University. When this happens, the entire school is accredited, and all its degrees may be called accredited degrees, or, more accurately, degrees from an accredited institution.

Or it may be the case that just the art department of Dolas University has been accredited by the relevant Professional Association, in this case the National Association of Schools of Art. If this happens, then only the art majors at Dolas can claim to have accredited degrees.

So if an accredited degree is important for you, the first question to ask is, "Has the school been accredited by one of the six Regional Associations?" If the answer is no, then the next question is, "Has the department in which I am interested been accredited by its relevant Professional Association?"

There are those jobs (psychology and nursing are two good examples) in which professional accreditation is more important than regional accreditation. In other words, even if a school is accredited by its regional association, unless its psychology department is also accredited by the American Psychological Association, its degrees will be less useful for psychology majors.

The final confusion in this matter is that some accrediting agencies are officially recognized by the U.S. Department of Education; some are recognized by the Council on Postsecondary Accreditation (the private non-governmental agency), some by both, and some by neither. There actually are situations where it is important to know which national agency has recognized an accreditor, although by and large, if either one has, that is good enough. Totally unrecognized agencies may still be quite legitimate, or they may be quite phony. Some of the unrecognized ones will be discussed after the following listing of the recognized ones. Each of the approved accreditors will gladly supply lists of all the schools (or departments within schools) they have accredited, and those that are candidates for accreditation and in correspondent status. They will also answer any questions pertaining to any school's status (or lack of status) with them.

THE TWO AGENCIES THAT RECOGNIZE ACCREDITING AGENCIES

Department of Education, Division of Eligibility and Agency Evaluation, Bureau of Postsecondary Education, Washington DC 20202, 202/245-9873

Council on Postsecondary Accreditation, One Dupont Circle N.W., Suite 760, Washington DC 20036, 202/452-1443

REGIONAL ACCREDITING ASSOCIATIONS AND THEIR GEOGRAPHICAL AREAS

Delaware, District of Columbia, Maryland, New Jersey, New York, Pennsylvania, Canal Zone, Puerto Rico, Virgin Islands.
Middle States Association of Colleges and Schools
3624 Market St., Philadelphia PA 19104, 215/662-5600.

Arizona, Arkansas, Colorado, Illinois, Indiana, Iowa, Kansas, Michigan, Minnesota, Missouri, Nebraska, New Mexico, North Dakota, Ohio, Oklahoma, South Dakota, West Virginia, Wisconsin, Wyoming.
North Central Association of Colleges and Schools
1221 University Avenue, Boulder CO 80302, 800/525-0840

Alaska, Idaho, Montana, Nevada, Oregon, Utah, Washington.
Northwest Association of Schools and Colleges
3700B University Way N.E., Seattle WA 98105, 206/543-0195

Alabama, Florida, Georgia, Kentucky, Louisiana, Mississippi, North Carolina, South Carolina, Tennessee, Texas, Virginia.
Southern Association of Colleges and Schools
795 Peachtree St., N.E., Atlanta GA 30365, 404/897-6126

Connecticut, Maine, Massachusetts, New Hampshire, Rhode Island, Vermont.
New England Association of Schools and Colleges
131 Middlesex Turnpike, Burlington MA 01803, 617/272-6450

California, Hawaii, Guam, Trust Territory of the Pacific.
Western Association of Schools and Colleges
Box 9990, Mills College, Oakland CA 94613, 415/632-5000

PROFESSIONAL ACCREDITING ASSOCIATIONS

Unless otherwise indicated, these associations are recognized by both the Department of Education and the Council on Postsecondary Accreditation.

Architecture
National Architecture Accrediting Board, 1735 New York Ave. N.W., Washington DC 20006, 202/783-2007

Art
National Association of Schools of Art, 11250 Roger Bacon Drive, Reston VA 22090, 703/437-0700

Bible College Education
American Association of Bible Colleges, Box 1523, Fayetteville AR 72701, 501/521-8164

Blind and Visually Handicapped Education
National Accreditation Council for Agencies Serving the Blind and Visually Handicapped (not COPA), 79 Madison Ave., New York NY 10016, 212/683-8581

Business
American Assembly of Collegiate Schools of Business, 11500 Olive Street Road, St. Louis MO 63141, 314/872-8481
Association of Independent Colleges and Schools (not COPA), 1730 M St. N.W., Washington DC 20036, 202/659-2460

Chemistry
American Chemical Society (COPA only), 1155 16th St. N.W., Washington DC 20036, 202/872-4589

Chiropractic
The Council on Chiropractic Education, 3209 Ingersoll Ave., Des Moines IA 50312, 515/255-2184

Clinical Pastoral Education
Association for Clinical Pastoral Education, 475 Riverside Drive, Room 450, New York NY 10027, 212/870-2558

Construction Education
American Council for Construction Education (COPA only), Box 1266, Manhattan KS 66502, 913/776-1544

Cosmetology
Cosmetology Accrediting Commission (not COPA), 1707 I St. N.W., Washington DC 20036, 202/331-9550

Dentistry
American Dental Association, 211 E. Chicago Ave., Chicago IL 60611, 312/440-2721

Dietetics
American Dietetic Association, 430 N. Michigan Ave., Chicago IL 60611, 312/280-5040

Engineering
Accrediting Board for Engineering and Technology, 345 E. 47th St., New York NY 10017, 212/705-7684

Forestry
Society of American Foresters, 5400 Grosvenor Lane, Washington DC 20014, 301/897-8720

Funeral Service Education
American Board of Funeral Service Education (not COPA), Box 2098, Fairmont WV 26554, 304/366-2403

Health Services Administration
Accrediting Commission on Education for Health Services Administration, One Dupont Circle N.W., Washington DC 20036, 202/659-4354

Home Economics
American Home Economics Association (COPA only), 2010 Massachusetts Ave. N.W., Washington DC 20036, 202/862-8355

Home Study Education
National Home Study Council, 1601 18th St. N.W., Washington DC 20009, 202/234-5100

Industrial Technology
National Association of Industrial Technology, Box 17074, Jacksonville FL 32216, 904/646-2684

Interior Design Education
Foundation for Interior Design Education Research, 242 W. 27 St., New York NY 10001, 212/929-8366

Journalism
American Council on Education for Journalism, 563 Essex Court, Deerfield IL 60015, 312/948-5840

Landscape Architecture
American Society of Landscape Architects, 1900 M St. N.W., Washington DC 20036, 202/466-7730

Law
American Bar Association, 735 W. New York St., Indianapolis IN 46202, 317/264-8071

Association of American Law Schools (COPA only), Suite 370, One Dupont Circle N.W., Washington DC 20036, 202/296-8851

Librarianship
American Library Association, 50 E. Huron St., Chicago IL 60611, 312/944-6780

Medical Assistant/Medical Laboratory Technician
Accrediting Bureau of Health Education Schools, 29089 U.S. 20 West, Elkhart IN 46514, 219/293-0124

Medicine
July 1 of odd-numbered years, through the following June 30: American Medical Association, 535 N. Dearborn St., Chicago IL 60610, 312/751-6310

July 1 of even-numbered years, through the following June 30: Association of American Medical Colleges, One Dupont Circle N.W., Washington DC 20036, 202/828-0670

Music
National Association of Schools of Music, 11250 Roger Bacon Drive, Reston VA 22090, 703/437-0700

Nursing
American Association of Nurse Anesthetists (not COPA), 111 E. Wacker Drive, Chicago IL 60611, 312/644-3093

National Association for Practical Nurse Education and Service, 254 W. 31 St., New York NY 10001, 212/736-4540

National League for Nursing, 10 Columbus Circle, New York NY 10019, 212/582-1022

Occupational, Trade, and Technical Education
National Association of Trade and Technical Schools, 2021 K St. N.W., Washington DC 20006, 202/296-8892

Optometry
American Optometric Association, 243 N. Lindbergh Blvd., St. Louis MO 63141, 314/991-4100

Osteopathic Medicine
American Osteopathic Association, 212 E. Ohio St., Chicago IL 60611, 312/280-5800

Paramedical Fields
The American Medical Association has separate accreditation programs for each of seventeen paramedical areas. The appropriate address is The American Medical Association, in care of one of the following programs, 535 N. Dearborn St., Chicago IL 60610, 312/751-6272.
Programs for the Blood Bank Technologist
Programs for the Cytotechnologist
Programs for the Histologic Technician
Medical Assistant Programs
Medical Laboratory Technician Programs
Programs for the Medical Record Administrator and Medical Record Technician
Programs for the Medical Technologist
Programs for the Nuclear Medicine Technologist
Programs for the Occupational Therapist
Programs for the Physical Therapist
Programs for the Assistant to the Primary Care Physician
Programs for the Radiation Therapy Technologist
Programs for the Radiographer
Programs for the Respiratory Therapist
Programs for the Surgeon's Assistant
Programs for the Surgical Technologist

Pharmacy
American Council on Pharmaceutical Education, One E. Wacker Drive, Chicago IL 60601, 312/467-6222

Physical Therapy
American Physical Therapy Association, 1156 15th St. N.W., Washington DC 20005, 202/466-2070 (see also PARAMEDICAL)

Podiatry
American Podiatry Association, 20 Chevy Chase Circle N.W., Washington DC 20015, 202/537-4970

Psychology
American Psychological Association, 1200 17th St. N.W., Washington DC 20036, 202/833-7600

Public Health
Council on Education for Public Health, 1015 15th St. N.W., Washington DC 20005, 202/789-1050

Rabbinical and Talmudic Education
Association of Advanced Rabbinical and Talmudic Schools (not COPA), 175 Fifth Avenue, New York NY 10010, 212/477-0950

Rehabilitation Counseling
Council on Rehabilitation Education (COPA only), 8 S. Michigan Ave., Chicago IL 60603, 312/332-7111

Social Work
Council on Social Work Education, 111 8th Ave., New York NY 10011, 212/242-3800

Speech Pathology
American Speech Language and Hearing Association, 10801 Rockville Pike, Rockville MD 20852, 301/897-5700

Teacher Education
National Council for the Accreditation of Teacher Education, 1919 Pennsylvania Ave. N.W., Washington DC 20006, 202/466-7490

Theology
The Association of Theological Schools in the United States and Canada, Box 130, Vandalia OH 45377, 513/898-4654

Veterinary Medicine
American Veterinary Medical Association, 930 N. Meacham Road, Schaumburg IL 60196, 312/885-8070

UNRECOGNIZED ACCREDITING AGENCIES

Although there are a great many so-called accrediting agencies that are not approved or recognized either by COPA or by the Department of Education, only one that is concerned with non-traditional schools is both clearly legitimate and pursuing such recognition. (Another, the Association of World Colleges and Universities, a highly reputable organization, has been dormant for some years.)

☐ National Association for Private Nontraditional Schools and Colleges
   1129 Colorado Ave., Grand Junction CO 81501

The National Association for Private Nontraditional Schools and Colleges (formerly the National Association for Schools and Colleges) is a serious and sincere effort to establish an accrediting agency specifically concerned with alternative schools and programs.

The National Association was established by a group of educators associated with Western Colorado University and still shares both office space and personnel with the University.

NAPNSC's standards for accreditation have grown stiffer and stiffer, over the years, and now are on a par with many traditional associations. They are still not recognized by either the Department of Education or by COPA, but that probably says as much about the confused state of the national education scene as it does about the National Association.

The National Association has plans to apply, again, for recognition, and no one can predict what will happen. In the meantime, it is fair to say that they are a legitimate, sincere, and respectable accrediting agency, with high standards.

OTHER ACCREDITING AGENCIES

There are several other accrediting agencies operating in the United States, that I find hard to recommend, for various reasons. Among them are the following:

☐ The International Accrediting Commission for Schools, Colleges and Theological Seminaries
   430 Geneva Avenue, Bellwood IL 60104

Formerly a part of the Accrediting Commission for Specialized Colleges (see next listing), IACSCTS separated from them in the late 1970's and moved from Indiana to Illinois.

The most curious thing about this agency is that they refuse to reveal the names of the schools they have accredited. It is hard to take such a group seriously. In past years, the Executive Director, Dr. George Reuter, acknowledged to me that he, too, was unable to find one of his accredited schools, when he went to St. Louis. (This particular school, National Graduate School, operates from a mail-forwarding service there — presumably a fully-accredited mail-forwarding service.)

Dr. Reuter says he is working to weed out the bad schools that have IACSCTS accreditation, but since he won't say who has been accredited, it is impossible to confirm this.

By its own definition, IACSCTS is essentially a religiously oriented organization. They request all member schools to state in their literature that the accreditor has "never requested listing by the Department [of Education] because of the philosophy of church and state conflict." This philosophy, however, has not prevented four legitimate religious accrediting agencies from seeking, and getting, such approval.

It also seems odd to me that an accreditor who falls back on the church-state separation argument will then go out and grant accreditation to a series of totally non-religious schools such as Century University, the International Institute for Advanced Studies, Kensington University, and California Western University. (All these schools, except Century, subsequently resigned from membership.)

☐ The Accrediting Commission for Specialized Colleges
   410 S. 10th St., Gas City IN 46933

ACSC was established by Bishop Gordon Da Costa and associates, from the address of Da Costa's Indiana Northern Graduate School. The above-described International Accrediting Commission separated from ACSC in the late 1970's and went its own way.

The accrediting procedures of ACSC seem superficial at best. The only requirement for becoming a candidate for accreditation is to mail in a check for $110. "Full accreditation" is only a little more difficult, it would appear. For instance, Century University in California received "full accreditation of all degree programs" less than two months after joining ACSC, and 34 days after its only on-site "visitation" — a one-day visit by the Executive Director of ACSC.

ACSC has written letters to the presidents of various independent unaccredited schools inviting them to pursue accreditation, pointing out that "to be accredited by us is good advertisement (sic) to have in your catalogue and other literature."

☐ Association of Career Training Schools
   (No address in their literature.)

A slick booklet provided to schools suggests, "Have your school accredited with the Association. Why? The Association Seal . . . could be worth many $ $ $ to you! It lowers sales resistance, sales costs [and] improves image."

☐ National Accreditation Association
   4606 Queensbury Rd., Riverdale MD 20840

Established in 1981 by Dr. Glenn Larsen, whose Doctorate is from the notorious Sussex College of Technology. His associate is Dr. Clarence Franklin, former President and Chancellor of American International University (see chapter on Diploma Mills). In a mailing to presidents of unaccredited schools, the N.A.A. offered full accreditation by mail, with no on-site inspection.

☐ International Commission for the Accreditation of Colleges and Universities
   8900 Edgewood Drive, Gaithersburg MD 20760

Established by United States University of America, primarily, it would appear, for the purpose of accrediting themselves.

☐ West European Accrediting Society
   Wachenheimerstr. 81, 6237 Liederbach, West Germany

A totally phony agency, set up solely to accredit various degree mills, such as Roosevelt University, Lafayette University, Loyola University, and others.

☐ Middle States Accrediting Board
   (No address available)

A non-existent accreditor, made up by Thomas University and other degree mills for the purpose of self-accreditation.

☐ National Council of Schools and Colleges
   (No address available)

Accreditation by this agency is claimed by International University, formerly of New Orleans, now of Pasadena, California. Despite many inquiries, the school has never provided the whereabouts of this agency, nor have I been able to locate it by other means.

☐ National Association of Open Campus Colleges
P.O. Box 207, Springfield MO 65801

Southwestern University in Tucson used to claim accreditation from this agency. The address is the same as that of Disciples of Truth, the organization that operated five schools in Oklahoma closed down as degree mills by Federal authorities in 1982.

☐ International Accrediting Association
601 Third Street, Modesto CA 95351

The address is the same as the Universal Life Church, the organization that sells Doctorates of all kinds, including the Ph.D., to anyone making a "donation" of $5 to $100.

BIBLE SCHOOL ACCREDITING AGENCIES

There are four recognized accreditors of religious schools, previously listed. There are also a great many unrecognized ones. Since many Bible schools readily acknowledge that their degrees are not academic in nature, accreditation of them has quite a different meaning. These associations may well be quite legitimate, but their accreditation has no academic relevance. Among the Bible school accreditors are:

☐ Accreditation Association of Christian Colleges and Seminaries
Drawer 609, Morgantown KY 42261

☐ Accrediting Association of Christian Colleges and Seminaries
Box 4174, Sarasota FL 33578

☐ International Accrediting Commission
7951 36th Ave., Kenosha WI 53142

☐ National Educational Accrediting Association
Formerly at 1156 Striebel Road, Columbus OH 43227; present location unknown

☐ Association of Fundamental Institutes of Religious Education (AFIRE)
Present location unknown

THE LAST WORD ON ACCREDITATION

Don't believe everything anyone says. It seems extraordinary that any school would lie about something so easily checkable as accreditation, but it is done. For instance, a degree mill called California Pacifica University unabashedly sent out thousands of bulletins announcing their affiliation with an accredited school. Not only was the affiliation a phony, the other school wasn't even accredited.

I have heard salespeople, while trying to recruit students, make accreditation claims that are patently false. Other schools ballyhoo their "fully accredited" status but never mention that the accrediting agency is unrecognized, and so the accreditation is of little or (in most cases) no value.

One accrediting agency (the aforementioned International Accrediting Association for Schools, Colleges and Theological Seminaries) boasts that two copies of every accreditation report they issue are "deposited in the Library of Congress." But for six dollars, anyone can copyright anything and be able to make the identical claim.

WORDS THAT DO NOT MEAN "ACCREDITED"

Some unaccredited schools use terminology in their catalogues or advertising that might have the effect of misleading unknowledgeable readers. Here are six of the common ways this is done:

1. "Pursuing accreditation"

A school may state that it is "pursuing accreditation," or that it "intends to pursue accreditation." But that says nothing whatever about its chances for achieving same. I can state just as accurately that I am practicing my tennis game, with the intention of playing John McEnroe in the finals at Wimbledon. Don't hold your breath.

2. Chartered

In some places, a charter is the necessary document that a school needs to grant degrees. A common ploy by diploma mill operators is to form a corporation, and state in the articles of incorporation that one of the purposes of the corporation is to grant degrees. This is like forming a corporation whose charter says that it has the right to appoint the Pope.

3. Licensed

This usually refers to nothing more than a business license, granted by the city or county in which the school is located, but which has nothing to do with the legality of the school, or the usefulness of its degrees.

4. Recognized

This can have many possible meanings, ranging from some level of genuine official recognition at the state level, to having been listed in some directory often unrelated to education, perhaps published by the school itself. (One ambitious degree mill once published an entire book as thick as this one, soley for the purpose of being able to devote a lengthy section to themselves as "the finest school in America."

5. Authorized

In California, this has the specific meaning that the state has authorized the school to grant degrees. It means the school is unquestionably operating legally, but it is not the same as accreditation.

6. Approval

In California, this has the specific meaning that the state has inspected a certain academic program at the school and found it worthy. It is one step higher than authorization and one step lower than accreditation. In other locations, it is important to know who is doing the approving. Some not-for-profit schools call themselves "approved by the U.S. Government," which means only that the Internal Revenue Service has approved their non-profit status for income taxes—and nothing more. At one time, some British schools called themselves "Government Approved," when the approval related only to the school lunch program.

Chapter 8

Scholarships and Other Financial Aid

Financial assistance comes in four forms:

Outside Scholarships: an outright gift of money, paid to you or the school by an outside source (government, foundation, corporation, etc.).

Inside Scholarships: the school itself reduces your tuition and/or other expenses.

Fellowship: money either from the school or an outside source, in return for certain work or services to be performed at the school (usually teaching or research).

Loans: from outside lenders, or from the school itself, to be paid back over a period of anywhere from one to ten years, generally at interest rates lower than current prime rate.

It is, sadly, the case that as college costs continue to rise substantially, the amount of money available for financial aid has diminished dramatically. Many loan and scholarship programs were either funded or guaranteed by the Federal government, and much of this money has been eliminated as part of the Reagan administration's cutbacks. After all, 300,000 cancelled full tuition scholarships can buy one nuclear powered aircraft carrier. And will.

Still, billions of dollars are available to help pay the college costs of people who need help. The vast majority of it goes to full-time students, under age 25, pursuing residential degrees at traditional schools.

Tapping into that particular fount is outside the scope of this book. There are several very useful books on this subject, which are described in the Reference Section. There are also some computerized services that have collected data on tens of thousands of individual scholarships. These match their clients' needs and interests with donors for a modest fee.

My favorite such service is called National Scholarship Research Service, at P.O. Box 2516, San Rafael CA 94912. They point out that each year, well over $100 million in scholarships goes unclaimed. Some of these are, admittedly, awfully peculiar scholarships: for rodeo riders with high G.P.A.'s; for Canadian petunia fanciers; for reformed prostitutes from Seattle; for people named Baxendale or Murphy; for people born on certain dates and/or in certain towns; and so on. But many are quite general, and a good many do not depend on financial need or net worth.

Other scholarship matching services are the College Scholarship Information Bank of the College Entrance Examination Board, 888 Seventh Ave., New York NY 10019, and Scholarship Search, 1775 Broadway, New York NY 10019.

Many students enrolled in non-traditional, even non-residential programs have their expenses paid, all or in part, by their employer. Thousands of large corporations, including nearly all of the Fortune 500, have tuition plans for their employees.

Many, but not all, corporations will pay for unaccredited programs. Some of the better unaccredited schools (e.g., Columbia Pacific, Pacific Western, Beverly Hills, California Coast, etc.) list in their school literature the names of hundreds of corporations that have paid students' tuition costs. costs.

Most non-traditional schools, accredited and unaccredited, offer Inside Scholarships to their students who need them. In other words, they will award a partial scholarship, in the form of tuition reduction (10% to 30% is the usual range), rather than lose a student altogether. Quite a few schools also offer an extended payment plan, in which the tuition can be paid in a series of smaller monthly installments, or even charged to a Master Card or Visa credit card.

There are schools, traditional and non-traditional, that offer tuition reduction in the form of commissions, or finders' fees, for bringing in other students. This quite ethical procedure can result in a tuition reduction of from $50 to several hundred dollars for each referral, when the referred student enrolls.

But the biggest single factors, by far, in financial aid for students at non-traditional schools are the speed of their education and the possibility of remaining fully employed while pursuing the degree. If even one year can be cut from a "traditional" four-year Bachelor's degree program, the savings (including revenue from a year of working for pay) are greater than 99% of all scholarship grants.

So, while it is nice to "win" money from another source, it is surely the case that to be able to complete an entire degree program for an out-of-pocket cost of from $1,000 to $4,000 (the typical range at non-traditional schools) is one of the great financial bargains of these difficult times.

"If you think *education* is expensive, try *ignorance*."
— Derek Bok
President of Harvard University

Chapter 9

Applying to Schools

HOW MANY SCHOOLS SHOULD YOU APPLY TO?

There is no single answer to this question that is right for everyone. Each person will have to determine his or her own best answer. The decision should be based on the following four factors.

(1) Likelihood of admission.

Some schools are extremely competitive or popular and admit fewer than ten percent of qualified applicants. Some have an ''open admissions'' policy and admit literally everyone who applies. Most are somewhere in between.

If your goal is to be admitted to one of the highly competitive schools (for instance, Harvard, Yale, Princeton, Stanford), where your chances of being accepted are not high, then it is wise to apply to at least four or five schools that would be among your top choices, and to at least one ''safety valve,'' an easier one, in case all else fails.

If your interest is in one of the good, but not world-famous, non-resident programs, your chances for acceptance are probably better than nine in ten, so you might decide to apply only to one or two.

(2) Cost.

There is a tremendous range of possible costs for any given degree. For instance, a respectable Ph.D. could cost around $2,000 at a good non-resident school, or as much as $50,000 at a well-known university — perhaps more when you consider lost salary. In general, I think it makes sense to apply to no more than two or three schools in any given price category.

(3) What they offer you.

Shopping around for a school is a little like shopping for a new car. Many schools either have money problems, or operate as profit-making businesses, and in either case, they are most eager to enroll new students. Thus it is not unreasonable to ask the schools what they can do for you. Let them know that you are a knowledgeable ''shopper,'' and that you have this book. Do they have courses or faculty advisors in your specific field? If not, will they get one for you? How much credit will they give for prior life experience learning? How long will it take to earn the degree? Are there any scholarship or tuition reduction plans available? Does tuition have to be paid all at once, or can it be spread out over time? If factors like these are important for you, then it could pay to shop around for the best deal.

You might consider investigating three to five schools that appear somewhat similar, because there will surely be differences.

> CAUTION: Remember that academic quality and reputation are probably the most important factors—so don't let a small financial saving be a reason to switch from a good school to a less-good school.

(4) Your own time.

Applying to a school can be a time-consuming process—and it costs money, too. Many schools have application fees ranging from $25 to $100. Some people get so carried away with the process of applying to school after school that they never get around to earning their degree(s)!

Of course once you have prepared a good and detailed resume, *Curriculum Vitae*, or life experience portfolio, you can use it to apply to more than one school.

Another time factor is how much of a hurry you are in. If you apply to several schools at once, the chances are good that at least one will admit you, and you can begin work promptly. If you apply to only one, and it turns you down, or you get into long delays, then it can take a month or two to go through the admissions process elsewhere.

SPEEDING UP THE ADMISSIONS PROCESS

The admissions process at most traditional schools is very slow: most people apply nearly a year in advance, and do not learn if their application has been accepted for four to six months. Non-traditional programs vary immensely in their policies in this regard. Some will grant conditional acceptance within a few days after receiving the application. ("Conditional" means that they must later verify the prior learning experiences you claim.) Others take just as long as traditional programs.

The following three factors can result in a much faster admissions process:

(1) Selecting schools by policy.

A school's admissions policy should be stated in its catalogue. Since you will find a range among schools of two weeks to six months for a decision, the simple solution is to ask, and then apply to schools with a fast procedure.

(2) Asking for speedy decisions.

Some schools have formal procedures whereby you can request an early decision on your acceptance. Others do the same thing informally, for those who ask. In effect what this does is put you at the top of the pile in the admissions office, so you will have the decision in, perhaps, half the usual time. Other schools use what they call a "rolling admissions" procedure, which means, in effect, that each application is considered soon after it is received instead of being held several months and considered with a large batch of others.

(3) Applying pressure.

As previously indicated, many schools are eager to have new students. If you make it clear to a school that you are in a hurry and that you may consider going elsewhere if you don't hear from them promptly, they will usually speed up the process. It is not unreasonable to specify a time frame. If, for instance, you are mailing in your application on September 1, you might enclose a note saying that you would like to have their decision mailed or phoned to you by October 1. (Some schools routinely telephone their acceptances; others do so if asked; some will only do so by collect call; and others will not, no matter what.)

HOW TO APPLY TO A SCHOOL

The basic procedure is essentially the same at all schools, traditional or non-traditional:

(1) You write (or telephone) for the school's catalogue or bulletin or other literature, and admissions forms.

(2) You complete the admissions forms and return them to the school, with application fee, if any.

(3) You complete any other requirements the school may have (exams, transcripts, etc.).

(4) The school notifies you of their decision.

It is step three that can vary tremendously from school to school. At some schools all that is required is the admissions application. Others will require various entrance examinations to test your aptitude or knowledge level; transcripts; letters of reference, a statement of financial condition, possibly a personal interview.

Happily, the majority of non-traditional schools have relatively simple entrance requirements. And all schools supply materials that tell you exactly what they expect you to do in order to apply. If it is not clear, ask. If the school does not supply prompt, helpful answers, then you probably don't want to deal with them anyway. It's a buyer's market.

It is advisable, in general, not to send a whole bunch of stuff to a school the very first time you write to them. A short note, asking for their catalogue, should suffice. You may wish to indicate your field and degree goal (''I am interested in a Master's and possibly a Doctorate in psychology...'') in case they have different sets of literature for different programs. It is unwise to write to a specific person, by name, at the school. If that person has left, the school may forward your materials on as if they were personal correspondences, delaying your application. On the other hand, it can do no harm to mention that you are a reader of this book; it might get you slightly prompter or more personal responses.

ENTRANCE EXAMINATIONS

Many non-resident degree programs, even at the Master's and Doctoral levels, do not require any entrance examinations. On the other hand, the majority of residential programs do require them. The main reason for this appears to be that non-residential schools do not have to worry about overcrowding on the campus, so they can admit more students. A second reason is that they tend to deal with more mature students who have the ability to decide which program is best for them.

There are, needless to say, exceptions to both reasons. If you have particular feelings about examinations—positive or negative—you will be able to find schools that meet your requirements. Do not hesitate to ask any school about their exam requirements if it is not clear from the catalogue.

Bachelor's admission examinations

Most residential universities require applicants to take part or all of the ''A.T.P.'' or Admissions Testing Program, run by a private agency, the College Entrance Examination Board (888 Seventh Ave., New York NY 10019). The main component of the A.T.P. is the S.A.T., or Scholastic Aptitude Test, which measures verbal and mathematical abilities. There are also achievement tests, testing knowledge levels in specific subject areas: biology, European history, Latin, etc. These examinations are given at centers all over North America several times each year, at modest fees.

A competing private organization, A.C.T. (American College Testing Program, P.O. Box 168, Iowa City IA 52240) offers a similar range of entrance examinations.

The important point is that very few schools have their own exams; virtually all rely on either the A.C.T. or the A.T.P.

Graduate degrees

Again, many non-residential schools do not require any entrance examinations. Many, but by no means all, residential Master's and Doctoral programs ask their applicants to take the G.R.E., or Graduate Record Examination, administered by the Educational Testing Service (Box 2815, Princeton NJ 08540). The G.R.E. consists of a three-hour aptitude test (verbal, quantitative, and analytical abilities) plus three-hour exams in a variety of specific fields (chemistry, computer science, music, philosophy, etc.).

Professional schools

Most law and medical schools also require a standard examination, rather than having one of their own. The M.S.A.T. (Medical School Admission Test) is given several times a year by A.C.T. while the L.S.A.T. (Law School Admission Test) is given five times a year by E.T.S.

There are many excellent books available at most libraries and larger bookstores on how to prepare for these various exams, complete with sample questions and answers. Some of these are listed in the bibliography, Chapter 27.

Chapter 10

Personal Recommendations

I used to receive a great many letters from readers who all asked essentially the same question: "You have written about hundreds of different schools. Now, can you tell me which one is really the best of all?"

In a word, no.

There are simply too many variables that make different schools appropriate or inappropriate for different people with different needs. These include accreditation status, residency requirements, tuition and fees, subject areas offered, educational philosophy, credentials of the faculty and the staff, length of time required to earn the degree, and methods for evaluating life experience learning.

Each person will have his or her own favorites, but it is truly impossible to select the single best school, or even to make a list of the "top ten" that will be suitable for everyone. That's one reason I started the personal consulting service which is described on page 274.

Still, I do have my favorites, and I'd like to share them. To make the list meaningful, I must organize the schools into various categories.

BACHELOR'S DEGREE

Accredited (or Candidate for Accreditation)/Non-Resident

1. University of the State of New York
2. Thomas Edison State College
3. University of Iowa
4. University of Minnesota
5. Indiana University
6. University of London
7. Western Illinois University

Accredited (or Candidate for Accreditation)/Short Residency

1. Skidmore College
2. University of Alabama
3. Empire State College
4. Elizabethtown College
5. Marywood College
6. Stephens College
7. The Evergreen State College

Unaccredited

None recommended, since there are so many good accredited ones. However, the schools listed under "Unaccredited Master's" all offer Bachelor's and combined Bachelor's/Master's programs, which may be considerably faster than the above schools for some people.

MASTER'S DEGREE

Accredited (or Candidate for Accreditation)/Non-Resident

1. California State University/Dominguez Hills
2. Beacon College
3. University of Waterloo
4. Antioch University

Accredited (or Candidate for Accreditation)/Short Residency

1. Syracuse University
2. Central Michigan University
3. Norwich University
4. University of Oklahoma
5. Goddard College
6. St. Mary's College
7. Canadian School of Management

Unaccredited/Non-Resident

1. Columbia Pacific University
2. Pacific Western University
3. Clayton University
4. California Coast University
5. Kensington University
6. University of Beverly Hills
7. California Pacific University

Unaccredited/Short Residency

1. Laurence University
2. University of Sarasota
3. International College

DOCTORATES

Accredited (or Candidate for Accreditation)/Non-Resident

1. University of South Africa
2. University of London
3. Open University (England)

Accredited (or Candidate for Accreditation)/Short Residency

1. Union Graduate School
2. Nova University
3. Fielding Institute
4. International Graduate School
5. Saybrook Institute

Unaccredited/Non-Resident

1. Columbia Pacific University
2. Pacific Western University
3. Clayton University

4. California Coast University
5. University of Beverly Hills
6. Kensington University
7. International Institute for Advanced Studies

Unaccredited/Short Residency

1. Walden University
2. Laurence University
3. University of Sarasota
4. International College

Part Two
Alternative Methods
of Earning Credit

Chapter 11

Equivalency Examinations

CLEP AND PEP

More than 1,500 colleges and universities in the United States and Canada award credit toward their Bachelor's degrees (and, in a few cases, Master's and Doctorates) solely on the basis of passing examinations. The exams are designed to be equivalent to the final exam in a typical college class, and the assumption is that if you score high enough, you get the same amount of credit you would have gotten by taking the class—or, in some cases, a good deal more.

Two independent national agencies administer about one hundred different exams. They are given at hundreds of testing centers all over North America and, by special arrangement, many of them can be administered almost anywhere in the world. The two organizations are known as CLEP and PEP.

CLEP is the College-Level Examination Program, offered by the College Entrance Examination Board (P.O. Box 1824, Princeton NJ 08540).

PEP is the Proficiency Examination Program, offered in the state of New York by the Regents External Degree–College Proficiency Programs (Cultural Education Center, Albany NY 12230), and everywhere else by the American College Testing Program (P.O. Box 168, Iowa City IA 52240).

Most of the tests offered by both CLEP and PEP consist of one-hour to three-hour, multiple choice examinations. Some are a combination of multiple choice and essay questions, and a few are essay only, some up to seven hours long.

Each college or university sets its own standards for passing grades, and also decides for itself how much credit to give for each exam. Both of these factors can vary substantially from school to school. For instance, the PEP test in anatomy is a three-hour multiple choice test. Hundreds of schools give credit for passing this exam. Here are three of them:

Central Virginia Community College requires a score of 45 (out of 80), and awards nine credit hours for passing.

Edinboro State College in Pennsylvania requires a score of 50 to pass, and awards six credit hours for the same exam.

Concordia College in New York requires a score of 47, but awards only three credit hours.

Similar situations prevail on most of the exams. There is even no predictability or consistency within a given school. For instance, at the University of South Florida, a three-hour multiple choice test in maternal nursing is worth 18 units while a three-hour multiple choice test in psychiatric nursing is worth only nine units.

So, with a hundred or more standard exams available, and well over one thousand schools offering credit, it pays to shop around a little and select both the school and the exams where you will get the most credit.

PEP exams are offered in the arts and sciences, criminal justice, business, education, and nursing. CLEP exams are offered in five general subject areas (English, math, science, social science, humanities), and in specific subject areas in the fields of business, dentistry, education, humanities, mathematics, medical technology, nursing, science, and social science.

CLEP exams are scored on a scale of either 20 to 80 or 200 to 800. This is done so that no score can have any intrinsic meaning. No one can say whether a score of 514, for instance, is either good or bad. Each school sets its own minimum score for which they will give credit, and in many cases all that is necessary is to be in the upper half of those taking the test.

PEP gives standard numerical or letter grades for its tests.

Anywhere from one to six credits may be earned for each hour of testing. The five basic CLEP tests, for instance, are one hour of multiple choice questions each, and are worth anywhere from 18 to 30 semester units, depending on the school. Thus it is possible to complete the equivalent of an entire year of college—30 semester units—in one day, by taking and passing these five tests.

Most exams cost between $20 and $30 an hour to take, and there are discounts for taking more than one at a time. CLEP tests are given over a two-day period once each month at more than 700 centers, most of them on college or university campuses. PEP tests are given for two days once every three months in about 100 locations, nationwide.

Persons living more than 150 miles from a test center may make special arrangements for the test to be given nearer home. And for those in a big hurry, the CLEP tests are given twice each week in Washington, DC.

There is no stigma attached to poor performance on these tests. In fact, if you wish, you may have the scores reported only to you, so that no one but you and the computer will know how you did. Then, if your scores are high enough, you can have them sent on to the schools of your choice. CLEP allows exams to be taken every six months; you can take the same PEP exam twice in any 12-month period.

HOW HARD ARE THESE EXAMS?

This is, of course, an extremely subjective question. However, I have heard from a great many readers who have attempted CLEP and PEP exams, and the most common response is, "Gee, that was a lot easier than I had expected." This is especially true of more mature students. The tests are designed for 18-to-20-year-olds, and there appears to be a certain amount of knowledge of facts, as well as experience in dealing with testing situations, that people acquire in ordinary life situations, as they grow older.

PREPARING FOR EXAMS

The testing agencies issue detailed syllabuses describing each test and the specific content area it covers. CLEP also sells a book that gives sample questions and answers from each examination.

At least four educational publishers have produced series of books on how to prepare for such exams, often with full-length sample tests. These can be found in the reference section of any good bookstore or library.

For years, the testing agencies vigorously fought the idea of letting test-takers take copies of the test home with them. But consumer legislation in New York has made the tests available, and a good thing, too. Every few months, it seems, someone discovers an incorrect answer, or a poorly-phrased question that can have more than one correct answer, necessitating a reissue of scores to all the thousands of people who took that test.

In recent years, there has been much controversy over the value of cramming for examinations. Many of my counseling clients have told me they were able to pass four or five CLEP exams in a single day by spending an intensive few days (or weeks) cramming for them. Although the various testing agencies have always denied that cramming can be of any value, in the last few years, there have been some extremely persuasive research studies that demonstrate the effectiveness of intensive studying. These data have vindicated the claims made by people and agencies that assist students in preparing for examinations. Such services are offered in a great many places, usually in the vicinity of college campuses, by graduate students and moonlighting faculty. The best place to find them is through the classified ads in campus newspapers and on bulletin boards around the campus.

THE STANLEY H. KAPLAN EDUCATIONAL CENTERS

Kaplan operates a nationwide chain of more that one hundred educational centers that offer intensive preparation for dozens of different tests, ranging from college admissions to national medical boards. Although the main method of preparation involves a good deal of classroom attendance at a center (from 20 to over 100 hours), almost all the materials can be rented for home study.

Residential tuition for most examination preparation courses is in the range of $150 to $300, but the cost goes as high as $850 for some medical exams. Rental for home study costs from $100 to $200 for most sets of materials.

Kaplan Centers operate in 40 states, the District of Columbia, Puerto Rico, and in Toronto, Canada. If you cannot locate a local one, you can communicate directly with Stanley H. Kaplan Educational Center Ltd., 131 West 56th St., New York NY 10019, 212/977-8200 or, outside New York, 800/223-1782.

OTHER EXAMINATIONS

There are two series of examinations that can be used to earn substantial credit toward many non-traditional degree programs.

The Graduate Record Examination

The GRE is administered by the Educational Testing Service, and is given at nationwide locations five times each year. The GRE Advanced Test is a three-hour multiple choice test, designed to test knowledge that would ordinarily be gained by a Bachelor's degree holder in that given field. The exams are available in the fields of biology, chemistry, computer science, economics, education, engineering, French, geography, geology, German, history, English literature, mathematics, music, philosophy, physics, political science, psychology, sociology, and Spanish.

Schools vary widely in how much credit they will give for each GRE. The range is from none at all to 39 semester units in the case of the University of the State of New York.

MLA Foreign Language Proficiency Tests

Although many schools will give credit for foreign language skills, the most credit is available through the MLA tests. Unfortunately they are normally given only under the auspices of three outstanding non-resident schools, at those schools' offices: the University of the State of New York, Edison State College of New Jersey, and Charter Oak College in Connecticut. (I have heard from a few readers who were able to arrange for schools in other locations to administer these tests, but there is no regular program for so doing.)

The MLA exams consist of two "batteries." Battery A is a half-day exam in either French, German, Italian, Russian, or Spanish, covering comprehension, speaking, reading, and writing. It is worth 24 semester hours at the University of the State of New York, less at most other schools. Battery B covers linguistics, civilization and culture, and language-teaching techniques. It also requires half a day, and is worth nine semester units at various schools.

Chapter 12

Correspondence Courses

There are two kinds of correspondence study, or home study, courses: vocational and academic. Vocational courses (meat cutting, locksmithing, appliance repair, etc.) often offer useful training, but rarely lead to degrees, so they are not relevant for this book. The National Home Study Council (1601 18th St. N.W., Washington DC 20009) offers excellent free information on the sources of vocational home study courses in many fields.

Sixty-eight major universities and teaching institutions offer academic correspondence courses — more than 12,000 courses in hundreds of subjects, from accounting to zoology. Virtually all of these courses can be counted toward a degree at almost any college or university. However most schools have a limit on the amount of correspondence credit they will apply to a degree. This limit is typically around 50%, but the range is from nothing to 100%.

"One hundred percent" means that it is indeed possible to earn an accredited Bachelor's degree entirely through correspondence study. This may be done, for instance, at the University of the State of New York, Edison State College, Charter Oak College, and Western Illinois University. Courses taken at any of the 68 schools can be applied to these degrees.

Each of the 68 institutions publishes a catalogue or bulletin listing their available courses. Some offer just a few while others have hundreds. All of the schools will accept students living anywhere in the United States, although some schools charge more for out-of-state students. About 80% accept foreign students, but all courses are offered only in English.

There is a helpful but frustrating directory that is, in effect, a master catalogue to all 68 schools. It lists the course titles of every course at each school. This directory is frustrating because it has a miserable index that makes finding many subjects difficult indeed. One must look under "C" for journalism (listed only under "Communication"); under "L" for biology ("Life Sciences") and so forth. The abbreviated one-line course titles are surprisingly informative: "Hist & phil of phys ed," "Fac career dev in schools," and 12,000 more.

The directory is called *Guide to Independent Study through Correspondence Instruction*, and it is revised every two or three years by the publisher, Peterson's Guides (Box 2123, Princeton NJ 08540).

Of course you can also write directly to the schools. All of them will send you their catalogue without charge. Many of the schools have popular subjects like psychology, business, and education, but some of the more esoteric topics may only be available at one or two schools, and this directory points you to them.

Correspondence courses range from one to six semester hours worth of credit, and can cost anywhere from $10 to $50 per unit. A typical course will consist of from five to 20 lessons, each one requiring either a short written paper, answers to questions, or an unsupervised test graded by the instructor. There is usually a supervised final examination. These can usually be taken anywhere in the world where a suitable proctor can be found (usually a high school or college teacher).

People who cannot go to a testing center, either because they are handicapped, live too far away, or are in prison, can usually arrange to have a test supervisor come to them. Schools can be extremely flexible. One correspondence program administrator told me he had two students — a husband and wife — working as missionaries on a remote island where they were the only people who could read and write. He allowed them to supervise each other.

Many schools set limits on how fast and how slow you can complete a correspondence course. The shortest time is generally three to six weeks, while the upper limit ranges from three months to two years. Some schools limit the number of courses you can take at one time, but most do not. Even those with limits are concerned only with their own institution. There is no cross-checking, and in theory one could take simultaneous courses from all 68 institutions.

THE 68 SCHOOLS

Coding as follows:
♥ = one of the dozen schools with the most courses
♠ = does not deal with foreign students
♦ = prefers not to deal with foreign students, but treats each case on its own merits.

ARIZONA STATE UNIVERSITY
University Continuing Education, ASB 110, Tempe AZ 85281, 602/965-6563

ARKANSAS STATE UNIVERSITY
Center for Continuing Education, Correspondence Department, State University AR 72467, 501/972-3052

AUBURN UNIVERSITY
Office of Extended Education and Human Development Services, 3002 Haley Center, Auburn AL 36830, 404/826-5979

AZUSA PACIFIC COLLEGE ♦
Universal College Program, Highway 66 at Citrus, Azusa CA 91702, 213/334-0212
All courses offered on videocassettes.

BALL STATE UNIVERSITY
School of Continuing Education, Muncie IN 47306, 317/285-5031

BRIGHAM YOUNG UNIVERSITY ♥
Independent Study, 210 HRCB, Provo UT 84602, 801/374-1211 ext. 2868

CALIFORNIA STATE UNIVERSITY
Department of Civil Engineering, 6000 J St., Sacramento CA 95819, 916/454-6142.
Offers two courses, both in wastewater treatment.

CENTRAL MICHIGAN UNIVERSITY
Office of Independent Study by Correspondence, School of Continuing Education, Mount Pleasant MI 48859, 517/774-3715

COLORADO STATE UNIVERSITY
Center for Continuing Education, Rockwell Hall, Fort Collins CO 80523, 303/491-5288.

EASTERN MICHIGAN UNIVERSITY
Director of Credit Programs, 323 Goodson Hall, Ypsilanti MI 48197, 313/487-0407

HOME STUDY INSTITUTE
Takoma Park, Washington DC 20012, 202/723-0800
Only institution offering courses from elementary school through college level.

INDIANA STATE UNIVERSITY
Independent Study, AC 220, Terre Haute IN 47809, 812/232-6311

INDIANA UNIVERSITY ♥
Independent Study Division, Owen Hall 001, Bloomington IN 47405, 812/337-3693

LOUISIANA STATE UNIVERSITY
Correspondence Study Department, Baton Rouge LA 70803, 504/388-3171

LOYOLA UNIVERSITY
Correspondence Study Division, 820 N. Michigan Ave., Chicago IL 60611, 312/670-3018

MASSACHUSETTS DEPARTMENT OF EDUCATION ♠
Supervisor of Correspondence Instruction, Bureau of Adult Services, 31 St. James Ave., Boston MA 02116, 617/727-5784

MISSISSIPPI STATE UNIVERSITY
Division of Continuing Education, Drawer 5247, Mississippi State MS 39762, 601/325-4030

MURRAY STATE UNIVERSITY
Extended Education, Sparks Hall, Murray KY 42071, 502/762-4159

NORTH DAKOTA DIVISION OF INDEPENDENT STUDY ♦
Box 5036, State University Station, Fargo ND 58105, 701/237-7182

NORTHERN MICHIGAN UNIVERSITY
Off-Campus Education, 410 Cohodas Administrative Center, Marquette MI 49855, 906/227-2101
Offers nine classes in history, criminal justice, geography.

OAKLAND UNIVERSITY ♦
Division of Continuing Education, Rochester MI 48063, 313/377-3120.
Offers non-credit courses only, in management, business, communication.

OHIO UNIVERSITY ♥
Independent Study, Tupper Hall 304, Athens OH 45701, 614/594-6721

OKLAHOMA STATE UNIVERSITY
Independent and Correspondence Study, 018 Classroom Building, Stillwater OK 74074, 405/624-6390

OREGON STATE SYSTEM OF HIGHER EDUCATION
Office of Independent Study, Division of Continuing Education, P.O. Box 1491, Portland OR 97207, 503/229-4865

PENNSYLVANIA STATE UNIVERSITY
Department of Independent Study by Correspondence, 3 Shields Building, University Park PA 16802, 814/865-5403

PURDUE UNIVERSITY
Division of Independent Study, 116 Stewart Center, West Lafayette IN 47907, 317/749-2227
Offers only two courses: one in pharmacy, one in pest control.

ROOSEVELT UNIVERSITY ♦
College of Continuing Education, 430 South Michigan Ave., Chicago IL 60605, 312/341-3864

SEMINARY EXTENSION HOME STUDY INSTITUTE
Southern Baptist Convention Building, 460 James Robertson Parkway, Nashville TN 37219, 615/242-2453
All courses are in religion and theology.

TEXAS TECH UNIVERSITY
Division of Continuing Education, P.O. Box 4110, Lubbock TX 74909, 806/742-2352

U.S. DEPARTMENT OF AGRICULTURE GRADUATE SCHOOL
Correspondence Study Programs, Room 6847, South Building, Washington DC 20250, 202/447-7123.
Designed for government employees but open to all.

UNIVERSITY OF ALABAMA ♥
Independent Study, P.O. Box 2967, University AL 35486, 205/348-7642

UNIVERSITY OF ALASKA
Correspondence Study, 101-D Eielson, Fairbanks AK 99703, 907/479-7222

UNIVERSITY OF ARIZONA
University Extension/Extended Study, 1717 E. Speedway, Babcock Building 3201, Tucson AZ 85721, 602/626-1896

UNIVERSITY OF ARKANSAS
Department of Independent Study, Division of Continuing Education, 346 West Ave., Fayetteville AR 72701, 501/575-3647

UNIVERSITY OF CALIFORNIA ♥
Independent Study Department, 2223 Fulton St., Berkeley CA 94720, 415/642-7268

UNIVERSITY OF COLORADO
Center for Lifelong Learning, Division of Continuing Education, 970 Aurora Ave., Room 206, Boulder CO 80302, 303/492-5141 ext. 206

UNIVERSITY OF FLORIDA ♥
Department of Correspondence Study, 2012 W. University Ave., Gainesville FL 32603, 904/392-1711

UNIVERSITY OF GEORGIA
Georgia Center for Continuing Education, Athens GA 30602, 404/542-3243

UNIVERSITY OF IDAHO
Correspondence Study Office, Moscow ID 83843, 208/885-6641

UNIVERSITY OF ILLINOIS
Guided Individual Study, 104 Illini Hall, 725 S. Wright St., Champaign IL 61820, 217/333-1321

UNIVERSITY OF IOWA
Center for Credit Programs, W400 East Hall, Iowa City IA 52242, 319/353-4963.
Also offers graduate-level courses in education.

UNIVERSITY OF KANSAS
Division of Continuing Education, Lawrence KS 66045, 913/864-4792

UNIVERSITY OF KENTUCKY ♥♦
Independent Study Program, Room 1, Frazee Hall 00031, Lexington KY 40506, 606/257-2966

UNIVERSITY OF MICHIGAN
Extension Service, Department of Independent Study, 412 Maynard St., Ann Arbor MI 48109, 313/764-5311.
Also offers graduate-level courses in several fields.

UNIVERSITY OF MINNESOTA ♥
Department of Independent Study, 69 Westbrook Hall, 77 Pleasant St. S.E., Minneapolis MN 55455, 612/373-3803

UNIVERSITY OF MISSISSIPPI
Department of Independent Study, University MS 38677, 601/232-7313

UNIVERSITY OF MISSOURI ♦
Center for Independent Study Through Correspondence, 514 S. Fifth St., Columbia MO 65211, 314/882-2491

UNIVERSITY OF NEBRASKA
Division of Continuing Studies, 511 Nebraska Hall, Lincoln NE 68588, 402/472-1926

UNIVERSITY OF NEVADA
Extended Programs and Continuing Education, Reno NV 89557, 702/784-4633

UNIVERSITY OF NEW MEXICO
Division of Continuing Education, 805 Yale Blvd., Albuquerque NM 87131, 505/277-2105

UNIVERSITY OF NORTH CAROLINA
Independent Study by Extension, 121 Abernethy 002A, Chapel Hill NC 27514, 919/933-1104

UNIVERSITY OF NORTH DAKOTA ♠
Correspondence Study, Box 8277 University Station, Grand Forks ND 58202, 701/777-3044

UNIVERSITY OF NORTHERN COLORADO
Continuing Education, Greeley CO 80639, 303/351-2891

UNIVERSITY OF NORTHERN IOWA ♦
Extension and Continuing Education, 144 Gilchrist, Cedar Falls IA 50613, 319/273-2121

UNIVERSITY OF OKLAHOMA ♥
Independent Study Department, 1700 Asp, Norman OK 73037, 405/325-1921

UNIVERSITY OF SOUTH CAROLINA
Correspondence Study, Center for Credit Programs, Columbia SC 29208, 803/777-2188

UNIVERSITY OF SOUTH DAKOTA
Statewide Educational Services, Vermillion SD 57069, 605/677-5281

UNIVERSITY OF SOUTHERN MISSISSIPPI
Department of Independent Study, Southern Station Box 5056, Hattiesburg MS 39401, 601/266-4267

UNIVERSITY OF TENNESSEE ♥
Center for Extended Learning, 447 Communications and Extensions Building, Knoxville TN 37916, 615/974-5135

UNIVERSITY OF TEXAS
Extension and Correspondence Studies, Education Annex F-38, Austin TX 78712, 512/471-5616

UNIVERSITY OF UTAH ♥
Division of Continuing Education, Correspondence Study, 1152 Annex, Salt Lake City UT 84112, 801/581-6472

UNIVERSITY OF WASHINGTON
Independent Study, Lewis Hall, Room 212, Mail Stop DW-30, Seattle WA 98195, 206/543-2350

UNIVERSITY OF WISCONSIN ♥

Independent Study, 209 Extension Building, 432 North Lake St., Madison WI 53706, 608/263-2055.

In addition to academic courses, the university offers a large number of non-academic vocational and technical courses.

UNIVERSITY OF WYOMING

Correspondence Study, Box 3294 University Station, Laramie WY 82071, 307/766-6323

UTAH STATE UNIVERSITY

Independent Study Division, Logan UT 84321, 801/752-4100 ext. 7394

WASHINGTON STATE UNIVERSITY

Continuing University Studies, 208 Van Doren Hall, Pullman WA 99164, 509/335-3557

WESTERN MICHIGAN UNIVERSITY

Department of Continuing Education, Kalamazoo MI 49008, 616/383-1860

WESTERN WASHINGTON UNIVERSITY

Independent Study Coordinator, Old Main 400, Bellingham WA 98225, 206/676-3320

Chapter 13

Credit for Life Experience Learning

The philosophy behind "credit for life experience" can be expressed very simply: Academic credit is given for what you know, without regard for how, when, or where the learning was acquired.

Consider a very simple example: Quite a few colleges and universities offer credit for courses in typewriting. For instance, at Western Illinois University, Business Education 261 is a basic typing class. Anyone who takes and passes that class is given three units of credit. But credit for life experience learning advocates say: "If you know how to type, regardless of how and where you learned, or even if you taught yourself at the age of nine, you should still get those same three units of credit, once you demonstrate that you have the same skill level as a person who passes Business Education 261."

Of course not all learning can be converted into college credit, but many people are surprised to discover how much of what they already know is, in fact, credit-worthy. With thousands of colleges offering hundreds of thousands of courses, it is a rare subject, indeed, that someone hasn't determined to be worthy of credit. And if even one college has, then many alternative programs will give it serious consideration.

Here are eight major classifications of life experiences that may be worth college credits in non-traditional, degree-granting programs:

1. WORK

Many of the skills necessary in paid employment are skills that are taught in colleges and universities. These include, for instance, typing, filing, shorthand, accounting, inventory control, financial management, map reading, military strategy, welding, computer programming, editing, planning, sales, and real estate appraisals, and literally thousands of other skills.

2. HOMEMAKING

Home maintenance, household planning and budgeting, child raising, child psychology, education, interpersonal communication, gourmet cooking, and much, much, more.

3. VOLUNTEER WORK

Community activities, political campaigns, church activities, service organizations, volunteer work in social service agencies, Big Brothers/Big Sisters, hospital volunteering, and so forth.

4. NON-CREDIT LEARNING IN FORMAL SETTINGS

Company courses, in-service teacher training, workshops, clinics, conferences and conventions, lectures, courses on radio or television, non-credit correspondence courses, etc.

5. TRAVEL

Study tours, significant vacation and business trips, living for extended periods in other countries or cultures, participating in activities related to sub-cultures or other cultures.

6. RECREATIONAL ACTIVITIES AND HOBBIES

Musical skills, aviation training and skills, acting or other work in a community theater, sports, arts and crafts, fiction and non-fiction writing, public speaking, gardening, attending plays, concerts and movies, visiting museums, designing and making clothing, and many other leisure-time activities.

7. READING, VIEWING, LISTENING

Any subject area in which a person has done extensive or intensive reading and study, but not for college credit.

8. DISCUSSIONS WITH EXPERTS

A great deal of learning can come from talking to, listening to, and working with experts, whether in ancient history, carpentry, or theology. Significant, extensive, or intensive meetings with such people may also earn credit.

THE MOST COMMON ERROR

The most common error people make when thinking about getting credit for life experience is to confuse time spent with learning. Being a regular church-goer for thirty years is not worth any college credit, in and of itself. But the regular church-goer who can document that he or she has taught Sunday school classes, worked with youth groups, participated in leadership programs, organized community drives, studied Latin or Greek, taken tours to the Holy Land, or engaged in lengthy philosophical discussions with a clergyman, is likely to get credit for those experiences.

It is crucial that the experiences can be documented to the satisfaction of the school. Two people could work side by side in the same laboratory for five years. One might do little more than follow instructions in running routine experiments, setting up and dismantling apparatus, and heading home. The other, ostensibly doing the same work, might do extensive reading in the background of the work being done, get into discussions with supervisors, make plans and recommendations for other ways of doing the work, propose or design new kinds of apparatus, or develop hypotheses on why the results were turning out the way they were.

So it is not enough just to say what you did, or to submit a short resume. The details and specifics must be documented.

DOCUMENTING YOUR LEARNING

The two most common ways that a learning experience is documented are by getting a letter of verification from someone who knows you and knows from first-hand experience what you have done; or by taking an equivalency examination to demonstrate knowledge gained.

PRESENTING YOUR LEARNING

Most schools that give credit for life experience learning require that a formal presentation be made, usually in the form of a life experience portfolio. Each school will have its own standards for the form and content of such a portfolio, and many, in fact, offer either guidelines or courses (some for credit, some not) to help the non-traditional student prepare the portfolio.

Many schools will suggest that you follow the procedures and descriptions recommended in a splendid manual on this subject, called *Assessing Prior Learning — A CAEL Student Guide*, by Aubrey Forrest, published by the Council for the Advancement of Experiential Learning, Lakefront North, Suite 300, Columbia MD 21004. The manual is sold by mail for $5. In 110 typewritten pages, Mr. Forrest tells you all you need to know about portfolios: identifying your relevant learning, documenting it, estimating how much credit you may get, and assembling your portfolio.

CAEL is also working on assembling a set of sample portfolios, but this project is moving slowly, and the result probably will not go on sale until sometime in 1984. However one of the good non-traditional schools will sell a set of sample portfolios and their own manual on portfolio preparation. The sample portfolio costs $9.50 (including postage), and the Portfolio Development Guide is $6. They are available from Marylhurst College for Lifelong Learning, Marylhurst OR 97036.

Here are 24 other means by which people have documented work they have done, leading to learning experiences, and thus credit for life experience learning:

slides   films or videotapes
audio tapes   certificates
official commendations   newspaper articles
films and photographs   official job descriptions
course outlines   copies of examinations taken
bills of sale   military records
programs of recitals and performances   samples of arts or crafts made
exhibitions   samples of writing
awards and honors   works of art
copies of speeches   designs and blueprints
licenses (pilot, real estate, etc.)   mementoes
interviews with others   testimonials and endorsements

HOW LIFE EXPERIENCE LEARNING IS TURNED INTO ACADEMIC CREDIT

It ain't easy. In a perfect world, there would be universally accepted standards, by which it would be as easy to measure the credit value in a seminar in refrigeration engineering as it is to measure the temperature in a refrigerator. Indeed, some schools and national organizations are striving toward the creation of extensive "menus" of non-traditional experiences, such that anyone doing the same thing would get the same credit.

There has been progress in this direction. Many schools have come to agreement, for example, on aviation experiences. A private pilot's license is worth four semester units; instrument rating is worth six units; and so forth.

The American Council on Education, a private organization, regularly publishes a massive, multi-volume set of books, in two series: *The National Guide to Educational Credit for Training Programs* and *Guide to the Evaluation of Educational Experiences in the Armed Forces.*

Many schools use these volumes to assign credit directly, and others use them as guidelines in doing their own evaluation.

A few examples will demonstrate the sort of thing that is done:

The Red Cross nine-day training course in The Art of Helping is evaluated as worth two semester hours of social work.

The John Hancock Mutual Life Insurance Company's internal course in technical skills for managers is worth three semester hours of business administration.

Portland Cement Company's five-day training program in kiln optimization, whatever that is, is worth one semester hour.

The Professional Insurance Agents' three-week course in basic insurance is worth three semester hours in principles of insurance, and three more in property and liability contract analysis.

The Army's 27-week course in Ground Surveillance Radar Repair is worth 10 semester hours of electronics and five more of electrical laboratory.

The Army Legal Clerk training course can be worth 24 semester hours, including three in English, three in business law, three in management, etc.

There are hundred of additional business and military courses that have been evaluated already, and thousands more that will be worth credit for those who have taken them, whether or not they appear in these A.C.E. volumes.

SOME INSPIRATION

There are always some people who say, "Oh, I haven't ever done anything worthy of college credit." I have yet to meet anyone with an I.Q. higher than room temperature who has not done at least some credit-worthy things. Just to inspire you, then, here is a list of one hundred and one things that could be worth credit for life experience learning. The list could easily be ten or a hundred times as long.

Playing tennis	Appraising an antique
Preparing for natural childbirth	Writing a speech
Leading a church group	Studying first aid or C.P.R.
Taking a body-building class	Organizing a union
Speaking French	Researching international laws
Selling real estate	Listening to Shakespeare's plays
Studying gourmet cooking	Designing a playground
Reading *War and Peace*	Planning a garden
Building model airplanes	Devising a marketing strategy
Touring through Belgium	Reading the newspaper
Learning shorthand	Designing a home
Starting a small business	Attending a seminar
Navigating a small boat	Playing the piano
Writing a book	Studying a new religion
Buying a Persian rug	Reading about the Civil War
Watching public television	Taking ballet lessons
Decorating a home or office	Helping a dyslexic child
Attending a convention	Riding a horse
Being a counselor at camp	Keeping tropical fish
Studying Spanish	Pressing flowers
Bicycling across Greece	Writing public relations releases
Interviewing senior citizens	Writing for the local newspaper
Living in another culture	Acting in little theater
Writing advertising	Running the P.T.A.
Throwing a pot	Flying an airplane
Repairing your car	Designing a quilt
Performing magic	Taking photographs
Attending art films	Building a table
Welding and soldering	Developing an inventory system
Designing and weaving a rug	Programming a home computer
Negotiating a contract	Helping in a political campaign
Editing a manuscript	Playing a musical instrument
Planning a trip	Painting a picture
Steering a ship	Playing war games

Serving on a jury
Volunteering at the hospital
Visiting a museum
Attending a great books group
Sewing and designing clothes
Playing golf
Having intensive talks with a doctor
Teaching a child to play the banjo
Reading the Bible
Leading a platoon
Learning Braille
Operating a printing press
Eating in an exotic restaurant
Running a store
Planning a balanced diet
Reading *All and Everything*
Learning sign language of the deaf

Teaching Sunday School
Training an apprentice
Being an apprentice
Hooking a rug
Learning yoga
Laying bricks
Making a speech
Being Dungeonmaster in Dungeons and
    Dragons
Negotiating a merger
Developing film
Learning calligraphy
Applying statistics to gambling
Becoming a ham radio operator
Taking care of sick animals
Reading about ancient Rome
Reading this book

Chapter 14

Credit by Learning Contract

A mainstay of many non-traditional degree programs is the learning contract, also known as a study plan, study contract, degree plan, etc. It is, essentially, a formal agreement between the student and the school, setting forth a plan of study the student intends to undertake, goals he or she wishes to reach, and the action to be taken by the school once the goals are reached—normally the granting either of a certain amount of credit, or of a degree.

A well-written learning contract is a good thing for both student and school, since it reduces greatly the chances of misunderstandings or problems after the student has done a great deal of work and the inevitable distress that accompanies such an event.

In my counseling practice, I regularly hear from people who are distressed, often devastated, to have discovered that some project on which they have been working for many months was really not what their faculty advisor or school had in mind, so they are getting little or no credit for it.

Indeed, I went through a similar sort of event myself. After I had worked nearly two years on my Doctorate, one key member of my faculty guidance committee died, and a second transferred to another school. No one else on the faculty seemed interested in working with me, and without a binding agreement of any sort, there was no way I could make it happen. I simply dropped out. (Three years later, a new department head invited me back to finish my degree, and I did so—but a lot of anguish could have been avoided if I had had a contract with the school.)

A learning contract is binding on both the student and the school. If the student does the work called for, then the school must award the predetermined number of credits. In case of disputes arising from such a contract, there are usually clauses calling for binding arbitration by an impartial third party.

A simple and then a more complex example of learning contracts should make clear how the concept works.

A SIMPLE LEARNING CONTRACT

In the course of discussing the work to be done for a Bachelor's degree, the student and the faculty advisor agree that it would be desirable for the student to learn to read in German. Rather than take formal courses, the student says that she prefers to study German on her own, with the help of an uncle who speaks the language. If the student had taken four semesters of German at a traditional school, she would have earned 20 semester hours of credit. So the learning contract might consist of these seven simple clauses:

1. Student intends to learn to read German at the level of a typical student who has completed four semesters of college-level German.

2. Student will demonstrate this knowledge by translating a 1000-word passage from *Drei Kameraden* by Erich Maria Remarque.

3. The passage will be selected and the translation evaluated by a member of the German faculty of the college.

4. If the student achieves a score of 85% or higher in the evaluation, then the college will immediately award 20 semester hours of credit in German.

5. If the student scores below 85%, she may try again after a 30-day interval.

6. The fee for the first evaluation will be $50 and, if necessary, $30 for any further evaluations.

7. If any dispute shall arise over the interpretation of this contract, it shall be settled by arbitration as follows. An arbitrator shall be chosen jointly by the student and the school. If they *cannot agree in choosing an arbitrator, then each* party will choose an arbitrator. The decision of the arbitrator(s) shall be final, and neither side will appeal the decision. If there are two arbitrators and they cannot agree, they shall jointly appoint a third arbitrator, and the majority decision of the panel of three shall be final and binding.

This contract has the three basic elements common to any learning contract:
1. The objectives or goals of the student.
2. The methods by which these goals are to be reached.
3. The method of evaluation of the performance.

The more precisely each of these items can be defined, the less likelihood of problems later. For instance, instead of simply saying, "The student will become proficient in German," the foregoing agreement defines exactly what "proficient" means.

A MORE COMPLEX LEARNING CONTRACT

What follows is an abridgement of a long learning contract, freely adapted from some of the excellent case histories provided in a recent catalogue of Beacon College.

Goals

At the end of my Master's program, I plan to have the skills, experiences, and theoretical knowledge to work with an organization in the role of director or consultant, and to help the organization set and reach its goals; to work with individuals or small groups as a counselor, providing a supportive or therapeutic environment in which to grow and learn.

I want to acquire a good understanding of and grounding in group dynamics, how children learn, how adults learn, developmental states, and what facilitates learning and what limits growth, how and why people come together to grow, learn, and work.

I am especially interested in alternative organizations. I want to have the skills to help organizations analyze their financial needs, and to locate and best utilize appropriate funding.

Methods

Theory and Skill Development (40% of work)

I shall take the following three courses at my local Community College (courses listed and described) = 20% of program.

After reading the following four books (list of books), and others that may be suggested by my faculty advisor, I shall prepare statements of my personal philosophy of education and growth, as a demonstration of my understanding of the needs of a self-directed responsible caring human = 10% of program.

I shall attend a six-lesson workshop on power dynamics and assertiveness, given by (details of workshop) = 10% of program.

Leadership and Management Practicum (30% of work)

I shall work with the Cooperative Nursery School to attempt to put into practice the things I have learned in the first phase of my studies, in the following way: (much detail here). Documentation shall be through a journal of my work, a log of all meetings, a self-assessment of my performance, and a commentary supplied by an outside evaluator = 15% of program.

I shall donate eight hours a week for 20 weeks to Women's Crisis Center, again endeavoring to put into practice the ideas which I have learned (many more details here) = 15% of program.

Organizational Development, Analysis, and Design (30% of work)

I shall study one of the above two groups (nursery school or crisis center) in great detail, and prepare an analysis and projection for the future of this organization, including recommendations for funding, management, and development = 20% of the program.

Documentation will be in the form of a long paper detailing my findings and recommendations, and relating them to my philosophy of growth and organization development = 10% of program. This paper will be read and evaluated by (name of person or committee).

The contract concludes with a standard arbitration clause, as in the first contract example.

Learning contracts are truly negotiable. There is no right or wrong, no black or white. So a skillful negotiator might well get more credit for the same amount of work, or the same degree for a lesser amount of work, when compared with a less-skillful negotiator.

Some schools will enter into a learning contract that covers the entire degree program, as in the second example. Others prefer to have separate contracts, each one covering a small portion of the program: one for the language requirement, one for science, one for humanities, one for the thesis, and so forth.

It is rare, but not unheard of, to seek legal advice in the preparation or the evaluation of a learning contract, especially for a long and complex one covering an entire graduate degree program. As the legal profession so often says, it is often better to invest a small amount of money in a lawyer's time now, rather than get into an expensive and protracted legal battle later, because of an unclear agreement. Dozens of colleges and universities are sued every year by students who claim that credits or degrees were wrongfully withheld from them. Most of these suits could be avoided by the use of well-drawn learning contracts.

Chapter 15

Credit for Foreign Academic Experience

There are many thousands of universities, colleges, technical schools, institutes, and vocational schools all over the world, whose courses are at least the equivalent of work at American universities. In principle, nearly all American universities are willing to give credit for work.

But can you imagine the task of an admissions officer faced with the student who presents the Advanced Diploma of the Wysza Szkola Inaynierska in Poland, or the degree of Gakuski from the Matsuyama Shoka Daigaku in Japan? Are these equal to a high school diploma, a Doctorate, or something in between?

Until 1974, the U.S. Office of Education offered the service of evaluating educational credentials earned outside the United States and translating them into the approximately comparable level of U.S. achievement. But this service is no longer available from the U.S. government. The government has chosen, instead, to recognize five private non-profit organizations that perform this evaluative service.

These services are used mostly by schools themselves to evaluate applicants from abroad or with foreign credentials, but individuals may deal with them directly at low cost.

Depending on the complexity of the evaluation, the costs run from $25 to $100, or more if there is non-school learning to evaluate. The services operate quickly. Less than two weeks for an evaluation is not unusual. While many schools accept their findings, there are some that do not, because they have their own evaluation procedures.

You may wish to use one of the services to get a good idea where you stand. But it may be wise, if this factor is important for you, to determine in advance whether or not the schools to which you may apply will honor the findings.

The reports of these services will give the exact U.S. equivalent of non-U.S. work, either by semester hours or degree equivalents. For instance, they would report that the Japanese Gakushi is almost exactly equivalent to an American Bachelor's degree.

The five U.S. Government-recommended services are:

EDUCATIONAL CREDENTIAL EVALUATORS, INC.
P.O. Box 17499, Milwaukee WI 53217, 414/964-0477

EDUCATION INTERNATIONAL
403 West 115th St., New York NY 10025, 212/662-1768

INTERNATIONAL CONSULTANTS OF DELAWARE
914 Pickett Lane, Newark DE 19711, 302/368-3018

INTERNATIONAL EDUCATIONAL RESEARCH FOUNDATION
Credentials Evaluation Service, P.O. Box 24679, Los Angeles CA 90024, 213/474-7313

WORLD EDUCATION SERVICES
P.O. Box 745, Old Chelsea Station, New York NY 10011, 212/679-0626

Chapter 16

The Credit Bank Service

A lot of people have very complicated educational histories. They may have taken classes at several different universities and colleges, taken some evening or summer school classes, perhaps some company-sponsored seminars, some military training classes, and possibly a whole raft of other, informal learning experiences. When it comes time to present their educational past, it may mean assembling dozens of diverse transcripts, certificates, diplomas, job descriptions, and the like, often into a rather large and unwieldy package.

There is, happily, an ideal solution to these problems: the Regents Credit Bank, operated by the enlightened Department of Education of the State of New York, and available to people anywhere in the world.

The Credit Bank is an evaluation and transcript service for people who wish to consolidate their academic records, perhaps adding credit for non-academic career and learning experiences. The Credit Bank issues a single widely-accepted transcript on which all credit is listed in a simple, straightforward, and comprehensible form. The transcript is for the University of the State of New York, but it is not necessary to be a student of the University to make use of the Credit Bank service.

The Credit Bank was originally established for students enrolling in the non-resident degree programs of the University of the State of New York, and is still given automatically to these enrollees. But for those not enrolling in New York's Bachelor's degree programs, the Credit Bank offers the best possible way to make sense and order out of a complex educational past.

There are six basic categories of learning experiences that can qualify to be "deposited" in an account at the Credit Bank, and, of course, various elements of these six can be combined as well.

1. College courses taken either in residence or by correspondence from regionally-accredited colleges and universities in the United States, or the equivalent in other countries.

2. Scores earned on CLEP (College-Level Proficiency Examinations), and other equivalency examinations administered by any of the major civilian or military testing authorities.

3. Military service schools, and Military Occupational Specialties that have been evaluated for credit by the American Council on Education (as described in Chapter 13).

4. Non-college learning experiences, offered as company courses or seminars or in-house training from many large and smaller corporations.

5. Pilot training licenses and certificates issued by the Federal Aviation Administration (formerly the Civil Aeronautics Administration).

6. Special assessment of learning in other fields.

The first five of these categories have predetermined amounts of credit. The CLEP basic science exam will always be worth six semester units. Fluency in Spanish will always be worth 24 semester units. Xerox Corporation's course in repair of the 9400 copier will always be worth two semester units. The Army's course in becoming a bandleader will always be worth 12 semester units. And so forth, for thousands of already evaluated, non-school learning experiences.

The sixth category can be extremely flexible and variable. Special assessment is a means of earning credit for things learned in the course of ordinary living or job experience. The Credit Bank assesses this learning by appointing a panel of two or more experts in the field. Except in rare cases, it is necessary to go to Albany, New York to meet with this panel.

The panel may wish to conduct an oral, a written, or (in the case of performers) a performance examination. They may wish to inspect a portfolio of writing, art, or documentation. Following the evaluation, whatever form it takes, the panel makes its recommendations for the amount of credit to be given. This has, in practice, ranged from zero to more than eighty semester units, although the typical range for each separate assessment is probably from 15 to 30 semester units.

Some typical areas of special assessment, according to the Credit Bank, have included work in journalism, ceramics, Hebrew language, electronics engineering, and Japanese culture studies.

To enroll in the Credit Bank, one first requests the necessary forms, then returns them to the Bank with a non-refundable payment of $125. This sum buys two years' worth of an unlimited number of evaluations and transcripts, but does not include special assessments. The fee for each special assessment is $300, and a separate assessment is required for each academic or vocational area assessed.

After the initial two-year period, there is an annual $50 maintenance fee to keep your Credit Bank account open.

One especially nice feature of the Credit Bank service is that only those courses the student wishes to be listed are actually listed. Thus any previous academic failures, low grades, or other embarrassments can be deleted from the Credit Bank transcript.

Also, if the student has done work that may be relevant for a certain job or situation, even if it is not assigned academic credit, that work may still be listed on the transcript as "non-credit" work.

The address is Regents Credit Bank, University of the State of New York, Cultural Education Center, Room 5D45, Albany NY 12230.

Part Three
Regular Alternative Schools

Each school has been rated on a scale of 😊 to 😣 , with regard to its non-traditional degree program. This is *not* necessarily a rating of the entire school. Thus, for instance, Harvard gets a lower rating only because they do little of a non-traditional nature.

Chapter 17

Non-Traditional Schools Offering the Bachelor's, Master's and Doctorate

In the listings that follow, the name of each school is followed by its mailing address, telephone number, accreditation status, the degrees offered, residency requirements, and then a narrative description of what it offers, and my opinion of it.

When a school claims accreditation from an unrecognized accrediting agency, I list them as unaccredited. Since accreditation does not exist outside the United States, foreign schools are simply identified as "foreign," instead of having an accreditation status. When a school requires residency, I indicate what it is that makes it non-traditional:

EW means evening and/or weekend (and occasionally summer) programs.
LE means unusually large amount of credit given for life experience learning.
IS means substantial elements of independent study as part of the program.

AALBORG UNIVERSITY CENTRE
Postbox 159, DK-9100, Aalborg, Denmark

Foreign
Bachelor's, Master's
Residency (IS)

After one year of residential study, students at this experimental Danish university combine work experience with independent study projects, reading, small group meetings, and field work. The degrees in economics, engineering, business administration, and social work are based on passing examinations.

ACADEMY OF OPEN LEARNING
426 S. Third St., Geneva IL 60134
312/232-6020

Accredited
Bachelor's
Residency (LE, IS)

Bachelor of Arts in Valuation Sciences for appraisers, offered in conjunction with Kendall College, Evanston, Illinois. The work is done through a combination of life experience credit and evening courses.

ACADIA UNIVERSITY
Wolfville, Nova Scotia BOP 1XO Canada
902/542-2201

Foreign
Bachelor's
Non-resident

Although it is not possible to complete all the degree requirements at Acadia, persons who have done work elsewhere can complete their degree non-residentially through Acadia. Work can be done by correspondence, work at other schools, Canadian armed forces classes, and examinations, which can be taken at remote locations. Credit for prior learning is assessed and awarded on the basis of Challenge for Credit examinations.

ADELPHI UNIVERSITY
Garden City NY 11530
505/227-0111

Accredited
Bachelor's, Master's
Residency or
"in transit" (EW, IS)

Bachelor of Arts in American Civilization, mathematics; Bachelor of Science in biology, chemistry, physics, through evening study. Up to 75% of credits can come through prior learning assessment, through the ABLE program.

Commuters in the New York City area can take advantage of Adelphi's unique "Classroom-on-Wheels" program, in which all classes required to earn the Bachelor's and the M.B.A. are taught on commuter trains and buses going to and from New York and its suburbs.

ALLAMA IQBAL OPEN UNIVERSITY
Sector H-8, Islamabad, Pakistan

Foreign
Bachelor's, Master's,
    Doctorates
Short residency

Pakistan's open university offers correspondence study, with some courses by radio, leading to degrees in science, social studies, mathematics, languages, education, gardening, and research and development. The awarding of the degrees is based largely on examinations. Some meetings with tutors at study centers may be required.

AMERICAN COLLEGE
270 Bryn Mawr Ave., Bryn Mawr PA 19019
215/896-4500

Accredited
Master's
Short residency

Offers an external Master of Science in financial services, through a combination of correspondence study and short residency, primarily for life insurance agents. Formerly known as the American College of Life Underwriters.

AMERICAN COLLEGE IN PARIS
31 Avenue Bosquet, 75007 Paris, France
551-2157

Accredited
Bachelor's
Residency (EW)

Bachelor's degrees are offered through summer or year-round study. Degrees are available in international business administration, international affairs, art history, French studies, and European culture. Tuition in excess of $4,000 per year.

AMERICAN GRADUATE UNIVERSITY
733 N. Dodsworth Ave., Covina CA 91724
213/331-5484

Unaccredited
Master's
Non-resident

Master of Business Administration in the specific area of contracting with the federal government. Courses may be taken entirely by correspondence, by video cassette, or by attending seminars given at various locations around the United States each year. The University, established in 1975, is accredited by the National Association for Private Nontraditional Schools and Colleges, a legitimate but unrecognized accreditor. Tuition is in excess of $4,000 for the degree program. A Bachelor's degree, or equivalent, and three years' experience in federal contracting are required for admission. Persons without the experience may take the courses, but the degree will not be awarded until the experience is acquired.

Comment: A.G.U. has a faculty with outstanding credentials, and appears to offer its hundred-or-more students an excellent course of study in this narrowly defined area. The 72-page catalogue provides extremely detailed information on the specific courses offered, and the history of the school and its faculty. The accreditation will only prove useful to students if the accrediting agency should be recognized.

AMERICAN INTERNATIONAL COLLEGE
Springfield MA 01109
413/737-5331

Accredited
Bachelor's, Master's
Residency (EW)

Bachelor of Arts in economics, liberal studies, social studies; Bachelor of Business Administration; Master of Arts in educational psychology, teaching, interdisciplinary social sciences; M.B.A., Master of Education, Master of Science, all offered through evening study. Not to be confused with the degree mill called American International University.

AMERICAN NATIONAL UNIVERSITY
3550 N. Central Ave., Phoenix AZ 85012
602/265-8657

Unaccredited
Bachelor's, Master's,
  Doctorates
Non-resident

Degrees in hundreds of fields are offered by correspondence study at a cost of around $2,000 for writing a very short thesis.

Comment: The University was established by Dr. Clarence Franklin, who had previously been President, Dean, and Chancellor of American International University, a diploma mill (described in Chapter 24), that uses an address in the same office building complex as American National. Dr. Franklin assures me that there is no connection whatsoever between American National and American International, and that he no longer has any connection with American International. Dr. Franklin further assures me that it is an error that his name appears in official state records as the incorporator of American International, and that someone has used his name without his permission. American National operates from a two-room office in Phoenix; Dr. Franklin lives in southern California. American National claims accreditation from the National Accreditation Association, an unrecognized agency of which Dr. Franklin is an officer, and which is described fully in Chapter 7.

AMERICAN TECHNOLOGICAL UNIVERSITY
P.O. Box 1416, Killeen TX 76541

Accredited
Bachelor's
Residency (LE)

It is possible to earn the Bachelor's degree in various technical subjects with a minimum of one semester in residence on the campus.

AMERICAN UNIVERSITY
McKinley Building, Washington DC 20016
202/686-2500

Accredited
Bachelor's
Residency (LE)

Wide range of Bachelor's degrees, offered through the APEL Program in the Division of Continuing Education. Up to 75% of the necessary units can be earned through a combination of credit for life experience and credit by examination. Two specially-designed courses are offered, during which the student prepares a life experience portfolio.

ANDREW JACKSON COLLEGE
4816 Jamestown Ave., P.O. Box 14891,
  Baton Rouge LA 70898

Unaccredited
Bachelor's, Master's
Non-resident

Correspondence courses leading to the Bachelor's and Master's correspondence programs in Asiatic disciplines (martial arts), parapsychology, and many traditional subjects (business, philosophy, political science, etc.). Courses are given in eight (page 8 of catalogue) or ten (page 84) languages including Arabic, Chinese, Japanese and Korean. The College was established in 1980 and maintains a residential program. It is recognized by the Louisiana Commission on Proprietary Schools. A list of faculty is given, and a list of schools from which the faculty earned degrees is given, but the two are not paired up. Tuition is $50 per credit hour.

Comment: It all appears legitimate, although it would be nice if the credentials of the faculty and staff were given. A lot of misspellings in the catalogue (''parapshychology,'' ''enterance,'' ''propritary'' etc.)

ANGLO-AMERICAN INSTITUTE OF DRUGLESS THERAPY

30 Kinloch Road, Renfrew, Scotland
041/886-3137

Unaccredited
Doctorates
Non-resident

Doctor of Naturopathy (N.D.) and Diploma in Osteopathy offered entirely though correspondence study. Established in Indiana in 1911 by a medical doctor. Moved to Scotland in 1939, to England in 1948, and back to Scotland in 1977. The degree involves completing about 50 lessons, ranging from anatomy and physiology to chiropractic and spondylotherapy (which appears to involve emptying the stomach and appendix by means of concussion, thus having effect, according to the catalogue, on heart trouble, bust development, syphillis, and impotence). The cost is under $500 for the lessons, including two wall charts. The Institute claims more than 8,000 graduates.

Comment: I wonder what that Indiana physician would have to say about spondylotherapy? The rather flamboyantly written 10-page catalogue is not my idea of a professional document. However, a number of correspondents have told me that if you are interested in these subject areas, A.A.I.D.T. is a good place to learn them. Holders of the degree in the United States certainly could not be licensed to practice medicine, and perhaps not even spondylotherapy.

ANNA MARIA COLLEGE

Paxton MA 01612
617/757-4586

Accredited
Master's
Residency (EW)

The Master of Business Administration can be earned in from 12 to 18 months of intensive weekend study, with classes meeting Saturdays in Boston.

SUSAN B. ANTHONY UNIVERSITY

6907 Sherman St., Philadelphia PA 19119
    or 7366 Princeton Ave., Kansas City MO 63130
No listed telephones

Unaccredited
Bachelor's, Master's,
  Doctorates
Non-resident

Established in the mid-1970's by Dr. Albert Schatz, discoverer of the antibiotic streptomycin. Bachelor's, Master's and Doctorates are offered in the areas of education, environmental studies, naturopathy, and ''peace and freedom.'' The catalogue also discusses a College of Naturopathy in Montreal, Canada, but there are no telephone listings there, either.

Comment: The catalogue is fairly impressive-looking, and one cannot dispute the credentials of the founder. And yet the school itself seems quite elusive, with at least some of the trappings of a spurious institution. They have never responded to my inquiries.

ANTIOCH UNIVERSITY

Yellow Springs OH 45387 (and various other locations)
513/767-7331

Accredited
Bachelor's, Master's, Law
Resident and Non-resident

The degrees are offered through programs of ''individualized study,'' which may take the form of residential work, internships, correspondence study, independent research and reading, plus credit for life and career experience learning. The programs change frequently, but dozens of subject areas have been offered in the social sciences, education, arts, urban affairs, and law, among others. Antioch International has operated as many as 32 learning centers all over the world, but recent financial problems have reduced this number substantially. There are major facilities or centers in cities from Honolulu to Philadelphia, as well as in England, France and Colombia. Tuition is in the range of $4,000 a year for the full-time student. All degree programs require a minimum of one academic year (nine months) to complete. The "At-A-Distance" program is especially designed for students who, for one reason or another, cannot visit the campuses. Antioch International's Individualized M.A. Program offers the opportunity to earn the Master's degree largely through independent study, with much of the work done outside the U.S. in the country of one's choice. Credit comes either through conversion of learning activities to graduate units, or through equivalency exams, or through a combination of the two.

Comment: Antioch is one of the pioneers of non-traditional education, and still offers excellent degrees with, in many cases, little or no residency. The University became quite over-extended in the late 1970's, and barely averted bankruptcy in 1979 when some trustees made emergency contributions. The prospective student still might be wise to ascertain the current financial situation before enrolling. Some of the campuses—especially the Law School in Washington, DC and Antioch/West in San Francisco—have become quite independent of the main campus and have discussed total separation, although degree-granting authority still comes only from Yellow Springs. The Master's programs seem good value for money, but the Bachelor's degrees are quite expensive when compared with other accredited alternatives that are available.

APPALACHIAN STATE UNIVERSITY
Boone NC 28608
704/262-2050

Accredited
Master's
Residency (LE, EW)

Bachelor of Arts in general studies, natural and physical sciences, social sciences, humanities, arts and business administration. More than 75% of the required units can come from credit for life experience or equivalency examinations. Oral interviews are required as part of this process. Master of Arts in education is offered through evening and weekend study, with only one full-time week required on campus.

AQUINAS COLLEGE
Grand Rapids MI 49506
616/459-8281

Accredited
Bachelor's, Master's
Short Residency (EW)

Aquinas offers its Bachelor's and Master's degrees in a Directed Study Program, requiring as little as ten days on campus per year. Participants come to campus one Saturday morning or afternoon each month for meetings and seminars. All the other work for the Bachelor of Science in business administration or the Bachelor of Arts in general education is done by independent study. Aquinas also offers Bachelor's degrees in accounting, business administration, communication arts and psychology, and a Master of Management program, with meetings one day or evening per week in Grand Rapids or Lansing.

ARMSTRONG COLLEGE
2222 Harold Way, Berkeley CA 94704
415/848-2501

Accredited
Bachelor's, Master's
Short residency (IS, EW)

Bachelor of Science and Bachelor of Business Administration largely through independent study; Master of Business Administration through regular evening courses. For the Bachelor's, six all-day Saturday meetings are held on the campus each year, and there are other evening meetings and seminars from time to time. Degree completion normally requires at least one year of enrollment. The cost is directly related to the time spent. Faculty meetings cost so much per hour, committee meetings three times the faculty rate, etc.

Comment: A good and very personal degree program. It is neither among the fastest nor the least expensive, but I have heard from quite a few satisfied alumni. The Policy Board for this program includes two past presidents of the American Association of Higher Education and the Director of the National Institute of Education—an impressive group.

ARMSTRONG STATE COLLEGE
11935 Abercorn St., Savannah GA 31406
912/925-4200

Accredited
Bachelor's, Master's
Residency (EW)

Bachelor of Arts, Bachelor of Science, Bachelor of Business Administration, Master of Business Administration, and Master of Educational Administration are offered entirely through evening study.

ARNOULD-TAYLOR ORGANISATION
Queen Street, Henley-on-Thames, Oxfordshire, England

Unaccredited
Bachelor's, Master's
Non-resident

Bachelor of Physiatrics and Master of Physiatrics, entirely through correspondence study. The course consists of seven lessons for each degree, with a paper to be written at the end of each lesson. The cost of each degree program is around $300. Physiatrics is the study of body weight and its effects on psychological well-being. Prospective students must be medical doctors, in paramedical professions, physiologists, or cosmetologists. The senior tutor is W. E. Arnould-Taylor, D.Ph. (presumably physiatrics).

Comment: The six-page typewritten prospectus does not inspire confidence. The degrees are neither authorized nor approved by Her Majesty's Department of Education and Science.

ARTHUR D. LITTLE MANAGEMENT EDUCATION
   INSTITUTE
35 Acorn Park, Cambridge MA 02140

Accredited
Master's
Residency (IS)

The Master of Science in International Management Education is offered primarily to people who hold managerial positions in business and government outside the United States. These people come to the U.S. for about ten months, in which the degree is earned through lectures, seminars, and case studies. The program is one of the few accredited profit-making graduate schools in the world.

ATHABASCA UNIVERSITY
14515 120th Ave., Edmonton, Alberta T5L 2W4, Canada
403/452-9990

Foreign
Bachelor's
Non-resident

Modeled along the lines of Britain's Open University, Athabasca offers its Bachelor of General Studies or Bachelor of Arts in interdisciplinary studies primarily through home study courses. Weekly telephone calls to a tutor at the main office are recommended. Some in-person lecture courses are offered, as well as "tele-lecture" courses in which students in remote locations interact with each other and the lecturer by conference telephone calls. More than 3,000 students are enrolled.

ATLANTIC UNION COLLEGE
South Lancaster MA 01561
617/365-4561

Accredited
Bachelor's
Short residency (LE)

Bachelor's degrees in natural and physical sciences, social science, business administration, and health sciences, computer sciences, and nursing. Students take one "unit" each semester. A "unit" is a six-month study project, requiring two weeks on campus, and the balance of the time in independent study. A minimum of two units hence four weeks of residency, is required to earn the Bachelor's degree. Up to 75% of the additional credit required may be earned from assessment of life experience learning. Bachelor's degrees are offered in art, business, behavioral science, communications, computer science, education, English, health science, history, home economics, interior design, modern languages, music, nursing, and physical education.

AURORA COLLEGE
347 Gladstone Ave., Aurora IL 60507
312/892-6431

Accredited
Bachelor's
Residency (EW)

Bachelor of Arts can be earned entirely through evening study with the continuing Education Program.

BABSON COLLEGE
Babson Park, Wellesley MA 02157
617/235-1200

Accredited
Master's
Residency (EW)

Babson offers its well regarded Master of Business Administration entirely through evening studies. Babson is known for its unique Center for Entrepreneurial Studies, where courses are offered and research is conducted in entrepreneurial activities.

BALDWIN-WALLACE COLLEGE
Berea OH 44017
216/826-2193

Accredited
Bachelor's, Master's
Residency (EW)

Bachelor of Arts in arts, business administration, English, history, political science, psychology, sociology, speech, theater arts; Bachelor of Science in elementary education, all through evening study. Master of Business Administration offered through intensive weekend or evening study, with courses offered on the main campus or in other centers in northern Ohio. The weekend degree is earned by taking courses from Friday afternoon through Saturday afternoon, every other week, for two years. The evening degree is earned by taking courses two evenings a week for two years. The evening program costs around $5,000, the weekend one (including room and board) about double that.

BALL STATE UNIVERSITY
Muncie IN 47306
317/289-1241

Accredited
Master's
Residency (EW)

Master of Education program, including a program in psychometrics, can be completed entirely through evening study.

BARAT COLLEGE
Lake Forest IL 60045
312/234-3000

Accredited
Bachelor's
Residency (LE)

Bachelor of Arts in natural and physical sciences, social science, humanities, arts, and business management, and a Bachlor of Fine Arts through a combination of coursework and credit for prior learning experiences. Up to 75% of the required units may be earned through prior learning, although the assessment procedures may take up to a year to complete. Barat offers an interesting proposition to deal with rising tuition. They will reduce their about-$5,000-a-year tuition by a third in exchange for 400 hours a year of work on campus.

BARD COLLEGE
Annandale-on-Hudson NY 12504
914/758-6822

Accredited
Bachelor's
Short-residency

Bachelor of Arts, Bachelor of Science, and Bachelor of Professional Studies, designed ''to meet the special needs of the many people who have left college without completing their studies and who wish to take them up again at a later date when their lives no longer fit the typical residential college structure.'' The program begins with an on-campus weekend each year. Students attend seminars or visit with their faculty advisor once a month. The minimum time to complete the degree is one academic year (nine months).

BARUCH COLLEGE
17 Lexington Ave., New York NY 10010
212/725-3131

Accredited
Bachelor's, Master's
Residency (EW)

This college of the City University of New York offers the Bachelor of Business Administration, Master of Business Administration, and Master of Public Administration entirely through evening study.

BEACON COLLEGE
2706 Ontario Road N.W., Washington DC 20009
202/797-9270

Accredited
Bachelor's, Master's
Non-resident

Bachelor's and Master's in almost any field, entirely through non-resident study. Students work with faculty advisors, who may or may not live in their vicinity. As needed, the Central Office provides services of the Academic Council (experienced educators who approve curriculum plans, award credit, and recommend awarding degrees), and Monitors (consultants to both the student and the advisor). Degrees may be earned in a minimum of nine months. Credit is given for all prior learning experiences. Each program is highly personal, and this is reflected by the degree titles, which can be selected by the student. Typical examples are B.A. in Urban Studies; M.A. in Dance Therapy; B.A. in Design Science; and so forth. Tuition is just over $1,000 per four-month term. Approximately 200 students are enrolled.

Comment: Beacon probably has the most flexible, most non-traditional Master's degrees ever to achieve traditional accreditation, which was granted in 1981. It offers an outstanding opportunity to earn an excellent degree at a relatively low cost. The catalog has many excellent examples of student programs and plans. Students outside the U.S. can only be accepted from countries in which Beacon has foreign program advisors. The school was formerly called Campus-Free College.

BELLARMINE COLLEGE
2000 Norris Place, Louisville KY 40205
502/452-8011

Accredited
Bachelor's
Residency (EW)

Bachelor of Arts and Bachelor of Science in Commerce available entirely through evening study.

BEMIDJI STATE UNIVERSITY
Center for Extended Learning, Deputy Hall 110,
    Bemidji MN 56601
218/755-2068

Accredited
Bachelor's
Residency (LE)

Bachelor of Arts and Bachelor of Science in English, geography, history, political science, sociology, community service, humanities, vocational education, industrial technology, and criminal justice. Up to 75% of the required credit is given for life experience and prior learning experiences. New credit is earned through on-campus classes, extension classes in other cities, and through independent guided home study. Learning packages (a syllabus, books, and sometimes audio or videocassettes) are provided. It is theoretically possible to earn the degrees without ever going to the campus, although an officer has written me, "We do normally expect to see them once in a while." Although the program was originally designed for students in northern Minnesota, there is no specific regulation governing residence, and there have been some out-of-state and out-of-country students.

BEN FRANKLIN ACADEMY AND INSTITUTE
    FOR ADVANCED STUDIES
P.O. Box 1776, Washington DC 20013
202/USA-1776

Unaccredited
Bachelor's, Master's,
    Doctorates
Non-resident

Bachelor of Arts, Master of Arts, and Doctor of Philosophy degrees, entirely through correspondence study. Degrees are awarded on the basis of credit for life experience, a "sworn statement detailing the years of actual experience a candidate has had in his chosen field,'' and completion of some sixty-odd correspondence courses offered. ''Deserving Americans'' may request Honorary Doctorates, which require a donation: ''It is through such an honorary degree program that this institution is able to embark on its continued development program.'' The 28-page catalogue lists 12 faculty members, half with traditional Doctorates.

Comment: The sales letter from the Director of Admissions, Donald Stephen, says, ''This is not just another degree mill, but a fully accredited degree-granting institution.'' The claimed accreditation is from the American Association of Accredited Colleges and Universities, an unrecognized accreditor of whom I can find no record. They say they are an educational affiliate of the Ben Franklin Society, the ''membership arm'' of the New Spirit of 76 Foundation. The address and the telephone number are surely the best part. At least they show the institution has influence somewhere.

BETHEL COLLEGE
McKenzie TN 38201
901/352-5321

Accredited
Bachelor's
Residency (EW)

Bachelor of Science in business administration, entirely through evening study.

BISCAYNE COLLEGE
University Without Walls
1150 N.W. 14th St., Suite 712, Miami FL 33136
305/324-8381

Accredited
Bachelor's
Residency (IS)

Bachelor's degrees may be earned with majors in a wide variety of fields, including sports administration, pre-medical, pre-dental, and pre-law, in a University Without Walls program. Credit is given for prior formal and informal learning experiences. Students work with a major professor to develop a plan of study covering the remaining work needed for the degree.

BLOOMSBURG STATE COLLEGE
Center for Experiential Learning
Bloomsburg PA 17815
717/389-2208

Accredited
Bachelor's
Little or no residency

Bachelor's degrees in natural and physical sciences, social sciences, humanities and arts, business administration, health science, and education. All of the necessary credit for the degree can be earned through assessment of prior learning, or a combination of this and equivalency exams and departmental challenge exams prepared by the college. The program requires 128 semester units.

BOSTON COLLEGE
Chestnut Hill MA 02167
617/969-0100

Accredited
Bachelor's
Residency (EW)

All of the courses required for the Bachelor of Arts degree in American Studies, business, economics, English, history, political science, psychology, or sociology can be earned entirely through evening study. Most courses are taught for two and a half hours, one evening per week.

BOSTON UNIVERSITY
Boston MA 02215
617/731-3300

Accredited
Bachelor's, Master's
Residency (EW, overseas)

Bachelor of Applied Science, Bachelor of Liberal Studies, Bachelor of Urban Studies, Master of Liberal Arts in history, Master of Liberal Studies, and Master of Urban Affairs may be earned entirely through evening study with the university's Metropolitan College. The Overseas Program offers Master's degrees in business administration, international relations, and education at centers in Germany, Italy, and Belgium.

BOWLING GREEN STATE UNIVERSITY
Bowling Green OH 43403
419/372-2531

Accredited
Master's
Residency (IS)

Master's degree program in organizational development, through an external degree plan involving a combination of on-campus study and independent study.

BRADLEY UNIVERSITY
College of Continuing Education
Peoria IL 61625
309/676-7611

Accredited
Bachelor's, Master's
Residency (EW)

Bachelor of Science in business administration, Master of Educational Administration, Master of Music Education, and Master of Business Administration, offered entirely through evening study.

BRANDON UNIVERSITY
270 18th St., Brandon, Manitoba R7A 6A9, Canada
204/728-9520

Foreign
Bachelor's
Residency (IS)

Brandon offers its Bachelor of Arts, Science, Teaching, and General Studies in remote locations in northern Canada. The Northern Teacher Education Programme is offered in eight residential centers, and also makes use of "traveling professors" who regularly fly in to remote villages to offer courses and advice. Many of the students are Indians.

BRIGHAM YOUNG UNIVERSITY
Independent Study Office, 206 Harman Continuing
   Education Building, Provo UT 84602
801/378-2868

Accredited
Bachelor's
Short-residency

Bachelor of Independent Studies program offered through independent study and a short period of on-campus study. The Bachelor's degree requires a maximum of attendance at five seminars on campus — one of each of five units of the program — but this may be shortened through credit for life experience or equivalency examinations. The total elapsed time can range from 16 to 60 months. Final exams must be supervised but may be taken anywhere in the world. The total cost is in excess of $3,000. There is a Hawaii campus at Laie, HI 96762.

Comment: The degree is both expensive and time-consuming, in comparison with some other accredited programs, but the school has an excellent reputation and is of particular importance to those of the Mormon faith. Brigham Young's home study courses comprise one of the largest offerings of any school. They may be taken at modest cost by students living anywhere in the world, whether or not they are working toward a degree.

BRYANT COLLEGE
Evening Division
Smithfield RI 02917
401/231-1200

Accredited
Bachelor's, Master's
Residency (EW)

Bachelor of Science in business administration and law enforcement; Master of Business Administration, offered entirely through evening study.

BURLINGTON COLLEGE
P.O. Box 2287, South Burlington VT 05401
802/862-5650

Accredited
Bachelor's
Very short residency

Bachelor of Arts, primarily through non-resident study. All students must attend a one-week workshop at Burlington, and are encouraged but not required to attend a one-week residential session twice a year. The degree may be completed in a minimum of six months. Because of the need to meet from time to time with advisors, students living far from Vermont are not encouraged to apply.

CALIFORNIA AMERICAN UNIVERSITY

230 W. 3rd Ave., Escondido CA 92025
714/741-6595

Unaccredited
Master's
Short-residency

Master of Science in Management involving either two eight-week summer sessions, or a series of weekend classes. The cost is more than $3,000 for one person, with a discount for a spouse attending at the same time. The faculty of ten all have earned traditional Doctorates. The school is authorized to grant degrees by the State of California.

CALIFORNIA COAST UNIVERSITY

700 N. Main St., Santa Ana CA 92701
714/547-9625

Unaccredited
Bachelor's, Master's,
  Doctorates
Non-resident

California Coast University, formerly called California Western University, was the first of California's many non-resident universities to open during the 1970's. Non-resident degrees at all levels are offered in the areas of engineering, education, behavioral science, and business. All four programs have been approved by the State of California. The university is accredited by the National Association of Private Nontraditional Schools and Colleges, a legitimate but unrecognized accrediting agency. Most degree programs cost between $2,000 and $3,000 and require a minimum of one year to complete. Credit is given only for actual in-school prior learning experiences, or for equivalency examinations that have been prepared by California Coast in a wide variety of fields. The founder and president is Thomas A. Neal, whose own Doctorate is from California Coast. The heads of the four schools all have traditional Doctorates. The University operates from its own building, a tastefully remodeled former bank building in a Los Angeles suburb.

Comment: For those persons willing to spend a year or more to earn their degree, California Coast University offers an excellent alternative. There are very few state-approved, totally non-resident Doctorates available. Combined programs are offered for earning the Bachelor's and Master's or the Master's and Doctorate simultaneously.

CALIFORNIA GRADUATE SCHOOL OF MARITAL
AND FAMILY THERAPY

39 Trellis Drive, Bldg. #5, San Rafael CA 94903
415/472-5511

Unaccredited
Doctorates
Residency (EW)

The Ph.D in Marital and Family Therapy and the D.M.F.C. (Doctor of Marital, Family and Child Therapy) are approved by the State of California, so graduates can take the state licensing examinations. A Ph.D. in clinical psychology is also available. Students meet either one or two days per week from 3 p.m. to 10 p.m., with an hour off for dinner.

CALIFORNIA INSTITUTE OF INTEGRAL
STUDIES

3494 21st St., San Francisco CA 94110
415/648-1489

Accredited
Master's, Doctorates
Residency (IS)

Master's degrees are offered in East-West Psychology, integral counseling psychology, and intercultural philosophy and religion. The Ph.D. is available in psychology and intercultural philosophy and religion. Most programs involve a combination of class study, personal experience of psycho-spiritual growth processes, and practical field work in counseling, community service, teaching, or creative independent study. Formerly called the California Institute of Asian Studies.

CALIFORNIA INSTITUTE OF THE ARTS
24700 McBean Parkway, Valencia CA 91355
805/255-1050

Accredited
Bachelor's
Residency (LE)

Bachelor of Fine Arts program in which up to 75% of the necessary units may be earned through an assessment of life experience and prior learning.

CALIFORNIA PACIFIC UNIVERSITY
920 Moreno Blvd., San Diego CA 92110
714/297-3880

Part accredited, part
 unaccredited
Bachelor's, Master's,
 Doctorates
Residency and Non-resident

California Pacific offers its own Master of Arts in Management and Human Behavior, a degree program that may be completed entirely by correspondence study, with two proctored examinations that may be taken anywhere. The degree program is approved by the State of California. The school's good reputation is enhanced by its partnerships with two excellent schools: a Bachelor's degree program is offered residentially in San Diego in conjunction with the accredited Alabama A & M University. C.P.U. does the teaching and Alabama awards the degrees. A doctoral program in psychology is offered residentially in cooperation with International College of Los Angeles.

CALIFORNIA SCHOOL OF PROFESSIONAL
PSYCHOLOGY
2152 Union St., San Francisco CA 94123
415/346-4500

Accredited
Master's, Doctorates
Residency (EW)

Master's and Ph.D. programs in psychology through evening and weekend study exclusively. There are branch campuses in Berkeley, Fresno, Los Angeles, and San Diego. Self-directed independent study is available. Some of the required classes can be waived (if similar work has been done elsewhere), or passed by a Challenge Examination.

CALIFORNIA STATE UNIVERSITY, CHICO
Chico CA 95926
916/895-6321

Accredited
Bachelor's, Master's
Residency (IS)

A part of California's "Thousand Mile Campus," Chico State offers the Bachelor of Arts in environmental planning, public administration and social science; Master of Arts in California Studies, environmental planning and social science; and the Master of Public Administration, with elements of independent study and credit for prior learning.

CALIFORNIA STATE UNIVERSITY,
DOMINGUEZ HILLS
1000 East Victoria St., Dominguez Hills CA 90747
213/516-3743

Accredited
Bachelor's, Master's
Non-resident

The External Degree Program in Humanities offers an outstanding and totally non-resident Bachelor of Arts and Master of Arts degree. Both programs encompass history, literature, philosophy, music, and art. The program is offered by "parallel instruction," which means the student does all the work that a residential student would do, in the same general time frame, but does not attend classes. The Master's requires 45 quarter hours for the degree, of which 80% must be earned after enrolling. Units are earned through independent study projects, correspondence courses, and completion of either a thesis or a creative project in the field of study. The programs emphasize communication with faculty advisors by mail and by telephone. A full-time student could finish the Master's in nine months, at a total cost under $3,000. The Bachelor's will take somewhat longer. Students living anywhere in the world are welcome to enroll.

Comment: One of the very rare opportunities to earn an accredited Master's degree entirely non-residentially, and surely among the least expensive. An outstanding program. (Of course I am biased. My wife will have completed her M.A. here in 1983, and is a walking testimonial to the program, its personal level of attention, and its professional staff.)

CALIFORNIA STATE UNIVERSITY, HAYWARD
25800 Hillary Road, Hayward CA 94542
415/881-3817

Accredited
Bachelor's
Residency (LE)

Bachelor's degrees in general studies, social science, science, humanities, arts, business administration and health administration, in which more than 75% of the units can come from assessment of prior learning.

CALIFORNIA STATE UNIVERSITY, NORTHRIDGE
18111 Nordhoff St., Northridge CA 91324
213/885-1200

Accredited
Bachelor's, Master's
Residency (IS)

Bachelor of Science in health science administration, and Master of Science in engineering are offered in a non-traditional mode, with elements of independent study, and credit for prior experience.

CALIFORNIA STATE UNIVERSITY, SACRAMENTO
6000 J Street, Sacramento CA 95819
916/454-6133

Accredited
Bachelor's
Residency (IS)

Bachelor of Arts in criminal justice and Bachelor of Science in nursing, with various non-traditional elements, including independent study and internships.

CALUMET COLLEGE
2400 New York Ave, Whiting IN 46394
219/473-4305

Accredited
Bachelor's
Residency (LE)

Bachelor's degrees in general studies, social sciences, humanities and arts, business administration, and other individualized programs. Up to 75% of the units required can come from an assessment of prior learning experience. A course is offered in the preparation of life experience portfolios.

CAMBRIDGE COLLEGE
Institute of Open Education,
    15 Mifflin Place, Cambridge MA 02138
617/492-5108

Accredited
Master's
Residency (EW)

The Master of Education is offered through an intensive 12-month program for working professionals. Each student must complete seven courses, participate in 12 one-day weekend workshops, participate in a year-long Professional Seminar, and produce a Master's Project (research paper, media presentation, community project, etc.). Courses are given one weekday evening per week. No grades are given, and no transfer credit is accepted. Tuition for the complete program is around $5,000. Some interest-free loans are available.

CANADIAN SCHOOL OF MANAGEMENT
S-245 OISE Building, 252 Bloor St. West,
    Toronto, Ontario M5S 1V5, Canada
416/960-3805

Candidate for
  accreditation
Bachelor's, Master's
Short-residency

Bachelor of Administration in health services and Bachelor of Management, primarily through non-resident independent study. Master of Business Administration through a combination of evening and weekend study and independent study. Courses are offered regularly in Toronto, but persons living in other areas may work with faculty advisors in their vicinity. The Bachelor's degree programs are affiliated with the Union for Experimenting Colleges and Universities, a consortium that is a candidate for accreditation. In special cases in the M.B.A. program, "experienced managers who wish to study at a distance can be admitted to a competency-based option," doing most of the work in their own area. Most degrees can be completed in four to six terms.

CANISIUS COLLEGE
Evening Division
Buffalo NY 14208
716/883-7000

Accredited
Bachelor's
Residency (EW)

A wide variety of Bachelor of Arts and Bachelor of Science degrees may be earned entirely through evening study.

CAPITAL UNIVERSITY
University Without Walls, 345 Renner Hall,
    Columbus Ohio 43209
216/236-6696

Accredited
Bachelor's
Non-residential

A University Without Walls program begun in 1976 by the Union for Experimenting Colleges and Universities was taken over in 1979 by the venerable Capital University. Beginning students must complete the equivalent of 41 courses, largely through guided independent study. A Bachelor of Arts, with various majors, or a Bachelor of General Studies, with no major, can be earned. All students must complete a Significant Project, showing Bachelor's-level abilities and serving as a learning experience. Tuition is in excess of $3,000 a year. The University maintains University Without Walls offices in Cleveland and Dayton as well.

CARDINAL STRITCH COLLEGE
Adult Education Division
6801 N. Yates Rd., Milwaukee WI 53217
414/352-5400

Accredited
Bachelor's
Residency (LE)

Bachelor's degree programs in many fields, in which more than 80% of the required units may be earned through an assessment of prior experience and learning.

CARSON-NEWMAN COLLEGE
Extension Division
Jefferson City TN 27760
615/475-9061

Accredited
Bachelor's
Residency (EW)

Bachelor of Arts and Bachelor of Science in many fields, available entirely through evening study.

CENTENARY COLLEGE
Shreveport LA 71106
318/869-5011

Accredited
Bachelor's
Residency (EW)

Bachelor of Arts, Bachelor of Science and Bachelor of Music degrees may be earned entirely through evening study.

CENTRAL MICHIGAN UNIVERSITY
Institute for Personal and Career Development, Rowe Hall,
    Mt. Pleasant MI 48859
517/774-3865

Accredited
Bachelor's, Master's
Short-residency

The Master of Arts programs offer an outstanding opportunity to earn this degree through intensive classes given at various locations, nationwide, plus independent guided research. The M.A. is offered in Management and Supervision (including administration, health care administration, logistics management, marketing management, personnel management, and environmental health, among other fields); Education; and Community Leadership (including, for instance, counseling, public administration, recreation and park administration, and urban and regional planning). All of the various programs are operated under the sponsorship of companies, military bases, or professional organizations. In nearly all cases, however, anyone may enroll, whether or not they have an association with the sponsoring group. Classes are offered in Michigan, Washington DC, Hawaii, and at locations throughout the Southeast and Midwest. In addition, there are three national programs, in which classes are offered in conjunction with national and regional meetings of the sponsoring groups. Only 15 units must be competed through Central Michigan at a cost just over $100 per unit. Up to a third of the required 30 units for the degree can come from experiential learning. The Bachelor's program is undergoing substantial change, development, and rethinking, and is currently available only to Michigan residents. A Bachelor of Arts, Science, or Individualized Studies is offered. At least 30 of the required 124 semester hours must be earned from Central Michigan.

Comment: One of the best of the short-residency accredited Master's programs. The Director of the Institute, Dr. Lawrence Murphy, used to run the splendid non-resident degree program at Western Illinois University — and believes very much in the personal approach in dealing with students and inquirers. In fact, Dr. Murphy suggests interested readers of this book write directly to him, so that he can be sure the proper person responds.

CENTRE DE TÉLÉ-ENSEIGNEMENT UNIVERSITAIRE
6, Avenue H. Maringer, B.P. 33.97, F-54015 Nancy, France

Foreign
Bachelor's, Master's
Non-resident

The Centre is a confederation of seven universities, offering degree studies by correspondence, based primarily on taped lectures (in French, of course), with supplementary written materials. The tapes are available by mail, and are also broadcast on the radio and available at various regional centers. Students must enroll first in one of the participating universities (Besançon, Dijon, Metz, Mulhouse, Nancy, Reims, Strasbourg), and then in the Centre. Even though all course work is done through the Centre, the degree is awarded by a participating university. Bachelor's (license) studies are offered in many fields, and Master's in only a few.

CENTRE NATIONAL DE TÉLÉ-ENSEIGNEMENT
12, Place du Pantheon, Paris 75005, France

Foreign
Bachelor's, Master's
Non-resident

Similar to the Centre just described, with programs available nationwide. The degrees are awarded solely on the basis of examinations, which must be taken in France. In the U.S., information is also available from the Embassy of France, Cultural Attache, 972 Fifth Ave., New York NY 10021.

CENTURY UNIVERSITY
9100 Wilshire Blvd., Beverly Hills CA 90212
213/278-1094

Unaccredited
Bachelor's, Master's,
Doctorates
Non-resident

Degrees at all levels are offered entirely through non-residential study, in a wide variety of fields, including business, education, engineering administration, and psychology. Accreditation is claimed from the International Accrediting Commission for Schools, Colleges and Theological Seminaries, an unrecognized agency (see Chapter 7). Century offers a combined Bachelor's/Master's and a Master's/Doctorate program. Their approach is very slick and professional, with well-designed materials and a businesslike approach. Degrees take a minimum of nine months to complete, at a cost between $2,000 and $3,000. The program is viewed by Century as the final year of traditional study for each degree, so candidates are expected to have substantial experience in their field. The school was established in 1978 by Donald Breslow, former President of the University of Beverly Hills. His Master's degree is from Pepperdine University. The school is authorized to grant degrees by the State of California.

Comment: Century appears to offer a good, sound approach to the non-residential unaccredited degree. Their claimed accreditation cannot be of use in any situation in which an accredited degree is required.

CHAMINADE COLLEGE
3140 Waialae Ave., Honolulu HI 96816
808/735-4711

Accredited
Bachelor's
Residency (LE)

The Bachelor of General Studies program, primarily for veterans, is advertised regularly in military newspapers. Credit is offered for military and other experience, and for equivalency examinations.

CHAPMAN COLLEGE
333 Glassell St., Orange CA 92666
714/997-6646

Accredited
Bachelor's, Master's
Residency (EW)

Bachelor of Arts in social science, and Master of Arts in education, primarily for government employees and military personnel, offered at Castle Air Force Base.

CHARTER OAK COLLEGE
340 Capitol Avenue, Hartford CT 06115
203/566-7230

Accredited
Bachelor's
Non-resident

This excellent program is available only to residents of Connecticut, Massachusetts, Rhode Island, New Hampshire, Vermont, and Maine. If you do not live in one of these states, please do not write to them, because then they write anguished letters to me and refuse to send me materials. But for residents of the New England states, the program is outstanding. The College is operated by the Connecticut Board for State Academic Awards, and offers the Bachelor of Arts and Bachelor of Science degrees, based entirely on units earned elsewhere. The student is responsible for amassing 120 semester units, which may come from courses taken elsewhere, equivalency examinations, military study, correspondence courses, or special in-person examinations of one's knowledge level. As soon as the 120 units are earned, with at least half in the arts and sciences, and 36 in a single subject or major area, the degree is awarded. The cost is under $1,000, but there is a fee of up to $500 for each special equivalency examination, in fields for which there are no standard exams. Vietnam veterans and people over 62 pay no fees at all. At least 60 semester units must be completed before you are admitted to the program.

Comment: This program, along with the University of the State of New York and Edison State College of New Jersey, are the only accredited non-resident Bachelor's programs in which 100% of the work can be done elsewhere, and before enrolling. The program was designed for New England residents only. (Charter Oak used to accept enrollments from people anywhere in the world, but it just didn't work out satisfactorily. New York and Edison still welcome out-of-state students.)

CHICAGO STATE UNIVERSITY
6800 S. Stewart St., Chicago IL 60621
312/995-2523

Accredited
Bachelor's
Short residency

A Bachelor of Arts is offered in two modes: either through a University Without Walls program, or through the Board of Governors Bachelor of Arts program. The former is based largely on learning contracts, negotiated between student and faculty, covering work to be done (courses, independent study projects, readings, internships, etc.). The latter can be completed entirely through off-campus study with the exception of 15 units to be earned in residence. The cost is in the range of $1,000 a year for Illinois residents and triple that for out-of-state people.

CITY UNIVERSITY LOS ANGELES
1111 Wilshire Blvd., Los Angeles, CA 90017
213/481-0950

Unaccredited
Bachelor's, Master's,
  Doctorates, Law
Non-resident

The degrees are offered in many fields, entirely through non-residential study, if desired. Residential seminars are also offered, primarily for students from outside the United States. (C.U.L.A. is authorized to issue I-20 forms for foreign students who wish to come to the U.S.) They offer a unique two-day "Challenge Examination" for the Bachelor's degree. It is designed for people who have already earned sufficient units for a degree elsewhere, but do not have the degree. If one passes, the degree is awarded at once. Other degree programs take an average of about six months, and cost between $2,500 and $4,500. The University also operates a non-resident law school. The founder and Chancellor is Henry L. N. Anderson, whose own Doctorate is from the University of California. City University has "external centers" throughout the United States and in 15 other countries, where students may deal with local representatives in their own language. Approximately 150 students are enrolled.

Comment: The Challenge Exam is an intriguing notion, but Dr. Anderson says not many people try it.

CLARK UNIVERSITY
The Evening College
Worcester MA 01610
617/793-7177

Accredited
Bachelor's
Residency (EW)

Bachelor of Fine Arts or Bachelor of Science in business or general studies offered entirely by evening study.

CLAYTON UNIVERSITY
P.O. Box 16150, St. Louis MO 63105
314/727-6100

Unaccredited
Bachelor's, Master's,
  Doctorates
Non-resident

Clayton offers degrees at all levels through their Interdisciplinary Program Institute (art, business, chemistry, music, and many other fields); the Behavior Sciences Institute (world-famous psychologist Carl Rogers appears on the letterhead as an advisor); and the Nutritional Science Institute (Linus Pauling and other well-known nutritionists are on the letterhead). The cost of the degree program is between $2,000 and $3,000. Clayton's credits have been accepted by some traditional universities, enabling the University to gain the government approval that qualifies students for veterans' benefits.

Comment: I continue to be impressed by the quality of the people Clayton attracts as advisors and consultants. The catalogue lists about 200 part-time faculty advisors, almost all with traditional Doctorates.

CLEVELAND STATE UNIVERSITY
E. 24th and Euclid, Cleveland OH 41115
216/687-2000

Accredited
Bachelor's, Master's
Residency (EW)

Bachelor of Arts, Science, and Business Administration; Master of Business Administration, Education, Engineering, and Laws, all available entirely through evening study.

COLBY-SAWYER COLLEGE
New London NH 03257
603/526-2010

Accredited
Bachelor's
Residency (EW)

Bachelor of Science program for women only, offered entirely through evening study.

COLLEGE OF CLINICAL HYPNOSIS
1481 S. King St., Suite 540, Honolulu HI 96814
808/947-3369

Unaccredited
Unspecified degrees
Non-resident

The catalog simply refers to the value of their $350 program by pointing out that "You will have a title, 'Clinical Hypnotherapist' and a degree to go with it." The degree is not specified. The Director of Operations, Alita Kurshals, reports that the founder and director, Mark R. Stephens, Ph.D., has his Doctorate from Thomas A. Edison College. This is a notorious degree mill whose founder has been convicted several times of selling fake Doctorates. The claim is made that the College is a chartered institution of learning under the laws of Colorado. This is definitely not so, according to the Colorado Commission on Higher Education. The only good part is their sales letter, which starts out, "Dear Beautiful Person."

COLLEGE MISERICORDIA
Dallas PA 18612
717/675-2181

Accredited
Bachelor's
Residency (EW)

Bachelor of Arts through weekend study; Bachelor of Science in Nursing and Bachelor of Music through evening study.

COLLEGE FOR HUMAN SERVICES
201 Varick St., New York NY 10014
212/989-2002

Unaccredited
Master's
Short residency

Master of Human Services, for persons over 21 whose family incomes fall below the poverty line. Over 90% of the students are either black or Hispanic. The school locates jobs for all students in one of 285 city agencies. Students work three days a week and take classes two days.

COLLEGE OF LIFE SCIENCE
8401 El Rey, Austin TX 78737
512/443-3155

Unaccredited
Doctorates
Non-resident

The College awards its Ph.D. in Nutritional Science on completion of 105 lessons, which will take a minimum of 48 weeks to complete. The lessons are detailed and comprehensive presentations of the viewpoint and methodologies of Administrator T. C. Fry and his associates. They see conventional medicine as "untrue in philosophy, absurd in science, in opposition to natural principles, contrary to common sense, disastrous in results, and a curse to humanity." In the course of the 105 lessons, the student learns about nutrition, physiology, diet, mental and emotional well being, and much more.

Comment: I confess to being suspicious when I first learned of the College, but I have reviewed hundreds of pages of the course material and find it comprehensive, and undoubtedly of value for those who agree with the philosophy. They rather delightfully justify giving the Ph.D. — "this symbol of supposed advanced intellect" — solely because they are convinced that it will make people pay more attention to their graduates.

COLLEGE OF MOUNT SAINT JOSEPH
Delhi Pike and Neeb Road, Mount Saint Joseph OH 45051
513/244-4312

Accredited
Bachelor's
Residency (EW)

The PM College offers degree programs in Paralegal Studies in classes that meet one or two evenings a week in this west Cincinnati suburb. The Weekend College offers the Bachelor of Arts in business (management or marketing), communication arts, human services (gerontology, mental health, management of human services), or liberal arts. Classes meet five weekends out of each 13-week term. Each class is three and a half hours long, and up to five can be taken between Friday evening and Sunday evening. Credit is available for experiential learning. There is also a Liberal Studies Program for women in transition, with substantial elements of specially-designed courses and independent study.

COLLEGE OF NEW ROCHELLE
New Rochelle NY   10801
914/632-5300

Accredited
Bachelor's
Short residency (EW, IS)

Bachelor of Arts in liberal studies or liberal arts for persons over 21. The program consists of core seminars on campus, life experience workshops, and independent study. All courses are available through evening study. The College's programs are offered at five branch campuses in various parts of New York City. One of these campuses is on the premises of and in association with a labor union, the American Federation of State, County and Municipal Employees, most of whom qualify for tuition refunds from the Union Benefit Fund. Courses for retired members are given during the day, and for working people in the evening.

COLLEGE OF ORIENTAL STUDIES
939 S. New Hampshire Ave., Los Angeles CA 90006
213/487-1235

Unaccredited
Bachelor's, Master's,
Doctorates
Residency (EW)

Degrees at all levels in Oriental Studies. Credit may be given for prior work, up to and including the equivalent of the Master's degree, by an advanced placement examination. The school is authorized to grant degrees by the State of California. The founder and president is the Venerable Thich Thien-An, former Chairman of the Department of Asian Studies at the University of Saigon. Many of the faculty have traditional American Doctorates.

COLLEGE OF SAINT FRANCIS
500 Wilcox St., Joliet IL 60435
815/740-3462, 800/435-0157

Accredited
Bachelor's
Residency (LE, EW)

Bachelor of Science program for registered nurses. Students are required to complete eight courses, which are given residentially at more than one hundred locations in 17 states, from California to Wisconsin. New locations are regularly added. Classes meet one evening a week. Full-time students may complete the degree in less than a year, while those remaining fully employed will normally take two years. One hundred twenty eight semester units are required for the degree, of which at least 32 must be earned after enrollment, at around $80 per unit. St. Francis also offers on-campus Bachelor's degrees in Joliet in which up to 80% of the required units may be earned through assessment of prior learning experience.

Comment: A good program for R.N.'s who prefer classroom instruction as part of the non-traditional degree program.

COLLEGE OF SAINT ROSE
432 Western Ave., Albany NY 12203
518/471-5143

Accredited
Bachelor's, Master's
Residency (LE)

Bachelor of Arts in which up to 75% of the required units may be earned through an assessment of prior learning experiences. The assessment may take six months or more, and costs around $200. Master of Arts in liberal studies, in which the work is a combination of credit for life experience, coursework on campus, independent study, and the writing of major papers.

COLLEGE OF STATEN ISLAND
130 Stuyvesant Place, Staten Island NY 10301
212/390-7937

Accredited
Bachelor's
Residency (IS, LE)

Bachelor's degrees in many fields, through a totally-individualized course of study. Credit is earned for on-campus classes, independent of study projects, work experience, and prior learning experiences. Non-credit workshops are offered to assist in the preparation of life experience portfolios. The College is a part of the City University of New York, and tuition is low.

COLORADO STATE UNIVERSITY
SURGE Program, Division of Continuing Education,
 Fort Collins CO 80523
303/491-5288

Accredited
Master's
Residency (IS)

Master of Business Administration and Master of Science in Engineering in an external program, involving a combination of coursework and independent study. The courses are available via taped lectures which are shipped to off-campus sites in Colorado and adjoining states.

COLORADO TECHNICAL COLLEGE
655 Elkton Drive, Colorado Springs CO 80907
303/598-0200

Accredited
Bachelor's
Short residency

Bachelor's degrees in electronic, biomedical and solar engineering technology, industrial management, and computer science. Although 30 quarter hours must be earned after enrolling, campus attendance may be waived.

COLUMBIA PACIFIC UNIVERSITY
1415 Third St., San Rafael CA 94901
In California, 800/552-5522; in Continental U.S.,
 800/227-0119; elsewhere 415/332-7832

Unaccredited
Bachelor's, Master's,
 Doctorates, Law
Non-resident

Columbia Pacific is the largest university in the United States and one of the largest in the world offering non-resident Bachelor's, Master's, and Doctorates. Despite the size, students report an extremely high level of personal attention from the faculty and staff. (The faculty numbers more than 200, nearly all with traditional Doctorates.) Two former presidents of major accredited universities serve as the two Deans of Columbia Pacific, and C.P.U.'s president, Richard Crews, is a prominent psychiatrist with his medical degree from Harvard. Work for the degrees is based largely on credit for prior learning experiences, plus completion of an independent study project, demonstrating competency or creativity in one's field. Degrees are offered in dozens of subject areas, including business, engineering, psychology, education, wholistic health, health sciences administration, architecture, and nutrition. Special programs are created for students wishing to work in specialized areas. Dual majors are encouraged. Combined degree programs (Bachelor's/Master's or Master's/Doctorate) are available. Work may be done in almost any language. Tuition is in the range of $2,000 to $3,000, with an extended payment plan possible. Columbia Pacific also operates an innovative School of International Law. The University has two campuses: a million-dollar university-owned urban campus in downtown San Rafael (just north of San Francisco), and a 13-acre North Campus in northern Marin County with library, student housing, and other facilities. There is a residential program in Santa Cruz, and an office in England.

Comment: No other non-resident, Doctorate-granting institution has a staff with the credentials, reputation, and experience of Columbia Pacific. Many major universities, including Harvard, Yale, and Princeton have expressed a willingness to accept C.P.U. degrees. I have had more positive, enthusiastic feedback from C.P.U. students and alumni than from any other school, accredited or not. These people praise the very personal approach, the valuable learning experience, and the comparatively low costs.

COLUMBIA UNION COLLEGE
Flower Ave., Takoma Park MD 20012
301/270-9200

Accredited
Bachelor's
Non-resident

The Bachelor of Arts can be earned entirely through correspondence study. Credit is given for standard equivalency examinations. At least 30 units must be earned after enrolling at Columbia Union (between eight and 12 courses). Students who believe they already have sufficient knowledge in a subject area may take the final exam for any course without taking the course. There are no majors, but courses must be taken in certain subject areas: English, a foreign language, science, art, and religion. All students must write a major paper, produce creative work in literature, science or the arts, and/or pass a comprehensive examination to qualify for graduation. The school is owned by the Seventh-Day Adventist Church, but non-church-members are welcome. Students may live anywhere in the world, but all work must be done in English. There is a $260 enrollment fee and tuition is $90 per unit, thus a range of $2,700 to more than $10,000.

Comment: The program is an excellent one, but potentially very expensive. The primary appeal, I think, is for persons who feel uncomfortable with self-directed or independent study situations.

COLUMBIA UNIVERSITY
New York NY 10027
212/280-1754

Accredited
Bachelor's, Master's
Residency (EW)

Bachelor of Arts, Bachelor of Science, Bachelor of Hebrew Literature, Bachelor of Religious Education (in conjunction with the Jewish Theological Seminary), Master of Arts in Teaching, and Master of Arts, all available entirely through evening study.

COOK'S INSTITUTE OF ELECTRONICS ENGINEERING
Highway 18, Box 20345, Jackson MS 39029
601/922-1833

Unaccredited
Bachelor's
Non-resident

Bachelor of Science in Electronics Engineering, entirely by correspondence study, involving completion of 36 courses, at a total cost in excess of $2,000. The student is entitled to skip up to half the courses if he or she feels that the material is already known (they take your word for it), but there is no reduction in tuition for so doing. Accreditation is claimed from the association of Career Training Schools, an unrecognized agency.

Comment: The literature is quite "hard sell," dwelling on the "superb Class Ring," the "beautiful and prestigious degree certificate," etc. Correspondents have told me that they find the course content generally useful, but those who have made a comparison often prefer the similar but accredited degree program at Grantham College. If you do not enroll in Cook's after making an initial inquiry, Mr. Cook may then try to sell you a franchise in his computerized dating service.

DALLAS BAPTIST COLLEGE
3000 Florina Ave., Dallas TX 75211
214/263-7595

Accredited
Bachelor's, Master's
Residency (LE)

The Bachelor of Career Arts program will award up to 80% of the necessary credits for the degree for prior learning experiences. The degree is offered in business administration, computer science, criminal justice, engineering management, fire protection management, real estate and secretarial science, and other areas. Credit is generously but realistically awarded for government, military, aviation and other career experience. (For instance, their brochure indicates a C.P.A. or C.L.U. certificate is probably worth thirty credit hours.)

DARTMOUTH COLLEGE
MALS Admissions, 10 Silsby Hall, Hanover NH 03775
603/646-1110

Accredited
Master's
Residency (IS)

Master of Arts in Liberal Studies, offered during summer sessions only. Dartmouth's program is designed for people over 22 who can come to New Hampshire for about two months each summer for three summers. (About 40% of the 150 participants are from out of the area.) The program combines lectures, a weekly colloquium, student-led seminars, independent study, and a final project assignment. Meals and housing are available on the Dartmouth campus, if desired. The total tuition for the degree is around $6,000; 85% of MALS students receive some form of financial assistance.

Comment: An opportunity to earn a graduate degree from one of America's best-known schools by non-traditional means.

DEAKIN UNIVERSITY   Foreign
Off-Campus Studies Programme   Bachelor's
P.O. Box 125, Belmont, Victoria 3216, Australia   Non-resident

Deakin operates as an open university, with voluntary attendance in classes, tutorials, weekend and vacation classes. The Bachelor of Arts is offered in humanities, social sciences, and education, and there is a Bachelor of Education degree as well. The Mature Entry Scheme offers the opportunity for adults without traditional qualifications to enroll. There are regional study centers at various locations for students who do wish to meet with faculty tutors.

DE LA SALLE UNIVERSITY   Foreign
2401 Taft Ave., Manilla 2801, Philippines   Master's
                                               Residency (IS)

The University offers a Master's degree in Public Administration in a part-time off-campus program, with evening study, independent study, and extensive field trips. It is designed for middle-management executives in public services, education, commerce and industry, and private agencies.

DE PAUL UNIVERSITY   Accredited
School for New Learning   Bachelor's
23 E. Jackson Blvd., Chicago IL 60604   Residency
312/321-7901

Bachelor's degrees in a wide variety of fields, in which up to 80% of the degree requirements can come through assessment of prior learning, for which there is a fee of $333. Tuition is under $2,000 per year.

DELAWARE VALLEY COLLEGE   Accredited
Doylestown PA 18901   Bachelor's
215/345-1500   Residency (EW)

The Bachelor of Science in business administration is available entirely through evening study.

DOMINION HERBAL COLLEGE   Foreign
7527 Kingsway, Burnaby, British Columbia V3N 3C1   Diplomas
   Canada   Non-resident
403/521-5822

The title of "Chartered Herbalist" is awarded to students who complete the 63 lessons of the correspondence course in herbalism. The cost of the program is under $200, including a plastic "anatomy kit." The school is apparently well-regarded in the profession.

DONSBACH UNIVERSITY   Unaccredited
7422 Mountjoy (P.O. Box 5550), Huntington Beach   Bachelor's, Master's,
   CA 92646   Doctorates
714/848-0774   Non-resident

Donsbach (pronounced DONS-baw) University offers degrees at all levels in the general areas of nutrition and health sciences. Programs are offered in nutrition, iridology, acupuncture, reflexology, and herbology. Residential courses and degrees are offered in the large university building, but all degrees are offered in the large university building, but all degrees may also be earned by correspondence. Multiple degree programs (Bachelor's/Master's, Master's/Doctorate), and all three degrees combined are available. Dr. Donsbach himself is a well known author and businesman in the field of nutrition. His staff and advisory board include a number of medical doctors, dentists, and persons well-known in nutrition research. Correspondence instruction is largely by tape cassettes and film-strips. Tuition is in the range of $2,000 to $3,000 for most programs. Around 3,000 students are enrolled in the residential or the correspondence programs. The university facilities include a sizeable auditorium, a 100-seat food preparation clinic, and a large Nutritional Training Clinic.

Comment: Donsbach offers what appears to be an excellent program for persons in the field of nutrition and health sciences.

DRAKE UNIVERSITY
2700 University Ave., Des Moines IA 50311
515/271-2181

Accredited
Bachelor's
Residency (LE, EW)

Bachelor of General Studies program, in which 75% of the required 124 semester units can be earned by alternative means, including credit for prior learning experiences, equivalency examinations, and correspondence study. The remaining 30 units can be taken by attending weekend, evening or summer courses on the Drake campus.

DREXEL UNIVERSITY
32nd and Chestnut, Philadelphia PA 19104
215/895-2000

Accredited
Bachelor's, Master's
Residency (EW)

Bachelor of Science in architecture, business administration, engineering, general studies; Master of Science in business administration, home economics, and library science, all through evening study.

DRURY COLLEGE
900 N. Benton Ave., Springfield MO 65802
417/865-8731

Accredited
Bachelor's
Residency (EW)

The Bachelor of Science in many fields may be earned entirely through evening study.

DUARTE COSTA UNIVERSITY
Somewhere in St. Louis MO
314/454-0459

The university is operated by the Servants of the Good Shepherd, whose headquarters is at 1529 Pleasant Valley Blvd., Altoona PA 16602. This is a "Western Rite Orthodox" order, which apparently stands between Roman Catholic and Eastern Orthodox. Several correspondents have told me that the Order operates a non-traditional university in Missouri, offering degrees for $992. Sure enough, there is a telephone listing in St. Louis (which never answered when I called), but this may be the first case in history of a university with an unlisted address. It does not appear in the St. Louis phone book, and the good fathers in Altoona would not give it to me.

DYKE COLLEGE
1375 E. 6th St., Cleveland OH 44144
216/696-9000

Accredited
Bachelor's
Non-resident or
short residency

Bachelor of Science, in which the student proceeds at his or her own pace through the completion of up to 21 learning modules under the guidance of faculty mentors. All work may be done non-residentially, but meetings with mentors on campus are almost certain to be necessary. Modules need not be taken if there is sufficient life experience or if equivalency exams have been passed. Modules are offered in humanities, science, mathematics, social science, business, and various electives. The cost is around $500 per module, hence a maximum cost of nearly $10,000. However this can be reduced greatly by use of equivalency exams.

EAST CENTRAL COLLEGE CONSORTIUM

Mount Union College, Alliance OH 44601
216/821-5320, ext. 314

Accredited
Bachelor's
Residency (LE)

The Consortium consists of seven colleges, cooperating to offer a non-traditional Bachelor's degree program in the fields of general studies, the sciences, humanities and arts, business administration, and health sciences. Substantial credit is given for prior learning experiences, and a credit course is offered to help prepare a life experience portfolio. A fee of about $300 is charged for the life experience assessment, regardless of the amount of credit awarded. The participating schools are Bethany College (West Virginia); Heidelberg College, Hiram College, Marietta College, Mount Union College and Muskingum College (all in Ohio); and Westminster College (Pennsylvania).

EAST CAROLINA UNIVERSITY

Greenville NC 27834
919/758-6212

Accredited
Master's
Residency (IS)

Master of Arts in elementary education, with a combination of residential courses and independent study in the course of one's teaching job.

EASTERN CONNECTICUT STATE COLLEGE

83 Windham, Willimantic CT 06226
203/456-2231

Accredited
Bachelor's, Master's
Residency (EW)

Master of Science programs are offered in a business, psychology, sociology, history, social science, and English, all available entirely through evening study. A Bachelor of General Studies degree program is available, as well. There is also a B.S. or B.A. program for registered nurses, in which the R.N. diploma is worth half the needed units.

EASTERN ILLINOIS UNIVERSITY

Charleston IL 61920
217/581-2021

Accredited
Bachelor's
Short residency

Bachelor of Arts, with a minimum of 15 units to be earned on campus, which can be done in four months or less. Eastern Illinois is one of five members of the Board of Governors Bachelor of Arts program, in which most of the work can be completed off-campus, through independent study, correspondence courses, equivalency examinations, and credit for life experience. (Two members of the B.O.G. program have no residency requirements at all: Western Illinois and Governors State.)

EASTERN MICHIGAN UNIVERSITY

Ypsilanti MI 48197
313/487-1849

Accredited
Master's
Residency (IS)

Master of Arts in educational administration, with much of the work possible through independent or off-campus study, combined with on-campus meetings and seminars.

EASTERN WASHINGTON UNIVERSITY

Cheney WA 99004
509/359-2398

Accredited
Bachelor's
Residency (LE)

Bachelor of Arts in general studies, specifically for persons with professional or paraprofessional experience. This includes, for instance, mechanics, computer programmers, police officers, nurses, secretaries, firefighters, draftspeople (look how hard I'm trying to be non-sexist) and others. Twenty-five percent of the work must be done after enrollment, which would normally require one academic year (nine months).

Comment: A main advantage is the school's willingness to give life experience credit to people in fields that other schools might not agree are credit-worthy. I have heard from a few people who enrolled in Eastern Washington long enough to get credit for, say, their secretarial experience, then transferred this credit to another, faster school.

ECKERD COLLEGE
St. Petersburg FL 33733
813/867-1166

Accredited
Bachelor's
Residency (IS, LE)

Bachelor of Arts and Bachelor of Science through an unusual approach to alternative education. Eckerd operates as a four-year college, but in each academic quarter, students may participate in either on-campus or off-campus or overseas independent study projects. Some of these are well-organized group activities while other are individually done, reflecting a student's own interests. Up to 75% of the necessary units for the degree may come from an assessment of prior learning experiences, through the P.E.L., or Program for Experienced Learners.

EDINBORO STATE COLLEGE
Edinboro PA 16444
814/732-2800

Accredited
Bachelor's
Residency (LE)

Bachelor's degrees in a wide variety of fields in which up to 75% of the necessary units can be earned through an assessment of prior experience. The assessment is done in Edinboro's Life Experience Center, and can take a month or less. For a small fee, they will conduct a brief inspection of one's resume or credentials and advise whether or not they think it is worthwhile to go ahead with the more expensive complete assessment.

ELIZABETHTOWN COLLEGE
Elizabethtown PA 17022
717/367-1151

Accredited
Bachelor's
Very short residency

Bachelor of Liberal Studies and Bachelor of Professional Studies, which may be earned with only three all-day seminars on campus to plan and discuss the independent study program. Credit is given for all prior learning experiences, both traditional and non-traditional. The tuition for the program is under $2,000. The college was chartered in 1899, and is affiliated with the Church of the Brethren.

Comment: The cost is quite modest for an accredited degree program.

EMERSON COLLEGE OF HERBOLOGY
11 St. Catherine St. East, Montreal, Quebec H2X 1K3
    Canada

Foreign
Master's
Non-resident

Master of Herbology title is awarded on successful completion of 33 correspondence lessons (a total of 550 pages), covering botanic medicine, phytotherapy, pharmabotanics and herbalism. Lessons are mailed in three at a time, graded, and returned with the next set of lessons.

ELMHURST COLLEGE
Office of the Evening Session
Elmhurst IL 60126
312/279-4100, ext. 354

Accredited
Bachelor's
Residency (EW, LE)

Bachelor's degree program in which up to 80% of the necessary units may be earned through an assessment of prior learning experiences. The assessment cannot be done until 12 units have been earned in residence, and can take as long as three months. Degrees in about 20 subjects can be completed entirely through evening study. Elmhurst also offers a Degree Completion Program for working registered nurses, with courses offered in hospitals in the Chicago area.

ELMIRA COLLEGE
Elmira NY 14901
607/734-3911

Accredited
Bachelor's, Master's
Residency (EW)

Bachelor of Science and Master of Science, both in education, available entirely through evening study.

ELYSION COLLEGE
Box 909, San Ysidro CA 92173
505/988-3800

Unaccredited
Bachelor's
Non-resident

The degrees are earned primarily by reading a small number of "concise texts from which all unnecessary material and wordage have been eliminated." Book reports and essays are submitted on various subjects, after which the degrees are issued. The cost is around $500. The literature says, "no classes or lectures, no meetings with an instructor, no tests, questions or examinations." The proprietor is Lane Williams, a lawyer who also claims a Doctorate from the now-defunct Golden State University, which is widely identified as a degree mill. The office is actually in Mexico, at Rosarito Beach, Baja California.

Comment: I cannot agree with Elysion's literature, that "We offer what we believe to be the best college degree plan available." When asked, Mr. Williams could supply no evidence to support his printed claim that "a number of consulates and embassies... actually endorse our program." If Elysion is legal, it must be because Mexico takes no interest in a school dealing only with Americans and California has no jurisdiction across the border. When Elysion was located in New Mexico, it was called Williams College.

EMPIRE STATE COLLEGE
Saratoga Springs NY 12866
518/587-2100

Accredited
Bachelor's
Non-resident or
   short residency

Bachelor of Arts or Bachelor of Science, based on a learning contract drawn between the student and the faculty mentors, taking into account work done in the past, and setting goals for future study. The work can be done entirely non-residentially through the Center for Distance Learning. The college operates learning centers throughout New York state for persons who wish to meet in person with mentors and use libraries. The degree program takes 32 months to complete, starting from scratch, but up to 26 months may be waived for prior experiential learning. Students work from learning modules, of which more than 100 have been developed in many subject areas, based in part on the courses of England's Open University. The cost of the program ranges from around $1,000 to over $3,000, depending on the number of modules taken.

Comment: Empire State is probably America's first college established solely to offer alternative degree programs within a state system. It is a unit of the State University of New York, which is not the same as the University of the State of New York (which also has an outstanding non-resident degree program). The academic program is very well regarded, but I've heard complaints from quite a few students who had a difficult time dealing with the business office.

EUROPEAN UNIVERSITY INSTITUTE
Via dei Roccettini, 5, San Domenico di Fiesole, Italy

Foreign
Doctorates
Residency (IS)

The Institute was established in 1976 by the nine member nations of the European Economic Community. Students are admitted primarily to undertake research in the areas of economics, history and civilization, law, political science, and social science. Students plan independent study projects, under the guidance of faculty tutors and research supervisors. About 10% of the students come from countries outside the Common Market. The degree of Ph.D. is awarded on completion and publication of the dissertation.

EVERGREEN STATE COLLEGE
Olympia WA 98505
206/866-6300

Accredited
Bachelor's
Residency (IS)

Students have the option of creating "independent contract" courses of study for supervised research under a faculty mentor. Groups of two or more students may work under a "group contract." Credit is given for internship programs, involving, for instance, work in local hospitals, clinics, or businesses. Regular courses are available on campus, as well, for those who want them. Students involved in independent study are still expected to visit the campus and meet with their faculty mentors at least once a month. All students must be enrolled for at least nine months before earning the degree. Total tuition for Washington residents is just under $2,000 a year, but is substantially higher for out-of-state students.

Comment: I have a personal bias, since my eldest daughter has chosen this school. Under the presidency of former Governor Dan Evans, Evergreen has developed a national reputation for its innovative approaches to undergraduate non-traditional education.

EVERYMAN'S UNIVERSITY
16 Kalusner Street, Ramat Aviv, Tel Aviv, Israel

Foreign
Bachelor's
Non-resident

Israel's first open university offers the Bachelor's degree on completion of 18 home study courses. Each course consists of a home study kit, which may include written materials, laboratory equipment, simulation games, and so forth. Many courses are supplemented by radio and television programs. Each course requires from 16 to 18 weeks to complete, working from 15 to 18 hours a week. Courses are available in mathematics, life sciences, natural sciences, social sciences, electronics, book-keeping, drafting, and humanities. Non-credit courses are available in Arabic, computers, and ecology. The University has been financed by the Rothschild Foundation, but the Israeli government is gradually assuming financial responsibility.

FAIRLEIGH DICKINSON UNIVERSITY
286 Madison St., Madison NJ 07940
201/933-5000

Accredited
Bachelor's, Master's,
Doctorates
Residency (EW, IS)

Bachelor of Arts, Bachelor of Science, Master of Arts, Master of Science and Doctor of Education programs, offered through centers at Madison, Rutherford and Teaneck, primarily through evening study. The Doctorate, in educational leadership, consists of formal courses, seminars, internships, plus independent study and research.

FAYETTEVILLE STATE UNIVERSITY
Box 156, Fort Bragg NC 28307
919/483-6144

Accredited
Bachelor's
Residency (EW)

Bachelor of Arts and Bachelor of Science for military personnel, their dependents, and local residents. All work can be completed through evening and weekend study. Some credit is given for prior learning experiences and for equivalency examinations.

FERNUNIVERSITÄT
Feithstrasse 152, D-5800 Hagen, West Germany
02331-8041

Foreign
Bachelor's, Master's,
Doctorates
Non-resident

West Germany's open university offers degrees at all levels, through completion of correspondence study units, plus examinations (which must be taken in Germany). Courses are offered in the fields of mathematics, electrical engineering, information science and computers, business administration, and education. Instruction is through a combination of written materials and audio tape cassettes. All courses are self-paced. The University operates about 30 study centers in Germany for the assistance and guidance of students. All instruction in German, although a nice color brochure is available in English. More than 300 of Fernuniversität's thousands of students live outside of Germany.

FERRIS STATE COLLEGE
Big Rapids, MI 49307
616/796-2641, ext. 3405

Accredited
Bachelor's
Non-resident or
    short residency

Bachelor of Science in environmental health offered through the Schools of Allied Health, External Degree Programs to people living anywhere in the United States. All of the requirements for the degree can be met through an assessment of prior learning experience, or a combination of that plus equivalency examinations, independent study, faculty-directed study, home study courses, and special projects. One year of work experience in the field of environmental health is required. The assessment of prior learning can take as long as nine months, and is done for a flat fee of around $250. A Bachelor of Science in Health Services Management is available in a similar model, but only to Michigan residents. The cost for new work done through Ferris State is a relatively modest $45 per unit.

FIELDING INSTITUTE
226 E. de la Guerra, Santa Barbara CA 93101
805/963-6601

Accredited
Master's, Doctorates
Very short residency

Fielding's programs offer the shortest required residency of any accredited doctoral program offered in America. However the degrees are neither fast nor easy. Only five days of residency are required for the Master's and Doctorate programs in psychology and in Human and Organization Development. The Master of Arts degree typically takes two years to complete, and the various Doctorates from three to five years. The psychology degrees (M.A., Ph.D., Psy.D.) are offered with specialties in clinical, counseling, or organizational psychology. The Master's is not offered separately, but is an integral part of the doctoral program. In Human and Organization Development, the degrees are M.A., Ph.D., Ed.D., and D.H.S. (Doctor of Human Services), with emphasis on human development, human services management, gerontological services, adult and continuing education, and human resources development. Participation in an Admissions Contract Workshop of five days in Santa Barbara is mandatory. Three are held each year. It is here that a learning contract is developed. Psychology students must gain the required knowledge on their own; Fielding does not offer classes, but tests the knowledge by comprehensive examination. Six hundred hours of practical training, 1600 hours of supervised internship, and a dissertation complete the doctoral requirement. In Human and Organization Development, students work concurrently on studying the prescribed curriculum, a training or internship program, and a thesis or dissertation. Tuition is around $5,000 per year.

Comment: Fielding's is the most non-traditional doctoral program yet to receive traditional accreditation. It is expensive when compared to unaccredited schools, but quite a bargain in comparison with most residential Doctorates.

FLAMING RAINBOW UNIVERSITY
P.O. Box 154, Tahlequah OK 74464
918/456-5662

Candidate for
    accreditation
Bachelor's
Residency (IS)

Bachelor of Arts primarily for Native Americans, or Indians, who comprise about 80% of the student body. Credit is given for prior learning experiences. After enrolling, learning comes from independent study, internships, group experiences, classes at other schools, travel, etc. "Traditional testing for academic achievement is not used in Flaming Rainbow, nor are grades assigned for work completed. A portfolio is kept on each student, that contains all forms and reports made by the student for the purpose of documentation and evaluation." The minimum period of enrollment is twelve months, but the average is considerably longer. Most students are on scholarships, covering from half to three-fourths of the tuition.

FLORIDA INTERNATIONAL UNIVERSITY
External Degree Program, Bay Vista Campus,
  North Miami FL 33181
305/940-5664

Accredited
Bachelor's
Residency (IS)

The Bachelor of Arts and Bachelor of Science may be earned through the State University System of Florida External Degree Program, administered by the Office of Academic Affairs at Florida International University. Students satisfy the requirements of the degree programs through an educational contract, which is a degree plan combining formal coursework with supervised independent study. Part of the formal coursework consists of individualized modules, which may be completed off-campus. The program is open only to persons who have lived in Florida at least one year and who have earned 60 semester hours (or the equivalent) elsewhere.

FORDHAM UNIVERSITY
School of General Studies
Bronx NY 10458
212/933-2233

Accredited
Bachelor's
Residency (EW)

Bachelor of Arts, Bachelor of Science, and Bachelor of Business Administration available entirely through evening study.

FORT WRIGHT COLLEGE
W. 400 Randolph Road, Spokane WA 99204
509/328-2970

Accredited
Bachelor's
Short residency (LE)

Bachelor's degrees in a wide variety of fields in which over 90% of the necessary units can come from an assessment of prior learning experiences, equivalency examinations, and transfer credit. Assessment is based on a portfolio, examinations, and/or interviews, and can take four months or longer.

FRAMINGHAM STATE COLLEGE
Framingham MA 01701
617/620-1220

Accredited
Bachelor's
Very short residency

Bachelor of Arts in liberal studies in which more than 80% of the required units may be earned through equivalency exams, independent study, correspondence study, prior learning experiences, and "non-credit educational experiences." The remaining units must be earned by taking courses on campus, taking a series of weekend or summer seminars, or making other arrangements satisfactory to the advisory committee. The only certain on-campus contact consists of oral examinations in each of four broad areas of study: humanities, social sciences, natural sciences and mathematics.

FRANKLIN AND MARSHALL COLLEGE
Separate Evening Division
Lancaster PA 17604
717/291-3911

Accredited
Master's
Residency (EW)

Master of Science in physics, entirely through evening study.

FRIENDS WORLD COLLEGE
Plover Lane, Huntington NY 11745
516/549-1102

Accredited
Bachelor's
Residency (IS)

The Bachelor's degree is earned through study in many centers, worldwide. A typical student will spend six semesters in six different countries. The first month in a new location, the student works out a course of study with the resident faculty at that location. After the six foreign experiences, the student returns to the "home base" to write a mini-thesis or major term paper on the experience. More than 50 countries have been included in the program over the years. Countries currently available are Mexico, Kenya, England, Israel, Costa Rica, Japan, and several centers in the United States. Tuition is about $4,000 a year, plus substantial travel and living expenses.

GEORGE MASON UNIVERSITY
Office of Extended Studies
4400 University Drive, Fairfax VA 22030
703/323-2342

Accredited
Bachelor's, Master's
Residency (LE, IS)

Bachelor of Individualized Studies degree in which 85% of the necessary units may be earned by alternative means: equivalency exams, credit for life experience learning, etc. If the student has knowledge in an area in which there is no standard equivalency exam, an ad hoc committee of three experts in that field may evaluate the student and assign credit. Applicants must have at least eight years of post-high-school experience. In conjunction with an academic advisor, the student designs and completes a program of study. A total of 30 units must be completed either at George Mason or at certain other northern Virginia colleges. A Master of Arts in Interdisciplinary Studies is available for adult students with at least three years of work in the area of proposed study. At least six hours of graduate-level work must be completed elsewhere before enrolling. A course of study is worked out with a member of the George Mason faculty, who supervises the performance of the work. A special project is required. Tuition is around $1,000 a year for Virginia residents and double that for carpetbaggers.

GEORGE WASHINGTON UNIVERSITY
706 20th St. N.W., Washington DC 20006
202/676-7065

Accredited
Bachelor's, Master's
Residency (EW)

Bachelor's and Master's degrees in many fields, including education, humanities, the social sciences, criminal justice, education, urban learning, forensics, telecommunication operation, and administration. Credit is given for all prior learning experiences, but at least one academic year (nine months) must be spent after enrolling at George Washington. Off-campus seminars and classes are held in many locations along the eastern seaboard, from Baltimore to Norfolk. Many of the students are in the military or government, but most courses are open to all.

GEORGIA SOUTHWESTERN COLLEGE
Americus GA 31709
912/928-1358

Accredited
Bachelor's
Residency (EW)

Bachelor of Arts, Bachelor of Science in social science and business administration, available entirely through evening study.

GLASSBORO STATE COLLEGE
Center for Experiential Education
Glassboro NJ 08028
609/445-5209

Accredited
Bachelor's
Residency (LE)

Bachelor's degrees in many fields, in which 75% of the required credit can come through an assessment of prior learning experiences, equivalency exams, and transfer credit. There is no fee for the assessment, once one has enrolled.

GODDARD COLLEGE
Plainfield VT 05667
802/454-8311

Accredited
Bachelor's, Master's
Residency (IS)

Goddard has been a pioneer in non-traditional education for nearly half a century — and the way in which they rebounded from their crisis of 1981 serves to demonstrate their innovative and pioneering spirit. In the throes of critical financial problems, Goddard sold four of its programs to Norwich University, put about half its campus land up for sale, and reduced its student body from more than 1,000 to fewer than 300. A year later, things were looking brighter. Goddard still offers some non-traditional options for studies in mathematics and science, human behavior, philosophy and religion, the visual and performing arts, and literature and writing. The first nine days of each term are spent in an All College Meeting, in which the work of the coming term is planned. Students may choose a "low residence" option, in which some, most, or all of their work is done off-campus, while maintaining contact by correspondence. Both Bachelor's and Master's programs require a minimum of one year's enrollment at Goddard. The costs, including room and board, are less than $3,000 a year for Low Residence students (who will only be on campus 18 days), and more than $8,000 a year for regular students.

GOLDEN GATE UNIVERSITY
536 Mission St., San Francisco CA 94105
415/442-7000

Accredited
Bachelor's, Master's
Residency

Bachelor of Arts in many fields; Bachelor of Science in accounting, insurance management and transportation; Master of Business Administration; Master of Public Administration; Master of Science in accounting and taxation; and a combined M.B.A. and law degree, all available entirely through evening study.

GOLDEN STATE UNIVERSITY
1699 Lake San Marcos Dr., San Marcos CA 92069
714/744-0270

Unaccredited
Bachelor's, Master's,
Doctorates
Non-resident

Degrees at all levels in the fields of nutrition, hypnoanalysis, human behavior, religion, business administration, communication, science, mathematics, the performing and visual arts, and international studies. Golden State was founded in 1979. The president, Warren Walker, was formerly president of Union University, a well-established non-traditional school. The statement in the catalogue on (lack of) accreditation is honest and straightforward. At least one full year of enrollment is required for all degrees at a cost in excess of $2,000 a year. There is no connection whatsoever with an alleged diploma mill of the same name that operated in California some years ago.

GOVERNORS STATE UNIVERSITY
Park Forest South IL 60646
312/534-5000

Accredited
Bachelor's
Non-resident

In the Board of Governors Bachelor of Arts program, the degree can be earned entirely by correspondence study. Fifteen units of credit must be earned after enrolling, but this can be done entirely by correspondence courses. The program is almost indentical to that of Western Illinois University, described in more detail later.

Comment: An excellent program. Of the five B.O.G. schools, only Governors State and Western Illinois have no residency requirement at all. Out-of-state students pay substantially more tuition than those in Illinois, but it is still a bargain.

GRADUATE SCHOOL OF HUMAN BEHAVIOR
368 42nd St., Oakland CA 94609
415/653-2868

Unaccredited
Doctorates
Residency (EW)

The Ph.D. is offered in clinical psychology and developmental/educational psychology, in a program offered entirely through late afternoon and evening study to currently employed professionals. The president is Alan Furhman, whose Doctorate is from the University of Chicago. The program requires two years of study, including courses, supervised clinical or field work, and the writing of a dissertation. The cost is around $2,500 per year. The school is authorized to grant degrees by the State of California, and state approval (which would permit graduates to sit for state licensing exams without further qualification) is being sought.

GRADUATE SCHOOL OF PATENT RESOURCES INSTITUTE
P.O. Box 19302, 20th St. Postal Station,
  Washington DC 20006
202/223-1175

Unaccredited
Master's
Residency (EW)

The school provides advanced study in patent-related matters for lawyers, engineers, and business-people. A Master of Science in Patent Practice and a Master of Patent Law are available, with all courses taught either in the evening or on Saturday morning. Tuition for the degrees is in excess of $5,000. The School is appropriately licensed in the District of Columbia.

GRANTHAM COLLEGE OF ENGINEERING
2500 La Cienega Blvd. (P.O. Box 35499),
  Los Angeles CA 90035
213/559-7101

Accredited
Bachelor's
Non-resident

Bachelor of Science in Engineering Technology entirely through correspondence study. The course consists of 344 lessons and four examinations. The exams must be supervised, but can be taken anywhere. In addition, the student must earn 26 semester units in English, social science, science, and elective subjects at other schools (by correspondence or in person) or by equivalency examination. Persons who already have substantial experience in electronics may apply for advanced standing, which is granted by passing an examination. The catalogue indicates that a part-time student will take between four and eight years to complete the degree at a cost of around $3,000.

Comment: There are not many accredited non-resident programs in the sciences, and this is a good one. However, the time required seems extremely long. All work is self-paced, so presumably the highly motivated student could finish faster. Grantham is accredited by the National Home Study Council, a recognized agency.

HARVARD UNIVERSITY
739 Holyoke Center, Cambridge MA 02138
617/495-4024

Accredited
Bachelor's
Residency (EW)

Bachelor of Arts in Extension Studies, requiring a minimum of two years instead of the usual four. Candidates must take and pass 16 full-year courses, of which at least five must be taken at Harvard, either during summer sessions or through evening study extension classes. There must be at least one course each in humanities, science, social science, English, and a foreign language.

HAWTHORNE UNIVERSITY
607 Mountain View Ave., Petaluma CA 94952
707/795-7168

Unaccredited
Bachelor's, Master's,
  Doctorates
Residency (IS)

Hawthorne opened in Fall, 1982, offering degrees at all levels in general studies, with an emphasis at the Master's level in humanistic computer studies. (The Bachelor's is offered as a convenience for those going on to higher degrees.) Hawthorne evolved from a state-approved school named Paideia, now apparently alive but dormant in Berkeley. Indeed, seven of the ten Hawthorne faculty have their highest degree from Paideia. They utilize the "Paideian process" in which interdisciplinary groups of 12 or so meet each week and the entire school meets one Saturday a month. Tuition is $1,200 per term. Hawthorne is authorized to grant degrees by the State of California.

HEADLANDS UNIVERSITY
10700 Ford St., P.O. Box 250, Mendocino CA 95460
707/937-4517

Unaccredited
Bachelor's, Master's
Resident and Non-resident

The Bachelor's and Master's degrees are offered in two fields: fine and performing arts, and science and technology. Full residential programs are available in Mendocino, a village on the ocean 150

miles north of San Francisco. All work can be completed by correspondence, if desired, with the exception of a final one-week session, for presentation of independent study projects and other work. All students pay a fixed fee of $1,200 (which covers the costs of three required courses, done in person or by correspondence; the initial evaluation of life experience learning; and the final week seminar), plus tuition of $600 per semester for residential students or $100 per semester for non-resident students. Some residential students will have their tuition paid by the local R.O.P. (Regional Occupational Program). The University is operated by the non-profit Educational Counseling Institute, whose assets include more than $200,000 worth of high technology equipment in the areas of computers, electronics, audio and video technology, design, and fabrication.

Comment: This highly innovative university is an outgrowth and extension of the non-traditional high school my three daughters have attended, so needless to say, I am biased in its favor. I am confident that the high quality of secondary education offered can be extended into the post-secondary realms. For people interested in "hands on" experience in these very popular developing fields, the opportunity for the low-cost residential program is especially appealing. The $1,200 fixed fee is not required until advancement to candidacy, which can occur anywhere from a few weeks to a few years after enrolling, depending on prior experience and training.

HEED UNIVERSITY
1720 Harrison St., Young Circle, Hollywood FL 33020
305/925-1600

Unaccredited
Master's, Doctorates
Short residency

Master of Arts, Master of Business Administration, Doctor of Philosophy, Doctor of Education and Doctor of Business Administration in a program requiring about six weeks of resident study at Heed locations in Florida or California. Seminars are held four times a year. The cost of degree programs is in the range of $4,000 to $6,000. Heed is a legal school, licensed by Florida's State Board of Independent Colleges and Universities.

Comment: The catalogue lists six pages of faculty and adjunct faculty, most with traditional Doctorates, and (an especially nice feature) ten pages of the names, addresses, and current jobs of their graduates — a generally impressive group of people.

HEIDELBERG COLLEGE
Tiffin OH 44883
419/448-2800

Accredited
Bachelor's
Residency (EW, LE)

Bachelor of Arts and Bachelor of Science in many fields, in which up to 75% of the necessary credits may be earned through an assessment of prior learning experiences, which is done on the basis of a portfolio prepared by the student. The assessment fee is around $300. Non-traditional courses are available, based on a learning contract model. There is also a weekend college which meets from Friday evening through Sunday morning during the fall, spring, and summer terms. Tuition for the full-time student is around $5,000 per year. (See also: East Central College Consortium.)

HIGHLAND UNIVERSITY
c/o Tennessee Wesleyan University, Athens TN 37303
615/745-5552

Unaccredited
Doctorates
Short residency

Doctor of Education program involving three four-week summer sessions, with independent study during the intervening months. An intensive residential session is held every July on the campus of Tennessee Wesleyan, but there is no affiliation with this school. The total cost is over $5,000. The 15 summer faculty all have traditional higher degrees; many are college teachers or administrators.

Comment: The program appears sound, although it will not meet teacher certification requirements in many areas. I am bothered by the way Highland's advertisements in professional journals leave the impression that they are a part of the accredited Tennessee Wesleyan University and not just a summer tenant. Highland originally was chartered in North Carolina, and was in Sweetwater, Tennessee, before going to Athens.

HIRAM COLLEGE
Hiram OH 44234
216/569-3211

Accredited
Bachelor's
Residency (EW)

Bachelor of Arts offered entirely through weekend study. The weekend college meets from Friday evening through Sunday noon. The degree can be completed in a minimum of one academic year. (See also: East Central College Consortium.)

HOFSTRA UNIVERSITY
Hempstead NY 11550
516/560-0500

Accredited
Bachelor's, Master's,
  Doctorates
Residency (IS, EW)

Bachelor of Arts degree through a mostly off-campus study program. At least one visit to campus per month is recommended. The program requires from one to four years, depending on the amount of prior learning and experience. Other Bachelor's degrees, Master of Arts, Master of Science, Master of Business Administration, Doctor of Education and Doctor of Philosophy degrees can be earned entirely through evening study.

HOLISTIC LIFE UNIVERSITY
1627 10th Ave., San Francisco CA 94122
415/665-3200

Unaccredited
Bachelor's, Master's
Residency (EW)

The University consists of a health institute, a life-death transitions institute, and a childbirth institute, each offering evening classes leading to the Bachelor or Master of Arts degree. The University's programs are approved by the State of California. In addition to seminars, coursework, and practical experience, students must have independently studied and practiced on a regular basis "an approved form of bodymind discipline and meditation" for a year or more.

HOLY NAMES COLLEGE
3500 Mountain Blvd., Oakland CA 94619
415/436-0111

Accredited
Bachelor's
Residency (EW)

Holy Names offers a Bachelor of Arts degree that can be earned entirely through weekend study. Degrees are available in business administration/economics, human services, and humanistic studies. Up to 27 units a year can be completed by attending classes every other weekend, on Friday evening and all day Saturday. Tuition for the student taking the maximum weekend load is between $3,000 and $4,000 a year.

HOOD COLLEGE
Frederick MD 21701
301/663-3131

Accredited
Bachelor's, Master's
Residency (EW, LE)

Bachelor's degrees in many fields in which more than 75% of the necessary units may be earned through an assessment of prior learning experiences, conducted by the college's Learning Assessment and Resource Center. Master of Arts in human sciences for in service teachers and others, through late afternoon, evening, and summer study.

HOWARD UNIVERSITY
University Without Walls, P.O. Box 662,
  Washington DC 20059
202/636-6100

Accredited
Bachelor's
Residency (IS)

A University Without Walls program leading to the Bachelor of Arts or Bachelor of Science degree, with a course of study determined by a learning contract negotiated between student and faculty, and involving substantial elements of independent study. Credit is given for prior learning experiences and for equivalency examinations. A bi-monthly seminar on campus is the main time for contacting advisors and faculty. Students are required to keep a daily log.

HUNTER COLLEGE
695 Park Ave., New York NY 10021
212/570-5566

Accredited
Bachelor's
Residency (EW)

Bachelor of Arts and Bachelor of Science degrees in many fields, available entirely through evening study.

ILLINOIS BENEDICTINE COLLEGE
Maple Ave. and College Road, Lisle IL 60532
312/968-7270

Accredited
Bachelor's
Residency (EW)

Bachelor of Arts in business economics, entirely through evening study. Credit is given for prior work and life experience learning. The school used to be known as St. Procopius College.

**ILLINOIS SCHOOL OF PROFESSIONAL
    PSYCHOLOGY**
14 E. Jackson Blvd., Chicago IL 60603
312/341-1198

Accreditation candidate
Doctorates
Residency (EW)

The Doctor of Psychology (D.Psy.) degree is offered through daytime or evening classes. The D.Psy. is offered, because it is felt that the traditional Ph.D. in psychology overemphasizes research skills to the detriment of counseling or clinical skills. Graduates who have two years of supervised experience in the field can qualify to take the state licensing examination in Illinois. The school is a closely held private corporation.

INDIANA CENTRAL COLLEGE
1400 E. Hanna Ave., Indianapolis IN 46227
317/788-3368

Accredited
Bachelor's, Master's
Residency (EW)

A variety of Bachelor's and Master's degrees can be earned entirely through evening study. The Executive M.B.A. program meets one Friday and three Saturdays each month. In this program, it is possible to earn the degree in two years (comprising 19 Fridays and 50 Saturdays).

**INDIANA NORTHERN GRADUATE SCHOOL OF
    PROFESSIONAL MANAGEMENT**
410 S. 10th St., Gas City IN 46933
317/674-9200

Unaccredited
Master's
Short residency

Master of Professional Management degree, primarily through independent study, with some class meetings in various cities in northern Indiana. Originally called Indiana Northern University. The "University" designation and the doctoral programs were dropped by agreement with the state of Indiana. Indiana Northern was founded by the Most Reverend Bishop Dr. Gordon A. Da Costa, Ph.D., Ed.D., D.Sc., D.C., whose only earned degree is from Indiana Northern. The School's telephone is answered, "Hello."

Comment: Some of Bishop Da Costa's other educational involvements are mentioned in Chapter 23, Bible Schools, under Burton and Pacific Western. The Bishop and his school were the subject of an extremely unfavorable front-page article in the *National Observer* (May 5, 1973). The article was based on three months of investigative reporting by Lawrence Mosher, who stands by what he wrote, despite vigorous disagreements by Dr. Da Costa. Indiana Northern claims accreditation from the Accrediting Commission for Specialized Colleges, founded by Bishop Da Costa.

INDIANA UNIVERSITY

External Degree Program, Division of Extended studies,
1300 W. Michigan St., Student Union G-025M,
Indianapolis IN 46205
317/923-1321

Accredited
Bachelor's, Master's
Non-resident,
residency (EW)

Bachelor of General Studies available entirely through non-residential study. The degree can be done without a major, or with a major in Labor Studies. One hundred twenty semester units are required, of which at least 24 must be earned from Indiana University, but this can be done through correspondence study, equivalency exams, or credit for "self-acquired competency." Most of the correspondence courses offered by Indiana may be passed by taking only the final examination, but if this is failed twice, then the entire course work must be taken if credit is desired. One quarter of the units must be upper division (junior or senior) level. The cost is around $40 per semester hour for Indiana residents and triple that for non-Hoosiers. Indiana also offers a Master of Science program for middle management employees with full-time jobs, with evening classes at various locations around the state, and a Master of Social Work program with all classes on Saturday, for workers in the field, whose regular jobs provide internship credit.

INDIANA UNIVERSITY OF PENNSYLVANIA

Indiana PA 15705
412/357-2262

Accredited
Doctorates
Residency (IS)

Indiana University, in the city of Indiana, which is in the state of Pennsylvania, offers a Ph.D. in English and American Literature and in English (Rhetoric and Linguistics) that can be completed in two summers of study, with independent study at home in between. The literature says that "our graduate programs are arranged to accommodate teaching schedules of secondary, community, and four-year college teachers. With this flexibility of scheduling, graduate students can pursue their studies without interrupting their careers." The student can choose from a number of areas related to the humanistic study of literature, including psychology, history, art, and music. A dissertation is required. It can take the form either of a book, or of five or six essays on a given subject. There is a language requirement, which can be met by coursework or exams in a foreign language, coursework in linguistics, or knowledge of a computer language. The Director of the program wants me to be sure to mention that his is a rigorous program for serious students who wish to be challenged intellectually. Done. Tuition is under $1,000 per semester. About one hundred students are participating in the program.

INSTITUTE FOR THE ADVANCED STUDY OF HUMAN SEXUALITY

1523 Franklin St., San Francisco CA 94109
415/928-1133

Unaccredited
Master's, Doctorates
Short residency

The state-approved degree programs of Master of Human Sexuality, Doctor of Philosophy, Doctor of Arts, and Doctor of Human Sexuality, enable graduates to take state psychological licensing exams in California. A minimum of nine weeks of residency is required for the Master's, and 15 weeks for the various Doctoral programs, although additional residency is encouraged. The Master's program requires three trimesters of enrollment and the Doctorate programs require five trimesters each, with a minimum of three weeks' residency each trimester. The Institute was established in 1976 by a group of prominent sexologists, including Kinsey's co-author, Wardell Pomeroy, in the belief that there is a "woeful lack of professionals who are academically prepared in the study of human sexuality. It is the Institute's intention to rectify this lack by the preparation of professional persons as sexologists." Many of the required lectures are available on videocassettes. A comprehensive examination and a basic research project are required. The tuition is around $5,000 per year. Each of the three Doctorates has a different emphasis: one in scientific inquiry, one in academic skills, and one in therapy and counseling.

INSTITUTO DE ESTUDIOS IBEROAMERICANOS
Guerrero 312 (Apartado Postal 358), Saltillo, Coah.,
   Mexico
Telephone 3-89-99

Foreign
Bachelor's, Master's,
   Doctorates
Residency

Bachelor's, Master's, Doctorates, primarily for Americans, through a combination of five-week summer sessions in Mexico and independent study during the year at home. The subjects available include Spanish language and literature, Latin American studies, bilingual nursing, bilingual social work, social sciences, fine arts, and intercultural education. Although the school is not accredited, its credits have been accepted at the undergraduate level by dozens of traditional colleges in the United States. Many courses are given in Spanish, some in English. Accreditation is claimed from the International Council of Academic Institutes, a legitimate but never-recognized and now-dormant organization. Room and board can be arranged for the Mexican residency.

INSTITUTO POLITECNICO NACIONAL
Unidad Profesional Zacatenco, Mexico 14 D.F., Mexico

Foreign
Bachelor's
Non-resident

Mexico's *sistema abierto de ensenanza* (open university system) offers the Bachelor's degree in economics and international trade. Study at a distance is accomplished through the use of printed materials, slides, movies, records, videocassettes, as well as group seminars held at various locations. Awarding of the degree is based primarily on passing the necessary examinations.

INTERNATIONAL COLLEGE
1019 Gayley Ave., Los Angeles CA 90024
213/208-6761

Unaccredited
Bachelor's, Master's,
   Doctorates
Residency and non-resident

The degrees are based on personal tutorial studies, often with world-famous scholars or artists, either in their own geographic areas, or by correspondence. The Bachelor's and Master's in Fine Arts and the Ph.D. in psychology programs are approved by the State of California; the school itself is authorized to grant other degrees by the State. The Master's requires one academic year of study, and the Doctorate two years (16 months). Tutors listed in the most recent catalogue include, among many others, Paolo Soleri (architecture), Buckminster Fuller (comprehensive anticipatory design science), George Leonard (transformation studies), Yehudi Menuhin and Ravi Shankar (music), Gary Snyder (poetry), Russell Kirk (political science), Judy Chicago (feminist studies), and Edward T. Hall (anthropology). Tuition is about $4,000 per academic year. Around 500 students are currently enrolled.

INTERNATIONAL GRADUATE SCHOOL
27 Maryland Plaza, St. Louis MO 63108
314/361-4840

Accreditation candidate
Doctorates
Short residency

I.G.S. was established as the Doctoral level affiliate of the accredited World University (Puerto Rico) in 1980, and received its candidacy status in the remarkably short time of one year. The Doctor of Education program requires a total of two six-week residency periods in St. Louis, which can take place during the summer. Applicants should have at least two years of experience in their field. Tuition is in the range of $5,000 to $7,000 for the entire program (not including meals and lodging).

INTERNATIONAL INSTITUTE FOR ADVANCED STUDIES
8015 Forsyth Blvd., Clayton MO 63105
314/725-6068

Unaccredited
Master's, Doctorates
Non-resident

Master's and Doctorates are available in a wide range of fields, entirely through non-residential study. IIAS is a non-profit institution whose administrative staff works without pay for this idea in which they believe. The degrees are earned by demonstrating competence in research, professional knowledge, and a "cognate field" competency (specific knowledge of one or more fields), plus a dissertation. Competency in a foreign language is required (or detailed knowledge of a non-American culture). There is an impressive list of adjunct faculty mentors. IIAS degrees have been recognized by a prominent Swiss institute of technology, so that graduates can take certain examinations in Switzerland and qualify for membership in the Swiss Association of Engineers and Doctors of Industrial Sciences. Tuition is under $2,000 for the program.

Comment: IIAS offers one of the better unaccredited non-resident graduate programs, and one of the least expensive. I have had a good deal of positive feedback from many students and alumni. The Institute remains quite small, with fewer than one hundred students. The founder and president is Alexander Niven, a professor of history at St. Louis Community College and a well known Civil War authority. His own Doctorate is earned from IIAS.

INTERNATIONAL UNIVERSITY (California)
39 N. Craig, Pasadena CA 91107
No listed telephone

Unaccredited
Bachelor's, Master's,
Doctorates
Non-resident

International University claims to have been chartered as a non-profit religious institution in Louisiana. Their literature was always mailed from Pasadena, California, using the same postage meter and address as Southland University. Southland's founder and president, James Kirk, wrote to me that he was just helping them out, but had no connection with them. The State of Louisiana insists that Dr. Kirk was a co-incorporator of International University. Accreditation is claimed from the North American Regional Accrediting Commission. I can find no record of the existence of this association. Dr. Kirk now reports that his wife and some of her friends started the school, which apparently is dormant. Dr. Kirk's own Doctorate is from International University.

INTERNATIONAL UNIVERSITY (Greece)
Adrianapoleos 47, Peristeri TT4, Athens, Greece

Foreign
Bachelor's, Master's,
Doctorates
Non-resident

Apparently affiliated with, or an organ of, the International Institute and Society of Human Sciences, Comparative Civilizations and Parapsychology, Inc. The claim is made that the degrees and the university are "fully recognized" by the government of Greece. This claim is not confirmed by the Embassy of Greece in Washington. Degrees are offered in many academic areas as well as in martial arts and parapsychology. Honorary Doctorates are offered to "distinguished scholars." The President is Rt. Rev. Bishop Dr. Jean El Khoury, Ph.D., Psy.D., Ed.D.

INTERNATIONAL UNIVERSITY (Missouri)
1301 S. Noland Rd., Independence MO 64095
816/461-3633

Unaccredited
Bachelor's, Master's,
Doctorates
Non-resident

The literature of this establishment describes it as "internationally accredited." There are no recognized international accrediting agencies. The catalogue indicates there are campuses in Japan,

England, and Washington D.C. Chancellor John Johnston told a visitor who said he had tried unsuccessfully to find the Washington campus that "it is just a paper campus at this time." The visitor found the University in one room of an old house in Kansas City; it subsequently moved to the suburbs. Chancellor Johnston has declined to identify the source of his own Doctorate. Tuition is in the range of $5,000. International University absorbed Mayer University, an unaccredited school established from a St. Louis address, in the late 1970's.

INTERNATIONAL UNIVERSITY (New York?)

505 Fifth Ave., New York NY 10017
212/687-0010

Generally reliable correspondents have told me that this is actually the International University of Antigua, apparently offering non-traditional studies leading to Master's and Doctorates in psycho-analysis, and that the man behind it is Dr. Benjamin Weisman, of Mercy College, New York. But none of my many letters asking for information has ever been answered.

INTERNATIONAL UNIVERSITY (Philippines and Switzerland)

Suite 2063, Boulevard Executive Suites, Roxas Blvd.,
    Ermita, Manila, Philippines
50-15-17

Foreign
Master's, Doctorates
Non-resident

The Master of Business Administration, Master of International Management and Doctor of Business Administration are offered entirely by correspondence study. Although the literature implies that the headquarters is the International University of St. Moritz, Switzerland (Karl Xavier Bleich, President), the Ambassador of Switzerland in Washington has written me that "International University at St. Moritz is not a legitimate and legal university in Switzerland." He ought to know. A colleague in Manila visited the premises, and investigated the school there. The small clean offices are located in a very old building near the American Embassy. The primary owner is one Emmanuel Santos, an attorney and the brother of an S.E.C. commissioner. Apparently the Ministry of Education accepts most foreign degrees without question, hence the Swiss connection. (The Registrar in Manila, Mireille Mathys, is a Swiss national.)

Comment: It would certainly appear there is little to recommend this institution, whose Swiss credibility appears to be based on its Philippines office and its Philippine credibility on its falsely-claimed Swiss recognition.

IONA COLLEGE

New Rochelle NY 10801
914/636-2100

Accredited
Bachelor's
Residency (EW)

Bachelor of Arts, Bachelor of Science in general studies, and Bachelor of Business Administration can be earned entirely through evening studies.

IOWA STATE UNIVERSITY

Ames IA 50010
515/294-4111

Accredited
Bachelor's, Master's
Non-resident,
    residency (IS)

See University of Iowa for combined non-resident Bachelor's degree program. Wide variety of Master's programs in agriculture, education, engineering, home economics and public administration offered externally through a combination of courses and seminars held at various locations around the state, and independent study. Radio and television courses are held statewide, with instructor contact by telephone and mail.

JOHN F. KENNEDY UNIVERSITY
12 Altarinda Road, Orinda CA 94563
415/254-0200

Accredited
Bachelor's, Master's
Residency (IS, EW)

Kennedy offers Bachelor's degrees in the arts and humanities, business and management. Master's degrees can be earned in parapsychology (the only accredited program in the U.S.), consciousness studies, religion, transpersonal counseling, museum studies, business and public administration. The university sees a major role for itself as assisting adults in mid-life career changes. More than half the students and nearly all the faculty are part-time. Instruction is by lectures, seminars, internships, community service work, and classes, held during the day, evenings, and weekends. Applicants must have completed two years of college (or equivalent) before enrolling.

JOHNS HOPKINS UNIVERSITY
Baltimore MD 21218
301/366-3300

Accredited
Bachelor's, Master's
Residency (EW)

Bachelor of Science in accounting, education, business, literature, nursing, psychology, mathematics, engineering and other areas; Master of Administrative Science; Master of Education, Master of Science in education, and Master of Liberal Arts all offered through evening study and weekend study.

JOHNSTON STATE COLLEGE
Johnson VT 05656
802/635-2356

Accredited
Bachelor's
Residency (EW, IS)

Bachelor's degrees in a variety of fields, in which credit is given for prior experiential learning, and new credit may be earned by evening or independent study.

KANSAS STATE UNIVERSITY
Manhattan KS 66506
913/532-5686

Accredited
Bachelor's
Non-resident

While it is theoretically possible to earn 100% of the requirements for the Bachelor of Arts degree through an assessment of prior learning experiences, in practice this simply does not happen. Some new work will inevitably be required. The assessment process takes less than one month. Because of staff cutbacks, at this time only Kansas residents can apply, but this policy may change.

KARMA UNIVERSITY
P.O. Box H
Little River CA 95456
No telephone

Unaccredited
Doctorates
Non-resident

All students are required to undergo a self-induced hypnotic regression, taking them through the experience of all their previous lives. Upon documentation of their reports, full credit is given for all past life experience.

KEAN COLLEGE
Morris Ave., Union NJ 07083
201/527-2163

Accredited
Bachelor's
Residency (EW)

Bachelor's degrees in many fields, for which up to 75% of the degree requirements can be earned through an assessment of prior learning experiences based on a portfolio prepared by the student.

KENSINGTON UNIVERSITY
512 E. Wilson Ave. (P.O. Box 2036), Glendale CA 91209
213/245-7224

Unaccredited
Bachelor's, Master's,
  Doctorates
Non-resident

Degrees at all levels, in many fields, entirely through non-residential study. Kensington gives credit for all prior learning experiences, and provides a useful little booklet on how to prepare a portfolio of such experiences. Most degree programs involve completion of correspondence courses (primarily by self-paced reading of assigned texts) and completion of a final project. Supervised examinations may be taken anywhere in the world. Most degree programs can be completed in less than one year. Kensington also offers residential programs in business at the Bachelor's and Master's level through the facilities of City Commercial College in London. Tuition is between $2,000 and $3,000 for the complete program. Kensington is authorized to grant degrees by the State of California. The enrollment is approaching 1,000 students.

KINGS COLLEGE
Center for Independent Learning
Wilkes-Barre PA 18711
717/824-9931, ext. 358

Accredited
Bachelor's
Residency (LE)

Bachelor's degrees in a wide variety of fields, in which 50% of the required credits can come through assessment of prior learning experiences, through the center. A credit-granting course is offered in the preparation of a portfolio of experiences. The cost of the assessment is a flat fee of $30 plus tuition for the special course. Assessment may be done before enrolling in the degree program.

LA JOLLA UNIVERSITY
8939 Villa La Jolla Dr., Suite 200, La Jolla CA 92037
714/452-7111

Unaccredited
Bachelor's, Master's,
  Doctorates
Very short residency

The University offers its degrees in the areas of business administration and human behavior. All work is done by correspondence study, in which students read assigned textbooks and write papers based on them. All students, without exception, must come to La Jolla for an oral discussion, which serves as an evaluation of their understanding of the work done. Tuition for the programs is around $2,000. The University is authorized to grant degrees by the State of California. About 150 students are enrolled. Eight of the eleven faculty members earned their own highest degrees at La Jolla University, an unusually high ratio.

LAKE ERIE COLLEGE
Painesville OH 44077
216/352-3361

Accredited
Bachelor's, Master's
Residency (EW)

Bachelor of Science offered through a weekend college program. Students attend every other weekend, from Friday evening through Sunday afternoon. The degree may be completed in three years or less, depending on the amount of credit given for prior experience. General majors, or "learning tracks" are available in business administration, or in the social sciences. Tuition is reduced by two thirds for people over 60. A Master of Arts and a Master of Business Administration are also available by similar means.

LAMAR UNIVERSITY
Box 10009, Lamar Tech Station, Beaumont TX 77710
713/838-7111

Accredited
Bachelor's, Master's
Residency (EW)

Bachelor of Arts, Bachelor of Science, Bachelor of Business Administration, Master of Arts and Master of Science degrees can be earned entirely through evening study.

LAURENCE UNIVERSITY
30 W. Mission St., Santa Barbara CA 93101
805/966-4811

Unaccredited
Master's, Doctorates
Short residency

Laurence offers the Master of Arts in Education, the Ph.D. in education, and the Doctor of Education degree. The programs require a minimum of three weeks of residency in Santa Barbara. The degree programs have been approved by the State of California. They require from one to two years to complete, at a cost between $3,000 and $5,000. The 12 resident faculty and more than 50 non-resident advisors all have traditional Doctorates. Laurence offers both independent study and correspondence study in many aspects of the field of education. Candidates for the degree must complete courses and independent study work, and pass an examination in each study area.

Comment: I like the school, even if they do write me snippy letters. They offer one of the better graduate degrees, with minimal residency, but only in the field of education. The state approval means that the degrees will have widespread but not universal acceptance in academic situations.

LESLEY COLLEGE
29 Everett St., Cambridge MA 02238
617/492-1700

Accredited
Bachelor's, Master's
Residency (IS, LE)

Lesley offers a program in cooperation with the National Audubon Society, involving a combination of coursework and expeditions. Audubon's Expedition Institute has a two-year program, or field component, which involves camping, hiking, canoeing, skiing, backpacking and cycling all over America. In the course of this, students gain practical knowledge of astronomy, anthropology, ecology, and many other areas. The balance of the time is spent in classes at Lesley. The Master's program involves a year or a year and a half on Audubon expeditions and three or four courses back at Lesley. Students may switch back and forth between Lesley and Audubon. Tuition is in the range of $6,000 to $8,000. Lesley also offers short residency M.A. programs in special education, psychology, and women's studies, primarily for residents of the New England states.

LINFIELD COLLEGE
McMinnville OR 97128
503/472-4121, ext. 269

Accredited
Bachelor's
Residency (LE)

Bachelor of Arts, Bachelor of Science in Business, home economics, and physical education, and Bachelor of Arts in Liberal Studies, in which nearly 80% of the necessary units can come from a combination of assessment of prior learning and equivalency examinations. The assessment can take place before enrollment and costs a flat fee of around $200, plus extra for each credit hour awarded. A required course assists the student in preparing the life experience portfolio.

LONG ISLAND UNIVERSITY
C. W. Post Center, Greenvale NY 11548
516/299-2501

Accredited
Bachelor's
Residency (EW)

Bachelor of Science in accounting, business, business education, distributive education, and secretarial science; Bachelor of Public Service in aviation management and in health care administration, all available through evening study.

LORETTO HEIGHTS COLLEGE
3001 S. Federal Blvd., Denver CO 80236
303/936-8441

Accredited
Bachelor's
Short residency

A University Without Walls program in which one can earn the Bachelor of Arts with little or no time spent on campus. The SAADP (Students-at-a-Distance) program is available to students of all ages in the Rocky Mountain area. One hundred twenty-eight semester units are required for the degree, of which at least 30 must be earned after enrolling. But these can all be earned through independent study projects or equivalency examinations. Students (except those in prison) are expected to register on campus and meet with faculty advisors. The faculty advisors may also visit students at their home locations. The program is available primarily to persons living in Colorado, Utah, New Mexico, Wyoming, Nebraska, Idaho, and Montana. Tuition is in the range of $6,000 a year for a full-time student.

LOUISIANA STATE UNIVERSITY
Department of Extramural Teaching
Baton Rouge LA 70803
504/388-6207

Accredited
Bachelor's, Master's
Residency (EW)

Bachelor of Science in general studies, law enforcement; Master of Business Administration, Master of Education, all through evening study, with courses offered at centers in Alexandria, Baton Rouge, Eunice, New Orleans, and Shreveport.

LOYOLA COLLEGE
4501 N. Charles, Baltimore MD 21210
301/323-1010

Accredited
Bachelor's, Master's
Residency (EW)

Bachelor of Arts, Bachelor of Science in physics and music through evening study. Master of Arts in psychology, afternoons, evenings, and weekends. Bachelor of Education, evenings and weekends. Master of Business Administration, evenings. Master's in education, afternoons, evenings, weekends.

LOYOLA UNIVERSITY (Illinois)
820 N. Michigan Ave., Chicago IL 60611
312/670-3000

Accredited
Bachelor's, Master's
Residency (EW)

Bachelor of Science in mathematics, psychology, education, business administration; Master of Arts in educational administration, all through evening study.

LOYOLA UNIVERSITY (Louisiana)
6363 St. Charles Ave., New Orleans LA 70018
504/866-5471

Accredited
Bachelor's
Residency

Bachelor of Liberal Studies available entirely through evening study in a program called Continuing Education for Women.

MADONNA COLLEGE
36600 Schoolcraft Road, Livonia MI 48150
313/591-1200

Accredited
Bachelor's
Residency (EW, LE)

Bachelor's degree programs in many fields, including criminal justice, nursing, home economics and family life, and computer science in which up to 75% of the required units can be earned through an assessment of prior learning. The assessment is by means of a life experience portfolio, tests, and oral interviews with the faculty. A portfolio development course is offered. Challenge examinations are available in many areas, to demonstrate previously acquired learning. Internships or practicums in health, business, journalism, criminal justice, and occupational safety can be arranged.

MADURAI UNIVERSITY
Madurai 625021, India

Foreign
Bachelor's, Master's
Non-resident

Bachelor of Arts, Bachelor of Commerce, Master of Arts and Master of Commerce through a combination of correspondence study and examinations. Indian universities generally award their degrees entirely by examination. Madurai offers a wide range of correspondence courses designed to prepare students for its own examinations, which must be taken in India. It is necessary to take the courses in order to be allowed to take the examinations. They are primarily designed for Indian nationals and others resident in India, and may be taken overseas by special permission.

MANCHESTER COLLEGE
North Manchester IN 46962
219/982-2141

Accredited
Master's
Residency (EW)

The Master of Arts in education can be earned entirely through evening study.

MANHATTAN COLLEGE
Riverdale, Bronx, New York 10471
212/548-1400

Accredited
Bachelor's
Residency (EW)

Manhattan offers the Bachelor of Science in general studies, radiological sciences and health, and the Bachelor of Business Administration, all through evening studies.

MARIETTA COLLEGE
5th and Putnam, Marietta OH 45750
614/373-4643

Accredited
Bachelor's
Residency (EW)

Bachelor of Arts in business communication and in interdisciplinary studies through evening study. See also: East Central College Consortium.

MARQUETTE UNIVERSITY
Milwaukee WI 53233
414/224-7700

Accredited
Bachelor's
Residency (EW)

Bachelor of Arts, Bachelor of Science in civil engineering, electrical engineering and mechanical engineering, through evening study.

MARTIN CENTER COLLEGE
3553 North College Ave., Indianapolis IN 46205
317/923-5349

Accreditation candidate
Bachelor's
Residency (IS, LE)

Martin Center was established in 1970 by the Rev. Boniface Hardin as an extension of his programs to develop and conduct training in the area of race relations. This well respected, non-traditional college offers the Bachelor's degree in business, communications, counseling, social problems management, and other areas. Up to 75% of the necessary credit can be earned for both formal and informal prior learning experiences. Much of the work can be done independently under a learning contract model. Martin Center is an affiliate member of the Union for Experimenting Colleges and Universities. Tuition is between $2,000 and $3,000 a year for the full-time student.

MARY BALDWIN COLLEGE
Staunton VA 24401
703/885-0811

Accredited
Bachelor's
Very short residency
(LE, IS)

Bachelor of Arts program for women only in which virtually all of the work can be done independently, or at a distance. The program is entirely non-residential. Students need to come to the campus only twice: once for a day of orientation, and once to present their degree plans. Advanced standing is given for work done at other schools, equivalency examinations, and the assessment of prior learning. The degree requires a minimum of nine months to complete, and the fee is under $2,000 per year.

Comment: An excellent opportunity for women to earn good degrees from a prestigious school at relatively modest cost, and with minimal residency.

MARYLHURST COLLGE FOR LIFELONG LEARNING

Marylhurst OR 97038
503/636-8141

Accredited
Bachelor's
Very short residency

Bachelor of Arts, Bachelor of Science, or Bachelor of Music degrees which may be earned almost entirely through non-residential study, although attendance at on-campus colloquia and meetings with faculty advisors may be necessary. Credit is earned by taking Marylhurst courses, courses at other schools, or by correspondence, and through independent directed studies. Twenty-two percent of the work for the degree must be done after enrollment. The minimum cost is between $2,000 and $3,000. Marylhurst sells a very useful guidebook on preparing a life experience portfolio, and a collection of sample portfolios. See Chapter 13 for details.

MARYMOUNT COLLEGE

Tarrytown NY 10591
914/631-3200

Accredited
Bachelor's
Residency (EW)

Bachelor of Arts earned by spending a minimum of 36 weekends on campus. Classes are given every third weekend, and go from Friday at dinner to Sunday afternoon. Degrees are offered in psychology, sociology, economics and business; $36 \times 3 = 108$ weeks, or just over two years for the program.

MARYVILLE COLLEGE

13550 Conway Road, St. Louis MO 63141
314/434-4100

Accredited
Master's
Residency (EW)

The Missouri school offers a Master of Arts in Education in which 16 of the required 30 semester hours are earned during a summer session in St. Louis and the remaining 14 are earned in courses given at International House in Caracas, Venezuela.

MARYWOOD COLLEGE

Scranton PA 18515
800/233-4186; in Pennsylvania 800/982-4354

Accredited
Bachelor's
Short residency

The Bachelor of Science in either business administration or accounting is earned through a combination of off-campus correspondence study and two two-week seminars held on the campus: one mid-way through the program, and one at the end. Sixty of the required 126 semester units must be earned after enrolling at Marywood. Credit is available by independent study projects, correspondence courses, equivalency exams, and credit for life experience as evaluated by the Portfolio Assessment Program of Thomas A. Edison State College of New Jersey. The minimum cost of the degree program is over $5,000.

Comment: Marywood represents an interesting alliance between an old Catholic women's college and the aggressive International Correspondence Schools. One of the benefits of modern-day marketing techniques is the toll-free telephone service, in which "an instructor is readily available for assistance" from 8 a.m. to 8 p.m. every day. The cost of the program is over $5,000.

MARY WASHINGTON COLLEGE

Box 3575, College Station, Fredericksburg VA 22401
703/899-4614

Accredited
Bachelor's
Residency (LE, IS)

Bachelor of Liberal Studies program in which up to 75% of the required units may be earned in an assessment of prior learning experiences. The remaining 25% of the work must be done after enrolling, either through Mary Washington classes, independent study, internships, or classes at other schools. One must be accepted as a student before the assessment can be done. There is a separate but modest assessment fee for each subject area.

Comment: Mary Washington's literature is among the best-written and most comprehensible I have seen. A pleasure to read. A brief extract: ''Anyone who has been married eight years and has two children knows a lot about marriage and the family without having taken Sociology 331. And anyone who has sold cars successfully for five years knows things about public speaking, personal relations, psychology, and finance that a college might teach in four courses. If what is taught in the college classroom has any meaning at all, it can also be learned outside the classroom.''

MASSEY UNIVERSITY
Centre for University Extra-Mural Studies,
    Palmerston North, New Zealand

Foreign
Bachelor's
Residency (IS)

Massey offers an external degree program, in which the majority of work can be completed by correspondence study, utilizing books, audio tape cassettes, and a telephone conference system. Students must attend part-time for one academic year (March to November), and the remaining work can be done at a distance. Degrees are offered in humanities, social sciences, science, business studies, agricultural science and education. (The latter three subjects may require some practical work experience as part of the degree program.)

MEMPHIS STATE UNIVERSITY
Memphis TN 38111
901/454-2716

Accredited
Bachelor's
Residency (LE, EW)

Bachelor of Arts, Bachelor of Business Administration, Bachelor of Fine Arts, Bachelor of Music and Bachelor of Science entirely through evening study. Also a Bachelor of Professional Studies and a Bachelor of Liberal Studies, in which more than 75% of the required units may be earned through assessment of prior learning experiences, through University College. The assessment must be done after enrollment and takes from two to five months. The cost is based on the number of units awarded.

METROPOLITAN STATE COLLEGE
1006 11th St., Denver CO 80204
303/629-3107

Accredited
Bachelor's
Residency (LE)

Up to half the units required for the Bachelor's degree can come from assessment of prior learning experiences. The assessment is based on a student-prepared portfolio, and the cost is based on the number of units awarded.

METROPOLITAN STATE UNIVERSITY
7th and Robert Streets, St. Paul MN 55101
612/296-3875

Accredited
Bachelor's
Short residency

Metropolitan is one of the pioneers in non-traditional programs. Their Bachelor of Arts requires one planning seminar on the campus, followed by a faculty-guided independent study program. After the initial course, no further campus attendance is mandatory, but occasional meetings with faculty advisors will almost certainly be necessary. Most of the students come from the Twin Cities area. The minimum time for completing the degree is nine months. The basic fee is very low, but students pay for university services as they use them, including faculty time and assessment of prior experience. Orientation meetings are held several times each week in the St. Paul-Minneapolis area. The school used to be called Minnesota Metropolitan State College.

MICHIGAN STATE UNIVERSITY
East Lansing MI 48824
517/355-1855

Accredited
Master's
Residency (EW)

Master of Business Administration and Master of Science in electrical and mechanical engineering, counseling and guidance, and nursing, offered entirely through evening study at East Lansing, Benton

Harbor, Bloomfield Hills, Grand Rapids and Saginaw. Also, Michigan State offers the M.A. in education through part-time and independent study at centers in Japan, England and Italy. This program is designed primarily for teachers living and working in those countries.

MILLIKIN UNIVERSITY
Decatur IL 62522
217/424-6335

Accredited
Bachelor's
Residency (EW)

Bachelor of Arts, Bachelor of Science and Bachelor of Music degrees are available entirely through evening study.

MILWAUKEE SCHOOL OF ENGINEERING
1025 N. Milwaukee St., Milwaukee WI 53202
414/272-8720

Accredited
Bachelor's, Master's
Residency (EW)

Bachelor of Arts, Bachelor of Science in engineering technology and industrial management; Master of Science in engineering management, entirely through evening study.

MOORHEAD STATE UNIVERSITY
External Studies Degree Program
Moorhead MN 56560
218/236-2161

Accredited
Bachelor's
Residency (LE)

Bachelor's degrees in many fields in which more than 75% of the required units may be earned through an assessment of prior learning experiences. The assessment is based on evaluation of a student-prepared portfolio and interviews with the faculty. The assessment fees, which are quite low, are based on the number of units awarded.

MORAVIAN COLLEGE
Division of Continuing Studies, Bethlehem PA 18018
215/861-1383

Accredited
Bachelor's
Residency (EW, IS)

Bachelor of Arts and Bachelor of Science in accounting, art, computer science, criminal justice, business, and the social sciences entirely through evening study. Credit is available for independent study projects and field studies, as well as equivalency examinations.

MOUNT UNION COLLEGE
1972 Clark Ave., Alliance OH 44601
216/821-5320, ext. 242

Accredited
Bachelor's
Residency (LE)

Bachelor's degree in many fields, in which 75% of the units can come from an assessment of prior learning experiences. The assessment, which is based on a portfolio prepared by the student, can be done before enrolling, at a fixed rate of around $250.

See also: East Central College Consortium

MUNDELEIN COLLEGE
6363 N. Sheridan Road, Chicago IL 60626
312/262-8100

Accredited
Bachelor's
Residency (LE, EW)

Bachelor's degrees in many fields, including management, home economics and the sciences, in which up to 75% of the required units can come from an assessment of prior learning experiences. The assessment is based on a portfolio, examinations, and/or faculty interviews. The assessment fee is based on the number of units awarded, and costs about a third the regular cost of earned units. Courses are also offered through a Weekend College program.

NATIONAL COLLEGE OF EDUCATION
25-361 Glen Park Rd., Lombard IL 60201
312/629-5320

Accredited
Bachelor's, Master's
Residency (LE, IS)

Bachelor of Arts in Applied Behavioral Sciences, in which up to 75% of the required units can be earned from assessment of prior learning and college transfer credit. Can cost up to $300. The College utilizes what they call the Field-Experience Model, combining an intense program of classes (one 4-hour session per week) and individual study, while remaining fully employed. The Master of Science in Management/Development of Human Resources combines independent study with 48 four-hour meetings (once a week for a year). Tuition is around $5,000 for the entire program.

**NATIONAL INSTITUTE FOR HIGHER
      EDUCATION**
Limerick, Ireland

Foreign
Bachelor's
Residency (IS)

The Institute was established to train workers for various Irish industries. The Bachelor's degrees in business administration, engineering and European Studies are earned through a combination of classes, on-the-job experience, and independent study.

NATIONAL UNIVERSITY
4141 Camino Del Rio South, San Diego CA 92108
714/563-0100

Accredited
Bachelor's, Master's
Residency (EW)

Bachelor's and Master's degrees in business administration, public administration and criminal justice, health care administration, human services management and real estate management. Classes are offered two evenings a week plus one or two Saturdays a month. Only one course is taken at a time, intensively for one calendar month. Sixteen courses, thus 16 months, are required for each degree. Tuition is over $4,000. Classes are offered in several off-campus locations, and seem to be moving in the direction of Los Angeles.

Comment: When National University was accredited in 1977, the traditional educators in the San Diego area were distressed and alarmed. They objected to the "limited curriculum" and "unkind advertising." National is run like a business, and their no-nonsense approach may have been threatening to the Higher Education Association of San Diego. Things seem to have calmed down now.

NAZARETH COLLEGE
Continuing Education Program
New Rochelle NY 10801
716/586-2525

Accredited
Bachelor's
Residency (EW)

Bachelor of Arts in liberal arts offered entirely through evening study, for persons over 21.

NEW COLLEGE OF CALIFORNIA
777 Valencia St., San Francisco CA 94109
415/626-1694

Accredited
Bachelor's, Master's
Residency (EW, IS)

This highly innovative school has offered its Bachelor of Arts and Master of Arts degrees in a variety of different approaches, including evening courses, weekend courses, and a series of long weekend seminars with independent study sessions in between, on-the-job practicums, tutorials, a weekend program, and credit for prior learning experience. The B.A. is offered in humanities (including art, writing, psychology, mathematics, chemistry, biology, and much more). There is an M.A. in psychology and in poetics (a unique non-literature approach to the subject). The Science Institute offers science courses designed for people planning to attend chiropractic or podiatric schools. New College was established in 1971 by Father John Leary, former president of Gonzaga University. Traditional courses are offered, generally in three-hour sessions.

Comment: The level of student enthusiasm and vitality is extremely high, and many letters from alumni have attested to their pleasure in earning the degree. (The name "New College," incidentally, comes from Oxford University where their New College was established in the 13th century!)

NEWPORT UNIVERSITY
3720 Campus Drive, Newport Beach CA 92660
714/556-0762

Unaccredited
Bachelor's, Master's,
Doctorates
Non-resident

Degrees at all levels are offered in business, the behavioral sciences, and religious education. The school is authorized to grant degrees by the State of California. Newport was established in the late 1970's as Newport International University by Reg Sheldrick, a hypnotist. In 1980, new management assumed control, under the presidency of Ted Dalton, whose Doctorate is from California Western University.

NEW SCHOOL FOR SOCIAL RESEARCH
66 Fifth Ave., New York NY 10003
212/741-5600

Accredited
Master's
Residency (EW, IS)

Master of Arts in media studies, for teachers, librarians and media specialists, offered through a combination of evening study and independent study.

NEW YORK INSTITUTE OF TECHNOLOGY
Wheatley Road (Box 170), Old Westbury NY 11568
516/686-7612

Accredited
Bachelor's
Non-resident or
short residency

Bachelor of Science in business or behavioral science, and Bachelor of Technology in electrical-mechanical-computer technology degrees, primarily through guided independent study in a learning contract model. Learning contracts consist of detailed course outlines, sequences of assignments, and alternate mechanisms by which students can complete their assignments. The technology program may involve laboratory work on campus, but the Institute may permit work at a facility in the student's vicinity (high school, college, business). Tuition is at the rate of $107 per semester unit earned, whether residentially or at a distance.

NEW YORK UNIVERSITY
Gallatin Division, 25 Waverly Place, 1st Floor,
  New York NY 10003
212/598-7077

Accredited
Bachelor's, Master's
Residency (IS, LE, EW)

A university without walls program offers the opportunity to earn the Bachelor of Arts in a program requiring no specific courses (however students are expected to be "thoroughly conversant" with a formidable list of great books as a graduation requirement). Internships, independent study, and credit for life experience are available. A cooperative education program offers the B.A. largely based on internships in education, arts administration, media, business, and public/social service. The Master of Arts in individualized study involves coursework, internships, and independent study, under the supervision of a faculty advisor. A scholarly, creative, or performance thesis is required. Credit is given for career experience learning.

NIAGARA UNIVERSITY
Niagara NY 14109
716/285-1212

Accredited
Master's
Residency (EW)

Master of Arts in education, English, history, philosophy; Master of Arts in Teaching, Master of Science in biology, chemistry, education; all through late afternoon or evening study.

NORDENFJORD WORLD UNIVERSITY
Skyum Bjerge, DK-7752, Snedsted, Thy, Denmark

Foreign
Bachelor's, Master's,
    Doctorate
Residency (IS)

An unusual institution, comprising six separate schools, where students come from all over the world to study for anywhere from a semester to an entire degree program. The New Experimental College is one of the six units, with the goal of developing a self-perpetuating community of scholars who will have a world-wide effect on technology, economics and social planning. The University is not officially recognized by the Danish government. Many of the students make arrangements with schools in their home countries to award Bachelor's, Master's, or Doctorates based on the work done at Nordenfjord. Education is largely through teacher-directed independent study, although there are some classes and seminars. Rules and plans are made in the "ting" — a group or community meeting with elements of group dynamics, sensitivity training, the Synanon Game, and maybe a little mysticism. Students nearing the end of their work may call for a "high ting" — a combined examination/celebration, in which the student presents his or her work and invites criticism and discussion from the group. Other units of Nordenfjord specialize in communications, arts and crafts, language, and philosophy.

NORTH ADAMS STATE COLLEGE
North Adams MA 01247
413/664-4511

Accredited
Bachelor's
Residency (LE)

Bachelor's degree programs in many fields, in which 75% of the required units may be earned by an assessment of prior learning experience. The assessment is based on a portfolio prepared by the student, and must be initiated after enrollment. The assessment requires less than a month, and is done without additional cost.

**NORTH AMERICAN COLLEGES OF NATURAL
    HEALTH SCIENCES**
817-B Fourth St., San Rafael CA 94901
415/459-4050

Unaccredited
Master's
Residency (IS)

Programs ranging from short courses in massage and nutrition to a 30-month program in homeopathy, and a Master's in nutrition in their Airola College. An independent study project is an element of the curriculum.

NORTH AMERICAN UNIVERSITY
1277 E. Missouri St., Phoenix AZ 85014
800/327-7006

Unaccredited
Bachelor's, Master's,
    Doctorates
Non-resident

According to the literature, all degrees are offered by correspondence study and credit for life experience. The cost is in the range of $2,000 for each program.

Comment: I find it really hard to get a handle on this school, and they don't make it easier, since they have never responded to any of my many letters. The literature, at first glance, is awfully impressive. Well written, nicely printed. However my first concern is that they aren't where they say they are. There is no listing for the school on the Missouri Street building directory. My research convinces me the school is really in Florida. The catalogues are mailed from Stuart, Florida, and that is where the "800" phone line apparently rings. There is a Gregory A. Miller (President of the University) listed in the Stuart, Florida phone book. Both Deans of the college have their Ph.D. from American International University, one of the two large degree mills exposed on *60 Minutes* a few years ago. And accreditation is claimed from the National Accreditation Association, an unrecognized agency that once offered automatic accreditation, without inspection, to any school willing to pay their fee. On the other side of the ledger, North American's President is a retired professor with 25 years experience at Michigan State University, and the catalogue lists about 100 faculty, nearly all with traditional degrees. Can they all have been duped by a less-than-wonderful institution, or is there more here than meets the eye? My research continues.

NORTH CONTINENTAL UNIVERSITY
P.O. Box 4468, Santa Rosa CA 95405
707/545-4686

Does not respond to letters or telephone calls; no street address given; unknown by Department of Education in Sacramento.

Comment: In the most recent of the many letters I have written to this impressively named institution, I said, ''The new edition of my book is now being written. Under North Continental University, I would certainly like to be able to say something other than, 'Does not respond to letters or telephone calls; no street address given; unknown by Department of Education in Sacramento.' '' No answer.

NORTH CAROLINA STATE UNIVERSITY
Box 5125, Raleigh NC 27650
919/737-2265

Accredited
Bachelor's, Master's
Residency (EW, LE)

Bachelor's degrees in many fields, including design, forest resources, and textiles, in which up to 75% of the units can be earned through an assessment of prior learning experiences. The assessment is done after enrollment. It normally takes less than a month, and there is no additional cost. Master of Public Affairs and Master of Industrial Engineering programs are offered through evening study at various centers around the state (Charlotte, Fayetteville, Greensboro, Greenville, Marion, and Raleigh).

NORTH DAKOTA STATE UNIVERSITY
State University Station, Fargo ND 58105
701/237-7014

Accredited
Bachelor's, Master's
Residency (LE, EW)

Bachelor's degrees in many fields, including agriculture and home economics, in which more than 75% of the units can be earned through an assessment of prior learning experiences. The assessment must be done after enrollment, and is based on a portfolio prepared by the student and submitted to the College of University Studies. There is no fee for the assessment. Master of Science in education is offered to in-service teachers (and others, by permission) entirely through evening study.

NORTHEASTERN ILLINOIS UNIVERSITY
5500 North St. Louis Ave., Chicago IL 60625
312/583-4050

Accredited
Bachelor's
Short residency

Bachelor of Arts, with a minimum residency requirement of 15 units, which can be completed in four months on campus. One of five Illinois universities participating in the Board of Governors Bachelor of Arts program. Credit is given for life experience and all prior learning experiences. New credit may be earned through regular courses at any of the five schools in the program, or by correspondence study and independent study.

Comment: The five Board of Governors schools started out with almost identical programs, but now two, Western Illinois and Governors State, offer totally non-resident programs.

NORTHEASTERN UNIVERSITY
360 Huntington, Boston MA 02115
617/437-2000

Accredited
Bachelor's, Master's,
Doctorate
Residency (EW, IS)

Northeastern offers what UNESCO calls ''the world's leading program in Cooperative Education.'' Most of Northeastern's more-than-50,000 students are employed half-time by companies all over the

United States. The academic year is divided into four equal quarters. While half the students are attending full-time (including evening study), the other half are working full-time. Every three months, they switch. There are many situations in which two students combine to hold a full-time job in business or industry. Bachelor's, Master's, Doctorates (Ph.D. and Doctor of Engineering) and Law degrees are offered in this manner, in a wide variety of subjects, from social science to engineering to pharmacy, nursing, and criminal justice.

NORTHERN UTAH MANAGEMENT INSTITUTE

312 Main St., Park City UT 84060
801/649-6207

Unaccredited
Master's
Non-resident

The Master of Business Administration or Master of International Management can be earned by taking correspondence courses, passing a comprehensive examination, and completing a thesis or major project. Although the literature states there is a one-week residency requirement in Utah, a subsequent newsletter says that this may be waived for persons with at least five years of work experience. The tuition is in excess of $3,000. A residency program has been offered in India.

Comment: Although no faculty or staff names are given in the literature, the newsletter lists half a dozen business and professional men with respectable titles as members of the Academic Policy Board. Several correspondents have told me there is a connection with Southeastern University/New Orleans, but neither organization has responded to my inquiries.

NORTHWESTERN COLLEGE

Orange City IA 51041
712/737-4821, ext. 19

Accredited
Bachelor's
Residency (LE)

Bachelor's degree in many fields, in which up to 80% of the units may be earned by assessment of prior learning experience. Only full-time students can be so assessed, on the basis of a portfolio they prepare. There is no additional fee for the assessment, which can take three to five months.

NORTHWOOD INSTITUTE

3225 Cook Road, Midland MI 48640
517/631-1600

Accredited
Bachelor's
Short residency

Bachelor of Business Administration degree, in either business or accounting, requiring a total of six days on the campus. Credit is given for prior learning experience and study, and for equivalency examinations. The External Plan of Study has many courses which can be passed by taking an open book examination. All students must attend two three-day seminars on campus, write a thesis, and pass a final oral examination ''which will last for several hours and be based on questions provided to the student in advance.'' Fees are quite variable, depending on the approach the student takes. Northwood has offered this program at other locations around the U.S., including Ohio, Texas, and California.

NORWICH UNIVERSITY

Vermont College, Montpelier VT 05602
802/229-0522

Accredited
Bachelor's, Master's
Short residency

When the excellent and well-regarded Goddard College fell on hard financial times in 1981, they sold some of their non-traditional programs to Norwich University. Norwich is permitted to use the Goddard name until 1984, and they have chosen to do so, for their bulletin is headlined ''The Goddard Graduate Program,'' with ''Vermont College'' in small type, and ''Norwich University'' in even smaller type only on the last page. This is probably because Norwich has a reputation as a straight-laced military school (a plaque at the entrance reads, ''Obedience to the law is liberty''). Goddard College continues to offer external programs, as well, as described earlier in this section. Norwich's Goddard programs begin with the selection of a committee of core faculty (faculty are located in Vermont, and in the New York, Los Angeles, San Francisco, Washington, Boston, and Philadelphia areas), and field faculty (mentors who may live anywhere). This committee "tries to meet at least twice" — once at the start and once near the end. In some parts of the country, clusters of students meet regularly; other students work mostly alone through independent guided study. Most students require one to two years to complete their degrees at a cost of around $4,000 per year.

NOVA COLLEGE

15006 78th Ave., P.O. Box 1878, Edmonton, Alberta,
   Canada T5J 2P2
403/487-3807

Foreign
Bachelor's, Master's,
Doctorates
Non-resident

Degrees at all levels are offered entirely through correspondence study. Nova is a small, new (established 1977) school. Many correspondence courses are offered in association with the National Extension College, a well-established non-degree-granting home-study school in England. The total cost of a degree program is quite variable, depending on the approach taken and the amount of prior work done. Challenge examinations are available. The founder and president is Reg Farley, who earned his Doctorate from the International Institute for Advanced Studies in Missouri. I've had positive feedback from Nova students, and from a couple of Canadian school boards that recognize Nova degrees. And there have been a few letters of concern from Canadians worried that Nova is not registered with the Minister of Advanced Education (Alberta) as a private vocational school. Nova is a member of a new national organization in Canada, the Federation of Independent Schools of Canada, and expects to join the Alberta Association of Independent Schools and Colleges.

NOVA UNIVERSITY

College Avenue, Fort Lauderdale FL 33314
305/587-6660

Accredited
Bachelor's, Master's,
Doctorates
Short residency

Nova University is one of the two most innovative and shortest-residency doctoral programs ever to receive regional accreditation. (Fielding Institute is the other.) Master's and Doctorates are offered in education, business administration, and public administration. The typical student attends one group meeting a month (generally for three or four days), plus two one-week residential sessions, and from three to six "practicums," or on-the-job learning experiences. The total time is generally around two years. Nova has offered its residential work at locations all over the United States, and will consider offering the program anywhere in the world that a large enough cluster can be formed — typically 40 students. The total cost is in excess of $8,000.

Comment: Nova's was the first alternative doctoral program to be accredited and, from most reports, the degree is an excellent and very useful one. However, many educational conservatives do not approve of the idea of a Doctorate with so little residency. According to its president, Abraham Fischler, Nova is forced to spend over $100,000 a year on legal battles to defend their good name, and enforce their right to offer programs nationally. Perhaps their landmark victory against the State of North Carolina, giving them the right to offer programs in that state, signifies a period of approaching calm. Still, every few months, a newspaper somewhere seems to "discover" that the local Superintendent of Schools has a Nova Doctorate, and an "exposé"-type article appears. This would appear to be one of the perils of innovation.

OHIO STATE UNIVERSITY

Division of Continuing Education, 2400 Olentangy River
   Road, Columbus OH 43210
614/422-6446

Accredited
Bachelor's, Master's
Residency (EW)

Bachelor of Arts in English, history; Bachelor of Science; Bachelor of Business Administration; Master of Arts in education, English, history and journalism, all available through evening study

OHIO UNIVERSITY
External Student Program, 301 Tupper Hall, Athens
  OH 45701
614/594-6569 (In Ohio, 800/282-4406)

Accredited
Bachelor's
Non-resident

The Bachelor of General Studies degree can be earned entirely through non-resident study. The External Student Program provides a counseling and advising service, and also acts as a liaison in dealing with other university offices. Credit for the degree can come from assessment of prior learning experiences, correspondence courses, independent study projects, and courses on radio or television. In many correspondence courses, you can take the examination only, and, if you pass, the credit is given. These exams can be administered anywhere in the world, and must be supervised. Forty-eight quarter hours of credit must be completed after enrolling at Ohio. Other Bachelor's degrees of Ohio University can be completed largely through external means, but some time on campus will almost certainly be required. Students from all over the United States and Canada are participating in the various offerings of the Office of Lifelong Learning.

OKLAHOMA CITY UNIVERSITY
Competency-Based Degree Program, N.W. 2501 North
  Blackwelder, Oklahoma City OK 73106
405/521-5265

Accredited
Bachelor's
Very short residency

The Bachelor of Arts or Science can be earned entirely through assessment of prior learning experiences. If these experiences are not sufficient for the degree, as is often the case, new learning takes place through correspondence courses and independent study, under a learning contract. Although no time on campus is required to do the work for the degree, each student must visit the campus once to meet with the faculty. After that, the mail and telephones are used. Degrees are available in six areas of concentration: communication skills, aesthetics and arts, comparative cultures, health ecology & life sciences, business & legal aspects of society, and experimental methodology. All students must be enrolled for at least 16 weeks before earning the degree. The University provides an extremely helpful Guidebook to the program — several hundred pages of detailed information, useful advice, and sample learning contracts. About 500 students are enrolled in the program.

OKLAHOMA STATE UNIVERSITY
Stillwater OK 74074
405/624-5000

Accredited
Master's
Residency (IS)

Master of Engineering programs are offered through the Cooperative Extension Service at various locations statewide, combining residential and independent study.

OPEN LEARNING FOR THE FIRE SERVICE
1750 New York Ave N.W., Washington DC 20006
602/659-2067

Accredited
Bachelor's
Short residency

Bachelor's degree program in fire science, primarily through independent study, for working fire-fighters and others interested in the field. Open Learning is a project of the International Association of Fire Fighters. They work with a number of accredited universities. Students take the Open Learning courses, mostly by correspondence, and then are awarded the Bachelor's degree by one of the participating schools.

OPEN UNIVERSITY
Walton Hall, Milton Keynes, Buckinghamshire, England

Foreign
Bachelor's, Master's,
  Doctorates
Non-resident

England's highly innovative non-traditional university has become the model for similar ventures worldwide. Degrees at all levels are offered through a combination of correspondence courses,

courses on radio and television, and some non-required week-long seminars during the summer months. The degrees offered are the Bachelor of Arts, Bachelor of Philosophy, Master of Philosophy, and Doctor of Philosophy in the fields of arts, education, mathematics, social sciences, science, and technology. A Bachelor's degree can take anywhere from three to six years of part-time study; a Doctorate from three to nine years. About 60 hours of courses are transmitted each week on BBC radio and television, but Open University is increasing its use of home-study materials, including books, tape cassettes and home laboratory kits for science students. Enrollment is approaching 100,000 students.

Comment: Started as an experiment in 1971, Open University has grown into the most elaborate correspondence school in the world. As at other British universities, credit is earned only by passing examinations. Thus it is theoretically possible to enroll in the University while in England (or using an English address), come back to the States, study at home, and return to England from time to time to take the examinations.

OPEN UNIVERSITY OF AMERICA

3916 Commander Drive, Hyattsville MD 20782
301/779-0220

Unaccredited
Bachelor's, Master's,
  Doctorates
Non-resident

Degrees at all levels, in all fields, entirely on the basis of work done elsewhere. Has operated branches in California and Nevada as California National Open University, etc. Most of the students come from the military, or from outside the United States.

Comment: In response to my routine request for information on the school and the credentials of the staff, Chancellor M. C. Rodgers, who runs the University from the basement of her home, wrote to me as follows: "Your attempt to extort data from me by blackmail method [sic] is reprehensible. . . . Be advised that you are not at liberty to criticize, extol, describe, interpret, or represent knowledge about the Open University of America in any way." Oh, dear. I'd better stop right now. Except to say that, as one might expect, I have received more complaint letters about this school than any other in the world. And perhaps I'd better mention that Open University was the subject of a devastating exposé by NBC television, which termed Open University "a diploma mill."

OPEN UNIVERSITY OF THE NETHERLANDS

Villa Zomerweelde, Heerten, Limburg, The Netherlands

Foreign
Bachelor's, Doctorates
Non-resident

Netherlands' first non-traditional university opens in late 1983 or early 1984, offering degrees in organizational science, engineering, natural science, English language and literature, behavioral science, history, sociology, political science, public and business administration. The main teaching method will be self-study, supported by printed course materials, audio or video tapes, computerized instructions, and radio and television programs. The model is based on Britain's Open University. Credit will be awarded solely by passing examinations. Tutoring will be available in study centers around the country, and by telephone.

OREGON TECHNICAL INSTITUTE

Klamath Falls OR 97601
503/882-6321

Accredited
Bachelor's
Residency (EW)

The Bachelor of Technology degree can be earned entirely through evening study. Credit is given for prior learning experience.

OTTAWA UNIVERSITY
605 W. 47th St., Kansas City MO 64112
816/753-1431

Accredited
Bachelor's
Short residency

Ottawa offers a Bachelor of Arts in health care administration, through a combination of independent study and attendance at four two-day seminars, either in Kansas City or at various locations around the U.S. The program is specifically designed for health care professionals: people from nursing, radiologic technology, respiratory therapy, nuclear medicine, nurse midwifery, etc. Up to 56% of the necessary credit for the degree can come from prior health care training. (R.N.'s, for instance, get 72 semester hours for the R.N. training.) Additional credit is available from assessment of prior learning. Credit is given for standard equivalency exams, and special exams will be prepared in fields not otherwise covered. The cost depends on how much experiential credit is given, but can range as high as $10,000.

OUR LADY OF THE LAKE UNIVERSITY
411 S.W. 24th St., San Antonio TX 78285
512/434-6711

Accredited
Bachelor's
Residency (EW, LE)

The university offers its Bachelor's degree in human sciences, management, public administration, liberal studies, or media communication arts, entirely through evening or weekend study. All classes are scheduled for Friday evening, Saturday or Sunday, every other week. A total of 18 weekends a year equals a full-time academic load. Up to 80% of the required units can be earned through a combination of credit for prior experience and work done before enrolling. The assessment itself takes from two to five months at a cost of $25 plus one-third the usual tuition for all units awarded.

PACE UNIVERSITY
Bedford Road, Pleasantville NY 10570
914/769-3200

Accredited
Bachelor's
Residency (LE)

Bachelor of Liberal Studies and Bachelor of Professional Studies, in which up to 75% of the required units may be earned by an assessment of prior learning experiences. A non-credit workshop is offered to help students prepare the portfolio on which the assessment is based. There is a flat fee of $100 for the assessment, which must be done after enrolling.

PACIFIC STATES UNIVERSITY
1516 S. Western Ave., Los Angeles CA 90006
213/731-2383

Unaccredited
Master's, Doctorate
Short residency

Master of Arts, Doctor of Education, Doctor of Product Development, and Ph.D. programs, primarily through non-residential independent study. A six-week summer session, either in Los Angeles or in London, England is required. The university was founded in 1928 as an engineering school, and still offers residential programs in various fields. The graduate degrees are offered with a specialty in administration, general education, psychology and counseling. They can be completed in less than a year, at a cost in excess of $3,000 plus travel expenses. Pacific States is accredited by the National Association for Private Nontraditional Schools and Colleges, a legitimate but unrecognized accrediting agency.

PACIFIC WESTERN UNIVERSITY
16200 Ventura Blvd., Dept. RDR-5, Encino CA 91436
213/995-0876

Unaccredited
Bachelor's, Master's,
  Doctorates
Non-resident

Pacific Western offers degrees at all levels, in many fields, entirely through non-residential study. The University provides its students with detailed and useful publications that make clear exactly what is required to complete the degree. (It is surprising how few schools do this.) Each degree program begins with the preparation of a Degree Program Warrant—a document requiring the student to identify his or her profession, and explain the student's role in the profession, and the profession's role in society. Next a portfolio of prior learning experiences is prepared. Pacific Western converts these into university credit units. (Bachelor's degree applicants with minimal formal training may be required to complete a six-to-nine-month home study program.) The final phase involves completion of a qualifying project, which can range from a short paper for the Bachelor's degree to a dissertation or other major project for the Doctorate. Pacific Western also offers an innovative approach to the Doctorate for in-service teachers. They take classes from traditionally-accredited schools (in person or by correspondence)—courses whose units must be acceptable to the teachers' districts for salary increases. On completion of a sufficient number of units, the Pacific Western Doctorate is awarded. Combined Bachelor's/Master's and Master's/Doctorate programs are available. The University is authorized by the State of California to award its degrees.

Comment: Pacific Western's catalogue has a long and impressive list of major corporations, government agencies and traditional universities where employees or staff are alumni or students of P.W.U. Pacific Western is doing a good job, at reasonable prices (in the vicinity of $2,000 for most programs).

PALO ALTO SCHOOL OF PROFESSIONAL PSYCHOLOGY
467 Hamilton Ave., Palo Alto CA 94301
415/329-0806

Unaccredited
Master's, Doctorates
Residency

The Ph.D. in clinical psychology is offered to working professionals, through classes offered in the late afternoon and evening. Normally, two years of classes, plus a lengthy period of supervised field work are required. Students who have knowledge in a specific subject area may take challenge examinations, rather than the entire course. The tuition is between $3,000 and $4,000 a year. The program is approved by the State of California, thus graduates can take the state licensing exams without further qualification.

PEPPERDINE UNIVERSITY
Malibu CA 90265
213/456-4000

Accredited
Bachelor's, Master's,
Doctorates
Residency (EW, IS)

Bachelor of Science in Management, M.B.A., Master of Science in Organization Development, and many Master's and Ed.D. programs in education, available through a combination of evening or weekend classes and independent study, at various centers in the Los Angeles and San Francisco area, and in Hawaii. Pepperdine is perhaps best known for its innovative M.B.A. programs, which have been offered at remote locations throughout the United States. These programs involve a 10-day intensive planning session, followed by evening and weekend classes. The M.B.A. Plan I is for the "emerging manager" while Plan II is for experienced managers. A Presidential/Key Executive program meets one weekend a month, and is limited to top executives and entrepreneurs. Tuition for the various programs can range from $8,000 to $13,000.

Comment: Pepperdine's reputation has been built largely on its non-traditional degrees. The school is affiliated with the Church of Christ, whose message appears in all the literature.

PHILADELPHIA COLLEGE OF TEXTILES AND SCIENCE
Evening Division, Philadelphia PA 19144
214/843-9700

Accredited
Bachelor's
Residency (EW)

The Bachelor of Science degree can be earned entirely through evening study.

PLYMOUTH STATE COLLEGE
Plymouth NH 03264
603/536-1550

Accredited
Master's
Residency (IS)

Master of Arts for classroom teachers, based on two eight-week summer sessions, with independent study during the nine months in between them.

POINT PARK COLLEGE
222 Wood St., Pittsburgh PA 15222
412/391-4100

Accredited
Bachelor's
Residency (EW)

Bachelor of Arts or Science in many fields, in a program requiring classes only on weekends, although evening classes are also available.

POLYTECHNIC INSTITUTE OF BROOKLYN
333 Jay St., Brooklyn NY 11201
212/643-5000

Accredited
Bachelor's
Residency (EW)

Bachelor of Science in engineering or science, available entirely through evening study.

PRACHATHIPOK UNIVERSITY
Thailand's open university is being planned, as a totally non-residential correspondence university, with courses by mail, by radio, and by television.

PRATT INSTITUTE
Ryerson St., Brooklyn NY 11205
212/636-3455

Accredited
Bachelor's
Residency (LE)

More than 80% of the units needed for the Bachelor's degree (available in many fields) can be earned through an assessment of prior learning experiences. The assessment cannot be done until the student has spent one semester in the Integrative Studies Program. Assessment is done by an analysis of a portfolio prepared by the student, and through oral interviews.

PROFESSIONAL STUDIES INSTITUTE
384 N. 2nd Ave., Phoenix AZ 85003
602/252-4049

Unaccredited
Bachelor's, Master's,
   Doctorates
Residency (IS)

Bachelor's, Master's and Doctorates are offered in psychology, holistic health, and clinical nutrition, through a combination of weekend classes, week-long intensive meetings, directed independent study, and off-campus study through taped lectures. Tuition ranges from around $3,000 to more than $7,000 depending on degree level and amount of prior experience. P.S.I. is affiliated with the University for Humanistic Studies of San Diego.

PROVIDENCE COLLEGE
Providence RI 02918
401/865-1000

Accredited
Bachelor's, Master's
Residency (EW)

Bachelor of Arts, Bachelor of Science in business administration and law enforcement, and Master of Business Administration, all available entirely through evening study.

PURDUE UNIVERSITY
Lafayette IN 47907
317/749-2108

Accredited
Master's
Residency (EW)

Master of Science in engineering for fully-employed engineers and Master of Science in education for persons already working in the field. Courses are held evenings and weekends in a number of Indiana cities.

QUAD CITIES GRADUATE STUDY CNETER
639 38th Ave., Rock Island IL 61201
309/794-7376

Accredited
Master's
Residency (EW)

Master of Arts, M.A. in Economics, Master of Science, M.S. in Education, and Master of Business Administration, all available entirely through evening study. The Center is sponsored by the University of Illinois, Northern Illinois University, the University of Iowa, Marycrest College and Augustana College. The degree is issued by one of these five, depending on the program selected.

QUEENS COLLEGE
Adult Collegiate Education, Flushing NY 11367
212/445-7500

Accredited
Bachelor's
Residency (IS, EW)

Bachelor of Arts degrees for persons over 30, consisting of short, long and weekend seminars, independent study, tutorials, exemption exams, work credit and supervised independent study. Classes are scheduled to fit the needs of students. One year of residency is usually required. Queens is a unit of the City University of New York.

RAMAPO COLLEGE
Office of Adult Learning, 505 Ramapo Valley Road,
   Mahwah NJ 07430
201/825-2800, ext. 213

Accredited
Bachelor's
Residency (EW, LE)

Bachelor's degrees in many fields, in which roughly two thirds of the units can be earned through assessment of prior learning experiences. Assessment is based on a portfolio, oral interviews, and possibly special tests. Students must have been out of full-time school for more than two years to qualify for this program. A Saturday College offers all courses needed to complete some degree programs on that day of the week.

RAMKAMHAENG UNIVERSITY
Hua-Mark, Bangapi, Bangkok 10, Thailand

Foreign
Bachelor's
Short residency

With over 200,000 students, Ramkamhaeng is one of the world's largest universities. Degrees are offered in business, humanities, education, science, political science, economics and law, through a combination of on-campus lectures, lectures on videotape at centers around the country, and courses broadcast nationally on 44 radio stations. It normally takes four years to earn a Bachelor's degree.

RAND GRADUATE INSTITUTE
1700 Main St., Santa Monica CA 90406
213/393-0411

Accredited
Doctorates
Residency (IS)

The Institute was established in 1970 to provide training leading to the Ph.D. in policy analysis (the application of scientific methods to problems of public policy in domestic, national security, and international affairs). Instruction is in the form of courses, workshops, and on-the-job training as an apprentice dealing with current Rand projects (which can range from hydrodynamics to juvenile justice to guided weapons systems). The cost is around $6,000 a year.

RANGOON ARTS AND SCIENCES UNIVERSITY
Department of University Correspondence Courses,
   Rangoon, Burma

Foreign
Bachelor's
Non-resident

Bachelor of Arts, Science, Economics, and Law can be earned entirely through correspondence study, plus passing necessary examinations. Some courses are also given through radio lectures. More than 25,000 students are enrolled in Burma's only non-traditional university.

RENSSELAER POLYTECHNIC INSTITUTE
East Windsor Hill CT 06028
203/549-3600

Accredited
Master's
Residency (EW)

The Master of Science is available entirely through evening study.

RIDER COLLEGE
Box 298, Trenton NJ 08602
609/896-0800

Accredited
Bachelor's
Residency (EW)

Bachelor of Arts in liberal studies, Bachelor of Science in business administration and in secretarial sciences, available entirely through evening study.

RIPON COLLEGE
Ripon WI 54971
414/748-8119

Accredited
Bachelor's
Residency (LE)

Bachelor's degree in many fields, in which up to 75% of the required units can come from an assessment of prior learning experiences. The assessment is based on analysis of a portfolio prepared by the student, which must be done after enrollment. The time required is less than one month, and there is no additional fee for the assessment.

ROANOKE COLLEGE
College Ave., Salem VA 24153
703/389-2351

Accredited
Master's
Residency (EW)

Master of Urban Affairs, Master of Business Administration, Master of Arts, Master of Science in clothing and textiles, computer science, human nutrition, all available through evening study at various locations throughout the state of Virginia.

ROBERT MORRIS COLLEGE
Pittsburgh PA 15108
412/264-9300

Accredited
Bachelor's
Residency (EW)

Bachelor of Science, in which all course work can be done in the evening.

ROCHESTER INSTITUTE OF TECHNOLOGY
1 Lomb Memorial Dr., Rochester NY 14623
716/464-2831

Accredited
Bachelor's, Master's
Residency (EW, IS)

Bachelor of Science in many technical fields, and Master of Science in engineering technology or business technology through a combination of evening study, independent study, and some field work. Master of Science in mathematical statistics requiring two short on-campus seminars plus independent study and a thesis.

ROCKFORD COLLEGE
5050 State, St., Rockford IL 61101
815/226-4000

Accredited
Bachelor's, Master's
Residency (EW)

Bachelor of Science in general education and Master of Arts in Teaching, both available through evening courses.

ROCKHURST COLLEGE
5225 Troost Ave., Kansas City MO 64110
816/363-4010

Accredited
Bachelor's
Residency (EW)

Bachelor of Science in business administration and Bachelor of Arts, available entirely through evening study.

ROCKWELL UNIVERSITY

4841 N. Scottsdale Rd., Scottsdale AZ 85251
602/941-1266

Unaccredited
Bachelor's, Master's,
  Doctorates
Non-resident

Rockwell offers its degrees in a wide range of fields, including business, data processing, education, personnel administration, psychology, arts, and humanities. Rockwell was established by five men with strong academic backgrounds, including a former President of Loyola University, Louisiana. For students with substantial academic backgrounds, the only degree requirement is writing a thesis or dissertation. Tuition is based on the length of time enrolled, and ranges from under $1,000 to about $2,500. Combined Bachelor's/Master's and Master's/Doctorate programs are also available.

Comment: Rockwell declines to reveal the number of students or the names of the 40 to 45 faculty. Accreditation candidacy had been claimed from the ''Alternative Institution Accreditation Association of Washington D.C.,'' an unrecognized and apparently no-longer existent organization.

ROGER WILLIAMS COLLEGE

Bristol RI 02809
401/255-2371

Accredited
Bachelor's
Residency (LE)

Bachelor's degrees in many fields, including engineering and industrial technology, in which up to 75% of the necessary units can be earned through an assessment of prior learning experiences, equivalency exams, etc. The assessment is based on a portfolio, oral interviews and tests. It takes two to five months, and there is no extra charge for it.

ROLLINS COLLEGE

Winter Park FL 32789
305/646-2000

Accredited
Bachelor's
Residency (EW)

Bachelor of Arts, Bachelor of Science and Bachelor of General Studies, available entirely through evening study.

ROOSEVELT UNIVERSITY

430 S. Michigan Ave., Chicago IL 60605
312/341-3500

Accredited
Bachelor's, Master's
Residency (EW)

Bachelor of General Studies with a major in urban problems and public administration. The degree is offered through the College of Continuing Education for persons over 25. Classes are held evenings and Saturdays in Chicago and several suburbs. Roosevelt also offers a ''Discovery Program,'' in which people with no Bachelor's degree can, through a year or less of testing and tutorials, enter the Master's degree programs directly. A Master of Arts in education is offered for Navy and civilian personnel at the Great Lakes Service School.

ROSKILDE UNIVERSITY CENTER

Postbox 260, DK-4000 Roskilde, Denmark

Foreign
Master's
Residency (IS)

An experimental university, specializing in interdisciplinary studies. Clusters of 60 students, five teachers and a secretary live together in a house for two years, during which time subgroups work together on interdisciplinary research and creative projects in humanities, social science, and natural science. Nearly 2,000 students are involved.

RUSSELL SAGE COLLEGE
The Evening Division, 140 New Scotland Road, Albany   Accredited
   NY 12208   Bachelor's, Master's
518/445-1717   Residency (EW)

Bachelor of Science and Master of Science in elementary education and health education available entirely through evening study. Up to 30 of the required 120 units come from credit for experiential learning.

RUTGERS — THE STATE UNIVERSITY   Accredited
New Brunswick NJ 08903   Bachelor's
201/932-1766   Residency (EW)

Bachelor of Arts, Bachelor of Science in accounting, home economics, management and vocational education available entirely through evening classes.

SACRED HEART UNIVERSITY   Accredited
Bridgeport CT 06604   Bachelor's
203/374-9441   Residency

Bachelor of Arts, Bachelor of Science in business and in liberal studies, available entirely through evening study.

SAINT BONAVENTURE UNIVERSITY   Accredited
St. Bonaventure NY 14778   Bachelor's
716/375-2000   Residency (EW)

Bachelor of Arts, Bachelor of Science, and Bachelor of Business Administration, which may be earned entirely through evening study.

SAINT CLOUD STATE UNIVERSITY   Accredited
St. Cloud, MN 56301   Bachelor's
612/255-0121   Short residency (LE)

Bachelor's degrees in many fields, in a program in which virtually all of the necessary course requirements and units may be earned through an assessment of prior learning experiences. Assessment is primarily through testing, and must be done after enrollment.

SAINT EDWARDS UNIVERSITY   Accredited
3001 S. Congress, Austin TX 78704   Bachelor's, Master's
512/444-2621   Short residency (EW)

Bachelor's degree program through New College, in business, humanities and social sciences, in which up to 99% of the degree requirements can be met through assessment of prior learning experiences. The assessment is based on analysis of a portfolio prepared by the student in a special course offered for that purpose, and on oral interviews. The cost is based on a fee for each credit awarded. St. Edwards also offers a Bachelor of Arts in behavioral sciences and criminal justice, Bachelor of Business Administration, and Master of Business Administration through evening study in the Center for Continuing Education.

SAINT FRANCIS COLLEGE   Accredited
180 Remsen St., Brooklyn NY 11201   Bachelor's
212/522-2300   Residency (EW)

Bachelor of Arts in special studies, available entirely through evening study in the School of Continuing Education.

SAINT JOHN'S UNIVERSITY
P.O. Box 357, Edgard LA 70049
No telephone

Unaccredited
Master's, Doctorates
Non-resident or residency

A very small school, established by Judge Thomas Malik of the District Court of Louisiana and some distinguished colleagues (the Director of the Louisiana Legislative Council, the Chairman of a New York Stock Exchange member firm, etc.) to offer non-resident degrees, and to offer residential classes in business administration and juvenile justice. There is also a Master of Laws program for people who have already earned a recognized law degree, and wish a second degree with various specializations. Tuition is between $500 and $1,000. Fewer than 30 students are enrolled, and St. John's grants less than half a dozen degrees each year. Accreditation is claimed from the International Accrediting Commission and the Accrediting Commission for Specialized Colleges, two unrecognized agencies described in Chapter 7. Judge Malik informs me that the University has no intention of ever getting a telephone, inasmuch as they have no daytime staff or faculty.

SAINT JOSEPH'S COLLEGE
107 Campbell Ave. S.W., P.O. Box 13486, Roanoke
   VA 24034
800/336-9622

Accredited
Bachelor's
Short residency

Bachelor of Science in Professional Arts, specifically oriented to registered nurses. There is a three-week residency required on St. Joseph's main campus in North Windham, Maine. All the remaining work is done by correspondence study. Students can major in business, health care administration, education, psychology or sociology. The non-traditional program is administered under contract by an "educational distributor" in Virginia, on behalf of the Sisters of Mercy who operate St. Joseph's. Only half of the credit toward the B.S. is given to holders of the R.N. — substantially less than most other non-traditional programs. The tution is in excess of $3,000 plus the costs of the Maine residency.

SAINT JOSEPH'S EVENING COLLEGE
54th and City Line Ave., Philadelphia PA 19131
215/879-7340

Accredited
Bachelor's, Master's
Residency (EW)

Bachelor of Arts, Bachelor of Science, Master of Arts in Education and Master of Science in chemistry, all through evening study.

SAINT LEO COLLEGE
P.O. Box 2248, Saint Leo FL 33574
904/588-8236

Accredited
Bachelor's
Residency (IS)

Bachelor of Arts degree in business administration, criminal justice, and a degree for registered nurses. The programs are available only to residents of Florida. Some of the work can be done by correspondence or independent study. The rest can be done at external facilities at various locations.

SAINT MARY-OF-THE-WOODS COLLEGE
Saint Mary-of-the-Woods IN 47876
812/535-4141

Accredited
Bachelor's
Very short residency

The Women's External Degree program offers Bachelor's degrees in creative writing, female studies, and various liberal arts fields, almost entirely through off-campus independent study.

SAINT MARY'S COLLEGE
Winona MN 55987
507/452-4430 (in Minnesota, 800/372-8176)

Accredited
Master's
Residency (IS)

Master of Arts or Science in human development or education, for persons living in one of the geographical areas in which Saint Mary's has regional advisors. These areas include a 75-mile radius around San Francisco, Washington D.C., Minneapolis, St. Paul, Boston, and Winona. All students must spend some time on the main campus in Minnesota, but this can be as little as one weekend. Credit is given for completion of learning contracts negotiated between the student and the advisor. Tuition for the degree is between $4,000 and $5,000. Most students complete the Master's in 18 to 24 months.

Comment: There are not too many opportunities for a short-residency accredited Master's degree, and this is a good one. I especially like the catalogue, with its excellent photography, quotations from the poetry and philosophy of Oriental philosphers, a haiku by the graduate Dean, a quote from the Red Zinger tea carton, and an all-time-great baboon picture.

SAINT MARY'S COLLEGE OF CALIFORNIA

P.O. Box 397, Moraga CA 94575
415/376-4411

Accredited
Bachelor's
Residency (EW, IS)

The Bachelor's degrees in management, social science, health services administration or humanities based on a learning contract. All students complete a core curriculum, a fieldwork project (and a comprehensive report on it), and various other courses comprising an area requirement. Credit is given for independent study and for equivalency exams. Tuition is around $3,000 per year.

SAINT PETER'S COLLEGE

2641 Kennedy Blvd., Jersey City NJ 07306
201/333-4400

Accredited
Bachelor's
Residency (EW)

Bachelor of Science and Bachelor of Science in Business Administration available entirely through evening study.

SAN FRANCISCO STATE UNIVERSITY

1600 Holloway Ave., San Francisco CA 94132
415/469-1207

Accredited
Bachelor's, Master's
Residency (IS)

Bachelor of Arts in liberal arts, and Master of Arts in environmental planning. The Bachelor's degree, which may be combined with a certificate program in criminal justice, gerontology, paralegal studies, or employment studies, requires three courses on campus. Other credit may be earned by evaluation of prior experience, or "parallel instruction" in which the student does the work of a regularly scheduled class without attending class meetings. The Master's degree requires completion of seven courses, either on campus or through parallel instruction. Although primarily for students in northern California, the brochure points out that "one of our first graduates completed his degree from Australia." All students, however, must earn 30 units in residence in San Francisco. This program is offered through the Consortium of California State Collges and Universities.

SAN FRANCISCO THEOLOGICAL SEMINARY

Advanced Pastoral Studies, 2 Kensington Ave.,
   San Anselmo CA 94960
415/453-2280

Accredited
Master's, Doctorates
Short residency

The Master of Arts in Values is a two-year program. In the first year, clusters of ten to twelve students meet regularly, under the guidance of a Seminary faculty member. These clusters can be formed anywhere in the country, subject to Seminary approval. Students pursue independent study courses, and discuss them in the group. The second year is an "externship" in which the student applies what has been learned in a vocational setting, and writes a thesis. The Doctor of Ministry is offered in many formats, all involving a six-week summer residency on campus, combined with independent study, supervised ministry, or local groups meeting together in various locations. A dissertation is required. The Doctor of the Science of Theology (S.T.D.) program is an advanced Doctorate, requiring from five to nine years, three "in parish" projects, and extensive additional work. Two six-week summer sessions in residency are required. Tuition for the complete programs ranges from $2,400 to over $5,000.

SANGAMON STATE UNIVERSITY
Springfield IL 62704
217/786-6626

Accredited
Bachelor's
Residency (IS)

The INO, or Individual Option program, is based partially on a university without walls model: a learning proposal is developed, a learning contract negotiated, and the student pursues the Bachelor's degree through selected off-campus study, internships, foreign study, independent study, or exchange with other institutions.

SAN JOSE STATE UNIVERSITY
San Jose CA 95192
408/277-3266

Accredited
Bachelor's
Residency (IS, EW)

Bachelor of Science in health care administration and Bachelor of Arts in community health education. They are called "external" degrees but a fair amount of on-campus or near-campus work is required. Credit is earned through coursework (evenings, summers), examinations, directed independent study, and parallel instruction (doing all the work of a required class without attending the class meetings). There is no opportunity for self-paced accelerated work. Students must have 56 semester units earned elsewhere before admission, and the remaining units can take three to four years of part-time study to earn. The program is offered through the Consortium of California State Universities and Colleges.

SANTA FE COLLEGE OF NATURAL MEDICINE
1590 Canyon Road, Santa Fe NM 87501
505/982-3038

Unaccredited
Bachelor's, Master's,
 Doctorates
Non-resident

The college is an alternative medical school, specializing in teaching drugless therapies with residential programs in health sciences, iridology, polarity, acupuncture, ayurvedic medicine, clinical herbology, and related areas. The non-residential student works with the school to design a program of independent guided study (there are no prepared correspondence courses). After a period of readings, assignments, case studies, etc., the student prepares a thesis, "oral dissertation," or other major project. Tuition is around $2,000 a year, with a nine-month minimum for completing a degree. Accreditation is claimed from the International Accrediting Commission on Accreditation of Schools, Colleges and Theological Seminaries, an unrecognized agency. (See Chapter 7 for more on them.) The President, Scott Gershen, lists an honorary N.D. from Brantridge Forest, which is described in Chapter 24, Diploma Mills.

Comment: Despite the last two items above, it appears to me that the College is totally legitimate and doing a good job in its field.

SARAH LAWRENCE COLLEGE
Bronxville NY 10708
914/337-0700

Accredited
Bachelor's, Master's
Residency (IS)

The Continuing Education for Women program offers the opportunity to earn the Bachelor and Master of Arts through part-time daytime study combined with independent study.

SAYBROOK INSTITUTE
1772 Vallejo St., San Francisco CA 94123
415/441-5034

Accreditation candidate
Master's, Doctorates
Short residency

Saybrook, until 1982 called the Humanistic Psychology Institute, offers a Master of Arts and Ph.D. in psychology, and a Ph.D. in human science. State approval of the programs means graduates are entitled to take state licensing examinations without further qualification. The only residency requirements are attendance at a four-day planning seminar for new enrollees, a week-long National Meeting held in San Francisco each summer, an oral examination for advancement to candidacy, and an oral defense of the required thesis or dissertation. Tuition is around $4,000 per year. Courses are offered in an independent study format: a course guide is provided, specifying the required readings, and including written lecture materials prepared by the faculty. Students may design their own courses as well. Student work focuses within four areas of concentration: study of the person, human systems, health studies, and consciousness studies. Many well-known psychologists are associated with Saybrook (Rollo May, Stanley Krippner, Richard Farson, Nevitt Sanford, Clark Moustakas, etc.). About 150 students are enrolled.

SCHOOL FOR INTERNATIONAL TRAINING
Brattleboro VT 05301
802/257-7751

Accredited
Master's
Residency (IS)

Master of Arts in Teaching offered by the academic arm of the Experiment in International Living. The program involves time in Vermont, in independent study, and in living with a family in another country.

SEATTLE UNIVERSITY
Seattle WA 98122
206/626-6200

Accredited
Master's
Residency (EW)

Master of Arts in education, English, history and teaching; Master of Education; Master of Business Administration and Master of Public Service, all through evening study.

SIENA HEIGHTS COLLEGE
17050 Dorset, Southfield MI 48075
313/569-6490 (In Michigan, 800/521-5346)

Accredited
Bachelor's
Residency (EW, IS, LE)

The degree completion program offers the opportunity to earn the Bachelor's degree in allied health, business administration, general studies, and many trade and industrial areas. Substantial credit is given for prior life experience. Up to 80% of the required 120 semester hours can be earned through the assessment (including coursework taken elsewhere). New work is done through a combination of evening classes, weekend courses, independent study, and extended weekend courses for out-of-town and out-of-state students. The cost of $77 per semester hour would mean nearly $10,000 for someone starting from scratch, but substantially less for those with prior experience.

SKIDMORE COLLEGE
Saratoga Springs NY 12866
518/584-5000

Accredited
Bachelor's
Very short residency

Skidmore is one of the pioneers of the non-traditional movement, having offered a university without walls program since 1970. It is possible to earn their well-regarded Bachelor of Arts or Bachelor of Science with a total of two days on campus: one for advising and planning, and the second to present a degree plan to a faculty committee. Skidmore makes it clear that they hold their graduates to "standards of knowledge, competence and intellectual attainment which are no less comprehensive and rigorous than those established by traditional . . . programs." After fulfilling requirements in the degree plan each student completes a final project—a project demonstrating competence in one's field. The basic tuition is only $850 a year, but additional fees and honoraria are paid directly to the faculty advisors. Students can major in any of the 69 fields offered by Skidmore, or can devise their own majors.

THE SONOMA INSTITUTE
17500 Bodega Lane, Bodega CA 94922
707/876-3116

Accredited program
Master's
Residency (IS)

Although the Institute itself is not accredited, it has a cooperative relationship with the University of Redlands, Johnston College, in which the work is done at Sonoma, and the degree is issued by Redlands. This meets the requirements for taking the Marriage, Family and Child Counselor licensing examination in California. The program is designed to humanize the process of counselor education. A group of 12 to 15 students work with a faculty advisor to construct a group curricular proposal, select instructors, and plan the course of study in areas such as existential psychotherapy, gestalt therapy, Jungian psychology, feminist therapy, body therapy, etc. The program requires two years, and costs more than $7,000. Classes are held in San Francisco as well as Bodega, but students must spend one or two days a week in Bodega.

SONOMA STATE UNIVERSITY
1801 E. Cotati Ave., Rohnert Park CA 94928
707/664-2411

Accredited
Master's
Short residency (IS)

Sonoma State offers a one-year external Master's degree in psychology. Although there is no requirement for taking any specific classes, students must attend occasional meetings with a faculty advisor. The program is designed jointly by student and faculty, and can include coursework, fieldwork, research, and independent study. Applicants must have a Bachelor's degree, one year of graduate-level experience in humanistic psychology, and nine units of credit previously earned (in residence or by extension) from Sonoma State. A requirement of basic knowledge of psychology can be met through courses or by an examination. The fee for the program is around $1,500, plus the cost of any courses or internships that may be part of the program. The total estimated cost is less than $3,000. About 40 new applicants are admitted each fall.

SOUTHEAST ASIA INTERDISCIPLINARY
    DEVELOPMENT INSTITUTE
Intramuros, Manila, Philippines

Foreign
Master's, Doctorates
Residency (IS)

The M.A. and Ph.D. are offered in organizational development and planning, and the M.A. in instructional development. Students work with a faculty committee to plan an independent study program, including field trips, simulations, Socratic and practicum conferences, etc. The program requires four years of part-time study, and one year in residence at the Institute.

SOUTHEASTERN MASSACHUSETTS UNIVERSITY
Old Westport Road, North Dartmouth MA 02747
617/999-8000

Accredited
Bachelor's
Residency

Bachelor's degree in history, sociology, psychology, political science, Portuguese, humanities, and other fields, in which up to 75% of the required number of units can be earned through an assessment of prior learning experience. The assessment is based on evaluation of a portfolio, which is prepared in a class given for that purpose. The assessment costs a flat fee of around $400, and is offered through the Division of Continuing Education.

SOUTHEASTERN UNIVERSITY (Louisiana)
5163 General de Gaulle Dr., New Orleans LA 70114
504/392-7157

Unaccredited
Doctorates
Short residency

Doctorates in philosophy, education, business administration, arts, ministry, and other fields, with one month of residency in New Orleans. The total cost is in excess of $3,000. The school used to be located in Myrtle Beach, South Carolina, and may be doing something in Park City, Utah.

Comment: I have been writing and telephoning Southeastern for more than four years, and they have never answered my questions. I have questioned their statement that they have ''met all the requirements for accreditation of the U.S. Department of Education,'' since the Department does not accredit schools. I have questioned their statement that they were taking the necessary steps ''to obtain full accreditation in the immediate future.'' Such a statement is either naive or misleading or both. I have tried to learn the source of the Doctorates claimed by university officers. And so on. Southeastern may indeed be a good and sincere alternative school, as several alumni have written me, but I do not have the evidence to say so at this time. Southeastern is attempting to sell the university to the alumni, and turn itself into a non-profit entity.

SOUTHEASTERN UNIVERSITY (Washington DC)   Accredited
501 I St. S.W., Washington DC 20024   Master's
202/488-8163   Residency (EW)

On Saturdays, Southeastern offers a Master of Business Administration and a Master of Science in accounting or taxation. On Sundays, there is a Master of Business and Public Administration. Classes last all day, once a week, and the degree can generally be earned after 48 to 64 days of classes, plus independent study in between.

SOUTHERN BIBLE COLLEGE   Accredited
Houston TX 77028   Bachelor's
713/675-2351   Residency (EW)

Bachelor's program of Christ-centered education for Christian missionaries, entirely through evening study.

SOUTHERN ILLINOIS UNIVERSITY   Accredited
Carbondale IL 62901   Master's
618/453-2121   Residency (IS)

Master of Science in administration of justice, through coursework, independent study, and work projects. Master of Science in engineering biophysics through coursework plus a field internship. Master of Arts in rehabilitation administration, with five weeks of independent study for each week spent on campus. Offered in Springfield, Centralia, and in Indianapolis and Evansville, Indiana.

SOUTHERN METHODIST UNIVERSITY   Accredited
Dallas TX 75222   Bachelor's, Master's
214/692-2000   Residency (EW)

Bachelor of Arts, Bachelor of Business Administration, Bachelor of Applied Sciences, and Master of Liberal Arts, all through evening study in the School of Continuing Education.

SOUTHERN OREGON STATE COLLEGE   Accredited
Ashland OR 97520   Bachelor's
503/482-6261   Residency (LE)

Bachelor's degree in any subject area offered at SOSC in which up to 75% of the required units may be earned by a combination of credit for prior learning experiences and equivalency examinations. The assessment is based on a portfolio prepared by the student after taking a course in the PLE (Prior Learning Experience) program. The entire process can take up to a year, at a cost dependent on the amount of credit given — generally between $400 and $600.

SOUTHWEST UNIVERSITY
12020 N. 35th Ave., Phoenix AZ 85029
602/978-0401

Unaccredited
Bachelor's, Master's,
Doctorates
Non-resident

Southwest University (unrelated to the equally new Southwestern University, also in Arizona) was established in 1982 by Reg Sheldrick, founder and former president of Newport University. Dr. Sheldrick is a professional hypnotist and hypnotherapist. Degrees at all levels are available in that field as well as in parapsychology, business administration, education, counseling & psychology, holistic health sciences, and an unusual program in entrepreneurship. Students may choose one of two models: a structured approach with assigned coursework plus a thesis or dissertation; or a self-development plan based on a student-designed, faculty-approved learning contract. Southwest maintains an office in Omaha, Nebraska, for curriculum development, and has a working relationship with several schools of hypnosis and hypnotherapy around the country.

SOUTHWESTERN UNIVERSITY
4621 N. First Ave., Tucson, AZ 85718
602/293-7737

Unaccredited
Bachelor's, Master's,
Doctorates
Non-resident

The degrees are awarded either based on a portfolio of life experiences, with no new work required, or, for those with no portfolio, a thesis of at least twenty double-spaced pages. The costs are between $575 and $1,050.

Comment: The 1982-1983 Bulletin of Southwestern University raised many doubts in my mind about the legitimacy of this school, which I expressed to Chairman of the Board Anthony Geruntino, whose Ph.D. is from Southwestern. Dr. Geruntino has written me a long letter in which he says he is "taking the lead in clearing up any clouded issue before it appears erroneously in your book, then later proven to be unfounded or untrue and avoiding the consequences thereafter."

Desirous of avoiding consequences whenever possible, I offer my concerns and Dr. Geruntino's responses.

Concern: Dr. Geruntino operates Adult Career and Education Services in Columbus, Ohio. The only telephone number appearing in the Bulletin of this Arizona school is Dr. G's phone in Ohio.

Response: "I do not believe it is too unusual."

Concern: In his counseling practice, Dr. G. has written to clients (more than a dozen have sent me the letters) recommending *only* American Western University and Northwestern College of Allied Science, and personally endorsing the Dean of these schools, James Caffee. Both schools were closed by federal authorities as degree mills, and the Tulsa *Daily World* identified Dr. Caffee as "a former convict who did prison time for grand larceny."

Response: Dr. G. says that he has "personally never met the man that you mention in your book James Caffee," and that "Northwestern has a bonafide charter and was in operation for 26 years," and "American Western was indeed legally chartered."

Concern: The closed degree mills were operated by Disciples of Truth, Box 207, Springfield, Missouri. Southwestern University's 1982-1983 Bulletin claims the school is accredited by the National Association of Open Campus Colleges of Box 207, Springfield, Missouri.

Response: "The original affiliation was an admitted mistake, and DO NOT recommend them to any person, organizations or schools." (sic)

Concern: The Program Manager of Southwestern, Dr. M. J. Jupinko, refuses to tell me where she earned her Ph.D.

Response: "Dr. Jupinko has a Ph.D. degree from University of Arizona." (sic)

New concern: The University of Arizona never awarded a Ph.D. to M. J. Jupinko.

New response: "The Dr. Jupinko I was referring to is a different Dr. Jupinko, Celeste, who is also on the staff, although not in the bulletin." (Celeste Jupinko does have a Ph.D. from Arizona.)

Concern: Only one of the 25 faculty members listed in the 1982-1983 Bulletin has a Ph.D. from an identified school.

Response: The sources of the degrees will be listed in the next edition of the Bulletin.

Concern: The diploma depicted in the bulletin shows the President to be John R. Thomas. Dr. Jupinko told me the real president was Robert J. LaFave, and said a false name was used on the diploma so if people counterfeited it, they would know. She said this was standard practice in universities. It is not.

Response: None.

Dr. Geruntino writes, "As a new school with growing pains, I'm sure we will be making our share of mistakes." At least. But if the next edition of the Bulletin corrects the above matters, and if the University moves into the 15,000 square-foot facility in late 1982, and begins offering residential programs, as Dr. G. says they will, then I shall be delighted to report these occurrences, and to suggest that Southwestern University may be a reasonable alternative for persons seeking a fast, easy, and relatively inexpensive degree.

SRI LANKA INSTITUTE OF DISTANCE EDUCATION	Foreign Bachelor's (equivalent)	
P.O. Box 1537, Maligawatte, Colombo, Sri Lanka	Short residency	

Higher National Diplomas in mathematics, science, technology and management through correspondence studies, with occasional face-to-face meetings with faculty at one of 12 national centers. Some fields require attending laboratory sessions. Instruction is given in English, Sinhala and Tamil.

STATE UNIVERSITY COLLEGE	Accredited	
Utica St., Brockport NY 14420	Bachelor's	
716/395-2851	Short residency	

Bachelor of Arts in Liberal Studies, with a minimum of three weeks on campus for an annual seminar. The degree is offered in science, natural science, and social science. Credit is given for all prior learning experiences, both formal and informal, as well as for equivalency exams, independent study, and correspondence courses. The minimum time of enrollment is one academic year (nine months).

STATE UNIVERSITY OF NEW YORK	Accredited	
Millard Fillmore College, 3435 Main St., Buffalo NY 14214	Bachelor's Residency (EW, IS)	
716/831-9000		

Bachelor of Arts for adults within commuting distance, through a combination of evening study and independent study based on learning contracts.

STATE UNIVERSITY OF NEW YORK	Accredited	
College at Old Westbury, Box 210, Old Westbury NY 11568	Bachelor's Residency (LE)	
516/876-4348		

Bachelor's degree program in which up to 60% of the required units can be earned through a combination of assessment for prior experience and equivalency examinations. The assessment takes place after a certain number of units have been earned, takes from two to five months, and is done without cost for enrolled students.

STEPHENS COLLEGE
College Without Walls, Campus Box 2083, Columbia
    MO 65201
314/442-2211, ext. 544

Accredited
Bachelor's
Short residency (IS)

Bachelor of Arts through a program primarily of independent study. The only firm residential requirement is attendance at a Liberal Studies Seminar. About 15 seminars a year are given, both on the Stephens campus, and in various locations around the U.S. (recently in Arizona, Florida, Illinois, Iowa, Louisiana, Pennsylvania and Tennessee). Stephens will consider conducting a seminar anywhere in the U.S. where 20 or more students enroll. The seminar requires two weekends of attendance, with a total of seven weeks of independent study before, between, and after the weekends. A total of 40 three-unit courses are required for the degree, of which at least ten must be completed after enrolling. Courses may be completed by independent guided study, contract study, or weekend courses at Stephens. The fee for each course is $365. More than 500 students, representing every state in the union, are enrolled in the program. Stephens also offers a program called Learning Unlimited, for women over 23 who wish to earn the Bachelor of Arts or Bachelor of Fine Arts through on-campus weekend and other classes.

STETSON UNIVERSITY
De Land FL 32730
904/734-4121

Accredited
Bachelor's
Residency (EW)

Bachelor of Arts and Bachelor of Science in many fields through evening study. Bachelor of Science in Medical Technology in conjunction with area hospitals.

STEWART UNIVERSITY SYSTEM
Centre AL 35960
No telephone

Unaccredited
Honorary degrees
Non-resident

Free tuition for all classes, and honorary Doctorates to anyone Mrs. Stewart finds deserving, but "they cannot be bought at any price." All courses at Frank Ross Stewart University are taught by Mrs. Frank Ross Stewart — from astrology to auto mechanics, from Bible study to law.

Comment: Mrs. Stewart, who seems to be enjoying herself immensely, writes a mean letter. Apparently there are no laws in Alabama to keep her from doing what she's doing. Then again, her first honorary Doctorate went to George Wallace.

SUFFOLK UNIVERSITY
41 Temple St., Boston MA 02144
617/723-4700

Accredited
Bachelor's, Master's
Residency (EW)

Bachelor of Arts, Bachelor of Science, Master of Business Administration, and Master of Education, all available entirely through evening study.

SWINBURNE COLLEGE OF TECHNOLOGY
P.O. Box 218, John St., Hawthorn, Victoria 3122,
    Australia

Foreign
Bachelor's
Residency (IS)

Swinburne is the major Australian institution following the cooperative plan of education, in which students alternate periods of up to six months of work in industry with taking classes. Degrees are offered in engineering, applied science, and graphic arts.

SYRACUSE UNIVERSITY
610 E. Fayette St., Syracuse NY 13202
315/423-3269

Accredited
Bachelor's, Master's
Short residency

Bachelor of Arts in liberal studies and in business administration; Master of Business Administration, Master of Fine Arts, and Master of Science in social science, all with minimal residency on campus, and long periods of independent study in between. The Master's in social science, for instance, requires two 12-day sessions on campus, each during the month of July (but not necessarily two consecutive sessions). The M.B.A. requires three eight-day sessions a year for either one or two years. The M.F.A., which has been taught by many of New York advertising's best-known art directors (Lubalin, Scali, Gargano, etc.), requires two two-week sessions on campus and several shorter sessions in New York City. The Bachelor's degree requires 24 days on campus. The minimum time for the Bachelor's is one year for people with substantial transfer credit, but in practice, most people take quite a bit longer. The cost of the various degree programs ranges from about $3,000 to $6,000.

TARKIO COLLEGE
330 Mansion House, Suite 316, St. Louis MO 63102
314/621-1018

Accredited
Bachelor's
Residency (EW)

Bachelor of Science in business administration, management and related fields, requiring evening classes that meet once a week for eight weeks.

TEMPLE UNIVERSITY
Evening Division, Philadelphia PA 19122
215/787-7000

Accredited
Bachelor's, Master's
Residency (EW)

Bachelor of Arts, Bachelor of Science in business education and technology, Master of Business Administration all available entirely through evening study.

TENNESSEE SOUTHERN UNIVERSITY
P.O. Box 731, Fayetteville TN 37334
615/433-0323

Unaccredited
Bachelor's
Non-resident

The Tennessee Southern University and School of Religion was established in late 1981 for the purpose, according to its founder, Dr. O. Charles Nix, of "developing students with a special sense of social responsibility, who can organize and apply knowledge for human betterment." The plan was to offer a Bachelor's degree in business and in religion.

TENNESSEE WESLEYAN COLLEGE
P.O. Box 40, Athens TN 37303
615/745-5872

Accredited
Bachelor's
Residency (IS)

The Bachelor of Applied Science program is designed for people who already have the equivalent of two years of college plus specialized technical skills. With the exception of a small required unit in philosophy and religion, the balance of the Bachelor's program can be completed under an independent study learning contract model. This program is also offered in Chattanooga, Knoxville and Cleveland, Tennessee. Tuition for a full-time student is around $3,000 a year.

TEXAS CHRISTIAN UNIVERSITY
Division of Continuing Education, Fort Worth TX 76129
817/921-7130

Accredited
Bachelor's
Residency (EW)

Bachelor of General Studies program, available entirely through evening study. At least 30 of the required 124 semester hours must be earned at T.C.U. Credit is given for prior academic work, and for equivalency exams, including a series of exams developed at the University. Some courses are offered on a closed-circuit television network connecting ten colleges and universities around the state.

TEXAS TECH UNIVERSITY
Box 4719, Tech Station, Lubbock TX 79409
806/742-7139

Accredited
Doctorates
Residency (IS)

Texas Tech offers its Doctor of Education in Higher Education with the possibility of much shorter residency than most traditional doctoral programs. It is necessary to earn 24 semester hours of credit in continuous enrollment during a given 12-month period. The shortest possible time frame, then, is about seven months: one semester plus one summer session. However, additional credit would have to be earned at other times, such as other summers, either in Lubbock, or in external courses Tech offers in El Paso, Abilene, and other west Texas cities.

THOMAS A. EDISON STATE COLLEGE
101 W. State St., Trenton NJ 08608
609/984-1100

Accredited
Bachelor's
Non-resident

Bachelor of Arts and Bachelor of Science degrees with no residential requirements whatsoever. The programs and approach are very similar to those at the University of the State of New York, with which Edison State used to be affiliated. Edison welcomes students living anywhere in the United States. Their policy on students living outside the U.S. varies from time to time. The Bachelor of Arts does not require a major. The Bachelor of Science may be earned with a major in business administration. Credit is given for career learning and experience, and all prior studies. New credit is earned through equivalency exams, correspondence courses at other schools (Edison State has none of its own), or residential courses at other schools. Edison State sometimes gives a little more credit for non-school learning achievements than does New York. (For instance, Edison State gives 30 semester units for the five basic CLEP exams, while New York gives 27.) The total fees are well under $1,000. Assessment of a life experience portfolio costs about $100, and is available whether or not one decides to enroll. Edison State operates counseling centers in various New Jersey cities for those who wish personal contact, but it is not necessary to visit them. There is, of course, no connection at all with a diploma mill of the same name in Florida and Arkansas.

THOMAS JEFFERSON UNIVERSITY (Missouri)
3113 Magnolia, St. Louis MO 63118
No listed telephone

Unaccredited
Bachelor's, Master's,
Doctorates
Non-resident

The literature is copied exactly, in wording and design, from that of Pacific Western University, a legitimate school that has nothing to do with Jefferson. They even copied the parts about California authorization, which are irrelevant for a Missouri institution. The address is a private residence, and the only response to a caller who knocked on the door during business hours was a barking dog. The literature is mailed from Denver, Colorado. Forms were enclosed for servicemen to pay their tuition directly through a deduction from their pay. There is certainly nothing recommendable here.

THOMAS JEFFERSON UNIVERSITY
Philadelphia PA 19107
215/829-8982

Accredited
Master's
Residency (EW, IS)

Master of Science in Clinical Microbiology, through evening classes, seminars, and a clerkship, for persons with prior laboratory experience.

TRINITY COLLEGE
Burlington VT 05401
802/658-0337

Accredited
Bachelor's
Residency (LE, IS)

The Program for Adult Continuing Education (PACE) offers men and women who have been out of high school at least four years the opportunity to earn the Bachelor of Arts or Bachelor of Science in a wide variety of fields, with up to 75% of the required units available through evaluation of prior learning experiences and credit by examination. At least 30 units must be earned after enrolling at Trinity. Trinity also offers a Weekend College, in which classes are held every other Saturday and Sunday for a total of eight weekends per semester. The Bachelor of Science in business administration and the Bachelor of Arts in human services administration can be earned in this manner. Tuition is $136 per semester hour, hence about $4,000 as the minimum cost for the Bachelor's.

TROY STATE UNIVERSITY
Troy AL 36081
205/566-3000

Accredited
Bachelor's, Master's
Residency (LE, IS)

Bachelor of Applied Science, Bachelor of Aviation Management, and Master of Science in education, public administration and criminal justice. Substantial credit is given for career and military experience and aviation training, as well as equivalency exams. Courses are given at various remote centers, mostly military bases, in Alabama and Florida.

UNION GRADUATE SCHOOL
Provident Bank Building, P.O. Box 85315, Cincinnati
   OH 45201
513/621-6444

Accreditation candidate
Bachelor's, Doctorates
Short residency

The school was established by the Union for Experimenting Colleges and Universities, a consortium of about 30 schools, including some large state universities to be, in effect, their alternative program. The main offices are in Ohio, with centers in northern and southern California and in Washington DC. The Bachelor's degree is based on an individualized degree program, and may involve independent study, directed reading, internships, on-the-job education, classroom instruction, tutorials, etc. Credit is given for all prior learning experiences. The required residency involves a weekend colloquium (held in various locations around the country) and occasional seminars. At least nine months are required to earn the degree. The Ph.D. begins with a 10-day "entry colloquium" held in various locations. The doctoral learner develops a committee of at least five, including two peers. The committee establishes a learning agreement, including an internship. All students must attend at least three five-day seminars at least six months apart, and another ten days in meetings of three or more learners. Thus a minimum of 35 days of residency are required. Each student produces a Project Demonstrating Excellence — a major project, which can be a dissertation, a creative work (art, music, literature), or other original contribution to human knowledge. A minimum of 24 months is required for the Ph.D. at a cost between $4,000 and $5,000 a year.

Comment: Union offers the best, most flexible, widely-accepted alternative Ph.D. available today. A lot of work is involved, since Union does not accept previously-done work, but except for the relatively short residency, it can all be done on one's own schedule. Union has been a candidate for accreditation since 1973 (perhaps a world's record). Their almost certain march to full accreditation was disrupted by a financial crisis in 1978, now over. Eventually, I think, accreditation must come. About 600 learners are enrolled, two-thirds in the Ph.D. program.

UNION UNIVERSITY
207 N. Breed St., Los Angeles CA 90033
213/263-6825

Unaccredited
Master's, Doctorates
Non-resident

Master of Arts and Ph.D. programs in business, economics, humanities, political science, religion, psychology and international studies, entirely through non-residential study. At least one year of enrollment is required at a tuition of about $2,000 a year. The school is operated by the W. U. M. Kose Foundation, an Oriental foundation dedicated to world peace and understanding through education. Union is authorized by the State of California to grant its degrees.

Comment: The catalogue has four pages of color photographs of faculty in action, but no faculty names are given, nor are the credentials of the administration offered. In 1979, the President and some staff members left Union to establish Golden State University.

UNITED NATIONS UNIVERSITY
Toho Seimi Bldg., 15-1 Shibuya 2-chome, Shibuya-ku,
   Tokyo 150, Japan
03/499-2811

Established in 1975, based on an idea of U Thant, as a worldwide network of advanced research and training institutions devoted to "pressing problems of human survival, development and welfare." UNU has considered granting degrees of its own, but has not yet done so. The Japanese government pledged $100 million of the $500 million endowment goal. Other large contributions have come from Venezuela and Ghana, with smaller amounts from many other nations.

Comment: The United States' contribution to this noble idea is, to date, $0. The Senate regularly votes down the proposal to contribute.

UNITED STATES UNIVERSITY OF AMERICA   Unaccredited
P.O. Box 4552, Washington DC 20017   Bachelor's, Master's,
202/783-4374   Doctorates
   Non-resident

The degrees are based on a minimal amount of correspondence study, working directly with adjunct faculty members. Tuition ranges from around $500 for the honorary Doctorates "awarded" to those who pay for them to over $2,000 for Doctorates. The 11-page typewritten catalogue sells for $5. Frank Pany, founder and president, declines to identify the source of his own Doctorate. He, and the University, are located in Florida. The Washington address is a secretarial service.

Comment: The catalogue states, "We stand on the excellent reputation and academic credentials of our carefully-selected faculty." I was able to learn (with some difficulty) the names of some of these faculty. Richard Schwartz, Ph.D., Dean of the College of Languages earned his Ph.D. from United States University of America. He told me, "USUA is strictly a paper operation; a convenience service, let us say." George Viertel, Ph.D., in charge of Marriage Counseling and Self-Improvement, earned his Doctorate from United States University of America. He stated, "You're in California. Why not deal with a degree service closer to home? I know there are a lot of them out there." And so it goes.

UNIVERSIDAD ESTATAL A DISTANCIA   Foreign
Calle 23 B 25, Av. 108, San José, Costa Rica   Bachelor's
   Non-resident

Costa Rica's state university for distance learning offers correspondence study consisting of written units, slides, audio cassettes and video cassettes, leading to the Bachelor's in education after about two years of study.

UNIVERSIDAD IBEROAMERICANA   Foreign
Av. Cerro de las Torres No. 395, Col. Campestre   Bachelor's
   Churubusco, Mexico 21, D.F., Mexico   Residency (IS)

The Bachelor's degree in sociology is based largely on individualized tutorials, with study guides backed up by telephone tutoring as required. The typical time involved is three to five years of part-time study.

UNIVERSIDAD MEXICANA DEL NORESTE
Sistema de Educación Abierta, 5a Zona No. 409, Apartado
   Postal No. 2191 "J", Col. Caracol, Monterrey, N.L.,
   Mexico

Foreign
Bachelor's
Non-resident

This open university program offers the Bachelor's degree in banking and finance, and in management of leisure time. Studies are based on learning guides and audio cassettes. About four years are required to complete the degree.

UNIVERSIDAD NACIONAL AUTONOMA DE
   MEXICO
Sistema Universidad Abierta, Circuito Exterior de la Ciudad
   Universitaria, Mexico 20, D.F., Mexico

Foreign
Bachelor's
Non-resident

Mexico's national open university has prepared elaborate and well-designed course units, each designed by a team including academics, audio-visual specialists, an editor, and a graphic designer. A unit consists of a work guide, written material, boxes of laboratory or field experiments, self-evaluation materials, and perhaps movies, tapes, and other audio-visual aids. An examination at the University must be taken after completing each course. There are courses offered in dental surgery; poultry, cattle and pig breeding; English literature; and most standard academic subjects.

UNIVERSIDAD NACIONAL ABIERTA
Apartado 8226, Caracas 101, Venezuela

Foreign
Bachelor's
Non-resident

Venezuela's open university offers the Bachelor's degree in social sciences, management, land and sea sciences, engineering, mathematics and physics. Students work at their own pace through teaching modules consisting of printed and audio-visual materials. Some courses are offered on radio or television. Laboratory work, where required, may be done at the University or at other institutions.

UNIVERSIDAD NACIONAL DE EDUCACION
   A DISTANCIA
Ciudad Universitaria, Madrid 3, Spain

Foreign
Bachelor's
Short residency

The national open university of Spain offers degrees in a wide range of academic subjects. Each group of 150 students has a professor-tutor responsible for guidance and personal contact. More than 40 centers around the country (including 11 within large business, government and military offices) are available for seminars, conferences and lectures. Most work is done at a distance by use of written and audio-visual materials.

UNIVERSIDAD NACIONAL DE EDUCACION
   "ENRIQUE GUZMAN Y VALLE"
San Felipe No. 640, La Cantuta, Chosica, Peru

Foreign
Certificates
Non-resident

Peru's open university pilot project is for working teachers, and offers them correspondence study in literature, science, Quechua language, geography, and mathematics. Some coursework is given by radio or in newspapers. Small group meetings at various locations are optional.

UNIVERSITÉ DE PARIS VIII — VINCENNES
Route de la Tourelle, F-75012, Paris, France

Foreign
Bachelor's, Master's,
   Doctorate
Residency (IS, EW)

The Vincennes campus of the University of Paris is known as the "university of second chance." It offers degrees in languages, linguistics, the social sciences, fine arts, theater, and cinematography, through evening study, small group study, and student-directed study. The more-than-30,000 students come from over 100 countries.

UNIVERSITI SAINS MALAYSIA
Minden, Penang, Malaysia

Foreign
Bachelor's
Residency (IS)

For the first four years of this five-year program, students study by correspondence and independent study, using printed materials, tapes, and slides mailed to them. They must come to the campus once a year for a seminar of a few weeks. The fifth year is done entirely in residence.

THE UNIVERSITY CENTER AT HARRISBURG
2986 N. 2nd St., Harrisburg PA 17110
717/238-9694

Accredited
Bachelor's, Master's,
Doctorates
Residency (EW)

The University Center is an educational consortium established in 1958 by five Pennsylvania institutions (the University of Pennsylvania, Pennsylvania State University, Temple University, Lebanon Valley College and Elizabethtown College) to offer various degree programs of all kinds, primarily through evening and weekend study. A wide variety of Bachelor's degree programs are offered. Among the other offerings are a Master of Science in Education from Temple, a Master of Governmental Administration from Penn, a Master of Liberal Arts from Temple, and Ed.D. programs in adult/continuing education and in elementary education, both from Temple.

Comment: This is such a splendid idea, it's a pity there aren't such Centers in a great many more locations around the country.

UNIVERSITY FOR HUMANISTIC STUDIES
2425 San Diego Ave., San Diego CA 92110
714/295-3355

Unaccredited
Bachelor's, Master's,
Doctorates
Non- or short residency

Degrees at all levels in psychology, community services, holistic health, and metaphysics, entirely through correspondence study. Degrees can be completed in a minimum of six months at a cost under $3,000. A thesis is required for graduate degrees.

Comment: The bulletin lists no names whatsoever, although reference is made to an experienced faculty of successful professionals. Some traditionalists (or even non-traditionalists) might quibble over the awarding of the Doctor of Philosophy for the study of astrology, divination, and pyramidology.

UNIVERSITY OF ALABAMA
New College External Degree Program, P.O. Drawer ED,
   University AL 35486
205/348-6000

Accredited
Bachelor's
Very short residency

The degrees of Bachelor of Arts or Bachelor of Science may be earned entirely by correspondence, with the exception of a two-to-five day seminar on the campus at the start of the program. At least 32 semester hours of work must be completed after enrolling at the University. This can be by contract learning, correspondence courses, television courses, weekend college, and prior learning evaluation. Students may major in human services, humanities, social sciences, natural sciences, applied sciences, administrative sciences, and communication. A final project is required of all students. Counseling is often done by telephone. Minimum tuition and fees are under $2,000.

Comment: An outstanding program from a major state university. Alabama used to offer a highly innovative Master of Science in Engineering, also requiring only two days in residence, but no new students are accepted into this program, which is a shame.

UNIVERSITY OF ALASKA

Fairbanks AK 99701
907/479-7581

Sadly, the University's highly innovative non-resident Ph.D. program in various scientific fields has been terminated, as "it has not lived up to our expectations." The University does have two non-traditional concepts that are relevant in pursuing degrees. One is the rule that the vast majority of courses can be challenged by examination. If the exam is passed, credit for the course is given. And they have introduced the delightful concept of "Academic Bankruptcy." Some students have such poor records, they cannot continue in school. Often the poor performance is due to outside factors, which can change. In such an event, a student may declare Academic Bankruptcy. All previous work is thereupon disregarded. Subject to the approval of the dean, the student is admitted to the University and begins with a clean slate.

UNIVERSITY OF ARIZONA

Tucson AZ 85712
602/884-2751

Accredited
Bachelor's, Master's
Residency (EW)

Bachelor of Science in public administration primarily for police officers, and Master of Teaching for military personnel at Davis-Monthan Air Force Base, available through evening study.

UNIVERSITY OF ARKANSAS

European Coordinator, USAFE, Box 6585, APO New
   York 09633
501/575-2000

Accredited
Master's
Residency (IS)

Programs are offered to military and civilian personnel at various military bases in Europe. The degrees include a Master of Arts in international relations and a Master of Science in management. The work has been offered at bases in England, Germany, Italy, Spain and Turkey.

UNIVERSITY OF BEVERLY HILLS

465 S. Beverly Dr., Beverly Hills CA 90212
213/556-0190

Unaccredited
Bachelor's, Master's,
  Doctorates
Non-resident

The degrees are offered in a wide variety of fields, in the broad areas of business and management, engineering, mass communications, health management, behavioral sciences, and fine arts. The program begins with an assessment of prior learning. Then a study plan contract is developed. The student then completes all work proposed in the study plan. Then a final project is designed and undertaken. Doctoral candidates must write a dissertation demonstrating superior proficiency in a narrow, advanced field. Students are expected to complete their work within 18 months in most cases. Tuition for most programs is between $3,000 and $4,000. The University is authorized to grant degrees by the State of California. The President is Julian Warner, a practicing attorney.

UNIVERSITY OF BRIDGEPORT

Bridgeport CT 06602
203/576-4000

Accredited
Bachelor's, Master's
Residency (EW)

Bachelor of Arts, Bachelor of Science, Master of Arts, Master of Science in education, engineering and nursing, all through evening study.

UNIVERSITY OF CALIFORNIA (Berkeley)

Berkeley CA 94720
415/642-6000

Accredited
Master's
Residency (EW)

Master of Business Administration, through the Graduate School of Business, available entirely through evening courses.

UNIVERSITY OF CALIFORNIA (Davis)
Davis CA 95616
916/752-1011

Accredited
Bachelor's, Master's
Residency (EW)

Davis has served as the pilot program of the University of California system for non-traditional students (as contrasted with non-traditional degrees). The Academic Re-entry Program exists to help and facilitate entry into various programs of students who are older or who have been out of school a long time or who don't have the usual academic background.

UNIVERSITY OF CALIFORNIA (Irvine)
Irvine CA 92717
714/833-5011

Accredited
Master's
Residency (EW)

Master of Science in educational administration, Master of Arts in social ecology and in the teaching of Spanish available through evening study.

UNIVERSITY OF CALIFORNIA (Los Angeles)
Los Angeles CA 90024
213/825-4321

Accredited
Master's
Residency (EW, IS)

Master of Business Administration, through the Graduate School of Management; Master of Engineering involving one afternoon and one evening a week, for employed engineers with five years' experience, through the Engineering Executive Program.

UNIVERSITY OF CALIFORNIA (Riverside)
Riverside CA 92502
714/787-1012

Accredited
Master's
Residency (EW)

Master of Administration program, offered in Riverside, Ontario, Palm Springs, San Bernardino and Ventura.

UNIVERSITY OF CALIFORNIA (San Diego)
La Jolla CA 92093
714/452-3410

Accredited
Bachelor's
Short residency

Bachelor of Arts based on a degree plan in which the student determines his or her educational goals and decides how best to reach them. Some students may reach their goals through non-residential study, although meetings with faculty tutors on campus will almost certainly be necessary. Credit is given for formal and informal prior learning experiences.

UNIVERSITY OF CALIFORNIA (San Francisco)
San Francisco CA 94122
415/666-9000

Accredited
Master's
Residency (EW)

Master of Science in Nursing, through the School of Nursing, with some courses through evening study with the Extension Division.

UNIVERSITY OF CALIFORNIA (Santa Barbara)
Santa Barbara CA 93106
805/961-2311

Accredited
Bachelor's, Master's
Residency (EW, IS)

Bachelor of Arts in law and society, through the College of Letters and Science; Master of Science in electrical engineering for advanced students requiring technical upgrading, and for U.S. Navy employees at Point Mugu.

UNIVERSITY OF CALIFORNIA (Santa Cruz)
Santa Cruz CA 95064
408/429-0111

Accredited
Bachelor's
Residency (EW)

Bachelor of Arts in community studies, available through evening study.

UNIVERSITY OF CINCINNATI
Cincinnati OH 45221
513/475-8000

Accredited
Bachelor's
Residency (EW)

Bachelor's degrees in general studies, science, social science, engineering, humanities, arts and business administration, which may be earned entirely through evening study.

UNIVERSITY OF CENTRAL CALIFORNIA
601 University Ave., Sacramento CA 95825
916/920-3451

Unaccredited
Bachelor's, Master's,
    Doctorates
Non-resident

Degrees in business, education, engineering, psychology, public administration and related fields, entirely by correspondence. A typical program consists first of responding to 100 to 200 multiple choice, true-false, and essay questions to demonstrate competency; then independent guided study, completion of a thesis, and a final oral examination. The University is authorized to grant degrees by the State of California.

Comment: Despite many requests over the past four years, the University has never responded to any of my letters asking basic questions about the operation of the school and the backgrounds and source of Doctorates of the President, Garrison Noble, and the Dean, Philip Smart.

UNIVERSITY OF CHICAGO
5801 Ellis Ave., Chicago IL 60637

Accredited
Master's
Residency (EW, IS)

The Master of Business Administration is offered in two non-traditional modes: entirely through evening study at a downtown Chicago location; and in an Executive Program requiring one day on campus every week for two years, plus a five-day residential seminar.

Comment: In 1978, the National Home Study Council reported that the University of Chicago was going back into the correspondence instruction business—a field in which they excelled until programs were terminated in the early 1960's. However my inquiries have not produced definitive information. The Dean of Students' office "can find no evidence of such a program." That doesn't mean it isn't happening. It is not uncommon in the course of my researches for one office of a school to deny flatly that a certain program exists, only to have it turn out that the program is offered by another office of the same school. But if Chicago is indeed returning to correspondence courses, I have not yet located the right people to ask.

UNIVERSITY OF DELAWARE
Clayton Hall, Newark DE 19711

Accredited
Bachelor's, Master's
Residency (EW)

Bachelor of Arts in liberal studies; Bachelor of Science; Master of Arts in economics and Master of Education, all through evening study.

UNIVERSITY OF DELHI
School of Correspondence Courses, 5 Cavalry Lines,
    Delhi 110007, India

Foreign
Bachelor's, Master's
Non-resident

Bachelor of Arts, Bachelor of Commerce, and Master of Arts in Hindi and in political science through correspondence study. All courses are available through correspondence, and some radio courses, for people anywhere in the world. Examinations must be taken to India, or at certain foreign centers.

UNIVERSITY OF DENVER

200 W. 14th St., Denver CO 80204
303/753-1964

Accredited
Doctorates
Residency (EW)

The Ph.D. in higher education may be completed entirely through evening study.

UNIVERSITY OF DETROIT

4001 McNichols Rd., Detroit MI 48221
313/927-1000

Accredited
Bachelor's, Master's
Residency (EW)

Bachelor of Arts, Bachelor of Science, Master of Public Administration, available entirely through evening study. A special Bachelor of Business Administration program requires one evening a week for six years.

UNIVERSITY OF GEORGIA

Athens GA 30601
404/542-3030

Accredited
Master's
Residency (EW)

The Master of Business Administration and Master's degrees in early childhood education and public administration, available through evening study.

UNIVERSITY OF HARTFORD

West Hartford CT 06117
203/243-4635

Accredited
Bachelor's
Short residency

Bachelor's degree program in which up to 75% of the required units can come from an assessment of prior learning experiences, credit by examination, etc. Assessment is based primarily on a portfolio prepared by the student. A non-credit course is offered to assist in this. The assessment may be done prior to enrollment. A fee of $100 plus a small amount for each credit awarded is charged.

UNIVERSITY OF HAWAII

2500 Dole St., Honolulu HI 96822
808/948-8207

Accredited
Bachelor's, Master's
Residency (EW)

Bachelor of Arts in history, mathematics, sociology; Bachelor of Business Administration; Master of Arts in educational administration, all through evening study in the College of Continuing Education. Some classes are given at Hickham Air Force Base.

UNIVERSITY OF IOWA

Division of Continuing Education, W400 Seashore Hall,
  Iowa City IA 52242
319/353-4963 (in Iowa, 800/272-6430; in neighboring
  states 800/553-6380)

Accredited
Bachelor's
Non-resident

The Bachelor of Liberal Studies degree may be earned entirely by correspondence from the University of Iowa and the University of Northern Iowa. Students must earn 62 semester hours of credit elsewhere before entering the program. (Those 62 hours can be done by correspondence through Iowa or any other recognized school.) At least 45 units must be earned at either the University of Iowa or certain other Iowa universities. Credit is given for equivalency exams, but not for life experience learning. There are no majors in the program, but students must earn 12 units in each of three of these five areas: humanities, communication and arts, science and math, social science, and professional fields (business, education, home economics). Credits may be earned through correspondence classes; Saturday and evening classes given at 23 cities around the state; or television, newspaper and radio courses. Iowa's "Telebridge" system is a statewide system of two-way audio conferencing, giving people the opportunity to hold seminars at remote locations, and even link various experts at third locations into the network. Seven Telebridge courses are offered at this time, with more to come. The B.L.S. program is open to people living anywhere in the U.S., and to U.S. citizens living outside the U.S. Tuition is $50 per semester hour, thus a minimum of $1,500 for the degree.

UNIVERSITY OF KANSAS
Lawrence KS 66045
913/864-2700

Accredited
Master's
Residency (EW)

Master of Public Administration and Master of Science in elementary education, through evening study.

UNIVERSITY OF KENTUCKY
103 Frazee Hall, Lexington KY 40506
606/258-9000

Accredited
Master's
Residency (EW)

Master of Business Administration offered through evening study, in University Extension.

UNIVERSITY OF LA VERNE
1950 Third St., La Verne CA 91750
714/596-3497

Accredited
Bachelor's
Residency (LE)

Bachelor's degrees in many fields, including business administration and the health sciences, in which up to 75% of the required units may be earned through an assessment of prior learning experiences. The assessment must be done after enrollment. The total cost of the degree program, including assessment, is over $4,000.

UNIVERSITY OF LONDON
Senate House, Malet St., London WC1E 7HU, England
01-636-8000

Foreign
Bachelor's, Master's,
  Doctorates
Non-resident

Good news. Five years after the University of London terminated its External Degree Programme for all but British citizens, they have once again opened it up to people living anywhere in the world. However the examinations for the degrees will only be given in England. For more than 100 years, London offered the only reputable non-resident degrees available worldwide. With one exception, the London degrees are based solely on examinations and a thesis. The University offers the examinations, but not the coursework to prepare one for the examinations. However there are a number of private non-degree-granting correspondence schools offering courses to prepare students for the London exams. Two such schools are the National Extension College (8 Shaftesbury Road, Cambridge CB2 2BP, England) and Metropolitan College (St. Peter's St., St. Albans, AL1 3NE, England). The one exception is the Bachelor of Science in Economics, for which the University offers its own correspondence courses. The total fee for this program is 600 pounds (about $1,000), and information is obtained from the University of London's Commerce Degree Bureau, 24 Russell Square, London WC1E 7HU, England. External students may study for Bachelor's, Master's, or Doctorates in theology, arts, laws, music, science, engineering, economics, and education. Note: there is a rigid and absolutely unchangeable rule that says all students seeking Master's or Doctorates must earn the University of London's Bachelor's degree first. It doesn't matter if you have three Doctorates from Harvard; if you don't have a London Bachelor's, you can't enroll for a London Master's or Doctorate, and that's final.

Comment: It's so nice to see the London degrees once again available outside England. Thus there is opportunity to earn these outstanding credentials with only one or two trips to England to take the required exams.

UNIVERSITY OF LOUISVILLE
2301 S.Third St., Louisville KY 40208
502/588-5555

Accredited
Bachelor's, Master's
Residency (EW)

Bachelor of Arts, Bachelor of Science, Master of Arts and Master of Science which may be earned entirely through evening study.

UNIVERSITY OF MAINE
14 Merrill Hall, Orono ME 04473
207/581-7011

Accredited
Bachelor's, Master's
Residency (EW)

Bachelor of Arts in elementary education, business administration, arts and sciences; Master of Arts in English, history, speech; Master of Science in education, business, library sciences, engineering; Master of Business Administration, and Master of Library Science, all of which may be earned through evening courses given at Orono and Portland.

UNIVERSITY OF MARYLAND
College Park MD 20742
301/454-2765

Accredited
Bachelor's
Non-resident

Maryland makes extensive use of both the philosophy and the actual materials of Britain's Open University in offering their Bachelor of Arts and Bachelor of Science programs. Students may visit learning centers throughout the Baltimore-Washington area, or may never visit them and do all the work at their home, with telephone or postal contact with the University's tutors. Credit is given for all prior learning experiences. Part-time students can earn 18 units a year, at a cost of less than $1,000. Thus for the student starting from scratch, it would require about six years to earn the degree.

Comment: Open University's courses and home laboratory equipment are excellent and rather demanding, so this program would be for students who really want to learn new material as well as earn the degree.

UNIVERSITY OF MASSACHUSETTS (Amherst)
Amherst MA 01002
413/545-0111

Accredited
Bachelor's
Short residency

UMass offers a University Without Walls program leading to the Bachelor of General Studies degree for people with full-time jobs, retired persons, and others, with courses involving independent study and at various locations around the state. Some visits to the main campus or other centers are required. In other University Bachelor's programs, up to 87% of the required units may be earned through an assessment of prior learning experiences. Degrees are offered in the sciences, social sciences, engineering, business administration and the health sciences. The assessment is based on a portfolio prepared by the student, oral interviews, and/or examinations. The assessment may be done anytime after enrollment, and takes from two to five months.

UNIVERSITY OF MASSACHUSETTS (Boston)
College of Public and Community Service, Boston
   MA 02125
617/287-1900

Accredited
Bachelor's
Residency (IS)

Bachelor's degree program in public and community service, human service, legal service and housing, and community development, in which 100% of the required units can come from an assessment of prior learning experience — but there is still the requirement of one year of residency at the University.

UNIVERSITY OF MIAMI
P.O. Box 8005, Coral Gables FL 33124
305/284-2211

Accredited
Bachelor's, Master's
Residency (EW)

Bachelor of Arts, Bachelor of Science in Business Administration, Bachelor of Continuing Studies and Master of Education, all through evening study. Master of Business Administration with classes held every other weekend, for fully-employed persons sponsored by their employers. (Miami's innovative M.D. program is described in Chapter 22.)

UNIVERSITY OF MICHIGAN
412 Maynard, Ann Arbor MI 48104
313/764-1817

Accredited
Master's
Residency (EW, IS)

Master of Business Administration, Master of Education, Master of Engineering and Master of Library Science offered entirely by evening study in Ann Arbor, Dearborn, Detroit, Flint and Grand Rapids, and through television courses.

UNIVERSITY OF MINDANAO
Bolton St., Davao City, Mindanao Island, Philippines

Foreign
Master's
Non-resident

The University's On-the-Air Project offers the Master's degree in education entirely through radio broadcasts. Students submit term papers, prepare workbooks, and take examinations at the University.

UNIVERSITY OF MINNESOTA (Minneapolis)
201 Westbrook Hall, Minneapolis MN 55455
612/373-3919

Accredited
Bachelor's
Non-resident

Bachelor of Arts or Bachelor of Science, which may be earned without visiting the campus. The program is open to students living anywhere in the world, subject to certain limitations. The University cannot serve distant students in technical fields (engineering, computer science) unless they have nearly completed a traditional degree. The same goes for certain areas of business administration. They cannot serve any students in fields requiring certification (teaching, nursing, etc.). The program is based on a curriculum plan drawn up by the student (who is expected to have a basic grasp of the meaning of a liberal arts education). Credit is given for prior learning of all kinds. At least 25% of the units must be earned after enrollment. Work for the degree may include equivalency exams, correspondence courses, and the completion of one or more independent study courses. Many courses are available on videotape. Tuition is $31 per credit, so the minimum cost can be around $1,000.

UNIVERSITY OF MINNESOTA (Morris)
Morris Learning Center, University Without Walls, Morris
   MN 56267
612/589-1041

Accredited
Bachelor's
Very short residency

Only students living in western Minnesota are encouraged to enter this program, in which up to 99% of the unit requirements can be met through an assessment of prior learning experiences. Degrees are not based on credits but on demonstrated learning, through learning contracts.

UNIVERSITY OF MISSOURI (St. Louis)
Evening College, 8001 Natural Bridge Rd., St. Louis
   MO 63121
314/553-5161

Accredited
Bachelor's
Residency

Bachelor of General Studies, which is available entirely through the Evening College. At least 24 semester hours of the 120 required must be completed in residence. Credit is given for equivalency exams, correspondence courses, community service projects, and cultural activities. There should be 30 semester hours in an area of "personal emphasis" — a subject of special interest to the student.

UNIVERSITY OF MISSOURI (Columbia)
College of Agriculture, Columbia MO 65201
314/882-6287

Accredited
Bachelor's
Short residency

Bachelor of Science in Agriculture, in which credit is given for all prior learning experiences, equivalency exams, correspondence courses, by evaluation of life experience, and by directed independent study projects. Prior college-level work is not required, but is strongly preferred. Only students who have not enrolled in any school full-time for at least five years are accepted. The program is designed primarily for farmers and those planning to farm.

UNIVERSITY OF NEBRASKA
P.O. Box 82446, Lincoln NE 68501
402/472-7211

Accredited
Bachelor's, Master's
Short residency

A "distance teaching program" of the University offers courses from many sources with credits leading to the Bachelor's degree. This is a student-planned Bachelor of General Studies program "to established adults only," with credit for life experience and "amnesty for past college failures." The College of Continuing Studies offers an external Master of Arts in civil engineering and water resources primarily for engineers in the Corps of Engineers.

UNIVERSITY OF NEW ENGLAND
Armidale, New South Wales 2351, Australia

Foreign
Bachelor's, Master's
Short residency

The University's External Studies Division does most of its instruction by correspondence, including printed lecture notes, course outlines and video cassettes. Students must attend residential vacation schools on campus or weekend schools in Sydney. The B.A. is offered in arts, economics, social science, and financial administration. Master's degrees are awarded in economics, accounting and education.

UNIVERSITY OF NEW HAMPSHIRE
Durham NH 03824
603/862-1234

Accredited
Bachelor's, Master's
Residency (EW)

Bachelor of General Studies, Master of Education in administration and supervision, which may be earned entirely through evening study.

UNIVERSITY OF NEW HAVEN
300 Orange Ave., West Haven CT 06516
203/934-6321

Accredited
Bachelor's, Master's
Residency

Bachelor of Arts, Bachelor of Science, Master of Business Administration, Master of Science in industrial engineering and criminal justice, and Master of Public Administration, all available entirely through evening study.

UNIVERSITY OF SOUTH WALES
P.O. Box 1, Kensington, New South Wales 2033 Australia

Foreign
Master's
Residency (IS)

The Division of Postgraduate Extension Studies offers various professional Master's degrees, primarily through radio and television courses, but most courses are also available as audio or video tapes. (The live lectures use "telephone talkback.") Students are expected to study together in groups of three or more.

UNIVERSITY OF NORTHERN IOWA
See University of Iowa for a shared non-resident Bachelor's degree program.

UNIVERSITY OF OKLAHOMA
1700 Asp Ave., Suite 226, Norman OK 73069
405/325-1061

Accredited
Bachelor's, Master's
Short residency

Bachelor of Liberal Studies and Master of Liberal Studies involving from four to 24 weeks on campus, with the balance of the time in directed independent study. B.L.S. students complete thematically organized studies in three areas: humanities, natural sciences, and social sciences. It is essentially a four-year degree, with each year requiring a three-week session on campus. (Sessions are held at least twice a year.) Three of the four years may be waived, either based on prior study, or by passing an equivalency examination. In the fourth year, the student completes a study in depth and attends a final mandatory seminar. Students who already have the equivalent of two years of college-level study can select an Upper Division Option, beginning with a two-day residential seminar, followed by completion of all three phases in about one year, and then the final ''inter-area'' seminar. Although there does not have to be a major subject, students can elect a special Legal Assistant Program, or the Open Learning for the Fire Service program described earlier in this chapter. The minimum cost for Oklahoma residents is about $1,500, and double that for people from other states and outside the U.S. The Master of Liberal Studies, designed in large measure for people with a specialized Bachelor's degree who wish a broader education, begins with a one-week seminar on campus. There follows a period of independent directed study at home, then a three-week colloquium on campus. Then comes another period of independent study and thesis planning, research, and writing, and finally a three-week advanced seminar after which the degree is awarded. The fees for the M.L.S. program are $1,250 for Oklahomans and $2,450 for everyone else.

Comment: Oklahoma is one of the pioneers in non-traditional education, with programs going way back to the early 1960's. And they are still one of the best.

UNIVERSITY OF PALM BEACH
660 Fern St., West Palm Beach FL 33402
305/833-5575

Unaccredited
Bachelor's, Master's
Short residency

Bachelor of Arts and Master of Business Administration through residential study, but with credit given for prior experience, it is possible to complete the Bachelor's degree in six months and the Master's in nine. The University is licensed by the State of Florida. It was begun in 1926 as Bell Isles College.

Comment: Five of the 10 faculty have their highest degree from Palm Beach, an unusually high ratio.

UNIVERSITY OF PENNSYLVANIA
Philadelphia PA 19174
215/243-5000

Accredited
Bachelor's, Master's
Residency (EW)

Bachelor of Arts and Master of Engineering, through evening study in the Division of Continuing Education.

UNIVERSITY OF PHOENIX
1427 N. Third St., Phoenix AZ 85004
602/258-3666

Accredited
Bachelor's, Master's
Residency (EW)

Qualified students can earn the Bachelor's degree in business administration, management or health services and the Master of Business Administration or M.A. in management entirely through evening study, in a minimum time period of one academic year. Classes meet one night a week in Phoenix, as well as in various cities in southern and northern California.

Comment: In earlier editions, I recounted the history of the University, and the running battles they had (now apparently over and won) with the Arizona Board of Regents. That listing brought a long letter from the University's law firm demanding that the listing be changed at once and all existing copies of this book be destroyed at once. Phooey.

UNIVERSITY OF PITTSBURGH
External Studies Program, 3808 Forbes Ave., Pittsburgh
   PA 15260
412/624-4102

Accredited
Bachelor's
Short residency (EW)

Bachelor of Arts and Bachelor of Science programs in a wide variety of fields. There is a three day workshop scheduled on campus for each 15-week course: one day at the beginning, one in the middle, and one at the end. However, except for a very few courses, it is not necessary to attend these workshops. In the College of General Studies, students can major in economics, psychology, public administration or social sciences entirely through non-residential study, and in many other fields by attending some evening or Saturday courses in those subjects. Self-designed non-residential majors are possible, too. Programs are also available (at much higher cost) in the School of Health Related Professions and the School of Education. Tuition is over $2,000 a year for Pennsylvania residents, double that for others. Tuition is 25% higher in health and 45% higher in education.

UNIVERSITY OF PUERTO RICO
Mayaguez PR 00708
809/765-6590

Accredited
Bachelor's
Residency (EW)

Bachelor of Arts in education for employed teachers, through weekend and summer classes; Bachelor of Secretarial Science through evening study.

UNIVERSITY OF PUGET SOUND
110 Prefontaine Place South, Seattle WA 98122
206/756-3100

Accredited
Bachelor's, Master's
Residency (EW)

Bachelor of Arts in business administration and public administration, Master of Business Administration, Master of Public Administration, all through late afternoon or evening study.

UNIVERSITY OF QUEBEC
Télé-Université, 3108 Chemin Sainte-Foy,
   Quebec G1X 1P8, Canada

Foreign
Bachelor's
Residency (IS)

Télé-Université is one of the ten units of the University of Quebec—a university without walls within the huge University. Programs are offered for the training of teachers of French and mathematics, and some general courses for the public. Instruction is largely by use of television, videotapes, textbooks, and experimental kits, all for home study, plus, in the teacher training programs, weekly three-hour group meetings. Instruction is in French.

UNIVERSITY OF REDLANDS
1200 Colton Ave., Redlands CA 92373
714/793-2121

Accredited
Bachelor's, Master's
Residency (LE, IS)

Bachelor's degrees in various fields, including business administration and management, in which up to 75% of the credit may be earned from an assessment of prior learning, based on a student-produced portfolio. The non-traditional programs are offered through Johnson College and Whitehead Center. Assessment takes from two to five months, and must be done after enrollment. The cost is a small fee for each unit awarded in the assessment. The Master of Arts in management can be earned by attending one four-hour class per week, in northern or southern California locations, through Whitehead College.

UNIVERSITY OF RHODE ISLAND

Providence RI 02908
401/792-2221

Accredited
Bachelor's, Master's
Residency (EW)

Bachelor of Arts in English (women only), Bachelor of Science, Master of Arts in English, Master of Business Administration, and Master of Public Administration, entirely through evening study at six cities around the state.

UNIVERSITY OF RICHMOND

7 West Franklin St., Richmond VA 23173
804/285-6000

Accredited
Bachelor's, Master's
Residency (EW)

Bachelor of Arts, Bachelor of Commerce, Master of Commerce, and Master of Humanities, all available entirely through evening study.

UNIVERSITY OF ROCHESTER

Rochester NY 14627
716/275-2121

Accredited
Bachelor's, Master's
Residency (EW)

Bachelor of Science and Master of Science in general study, through evening study.

UNIVERSITY OF SAN FRANCISCO

Continuing Education, 2130 Fulton St., San Francisco
  CA 94117
415/666-0600

Accredited
Bachelor's
Residency (LE)

Bachelor of Arts in the social sciences, in which about 80% of the required units may be earned through an assessment of prior learning experiences. This program requires that 30 units be earned after enrollment, including a special course to help prepare the life experience portfolio. The assessment takes from two to five months and costs $500.

UNIVERSITY OF SARASOTA

2080 Ringling Blvd., Sarasota FL 33577
813/955-4228

Unaccredited
Bachelor's, Master's,
  Doctorates
Short residency

The University offers programs leading to the Bachelor and Master of Business Administration, Master of Arts in Education, Master of Educational Development, Master of Human Services, Doctor of Educational Development, Doctor of Human Services, and Doctor of Education. Some residency in Sarasota is required for each degree, but the amount depends on a combination of degree requirements and students' personal and professional responsibilities. The school of Management and Business holds intensive residential sessions of five eight-hour days; the School of Education holds three two-week terms each summer. Master's and doctoral students must complete a "criterion-referenced evaluation" — a two-day comprehensive written examination in their field. Tuition is based on the number of credits taken with Sarasota; a minimum would be in excess of $4,000. The University is accredited by the National Association for Private Non-traditional Schools and Colleges, and I wish their literature pointed out that this is an unrecognized, albeit legitimate accreditor. The University began a building program on a new campus site in mid-1982. About 400 students are enrolled, three-fourths of them doctoral students in education (mostly teachers and administrators seeking to upgrade themselves). The catalog lists about 100 adjunct faculty and consultants, all with impressive credentials.

UNIVERSITY OF SASKATCHEWAN

Saskatoon, Saskatchewan S7N 0W0 Canada
306/343-3761

Foreign
Bachelor's
Residency (IS)

Bachelor of Commerce in health care administration, in an alternative program that may require up to six years of part-time independent study. A total of one year of residency is required during those six years.

UNIVERSITY OF SOUTH AFRICA

Box 392, Muckleneuk Ridge, Pretoria, South Africa 0001
48-2811

Foreign
Bachelor's, Master's,
 Doctorates
Non-resident

UNISA, as the University is known worldwide, offers the opportunity to earn outstanding, universally recognized and accepted degrees from a major university, entirely by correspondence, with the exception of final examinations, which may be taken at South African government offices in New York, Washington, Houston or Los Angeles. Degrees at all levels are offered in a wide variety of fields, through a technique called "tele-tuition," involving course materials, tapes, slides, etc. For admission the applicant must give "full reasons why he cannot pursue his studies at a university in his own country." The most acceptable reasons are either living far from any university, or wishing to study subjects offered uniquely by UNISA (e.g., range management, African archaeology, African languages, etc.). Applicants are asked to sign a statement saying they will go to Pretoria for examinations if required, but in practice this is only asked for if there is some suspicion of irregularities. Indeed, of the 20-or-so American alumni to whom I have spoken, none had to go, and, in fact, several were in prison. The program is modeled closely on the University of London's external degrees, with the significant exception that one does not need to earn UNISA's Bachelor's degree before going on for their graduate degrees. The cost of the programs, government subsidized, is extremely low — probably under $1,000 for most programs. The catalog is highly informative, and will be sent by air mail on receipt of payment of five South African rand (about $5).

Comment: When I visited UNISA, I was extremely impressed by the scope (more than 50,000 students), and quality of education offered (and by the extraordinary architecture of the buildings). The racial issue must be addressed. Some Americans tell me they feel a little uncomfortable with a South African degree — but by and large, schools are evaluated outside the political climate of their countries. About 12% of UNISA's students are black Africans, and many black African leaders, such as Robert Mugabe of Zimbabwe, have earned UNISA degrees.

UNIVERSITY OF SOUTH CAROLINA

College of Applied Professional Sciences, Columbia
 SC 29208
803/777-0411

Accredited
Bachelor's, Master's
Residency (IS, EW)

Bachelor of Arts in Interdisciplinary studies, utilizing a student-designed curriculum, which must be approved in advance by the faculty. The last 30 semester hours must be earned after enrolling. Students must have earned at least 45 semester hours before entering the program. There are no specific course requirements. The MBA-ETV program offers a Master of Business Administration statewide with courses held on educational television supplemented by eight on-campus sessions at Columbia on Friday evenings and Saturday mornings.

UNIVERSITY OF SOUTHERN CALIFORNIA
Los Angeles CA 90007
213/746-6750

Accredited
Bachelor's, Master's,
    Doctorate
Residency (EW, IS)

U.S.C. offers a wide range of alternative approaches to earning degrees at various locations around the state, and in Washington D.C. The Bachelor's degrees are generally offered through evening classes in the Los Angeles area. Their "Flex Ed" system is based on cassette tapes, workbooks, and a one-on-one tutorial system, with hours set to the students' convenience. A Master of Science in Safety is offered through weekend study in the San Francisco bay area. Graduate degrees in education and public administration are offered in the San Francisco and Sacramento areas. The Doctor of Education for teachers and administrators is available through summer residency plus independent study. The Doctor of Administration is offered in Washington D.C. as well. Two Master's degrees are given in Europe: an M.A. in International Relations open to anyone in London; and an M.S. in education, an M.S. in systems management and an M.A. in International Relations for the "military community" in Germany. American citizens not in said community may obtain special permission to attend.

UNIVERSITY OF SOUTH FLORIDA
Bachelor of Independent Studies External Program, Tampa
    FL 33620
813/974-2403

Accredited
Bachelor's
Short residency (IS)

The Bachelor of Independent Studies program requires from three to nine weeks on campus, spread out over anywhere from 14 to 69 months. All students must have knowledge in three broad areas of study: social sciences, natural sciences, and humanities. Each of the three areas has an extensive program of guided independent study and a three-week on-campus seminar for research, writing, peer interaction, and, when relevant, laboratory experience. Up to two of the areas can be waived for students who have already had sufficient work and background, and pass an equivalency examination in the field. All students must write a thesis, and defend it orally in a one-day examination on campus. The average student takes more than five years to earn the degree, but there is a wide range. The total cost, not including travel and housing, is around $4,000.

UNIVERSITY OF TENNESSEE
Chattanooga TN 37402
615/755-4011

Accredited
Bachelor's, Master's
Residency (EW)

Bachelor of Arts, Bachelor of Science, Master of Business Administration, Master of Science and Master of Education, all available entirely through evening study. Some credit is given for prior work and volunteer experience through the Individualized Education Program.

UNIVERSITY OF TEXAS
Arlington TX 76010
817/273-2011

Accredited
Bachelor's, Master's
Residency (EW)

Bachelor of Arts and Master of Arts in many fields, available through evening study.

UNIVERSITY OF THE PACIFIC
University College, Stockton CA 95211
209/946-2264

Accredited
Bachelor's
Residency (IS)

The Bachelor of Liberal Studies program is designed for adult students (25 and over), and involves a good deal of directed independent study. Personal visits with the faculty are required "on a fairly regular basis"—but the University solicits students living as far away as Denver and Los Angeles. Up to 60 of the required 132 semester hours can be earned through a combination of non-traditional courses and prior experiential learning. The cost of the program for a full-time student is more than $6,000 a year, which is one reason fewer than a dozen people are enrolled in this program.

UNIVERSITY OF THE STATE OF NEW YORK
Cultural Education Center, Albany NY 12230
518/474-3703

Accredited
Bachelor's
Non-resident

Bachelor of Arts and Bachelor of Science degrees, entirely through non-resident study, at a cost that can be under $1,000. The university is the oldest state educational agency in America, yet it has no faculty, no campus, and no courses of its own. It is in the business of evaluating work done elsewhere, and awarding its own fully-accredited degrees to persons who have accumulated sufficient units, by whatever means. Credit is given for all prior college courses, as well as for a great many non-college learning experiences (such as company-sponsored courses, military training, classes within government agencies, and so forth). The university recognizes many different equivalency examination programs, and offers its own, as well, given at nearly 100 locations around the country at regular intervals, and, by special arrangement, at foreign locations as well. Each of the degrees has its own requirements with regard to areas of emphasis, however they are not restrictive. They require, for instance, a certain minimum number of units in science, in social science, and in humanities. Degrees are available without specific majors, or with a major in either business or nursing. Special concentrations are available in computer science, mathematics, physics, geology, geography, sociology, history, political science, English, French, Spanish, and philosophy. Admission is open to all students. The program is described in great detail in the excellent 300-page catalogue, which is sent free to all who request it. (Outside North America, the catalogue is sent surface mail, which can take months to arrive. The University will send it by air on payment of a postal fee: $7 to South America, $11 to Europe, and $15 elsewhere.) The catalogue is like a textbook in non-traditional education. Credit is given for non-school learning experiences. Those that cannot easily be assessed at a distance, or by examination, may require the student to come to New York for an oral examination. The University, incidentally, is entirely self-supporting and does not draw any public funds. It is an academic success, as well, with more than 22,000 students currently enrolled.

Comment: Quite simply, the best non-traditional Bachelor's degree available non-residentially anywhere in the world. Accredited, prestigious, inexpensive, fast, efficient, and available to anyone, anywhere in the world.

UNIVERSITY OF TOLEDO
Adult Liberal Studies, University College, Toledo
OH 43606
419/537-2051

Accredited
Bachelor's, Master's
Residency (EW, IS)

Toledo's Adult Liberal Studies program offers people over 25 the opportunity to earn the Bachelor's degree through a combination of independent study, evening or weekend classes, regular coursework, plus a thesis. All students begin with an introductory planning seminar. Generous credit is given for CLEP exams. Nine seminars are given in various fields of study, usually one evening a week, for a total of 54 of the required 186 quarter hours needed. Thirty-five hours of traditional courses must be taken, before writing a thesis in an area of special interest. Toledo also offers a Bachelor of Education degree specifically for Registered Nurses, with substantial credit for nursing training, and the option of designing a program to meet individual needs.

UNIVERSITY OF TULSA
Tulsa OK 74104
918/939-6351

Accredited
Doctorate
Residency (EW)

The Doctor of Education degree may be completed in about two years of evening study, plus writing a dissertation.

UNIVERSITY OF UTAH
Salt Lake City UT 84110
801/581-7200

Accredited
Master's
Residency (EW)

Master of Business Administration, Master of Engineering and Master of Administration, which may be earned entirely through evening study.

UNIVERSTIY OF WATERLOO
200 University Ave. West, Waterloo, Ontario N2L 3G1
　Canada
519/885-1211

Foreign
Bachelor's, Master's
Non-resident, Residency

Bachelor of Arts, Bachelor of Science, Bachelor of Mathematics, Master of Science in Physics, and Master of Mathematics, which may be earned entirely through correspondence study from this large, provincially chartered university. The science degree is offered without a major. The Bachelor of Arts can be in economics, history, psychology, or classics. Credit is given for prior academic experience, but little or none for other learning experience. The full-time student, starting from scratch, can complete most degrees in three years. Waterloo is also Canada's major university offering cooperative education plans. Thousands of the undergraduates participate by alternating four-month terms on campus and in paid employment off campus. Generally eight terms on campus and six terms off are required for the degree.

UNIVERSITY OF WEST LOS ANGELES
10811 Washington Blvd., Culver City CA 90230
213/204-0000

Accreditation candidate
Bachelor's
Residency (EW)

Bachelor of Science in paralegal studies, which can be earned through two years of evening classes. Tuition is more than $3,000.

UNIVERSITY OF WISCONSIN (Green Bay)
Individualized Learning Programs Office, Green Bay
　WI 54302
414/465-2000

Accredited
Bachelor's
Short residency (IS)

Two non-traditional programs are available primarily for Wisconsin residents. (Persons in other states used to be encouraged to enroll; now they are discouraged.) The Bachelor of Arts in General Studies degree begins with structured independent study, and becomes more individualized with time. There are self-paced learning modules, field experiences, radio and television courses, internships, and research projects, based on learning contracts. An entrance seminar is required, to provide a detailed overview of the program. A University Without Walls degree program operated entirely through learning contracts, drawn up with faculty in the area of study interest. Students may work in any of the many majors available to on-campus students. Enrollment in both programs is for students with 62 or more semester hours. Tuition and fees are around $600 a semester for Wisconsin residents and triple that for out-of-staters.

UNIVERSITY OF WISCONSIN (Oshkosh)
Oshkosh WI 54901
414/424-1095

Accredited
Bachelor's
Residency (EW)

Bachelor's degrees in many fields, including engineering, business, and health sciences, in which up to 75% of the required units can come from an assessment of prior learning experiences. The assessment must be done after enrollment, and is based on an oral interview, a portfolio prepared by the student, and on examinations. The cost is based on the number of examinations and the number of credits awarded.

UNIVERSITY OF WISCONSIN (Superior)

Center for Continuing Education, Superior WI 54880
715/392-8101, 800/472-7353 (Wisconsin only),
  800/826-7122 (adjoining states)

Accredited
Bachelor's
Short residency

The Superior campus of the huge University of Wisconsin system offers a Bachelor of Arts degree which can be completed entirely through off-campus independent faculty-guided study. However on-campus conferences with faculty are required every few months. While most students live in northern Wisconsin or northern Minnesota, anyone who is willing to come to Superior three or four times a year may enroll. The student designs a degree program around the competency-based self-paced home study courses developed by the university in a wide variety of fields. Additional credit can be earned through assessment of prior learning, correspondence study of a more traditional sort, and on-campus courses if desired. The annual fee is under $400 a year for off-campus students.

UNIVERSITY OF WISCONSIN (Platteville)

Extended Degree Program, Pioneer Tower 513, Platteville
  WI 53818
608/342-1468

Accredited
Bachelor's
Residency (IS)

The Bachelor's degree in business administration is open to students who already have 60 to 65 semester hours of work. The remaining half of the degree work can be accomplished through independent study, workshops, field experiences, guided work with a tutor, research projects, programmed learning, and eventual completion of a major project: either a thesis, an apprenticeship, or significant study in a related academic area.

UPPER IOWA UNIVERSITY

Fayette IA 52142
800/553-4150 (Iowa), 800/632-5954 (other states)

Accredited
Bachelor's
Short residency (IS)

Upper Iowa's Coordinated Off-Campus Degree Programs offers the opportunity to earn a Bachelor of Arts in either business administration or public administration with only two to four weeks of residency. The balance of the program is conducted through directed independent study, with learning modules containing assignments and other course materials. Frequent interaction with the faculty is encouraged by toll-free phone lines or by mail. Students entering the program with 60 or more semester units must spend one two-week session on campus. Those with fewer than 60 units must attend two two-week sessions. The residency requirement may be waived for students outside the United States. Home study modules are available in a wide variety of fields, from accounting to chemistry, history to fine arts. Tuition is around $75 for each unit earned in a module, and $110 for units earned on campus. There is a text and materials fee of $40 to $70 per module as well. About 2,000 students worldwide are enrolled in this program.

UPPSALA UNIVERSITY

Long Distance Education Program, Box 256, S-751
  Uppsala, Sweden

Foreign
Bachelor's
Non-resident

The program was originally designed for Scandinavians living in other countries, and offers the opportunity to earn the Bachelor's degree in business administration, environmental studies, political science, and developmental studies entirely by correspondence, and at no cost. Uppsala offers two-thirds of the necessary courses for the degree; the remaining third come from Hermods, the Swedish National Correspondence Institute. Books, correspondence materials, taped lectures and assignments are mailed to students anywhere in the world. Examinations may be taken at any Swedish embassy or consulate. Around 500 people are enrolled in the program.

Comment: this may be the only totally free degree offered non-residentially by a major university. One might consider learning Swedish just to take advantage of the opportunity.

UPSALA COLLEGE
40 Clinton St., East Orange NJ 07019
201/266-7000

Accredited
Bachelor's
Residency (EW)

Bachelor of Arts and Bachelor of Science degrees can be earned entirely through evening study in the Division of General Studies.

VERMONT STATE COLLEGE SYSTEM
External Degree Program, Box 823, Montpelier VT 05602
802/828-2401

Accredited
Bachelor's
Residency (IS, LE)

Three Vermont schools cooperate to offer a non-traditional Bachelor's degree program, combining independent study, experiential learning credit, correspondence courses, courses by radio and television, and some traditional courses at Windham College (Putney), Johnson State College (Johnson), or Castleton State College (Castleton). The program is primarily for Vermont residents. A course in educational assessment and portfolio presentation helps students prepare their life experience portfolio.

VIRGINIA COMMONWEALTH UNIVERSITY
Richmond VA 23220
804/770-6472

Accredited
Master's
Residency (IS)

Master of Science in rehabilitation counseling for employed professionals in the field. The course is composed of alternate periods of intensive instruction and supervised clinical field research.

WALDEN UNIVERSITY
801 Anchor Rode Drive, Naples FL 33940
813/261-7277

Unaccredited
Doctorates
Short residency

Walden offers the Ph.D. and the Doctor of Education for professionals from the fields of business, education, government, health, psychology and social service. All students must attend a four-week summer residency session, which has been held at various locations around the country; in 1982, for instance, in southern California and in Minnesota. The residential session is used primarily to plan the doctoral dissertation, and to take various ''core courses'' in research methodology and related areas. Each student is then assigned a research advisor and a reader, under whose guidance the dissertation is written. Walden's Doctorates are widely accepted and recognized — a testimony to the quality of the program and the impressive staff. The degree program is approved by the State of California, and is the first out-of-state program approved by the notoriously tough state of Minnesota. (Walden has moved its main academic office to Minneapolis, while administrative offices remain in Florida.) Walden's Academic Policy Board is chaired by Harold Hodgkinson, former Director of the National Institute of Education. At least four former college and university presidents are affiliated with Walden as faculty or board members. Students may enroll and begin work at any time of the year. Those wishing to begin before a summer residency may take an optional Guided Independent Study Program, containing self instructional modules to help prepare for the summer work. Many of Walden's 150-or-so students are school teachers and administrators who have determined they will benefit from the Walden Doctorate. Many students will complete the degree in about a year, at a cost approaching $10,000.

WASHBURN UNIVERSITY
Special Instructional Programs
Topeka KS 66621
913/235-5341

Accredited
Bachelor's
Residency (EW)

Bachelor of Arts or Science in many fields, available entirely through evening study.

WASHINGTON UNIVERSITY
St. Louis MO 63130
314/863-0100

Accredited
Bachelor's
Residency

Bachelor of Science and Bachelor of Technology in computer applications, computer electronics, electrical power, mechanical design, structural design and thermomechanical energy, all available through evening study, in the School of Continuing Education of University College.

WAYLAND BAPTIST COLLEGE
Plainview TX 79072
806/296-5521

Accredited
Bachelor's
Residency (LE)

Bachelor of Science in Occupational Education in which more than 75% of the necessary units can be earned through an assessment of prior learning experiences. The assessment is done after enrollment, and is based on a portfolio prepared by the student. The time required for the assessment is less than one month and there is no additional cost for it.

WAYNE STATE UNIVERSITY
University Studies and Weekend College, 468 W. Ferry,
   Detroit MI 48202
313/577-2424

Accredited
Bachelor's
Residency (EW, IS)

The Bachelor of General Studies is offered through a combination of television courses broadcast in the early morning or late evening, four-hour evening workshops, and a weekend conference every few months. Students must complete the equivalent of a year of studies in social science, natural science, and humanities, and a final year of interdisciplinary advanced studies. The residential sessions are held at a variety of locations, such as public libraries, union halls, and in the Jackson State Prison.

WEBSTER COLLEGE
Webster Center, St. Louis MO 63119
314/968-0500

Accredited
Bachelor's
Short residency

Bachelor's degree in many fields, in which virtually all the necessary credit can come from an assessment of prior learning experiences. The assessment is based on a portfolio prepared by the student. A credit course is offered, optionally, for this purpose. The fee for an assessment is on a sliding scale, with a maximum around $600.

WEST COAST UNIVERSITY
440 S. Shatto Pl., Los Angeles CA 90020
213/487-4433

Accredited
Bachelor's, Master's
Residency (EW)

Bachelor of Science in administration, engineering, applied mathematics, applied physics, and computer science; Master of Science in systems engineering, applied mathematics, management science, and environmental science, all entirely through evening study.

WESTERN AUSTRALIAN INSTITUTE OF TECHNOLOGY
Department of External Studies, Hayman Road, South
   Bentley, Western Australia 6102, Australia

Foreign
Bachelor's, Master's
Non-resident

Both Australians and overseas students can enroll in the correspondence degree programs, with instruction via individualized study materials, audio tapes, course guides, and lecture notes. Radio programs are used in the Perth area, too. All students must take their examinations on the campus. Bachelor's and Master's degrees are available in business, the social sciences, and the arts. More than 1,500 students are enrolled in the external program.

WESTERN COLORADO UNIVERSITY
1129 Colorado Ave., Grand Junction CO 81501
303/245-3880

Unaccredited
Bachelor's, Master's,
   Doctorates
Non-resident

Western Colorado University offers non-resident degrees at all levels, in business administration, criminal justice, education, and a Ph.D. in counseling psychology. Credit is earned by completion of learning modules, which may be done through independent study, guided study, annotating a bibliography in the field, or passing a proctored challenge examination. At the Master's level, at least 18 units (three modules plus a thesis) must be earned after enrolling. At the doctoral level, the minimum is six modules plus a dissertation. The normal period of registration for the Bachelor's is two years for people who already have the equivalent of two years' academic experience. The minimum enrollment for graduate degrees is one year. The cost of the degree programs is between $2,500 and $3,000. Western Colorado is accredited by the National Association for Private Nontraditional Schools and Colleges, a legitimate but unrecognized accrediting agency founded by the faculty of Western Colorado, and with whom they still share offices and staff.

Comment: I have had some good feedback from satisfied alumni of Western Colorado. I wish that their catalogue informed prospective students that the accreditation is from an unrecognized agency. The founders, Doctors John and Sybil Curtis, have Doctorates from East Coast University, a school that I believe to be a degree mill as it now operates, but which they assure me was a legitimate fundamentalist Bible school when they attended in the early 1970's.

WESTERN ILLINOIS UNIVERSITY
Non-Traditional Programs, 309 Sherman Hall, Macomb
   IL 61455
309/298-1929; in Illinois, 800/322-3902

Accredited
Bachelor's
Non-resident

The Board of Governors Bachelor of Arts is offered through five Illinois universities, with the degree actually being awarded by the Board of Governors of State Colleges and Universities. Requirements for the degree are 120 semester hours, of which 15 must be earned at a B.O.G. university, and 40 must be upper division. The 15 units that must be earned after enrolling can be done entirely by correspondence, or through extension courses at Macomb and other locations around the state. All students who did not graduate from an Illinois high school must either pass an examination in the U.S. and the Illinois state constitution, or take a course in political science. All students must also pass a University Writing Examination. Western Illinois provides a helpful guide to the preparation of an experiential learning portfolio. Credit is given for a variety of learning experiences and for many equivalency exams. (Unlike many schools, they publish a very helpful list of the available exams, the minimum score necessary to earn credit, and the amount of credit given.) The total cost of the program depends on the number and type of courses taken, but they are generally remarkably low. The minimum cost is well under $1,000 (more for out-of-state students), and the cost of assessing a life experience portfolio is only $30.

Comment: I have had a great deal of favorable feedback from satisfied students in this program, particularly stressing the personal attention received. Their literature is among the most understandable of any non-traditional program, for which I am grateful.

WESTERN INTERNATIONAL UNIVERSITY
10202 N. 19th Ave., Phoenix AZ 85021
602/997-1072

Accreditation candidate
Bachelor's, Master's
Residency (EW)

Bachelor's and Master's degrees in arts, public administration, and "TTT" (Travel, Tourism and Transportation). Each residential course in Phoenix lasts for one calendar month, and two courses may be taken at a time. A total of 40 courses (thus 20 months) is required for the Bachelor's degree, and 12 courses (six months) for the Master's, when starting from scratch. Many courses may be waived if the student can demonstrate knowledge of their content, from prior learning or career experience. The cost ranges from $3,000 to $5,000.

Comment: A straightforward, no-nonsense approach to the alternative degree, along the lines of San Diego's National University. A few readers have reported high levels of frustration in bureaucratic involvements with the University.

WESTERN MARYLAND COLLEGE
College Hill, Westminster MD 21157
301/848-7000

Accredited
Master's
Residency (IS)

Master of Education in the education of the deaf, which is earned by completing three consecutive eight-week summer sessions, with independent study at home in between.

WESTERN MICHIGAN UNIVERSITY
Kalamazoo MI 49001
616/383-1600

Accredited
Bachelor's
Residency (EW)

Bachelor of Arts and Bachelor of Science, available entirely through evening study in the Division of Continuing Education.

WESTERN NEW ENGLAND COLLEGE
School of Continuing Higher Education, 1215 Wilbraham
   Rd., Springfield MA 01119
413/783-6131

Accredited
Bachelor's
Residency (EW, IS)

Bachelor of Arts in Liberal Studies and Bachelor of Science in Law Enforcement are offered to part-time students, entirely through evening study.

WESTERN REGIONAL LEARNING CENTER
1855 Folsom St., San Francisco CA 94103
415/431-5394

Unaccredited
Bachelor's, Master's,
   Doctorates
Residency (IS)

Degrees at all levels, through a combination of residential and independent study, for persons involved in community change and educational innovation. The degree programs have been approved by the State of California. The typical student is enrolled for 15 months or more, which must include two months in residency in San Francisco. The approach involves intensive study in small groups, and meaningful involvement in community activities and projects, working with other community change organizations. Tuition is around $3,000 a year.

Comment: I was very impressed by the enthusiastic report prepared by the committee appointed by the state to make recommendations on state approval.

WESTMINSTER COLLEGE (Pennsylvania)
New Wilmington PA 16142
412/946-8761

Accredited
Bachelor's
Residency (LE)

Bachelor's degrees in many fields, in a program in which up to 75% of the necessary units may be earned by an assessment of prior learning experiences. The assessment may be done before enrollment, and costs a flat fee of $225, regardless of the amount of credit awarded. The time for the assessment is less than one month.

WESTMINSTER COLLEGE (Utah)
Office of Adult and Extended Education,
   1840 S. 13th St. East, Salt Lake City UT 84105
801/484-8831

Accredited
Bachelor's
Residency (LE)

Bachelor's degrees in many fields, in which up to 75% of the required units may be earned from an assessment of prior learning experiences, transfer credits, or equivalency examinations. The assessment is done after enrollment, at a cost based on the number of units awarded, but generally under $500.

**WEST VIRGINIA BOARD OF REGENTS DEGREE
   PROGRAM**
203 Student Services Bldg., West Virginia University,
   Morgantown WV 26506
304/293-5441

Accredited
Bachelor's
Short residency

Bachelor of Arts program, requiring a minimum of 15 semester hours in residence at any of the member schools in the state. "As long as the student can provide evidence that he/she possesses college equivalent knowledge or skills, his/her achievements will be credited and recognized as applicable toward this degree program." The evaluation of life experience costs a modest $50, regardless of the amount of credit granted. The cost of the degree can be under $1,000. The member schools are:

        Bluefield State College, Bluefield 26554
        Concord College, Athens 24712
        Fairmont State College, Fairmont 26554
        Shepherd College, Shepherdstown 25443
        West Liberty State College, West Liberty 26074
        West Virginia State College, Institute 25112
        West Virginia Tech, Montgomery 25136
        West Virginia University, Morgantown 26506

WEST VIRGINIA UNIVERSITY
Morgantown WV 26506
304/293-5531

Accredited
Bachelor's, Master's
Residency (EW, IS)

Bachelor of Arts through the West Virginia Board of Regents Degree Program, just described. Master of Arts in education and Master of Business Administration available through evening study.

WICHITA STATE UNIVERSITY
Wichita KS 67208
316/689-3100

Accredited
Bachelor's
Residency (LE)

Bachelor's degree program in which more than 80% of the required units can be earned through an assessment of prior learning experiences, in the External Credit Program. The assessment is based on a portfolio provided by the student, and must take place after enrollment. A flat fee of $25 is charged, regardless of the amount of credit given.

WINONA STATE COLLEGE
Winona MN 55987
507/457-2110

Accredited
Bachelor's, Master's
Residency (EW)

Bachelor of Arts in arts and science and business administration; Bachelor of Science in education; Master of Arts in English and history; Master of Science in education, educational administration; all available entirely through evening study.

WITTENBERG UNIVERSITY
School of Community Education, P.O. Box 720,
    Springfield OH 45501
513/327-7012

Accredited
Bachelor's
Residency (EW)

The degrees of B.A. in Liberal Studies, B.A. in Business Administration, and a B.A. degree completion program for registered nurses, can be done entirely through evening study. Credit is given for standard equivalency exams, and special exams will be devised in areas not covered by standard tests.

WORLD OPEN UNIVERSITY
Drawer 5505, Orange CA 92667
714/633-3377

Unaccredited
Bachelor's, Master's,
    Doctorates
Non-resident

Degrees at all levels in engineering, science, humanities, languages, literature, mathematics and other subjects, entirely by correspondence study. The cost of the Master's program is over $4,000 and the Doctorate ranges from $7,000 to $10,000, depending on the amount of prior experience. The typewritten prospectus is sold for $5 for each of the 29 divisions of the university (thus the entire catalogue would cost $145!). The founder and president is Shu-Tien Li, who earned his Doctorate at Cornell University in 1926. The school was originally established in South Dakota as the Li Institution of Science and Technology. The literature says Dr. Li previously served as president of several engineering schools in China. The main emphasis appears to be in engineering, where there are 18 separate divisions, each in a highly-specialized area. The literature states, "WOU has faculties of excellence by providing only profoundly learned and experienced [people] who are well qualified as full professors. She has no associate professors. She has no assistant professors. She has no instructors. She is mainly a graduate school. Her operations are entirely regardless of distance, nationality, race, and creed."

Comment: It may be that the faculty is so eminent in its specialties that it can be beneficial to a student's career merely to have worked with such people, regardless of the quality of the degree itself. But whether or not this is so, she is extremely expensive for an unaccredited school.

WORLD UNIVERSITY OF AMERICA
107 N. Ventura St., Ojai CA 93023
805/646-1444

Unaccredited
Bachelor's, Master's,
    Doctorates
Residency (IS)

The University is concerned with "personal unfoldment and spiritual growth within the traditional framework of an academic curriculum." The University Secretary informed me that "World University is fully accredited in all its programs. Full accreditation was awarded the University in January 1981." Not so. Some of the Bachelor's programs are state approved; the school itself is authorized to grant degrees. The President is Benito F. Reyes, Ph.D. Despite several requests, the school has not supplied the source of Dr. Reyes' degree. The only faculty member with a Doctorate other than from World University claims it from San Gabriel College, a school of which I can find no record of existence. World University's plan is to establish a campus "in every state in the United States and every country of the world."

XAVIER EVENING COLLEGE
College of Continuing Education, Cincinnati OH 45207
513/745-3355

Accredited
Bachelor's, Master's
Residency (EW)

Xavier offers a Bachelor of General Studies, a Bachelor of Science in Business Administration, and other Bachelor's degrees in nuclear medical technology, modern foreign languages, computer science, and communication arts, either through weekend study or evening study. Extremely low tuition is available for people over 60.

Chapter 18

Schools Requiring One Year or Less on Campus

Many traditional colleges and universities require only one academic year, or less, on campus. The first three years can be earned at other schools, or by independent study, or correspondence study, or equivalency exams (although most schools have limits on the amount of credit they will accept by these latter two means). The following data come from many sources including, primarily, college catalogues and bulletins. Because this information is so time-consuming to collect, I am not able to update it as often as I revise the rest of the book. Therefore, since rules and regulations do change, this list should be taken as an indication of the kinds of things that have been available, and not as the final word on the subject. Direct inquiry should be made to any school that has possible interest for you.

On each line is listed the name of the school, its location (unless that is part of the name), and the minimum period of on-campus residency required to earn a traditional Bachelor's degree. Bear in mind that these are minimums, and more time may well be required in individual cases. "1" means one academic year (actually 8 or 9 months in most cases). Fractions like 30/124 mean that 30 out of a total of 124 credits for the degree must be earned at this school. "U" stands for University, "C" for College, and "S" for State.

ALABAMA

Alabama C, Montevallo, 1
Alabama S, Montgomery, 1
Athens C, Athens, 1
Birmingham Southern C, 1
Florence S C, 1
Huntingdon C, Montgomery, 1
Jacksonville S U, 36 weeks
Judson C, Marion, 1
Livingston S C, 3 qtrs.
Oakwood C, Huntsville, 1
St. Bernard C, 1
Samford U, Birmingham, 1
Spring Hill C, Mobile, 1
Troy S U, 1
Tuskeegee Institute, 1
U of Alabama, 25% of credits

ALASKA

Alaska Methodist U, Anchorage, 2 sem.
U of Alaska, College, 1

ARIZONA

Arizona S U, Tempe, 1
Northern Arizona U, Flagstaff, 1

ARKANSAS

A M & Normal, Pine Bluff, 1
Arkansas A & M, College Hts., 1
Arkansas C, Batesville, 1
Arkansas Poly C, Russellville, 1
C of the Ozarks, Clarkesville, 30/124
Henderson's S C, Arkadelphia, 1
Hendrix C, Conway, 30/124
John Brown U, Siloam Springs, 30/124
Little Rock U, 30/124
Ouachita Baptist U, Arkadelphia, 30/124 or 1
Southern S C, Magnolia, 30/124
S C of Arkansas, Conway, 1
U of Arkansas, Fayetteville, 30/124

CALIFORNIA

Armstrong C, Berkeley, 3 qtrs.
Azusa Pacific C, Azusa, 1
Bethany Bible C, Santa Cruz, 1
Biola C, La Mirada, 1
Calif. C of Arts & Crafts, Oakland, 1
Calif. Inst. of Arts, Los Angeles, 1
Calif. Inst. of Technology, Pasadena, 1
Calif. Lutheran C, Thousand Oaks 9/46
Calif. S C
    Dominguez Hills, 1

Fullerton, 1
Hayward, 2 qtrs.
Long Beach, 1
Pomona, 1
San Bernardino, 1
Calif. S Poly C, San Luis Obispo, 1
Chapman C, Orange, 25/144
C of Holy Names, Oakland, 24/120
C of Notre Dame, Belmont, 24/128
C of Our Lady of Mercy, Burlingame, 1
Dominican C, San Rafael, 1
Dominican C of Philosophy, Oakland, 1
Fresno Pacific C, 1
Fresno S C, 24/124
Golden Gate C, San Francisco, 24/124
Humbolt S U, Arcata, 36/186
Immaculate Heart C, Los Angeles, 30/124
Loma Linda U, 24/128
Loyola U, Los Angeles, 1
Mills C, Oakland, 1
Mt. St. Mary's C, Los Angeles, 1
Northrop Inst., Inglewood, 1
Occidental C, Los Angeles, 33 wks.
Pacific Oaks C, Pasadena, 2 sum'rs
Pacific Union C, Angwin, 1
Pasadena C, 1

Pepperdine C, Malibu, 1
Sacramento S C, 1
St. Mary's C, St. Mary's, 1
San Diego S C, 24/124
San Fernando Valley S C, 24/124
San Francisco C for Women, 1
San Francisco S U, 24/124
San Jose S U, 24/124
San Luis Rey C, 1
Southern Calif. C, Costa Mesa, 24/124
Stanislaus S C, Turlock, 2 qtrs.
U of Redlands, 1
U of San Diego, 20/128
U of San Francisco, 1
U of Santa Clara, 1
U of Southern Calif., Los Angeles,
   24/128
Westmont C, Santa Barbara, 3 qtrs.
Whittier C, 1

COLORADO

Adams S C, Alamosa, 1
Colorado School of Mines, Golden, 1
Colorado S U, Ft. Collins, 48/192
Colorado S C, Greeley, 45/186
Regis C, Denver, 30/128
Southern Colorado S C, Pueblo, 1
Temple Buell C, Denver, 30/120
U of Colorado, Boulder, 30/124
U of Denver, Denver, 3 qtrs.
Western S C, Gunnison, 45/180

CONNECTICUT

Central Conn. S C, New Britain, 1
Eastern Conn. S C, Willimantic, 1
New Haven C, 1
Quinnipiac C, Hamden, 1
Southern Conn. S C, New Haven,
   32/128
U of Conn., Storrs, 2 sem.
U of Hartford, 30/120
Wesleyan U, Middletown, 1
Western Conn. S C, Danbury, 1

DELAWARE

Delaware S C, Dover, 30/121
U of Delaware, Newark, 30/121

DISTRICT OF COLUMBIA

American U, 30/120
George Washington U, 30/124
Howard U, 1
U of District of Columbia, 1

FLORIDA

Bethune-Cookman C, Daytona, 1
Florida A & M, Tallahassee, 3 qtrs.
Florida Atlantic U, Boca Raton, 45/180
Florida Institute of Technology,
   Melbourne, 45/215
Florida Memorial C, Miami, 30/124
Florida Southern C, Lakeland, 1
Florida S U, Tallahassee, 45/184

Jacksonville U, 1
Rollins C, Winter Park, 1
St. Leo C, St. Leo, 1
Stetson U, DeLand, 32/128
U of Florida, Gainesville, 45/192
U of South Florida, Tampa, 45/180

GEORGIA

Albany S C, 1
Augusta C, 45/180
Berry C, Mt. Berry, 1
Brenau C, Gainesville, 1
Clark C, Atlanta, 1
Fort Valley S C, 1
Georgia Inst. of Tech., Atlanta, 1
Georgia Southern C, Statesboro, 3 qtrs.
Georgia S C, Atlanta, 3 qtrs.
Mercer U, Macon, 3 qtrs.
North Georgia C, Dahlonega, 3 qtrs.
Morehouse C, Atlanta, 1
Paine C, Augusta, 30/124
Piedmont C, Demorest, 1
Savannah S C, 1
Shorter C, Rome, 30/124
Spelman C, Atlanta, 1
Tift C, Forsyth, 1
Valdosta S C, 1
Wesleyan C, Macon, 1

HAWAII

Chaminade C, Honolulu, 1
Church C of Hawaii, Laie, 1
U of Hawaii, Honolulu, 30/120

IDAHO

C of Idaho, Caldwell, 30/124
Idaho S U, Pocatello, 32/128
Northwest Nazarene C, Nampa, 1
U of Idaho, Moscow, 1

ILLINOIS

Augustana C, Rock Island, 1
Aurora C, 1
Blackburn C, Carlinville, 1
Bradley U, Peoria, 30/124
Chicago S C, 30/128
C of St. Francis, Joliet, 1
Concordia Teachers C, River Forest, 1
DePaul U, Chicago, 1
Elmhurst C, 1
Eureka C, 32/128
George Williams C, Downers Grove,
   48/192
Greenville C, 30/120
Illinois C, Jacksonville, 1
Illinois Inst. of Tech., Chicago, 1
Illinois S U, Normal, 32/128
Illinois Wesleyan U, Bloomington, 1
Lewis C, Lockport, 32/128
MacMurray C, Jacksonville, 30/128
Maryknoll C, Glen Ellyn, 1
Millikin U, Decatur, 1
Monmouth C, 1
Mundelein C, Chicago, 1

North Central C, Naperville, 30/128
North Park C, Chicago, 1
Northeast Illinois S C, Chicago, 1
Northern Baptist Seminary,
   Oak Brook, 1
Northern Illinois U, DeKalb, 30/124
Olivet Nazarene C, Kankakee, 1
Quincy C, 30/127
Rockford C, 30/120
Roosevelt U, Chicago, 1
St. Xavier, Chicago, 1
School of the Art Institute, Chicago, 1
Southern Illinois U, Carbondale, 1
U of Chicago, 3 qtrs.
Western Illinois U, Macomb, 1
Wheaton C, 1

INDIANA

Anderson C, 1
Ball S U, Muncie, 3 qtrs.
Butler U, Indianapolis, 1
Concordia Senior C, Ft. Wayne, 1
DePauw U, Greencastle, 1
Earlham C, Richmond, 1
Franklin C, Franklin, 1
Goshen C, Goshen, 30/120
Hanover C, 1
Huntington C, 30/128
Indiana Inst. of Tech., Ft. Wayne, 3
   qtrs.
Indiana S U, Terre Haute, 30/124
Indiana U, Bloomington, 1
Manchester C, 1
Marian C, Lafayette, 1
Purdue U, Lafayette, 1
Rose Polytech. Inst., Terre Haute, 1
St. Francis C, Ft. Wayne, 1
St. Joseph's C, Rensselaer, 1
St. Mary-of-the-Woods C, St. Mary, 1
St. Meinrad C, 24/135
Taylor U, Upland, 1
Tri-State C, Angola, 45/193
U of Evansville, 1
Valparaiso U, 1
Wabash C, Crawfordsville, 1

IOWA

Briar Cliff C, Sioux City, 1
Buena Vista C, Storm Lake, 1
Central C, Pella, 1
Clarke C, Dubuque, 1
Coe C, Cedar Rapids, 1
Cornell C, Mt. Vernon, 1
Drake U, Des Moines, 30/124
Graceland C, Lamoni, 1
Grinnell C, 1
Iowa S U, Ames, 45/198
Iowa Wesleyan C, Mt. Pleasant, 1
Loras C, Dubuque, 1
Luther C, Decorah, 1
Morningside C, Sioux City, 1
Mt. Mercy C, Cedar Rapids, 1
Northwestern C, Orange City, 30/126
St. Ambrose C, Davenport, 1
Simpson C, Indianola, 1

U of Dubuque, 1
U of Iowa, Iowa City, 1
U of Northern Iowa, Cedar Falls, 36
    weeks
Upper Iowa C, Fayette, 1
Wartburg C, Waverly, 1
Westmar C, LeMars, 1
William Penn C, Oskaloosa, 30/124

KANSAS

Baker U, Baldwin, 7/32 courses
Lindsborg C, 24/126
Friends U, Wichita, 1
Kansas S Teachers C, Emporia, 30/124
Kansas S U, Manhattan, 30/120
Kansas Wesleyan U, Salina, 6/24
    courses
McPherson C, 1
Mt. St. Scholastica C, Atchison, 1
Ottawa U, 1
Pittsburg S U, 30/124
Sacred Heart, Wichita, 1
St. Benedict's C, Atchison, 1
St. Mary C, Xavier, 30/128
St. Mary of the Plains, Dodge City, 1
Sterling C, 30/124
U of Kansas, Lawrence, 1
Washburn U, Topeka, 30/124
Wichita S U, 30/124

KENTUCKY

Bellarmine C, Louisville, 1
Berea C, 1
Brescia C, Owensboro, 32/128
Campbellsville C, 1
Spalding C, Louisville, 32/128
Centre C, Danville, 1
Cumberland C, Williamsburg, 1
Eastern Kentucky U, Richmond, 1
Georgetown C, 30/128
Kentucky S C, Frankfort, 1
Kentucky Wesleyan C, Owensboro, 1
Morehead S U, 32/128
Nazareth C, 1
Pikeville C, 30/128
Thomas More C, Ft. Mitchell, 1
Transylvania C, Lexington, 1
Union C, Barbourville, 30/128
U of Louisville, 30/122
Ursuline C, Louisville, 1
Western Kentucky U, Bowling Green,
    36 weeks

LOUISIANA

Centenary C, Shreveport, 1
Nicholls State C, Thibodaux, 2 sem.
Grambling C, 1
Louisiana C, Pineville, 1
Louisiana Poly. Inst., Ruston, 36 wks.
Louisiana S U, Baton Rouge, 2 sem.
Loyola U, New Orleans, 1
New Orleans Baptist Seminary, 1

St. Mary's Dominican C, New Orleans,
    30 weeks
Southeastern Louisiana S C, Hammond,
    36 weeks
Southern U & A & M, Baton Rouge, 2
    semesters
Tulane U, New Orleans, 1 year
U of Southwestern Louisiana,
    Lafayette, 30/133

MAINE

Bates C, Lewiston, 1
Bowdoin C, Brunswick, 1
Farmington S C, 1
St. Joseph's C, North Windham,
    30/132
U of Maine, Orono, 1
U of New England, Biddeford, 1

MARYLAND

Bowie S C, Bowie, 1
Columbia Union C, Takoma Park, 1
Coppin S C, Baltimore, 1
Frostburg S C, 1
Hood C, Frederick 1
Loyola C, Baltimore, 1
Maryland S C, Princess Anne, 30/124
Morgan S C, Baltimore, 32/128
Mt. St. Mary's C, Emmitsburg, 1
St. Joseph C, Emmitsburg, 1
Salisbury S C, 30/128
Towson S C, 1
U of Maryland, College Park, 30/120
Washington C, Chestertown, 1
Western Maryland C, Westminster,
    30/124

MASSACHUSETTS

American International C, Springfield,
    30/120
Assumption C, Worcester, 1
Atlantic Union C, S. Lancaster, 30/128
Boston U, 1
Eastern Nazarene C, Quincy, 1
Emerson C, Boston, 1
Hebrew Teachers C, Brookline, 1 sem.
Lesley C, Cambridge, 1
Lowell Tech. Inst., 1
Mass. Inst. of Tech., Cambridge, 1
New England Conservatory of Music,
    Boston, 1
Nichols C of Business Administration,
    Dudley, 1
Northeastern U, Boston, 1
Springfield, C, 1
State College
    Boston, 1
    Fitchburg, 30/124
    Framingham, 30/123
    Lowell, 1
    N. Adams, 1
    Salem, 1

Westfield, 1
Suffolk U, Boston, 1
U of Mass., Amherst, 1
Western New England C, Springfield,
    30/124

MICHIGAN

Alma C, 1
Andrews U, Berrien Spgs, 45/190
Calvin C, Grand Rapids, 1
Central Michigan U, Mt. Pleasant,
    30/124
Eastern Michigan U, Ypsilanti, 30/124
Ferris S C, Big Rapids, 48/200
Hillsdale C, 1
Hope C, Holland, 1
Lawrence Inst. of Technology,
    Southfield, 3 qtrs.
Madonna C, Livonia, 1
Mercy C, Detroit, 1
Michigan S U, E. Lansing, 45/183
Michigan Tech. U, Houghton, 1
Northern Michigan U, Marquette, 4/32
Sacred Heart Seminary, Detroit, 1
Siena Heights C, Adrian, 1
Spring Arbor C, 2 sem.
U of Detroit, 32/128
U of Michigan, Ann Arbor, 24/120
Wayne S U, Detroit, 45/180
Western Michigan U, Kalamazoo,
    15/124

MINNESOTA

Augsburg C, Minneapolis, 1
Bethel C, St. Paul, 30/125
C of St. Benedict, St. Joseph, 1
C of St. Scholastica, Duluth, 1
C of St. Thomas, St. Paul, 1
Gustavus Adolphus C, St. Peter, 1
Concordia C, Moorhead, 1
Concordia C, St. Paul, 1
Mankato S C, 45/192
Minneapolis School of Art, 1
Moorhead S C, 3 qtrs.
St. Cloud S C, 3 qtrs.
St. John's U, Collegeville, 1
St. Mary's C, Winona, 1
St. Paul Seminary, 1
U of Minnesota, Minneapolis, 1
Winona S C, 45/192

MISSISSIPPI

Alcorn A&M, Lorman, 30/127
Belhaven C, Jackson, 30/124
Blue Mountain C, 36 weeks
Delta S C, Cleveland, 2 sem.
Jackson S C, 48/193½
Milsaps C, Jackson, 3 summers
Mississippi C, Clinton, 30/120
Mississippi C for Women, Columbus,
    30/120
Mississippi S U, State College, 32/128

Tougaloo C, 1
U of Mississippi, University, 1
U of Southern Mississippi, Hattiesburg, 45/192
William Carey C, Hattiesburg, 1

MISSOURI

Avila C, Kansas City, 1
Cardinal Clennon C, St. Louis, 1
Central Methodist C, Fayette, 1
Culver Stockton C, Canton, 30/124
Drury C, Springfield, 1
Evangel C, Springfield, 1
Fontbonne C, St. Louis, 32/128
Harris-Stowe C, St. Louis, 30/135
Immaculate Conception C, Conception, 1
Lincoln U, Jefferson City, 30/120
Missouri Southern C, Joplin, 1
Missouri Valley C, Marshall, 30/120
Northeast Missouri S C, Kirksville, 3 qtrs.
Northwest Missouri S C, Maryville, 30/120
Park C, Parkville, 1
Rockhurst C, Kansas City, 1
St. Louis C of Pharmacy, 1
St. Louis U, 1
School of the Ozarks, Pt. Lookout, 1
Southeast Missouri S C, Cape Girardeau, 30/124
Southwest Baptist C, Bolivar, 30/124
Southwest Missouri S C, Springfield, 30/124
Stephens C, Columbia, 1
U of Missouri
    Columbia, 1
    Kansas City, 30/124
    St. Louis, 1
Washington U, St. Louis, 1
Webster C, St. Louis, 1
Westminster C, Fulton, 1
William Woods C, Fulton, 1

MONTANA

Carroll C, Helena, 1
C of Great Falls, 1
Eastern Montana C, Billings, 1
Northern Montana C, Havre, 3 qtrs.
Rocky Mountain C, Billings, 30/124
U of Montana, Missoula, 3 qtrs.
Western Montana C, Dillon, 1

NEBRASKA

Chadron S C, 1
C of St. Mary, Omaha, 30/128
Concordia Teachers C, Seward, 30/128
Creighton U, Omaha, 1
Dana C, Blair, 1
Doane C, Crete, 1
Kearney S C, 36 weeks
Midland Lutheran C, Fremont, 1

Nebraska Wesleyan U, 30/125
Peru S C, Peru, 30/125
U of Nebraska, Lincoln, 1
U of Nebraska, Omaha, 30/125
Wayne S C, 1

NEVADA

U of Nevada, Las Vegas, 32/128

NEW HAMPSHIRE

Keene S C, 1
New England C, Henniker, 1
Plymouth S C, 1
U of New Hampshire, Durham, 1

NEW JERSEY

Bloomfield C, 32/124
Don Bosco C, Newton, 1
Fairleigh Dickinson U, Rutherford, 32/128
Glassboro S C, 1
Jersey City S C, 1
Monmouth C, W. Long Branch, 1
Montclair S C, Upper Montclair, 1
Newark C of Engineering, 1
Paterson S C, Wayne, 32/124-8
Rutgers U, New Brunswick, 30/120
St. Peter's, Jersey City, 1
Trenton S C, 1
Upsala C, East Orange, 1

NEW MEXICO

C of Santa Fe, 30/132
Eastern New Mexico U, Portales, 32/128
New Mexico Inst. of Mining, Socorro, 30/130
New Mexico S U, Las Cruces, 30/132
U of Albuquerque, 30/124
U of New Mexico, Albuquerque, 30/124
Western New Mexico U, Silver City, 30/128

NEW YORK

Adelphi U, Garden City, 30/120
Alfred U, 1
Canisius C, Buffalo, 1
City U of New York
    Brooklyn C, 1
    City C, 1
    Hunter C, 1
    Queens C, 30/128
Elmira C, 1
Hartwick C, Oneonta, 1
Hobart & Wm. Smith, Geneva, 1
Hofstra U, Hempstead, 1
Houghton C, 1
Ithaca C, 1
Julliard School, New York, 1
Klempner Institute, New York, 1

LeMoyne C, Syracuse, 1
Long Island U, Greenvale, 32/128
Manhattan School of Music, New York, 1
Marist C, Poughkeepsie, 1
Maryknoll Seminary, 1
Medaille C, Buffalo, 1
Mills C, New York, 30/125
New York U, New York, 1
Nyack Missionary C, 1
Pace C, New York, 1
Pratt Institute, Brooklyn, 32/132
Rensselaer Poly. Inst., Troy, 1
Roberts Wesleyan C, North Chili, 8/36
Rochester Inst. of Tech., 45/180
St. Bonaventure U, 1
St. Francis C, Brooklyn, 32/132
St. John's U, Jamaica, 1
St. Joseph's Seminary, Yonkers, 1
St. Lawrence U, Canton, 30/120
Skidmore C, Saratoga Springs, 2 sem.
State U of New York
    Binghamton, 7½/31
    Buffalo, 1
    Stony Brook, 1
State U C at
    Brockport, 1
    Fredonia, 1
    New Paltz, 1
    Oswego, 1
    Plattsburgh, 1
    Potsdam, 1
Syracuse U, 30/120
Union C & U, Schenectady, 1
Wagner C, Staten Island, 1

NORTH CAROLINA

Appalachian S U, Boone, 45/195
Atlantic Christian C, Wilson, 1
Barber-Scotia C, Concord, 1
Bennett C, Greensboro, 1
Campbell C, Buie's Creek, 1
Catawba C, Salisbury, 1
Duke U, Durham, 1
Eastern Carolina U, Greenville, 1
Elizabeth City S U, 1
Elon C, 1
Fayetteville S U, 1
Greensboro C, 1
Guilford C, Greensboro, 1
Johnson C. Smith C, Charlotte, 1
Lenoir Rhyne C, Hickory, 1
Mars Hill C, 1
North Carolina S U, Raleigh, 1
North Carolina C, Durham, 1
Pembroke S C, 32/128
Pfeiffer C, Misenheimer, 1
Queens C, Charlotte, 30/124
St. Andrews Presbyterian C, Laurinburg, 1
Salem C, Winston-Salem, 24/126
Shaw U, Raleigh, 1
U of North Carolina, Wilmington, 1

Western Carolina U, Collowhee, 3 qtrs.
Winston-Salem S U, 30/127

NORTH DAKOTA

Dickinson S C, 1
Jamestown C, 1
Mayville S C, 3 qtrs.
Minot S C, 45/196
North Dakota S U, Fargo, 1
U of North Dakota, Grand Forks,
    30/125
Valley City S C, 3 qtrs.

OHIO

Ashland C, 1
Athenaeum of Ohio, Norwood, 1
Bluffton C, 30/124
Capital U, Columbus, 1
Case Western Reserve, Cleveland, 1
Central S U, Wilberforce, 30/186
Cleveland S U, 45/192
C of Mt. St. Joseph, 30/128
C of Steubenville, 1
C of Wooster, 1
Defiance C, 1
Findlay C, 32/128
Heidelberg C, Tiffin, 1
Kent S U, 3 qtrs.
Lake Erie C, Painesville, 1
Marietta C, 1
Mary Manse C, Toledo, 1
Miami U, Oxford, 1
Mt. Union C, Alliance, 9/36
Muskingum C, New Concord, 1
Notre Dame, C, Cleveland, 1
Oberlin C, Oberlin, 24/112
Ohio Dominican C, Columbus, 1
Ohio Northern U, Ada, 3 qtrs.
Ohio S U, Columbus, 3 qtrs.
Ohio U, Athens, 1
Otterbein C, Westerville, 1
Our Lady of Cincinnati C, 1
St. John C of Cleveland, 32/128
U of Acron, 1
U of Cincinnati, 1
U of Dayton, 1
U of Toledo, 1
Western C for Women, Oxford, 1
Wilberforce U, 30/124
Wilmington C, 30/124
Wittenberg U, Springfield, 8/36
Xavier U, Cincinnati, 32/128
Youngstown S U, 45/190

OKLAHOMA

Bethany Nazarene C, 30/124
Central S C, Edmond, 30 wks.
Langston U, 30/124
Northeast S C, Tahlequah, 30/124
Oklahoma Baptist U, Shawnee, 1
Oklahoma Christian C,
    Oklahoma City, 30/126

Oklahoma City U, 2 sem.
Oklahoma C of Liberal Arts,
    Chickasha, 30/124
Oklahoma S U, Stillwater, 1
Phillips U, Enid, 30/128
Southeastern S C, Durant, 30/124
U of Oklahoma, Norman, 1
U of Tulsa, 1

OREGON

Cascade C, Portland, 45/186
Eastern Oregon C, La Grande, 45/192
George Fox C, Newberg, 45/189
Lewis & Clark C, Portland, 9/37
Linfield C, McMinnville, 1
Marylhurst C, 24/128
Mt. Angel C, 30/128
Mt. Angel Seminary, St. Benedict, 1
Northwest Christian C, Eugene, 1
Oregon C of Education,
    Monmouth, 45/192
Oregon S U, Corvallis, 45/192
Pacific U, Forest Grove, 30/124
Portland S U, 45/186
Reed C, Portland, 1
Southern Oregon C, Ashland, 1
U of Oregon, Eugene, 45/186
Warner Pacific C, Portland, 1

PENNSYLVANIA

Albright C, Reading, 1
Alliance C, Cambridge Springs, 30/128
Bucknell U, Lewisburg, 1
California S C, California, 1
Carnegie-Mellon U, Pittsburgh, 1
Cedar Crest C, Allentown, 1
Cheyney S C, 1
Clarion S C, 1
C Misericordia, Dallas, 32/128
Drexel Inst. of Technology,
    Philadelphia, 1
Duquesne U, Pittsburgh, 1
E. Stroudsburg S C, 1
Eastern Baptist C, St. Davids, 32/127
Edinboro S C, 32/128
Elizabethtown C, 30/128
Franklin & Marshall C, Lancaster, 1
Gannon C, Erie, 30/128
Geneva C, Beaver Falls, 30/126
Gettysburg C, 1
Haverford C, 1
Holy Family C, Philadelphia, 1
Indiana U, Indiana, 1
Juniata C, Huntingdon, 1
Kutztown S C, 1
La Salle C, Philadelphia, 2 sem.
Lebanon Valley C, Annville, 1
Lehigh U, Bethlehem, 1
Lock Haven S C, 1
Mansfield S C, 1
Millersville S C, 1
Moor C of Art, Philadelphia, 1

Mt. Mercy C, Pittsburgh, 30/128
Muhlenberg C, Allentown, 1
Pennsylvania S U, University Park,
    36/124+
St. Francis C, Loretto, 1
S. Joseph's C, Philadelphia, 1
Shippensburg S C, 1
Slippery Rock S C, 1
Temple U, Philadelphia, 1
Thiel C, Greenville, 30/124
U of Pittsburgh, 2 terms
Waynesburg C, 1
West Chester S C, 1
Wilkes C, Wilkes-Barre, 1

RHODE ISLAND

Barrington C, 1
Bryant C, Providence, 1
Rhode Island C, Providence, 1
Salve Regina C, Newport, 1
U of Rhode Island, Kingston, 1

SOUTH CAROLINA

Benedict C, Columbia, 1
Claflin C, Orangeburg, 30/124
Coker C, Hartsville, 1
C of Charleston, 1
Columbia C, 30/127
Converse C, Spartanburg, 1
Furman U, Greenville, 8/32
Lander C, Greenwood, 1
Limestone C, Gaffney, 1
Newberry C, Newberry, 1
Presbyterian C, Clinton, 24/126
South Carolina S C, Orangeburg, 1
U of South Carolina, Columbia, 30/120
Winthrop C, Rock Hill, 1
Wofford C, Spartanburg, 1

SOUTH DAKOTA

Augustana C, Sioux Falls, 1
Black Hills S C, Spearfish, 32/128
Dakota Wesleyan C, Mitchell, 30/130
General Beadle S C, Madison, 1
Huron C, 24/128
Mt. Marty C, Yankton, 1
Sioux Falls C, 1
South Dakota School of Mines,
    Rapid City, 1
South Dakota S C, Brookings, 1
Yankton C, 1

TENNESSEE

Austin Peay S U, Clarksville, 3 qtrs.
Belmont C, Nashville, 24/128
Bethel C, McKenzie, 1
Carson-Newman C, Jefferson City,
    30/128
David Lipscomb C, Nashville, 3 qtrs.
East Tennessee S U,
    Johnson City, 3 qtrs.

Fisk U, Nashville, 1
George Peabody C for Teachers,
   Nashville, 2 sem.
King C, Bristol, 1
Knoxville C, 1
Lambuth C, Jackson, 1
Lane C, Jackson, 2 sem.
Le Moyne C, Memphis, 1
Lincoln Memorial U, Harrogate, 1
Memphis Academy of Arts, 1
Memphis S U, 24/132
Middle Tennessee S U,
   Murfreesboro, 1
Milligan C, 2 sem.
Siena C, Memphis, 1
Southern Missionary C,
   Collegedale, 30/128
Tennessee A&I, Nashville, 1
Tusculum C, Greeneville, 2 sem.
Union U, Jackson, 1
U of Tennessee, Knoxville, 45/194+

TEXAS

Abilene Christian U, Abilene, 1
Angelo S C, San Angelo, 30/128
Austin C, Sherman, 8/35
Bishop C, Dallas, 1
East Texas Baptist C, Marshall, 30/128
Hardin Simmons U, Abilene, 30/124
Howard Payne C, Brownwood, 24/134
Huston-Tillotson C, Austin, 30/124
Incarnate Word C, San Antonio, 1
Jarvis Christian C, Hawkins, 1
Lamar S C, Beaumont, 30/126
Mary Hardin-Baylor, Belton, 1
McMurry C, Abilene, 1
Midwestern U, Wichita Falls, 30/126
North Texas S U, Denton, 2 sem.
Our Lady of the Lake C,
   San Antonio, 30/128
Pan American C, Edinburg, 24/124
Rice U, Houston, 1
Sacred Heart Dominican C, Houston, 1
St. Mary's U, San Antonio, 1
Sam Houston S C, Huntsville, 30/130
Southwest Texas S C, San Marcos, 2 s.
Southwestern U, Georgetown, 1
Sul Ross S C, Alpine, 30 weeks
Texas A&I U, Kingsville, 30/124
Texas Tech, Lubbock, 30/124
Texas Wesleyan C, Ft. Worth, 1
Trinity U, San Antonio, 30/128+
U of Corpus Christi, 30/124
U of Dallas, 1
U of Houston, 30/122
U of Texas
   Austin, 2 sem.
   Arlington, 30/122
   El Paso, 24/123+
Wayland Baptist C, Plainview, 30/124
Wiley C, Marshall, 1

UTAH

Brigham Young U, Provo, 30/128
Southern Utah S C, Cedar City, 1
Westminster C, Salt Lake City, 1

VERMONT

Castleton S C, 30/124
Goddard C, Plainfield, 2 summers
Johnson S C, 1
Lyndon S C, Lyndonville, 30/124+
Marlboro C, 1
St. Michael's C, Winooski, 1
Trinity C, Burlington, 1
U of Vermont, Burlington, 30/120
Windham C, Putney, 24/124

VIRGINIA

Bridgewater C, 30/128
C of Wm. & Mary,
   Williamsburg, 30/120
Eastern Mennonite C, Harrisonburg, 1
Hampden-Sydney C, 1
Hampton Institute, 1
James Madison U, 2 sem.
Longwood C, Farmville, 1
Lynchburg C, 1
Old Dominion C, Norfolk, 2 sem.
Radford C, 1
Richmond Prof. Institute, 30/124
Roanoke C, Salem, 1
St. Paul's C, Lawrenceville, 30/125
Virginia Poly. Inst., Blacksburg, 1
Virginia S U, Petersburg, 1
Virginia Union U, Richmond, 1
Washington & Lee, Lexington, 1

WASHINGTON

Central Washington S C,
   Ellensburg, 45/192
Eastern Washington S C,
   Cheyney, 45/192
Fort Wright C, Spokane, 1
Gonzaga U, Spokane, 1
Pacific Lutheran U, Tacoma, 30/128
St. Martin's C, Olympia, 1
Seattle Pacific C, 45/192
U of Puget Sound, Tacoma, 30/124
U of Washington, Seattle, 1
Walla Walla C, College Place, 1
Washington S U, Pullman, 30/120
Western Wash. S C, Bellingham, 1
Whitworth C, Spokane, 1

WEST VIRGINIA

Alderson Broaddus C, Philippi, 30/120
Bethany C, Bethany, 1
Bluefield S C, 36 weeks
Davis & Elkins, Elkins, 1
Fairmont S C, 32/128
Marshall U, Huntington, 1
Morris Harvey C, Charleston, 32/128

Salem C, 1
Shepherd C, Shepherdstown, 32/128
West Liberty S C, 32/128
West Virginia Inst. of Technology,
   Montgomery, 30/128
West Virginia S C, Institute, 30/125+
West Virginia U, Morgantown, 30/128
West Virginia Wesleyan C,
   Buckhannon, 32/128

WISCONSIN

Alverno C, Milwaukee, 32/128
Beloit C, 6/30
Cardinal Stritch C, Milwaukee, 30/128
Carroll C, Waukesha, 1
Edgewood C, Madison, 32/128
Holy Family C, Manitowoc, 30/128
Lakeland C, Sheboygan, 1
Marian C, Fond du Lac, 1
Marquette U, Milwaukee, 1
Mt. Mary C, Milwaukee, 1
Northland C, Ashland, 45/180
Ripon C, Ripon, 1
St. Francis Seminary, Milwaukee, 1
Stout S U, Menomonie, 32/128+
U of Wisconsin, Madison, 30/120
Viterbo C, La Crosee, 30/128+
Wisconsin S U
   Eau Claire, 1
   La Crosse, 32/128
   Osh Kosh, 30/128
   Platteville, 32/128
   River Falls, 1
   Stevens Point, 30/124
   Superior, 30/124
   Whitewater, 32/130

WYOMING

U of Wyoming, Laramie, 30/128+

Chapter 19

Weekend Colleges

As one answer to ever-increasing expenses, many colleges attempt to make more efficient use of their facilities. A multi-million-dollar campus standing virtually empty for three months each summer, and for 18 hours each weekday during the term, and all weekend long, is a terrific waste.

That is one reason we have summer school, all-year school, night school, and, a fairly recent development, the weekend college.

Weekend college is a degree program in which all the courses are taught intensively, on Friday evening, Saturday, and/or Sunday. In some cases, the student actually moves into a dormitory room on campus on Friday afternoon, remaining until Sunday afternoon, living the life of a student for 48 hours each week.

The number of weekend colleges has grown rapidly in the last few years, and doubtless will continue to do so. Some schools offer courses every weekend; others have programs one or two weekends per month, with independent study in between. In most cases, it will take just about as long to earn a Bachelor's degree at a weekend college as at a regular college — around four years, starting from scratch — but of course with a great deal less time on campus, and with the opportunity to hold a full-time job as well.

The following schools have well-established weekend programs. Details of their offerings can be found in the alphabetical listings in Chapter 17.

Anna Maria College
Aquinas College
Baldwin-Wallace College
City College (Seattle)
College Misericordia
C. W. Post College
Elizabeth Seton College
Heidelberg College
Hiram College
Holy Names College
Lake Erie College

Marymount College (New York)
Mount Saint Joseph College
Mundelein College
Our Lady of the Lake College
Pace College
Point Park College
Southeastern University (Washington, D.C.)
Texas Southern University
Trinity College
Wentworth Institute of Technology (Boston)
Xavier University

Chapter 20

High School and Associate Degrees

HIGH SCHOOL DIPLOMAS BY MAIL

The first thing to say is that, even if you have not completed high school, you probably will not need to do so in order to enroll in a non-traditional degree program or a non-traditional school.

The high school diploma is the usual "ticket of admission" to a traditional university. However, many universities, both traditional and non-traditional, believe that anywhere from two to seven years of life experience or job experience is at least the equivalent of a high school diploma. So if you are over age 25, you should have no trouble finding schools that do not require a high school diploma. If you are between 20 and 25, you may have to shop around a bit, and if you are under 20, it may well be necessary to complete high school first.

Here are the three ways to do it by mail. Each has its merits, although the first category is probably the best for most people.

1. The High School Division of a University

While many of the universities with correspondence programs listed in Chapter 12 offer high-school-level correspondence study as well, only three major universities actually award high school diplomas by mail. The diplomas are the exact equivalent of a traditional high school diploma, and are accepted everywhere. The first school offers the diploma work in cooperation with a local school district; the second and third issue their own high school diploma.

Brigham Young University
Adult High School Diploma Program
206 Harman Continuing Education Building
Provo UT 84602

University of Arkansas
External High School Diploma Program
Division of Continuing Education
346 West Avenue
Fayetteville AR 72701

University of Nebraska
High School Completion Program
Division of Continuing Studies
511 Nebraska Hall
Lincoln NE 68588

2. State Equivalency Examinations

Each of the 50 states offers a high school equivalency examination which is the equivalent of a high school diploma for virtually all purposes. Although each state's procedures differ, in general the examination takes from three to five hours and covers the full range of high school subjects: mathematics, science, language, history, social studies, etc. It must be taken in person (not by mail). For details for any given state, write to that state's Department of Education at the state capital.

3. Private Correspondence Schools

There are a number of private, usually profit-making, schools or institutes that award high school diplomas or equivalency certificates through correspondence study. They tend to be more expensive and not quite as widely accepted as the university programs or the state equivalency exams. On the other hand, they may be faster and more generous in the credit given for prior experience. There are three accredited schools offering this program:

American School
850 E. 58th St.
Chicago IL 60637

Home Study Institute
6940 Carroll Ave.
Takoma Park MD 20912

International Correspondence Schools
Scranton PA 18515

THE ASSOCIATE DEGREE

The Associate Degree, a relatively recent innovation, is awarded at the conclusion of two years of successful study by community and junior colleges, as well as being given halfway through the Bachelor's degree program by some (but not too many) four-year colleges.

The standard degree is either the A.A. (Associate of Arts) or the A.S. (Associate of Science), but many other titles are used.

Literally thousands of different Associate programs exist, that are available by part time, evening, or correspondence work, or that take into account life experience, previous coursework, or credit by examination.

To describe, or even to list, them all would have doubled the size of this book, and my research has shown that only a tiny percentage of readers have interest. Fortunately, for those who are interested, there is a good directory of existing programs. It is called *A Directory of U.S. College and University Degrees for Part-Time Students,* and it costs $2.95 postpaid from:

National University Extension Association
One Dupont Circle, Suite 360
Washington DC 20036

The Directory is alphabetically arranged by states and cities, but has no index to degrees or subject matter. More than 2,000 Associate degree programs in all 50 states are covered.

Part Four
Specialized Alternative Schools

Chapter 21

Law Schools

The law is a curiosity of the academic world. On one hand, it is possible to graduate from a world-famous law school and not be able to practice law. And on the other hand, it is possible to practice law without ever having seen the inside of a law school.

What makes this unusual set of circumstances possible is, of course, the Bar Exam. In all fifty states of this union, the way most people are "admitted to the Bar" is by taking and passing the Bar Exam. Each state administers its own exam, and there is the Multi-State Bar Exam, which is accepted by a majority of states.

Until the twentieth century, most lawyers learned the law as Abraham Lincoln did — by apprenticing themselves to a lawyer or a judge, or studying on their own, and when they had learned enough, taking the Bar. Although a few states theoretically still permit this practice, for all intents and purposes, this practice survives only in California, where the study of law is, in many aspects, different from the rest of the U.S. I will consider California separately.

In five states, it is possible to be admitted to the practice of law without taking the Bar Exam at all, but only if one has graduated from a law school in that state. These states are Mississippi, Montana, South Dakota, West Virginia, and Wisconsin.

THE BAR EXAM

The Bar Exam has come under increasing criticism in recent years on a number of grounds. One is that there often seems to be little correlation between performance on the Bar and performance as a lawyer. (The exam, for instance, does not test ability to do legal research, conduct interviews, or argue in court.) Another reason is that whites tend to do about twice as well as blacks or Hispanics on the test. (In California, for instance, the pass rate is about 70% whites, 40% Hispanics, and 30% blacks.) Perhaps most damning is this: although the quality of law education continues to improve, the percentage of people passing the Bar has steadily declined in recent years. Can it be, some ask, that there are already too many lawyers in the world, and the already established ones are trying to limit new competition? (Between 1970 and 1980, the number of lawyers in the U.S. increased from 355,000 to 500,000 — a rate of growth more than double that of the population. There are more lawyers in Chicago than in all of Japan.)

THE LAW DEGREE

Until the early 1960's, the law degree earned in America was the LL.B., or Bachelor of Laws. Many lawyers didn't like the idea that lots of other professionals (optometrists, podiatrists, civil engineers, etc.) put in three years of study after college and got a Doctorate, while lawyers put in the same time and got a second Bachelor's. Law schools took heed, and almost universally converted the title of the law degree to a J.D. (which can stand for Doctor of Jurisprudence or Juris Doctor). Most schools offered their alumni the opportunity to convert their old LL.B.'s into nice shiny new J.D.'s, and, naturally, about 99% of them accepted.

THE SITUATION IN CALIFORNIA

California is the only state that permits study of law by correspondence, and it is one of two states (Georgia is the other) that allows graduates of unaccredited law schools to take the Bar Exam.

To study law in California, you must meet two standards: documented study of 864 hours a year for four years, and passing the "Baby Bar" at the end of the first year. The Baby Bar, or, as it is officially known, the First Year Law Students' Qualifying Exam, is given one fourth of the way through, both to help the student determine if he or she is on the right track, and to keep a lot of unqualified people from cluttering up the regular Bar Exam. Only the first 864 hours of study can count toward the grand total of 3,456 required (4 × 864) until the Baby Bar has been passed. (There is some pressure to make the Baby Bar an optional requirement, not a mandatory one, and a bill to that effect has been introduced into the state legislature.)

Incidentally, 864 hours a year works out to nearly 3½ hours of study a day, five days a week. This is surely no short cut. It is, however, a means of bypassing traditional law schools.

California has about thirty traditionally accredited law schools, which are hard to get into, quite expensive, and require three years of full-time study. California also has about thirty unaccredited law schools, which are generally less expensive, easier to get into, and require either three or four years of study, often available entirely by evening or weekend study, and in the case of a few schools, entirely by correspondence.

Law Degrees by Correspondence

Correspondence law school study also requires 3,456 hours of study. The Baby Bar and the regular Bar must be taken in person. However all of the study can be done by mail. The courses have been designed to take that much time for the typical student; some will go faster, some slower. A couple of schools offer a much faster law degree program (two or three years of correspondence study), leading to the Doctor of Jurisprudence degree, but not qualifying the holder to take the Bar. Such programs are popular with businesspeople, medical doctors, and others for whom legal knowledge is important (and the prestige of a law degree desirable), but who have no intentions of practicing law.

Five correspondence law schools are currently active in California, none of them accredited.

BERNADEAN UNIVERSITY
13615 Victory Blvd., Suite 114, Van Nuys CA 91401
213/988-5710

Bernadean is a part of the Church of Universology. It operates from two rooms in a converted motel in a Los Angeles suburb. A full four-year correspondence law program, qualifying students to take the California Bar, is offered for a total tuition of $8,400. The President and Dean is Joseph M. Kadans, who earned his law degree at the University of Baltimore, and is a member of the Bar in Maryland and Michigan, as well as the Bar of the Supreme Court. Kadans claims a Ph.D. from International University—"somewhere in India" he recalls. No law faculty is listed in the typewritten catalogue.

CITY UNIVERSITY LOS ANGELES
1111 Wilshire Blvd., Los Angeles CA 90017
213/481-0950

City University used to operate a residential law program, but now it is all done by correspondence. This is a four-year program, leading to the degree of Juris Doctor. The first three years are the same for all students. In the fourth year, students preparing to take the Bar concentrate on Bar preparation, while others concentrate on an area of specialization. Tuition for the entire degree program is around $7,000. The president of City University Los Angeles is Henry Anderson, whose Doctorate is from the University of California.

COLUMBIA PACIFIC UNIVERSITY

1415 Third St., San Rafael, CA 94901

415/332-7832

Columbia Pacific University offers only a non-Bar, two-year law degree, the Doctor of Jurisprudence, with a specialty in International Law. A combined international law/international business (M.B.A. or Ph.D.) program is also available. Tuition for the law program is around $5,000. The President of Columbia Pacific, Richard Crews, has his Doctorate from Harvard. The Dean of the School of International Law is Michael Bloom, a practicing lawyer. The faculty includes nine practicing lawyers.

SOUTHLAND UNIVERSITY

35 N. Craig, Pasadena CA 91107

213/795-5558

Southland was established as a religious school in Louisiana, and relocated to California in the late 1970's. It offers both a four-year Bar-qualifying program and a three-year non-Bar-qualifying program. Tuition is around $7,000. Southland also offers a combined law/M.B.A. program. According to Southland's founder and President, James V. Kirk, the university "is operated as an educational arm of the Trinitarian Church. Its sole purpose is to follow one of the directions of Christ which is to 'go forth and teach.' " Dr. Kirk earned his law degree at Valley University School of Law, a name not known to the State Bar of California. His Bachelor's and Master's are from Southeastern University of South Carolina (see the "Goodbye/Hello" index) and his Ph.D. is from International University, which operates from the same address as Southland. Three lawyers with traditional law degrees are on the Southland staff.

THOMAS JEFFERSON COLLEGE OF LAW

3923 W. 6th St., Los Angeles CA 90020

213/895-0962

Jefferson apparently offers a four-year correspondence program qualifying students to take the bar. (I say "apparently" because on several visits to the address and on many phone calls, I've never found anyone there.) The brochure, mailed from Hollywood, Florida, describes various law-related programs, ranging from a Bachelor of Science in Law to a Doctor of Juridical Science. Tuition for the four-year program is in excess of $5,000. Jefferson may be affiliated with Heed University.

INTERSTATE LEGAL STRATEGIES

Since the rules for becoming a lawyer can vary so from state to state, the question often arises: What about qualifying to practice law in one state, and then moving to another state to practice?

It is possible, but it isn't easy. All but a few states have reciprocal agreements, in which lawyers from one state are allowed to practice in another state—but only after they have practiced in their "home" state for a number of years, and after passing the Bar exam in the second state. Most states say that you have to have been a practicing lawyer for at least five years before you can move; for a few states, it is three or four years.

So if, for instance, your ultimate goal is to practice law in the state of Illinois, but you do not wish to go to law school, the only solution is to study by correspondence with a California school (or with a lawyer or judge in one of the states permitting apprenticeship), take the Bar in California (or the other state), practice law for five years, and then go to Illinois.

Another thing one can do with the California correspondence law degree is take the qualifying exam to be permitted to practice before various Federal agencies (patent, interstate commerce, etc.) and before Federal courts.

The current standards for admission to the Bar in each state may be learned from the Attorney's

"Desk Book," which can be found in many public libraries, and in a free booklet entitled Rules for Admission to the Bar in the United States and Territories, available from West Publishing Co., 50 W. Kellogg Blvd., St. Paul MN 55102.

STUDYING LAW AT NIGHT

A number of traditional, accredited law schools have programs that make it possible to earn the law degree entirely through evening classes. Ostensibly it is possible to do so while remaining fully employed, although the amount of time involved is great. The evening law degree programs are:

ANTIOCH SCHOOL OF LAW (Washington DC)

BROOKLYN LAW SCHOOL (Brooklyn NY)

CAPITAL UNIVERSITY (Columbus OH)

CATHOLIC UNIVERSITY (Ponce PR)

CHICAGO KENT COLLEGE OF LAW (Chicago IL)

CLEVELAND STATE UNIVERSITY (Cleveland OH)

COOLEY SCHOOL OF LAW (Lansing MI)

DE PAUL UNIVERSITY (Chicago IL)

DUQUESNE UNIVERSITY (Pittsburgh PA)

FORDHAM UNIVERSITY (Bronx NY)

GOLDEN GATE UNIVERSITY (San Francisco CA)

GONZAGA UNIVERSITY (Spokane WA)

INDIANA UNIVERSITY (Indianapolis IN)

INTERAMERICAN UNIVERSITY (Hato Rey PR)

JOHN F. KENNEDY UNIVERSITY (Orinda CA)

LEWIS & CLARK COLLEGE (Portland OR)

LOYOLA UNIVERSITY (Los Angeles CA)

LOYOLA UNIVERSITY (New Orleans LA)

MEMPHIS STATE UNIVERSITY (Memphis TN)

NEW COLLEGE (San Francisco CA)

NEW ENGLAND SCHOOL OF LAW (Boston MA)

NEW YORK LAW SCHOOL (New York NY)

NORTHEASTERN UNIVERSITY (Boston MA)

PEOPLE'S LAW SCHOOL (Los Angeles CA)

ST. JOHN'S UNIVERSITY (Jamaica NY)

SALMON P. CHASE COLLEGE OF LAW (Covington KY)

SAMFORD UNIVERSITY (Birmingham AL)

SETON HALL UNIVERSITY (Newark NJ)

SOUTH TEXAS COLLEGE OF LAW (Houston TX)

SOUTHWESTERN UNIVERSITY SCHOOL OF LAW (Los Angeles CA)

SUFFOLK UNIVERSITY (Boston MA)

TEMPLE UNIVERSITY (Philadelphia PA)

UNIVERSITY OF AKRON (Akron OH)

UNIVERSITY OF BALTIMORE (Baltimore MD)

UNIVERSITY OF BRIDGEPORT (Bridgeport CT)

UNIVERSITY OF CONNECTICUT (West Hartford CT)

UNIVERSITY OF DENVER (Denver CO)

UNIVERSITY OF DETROIT (Detroit MI)

UNIVERSITY OF HOUSTON (Houston TX)

UNIVERSITY OF LOUISVILLE (Louisville KY)

UNIVERSITY OF MIAMI (Miami FL)

UNIVERSITY OF MISSOURI (Kansas City MO)

UNIVERSITY OF PUERTO RICO (Mayaguez PR)

UNIVERSITY OF SAN DIEGO (San Diego CA)

UNIVERSITY SANTA CLARA (Santa Clara CA)

UNIVERSITY OF TOLEDO (Toledo OH)

UNIVERSITY OF TULSA (Tulsa OK)

WAYNE STATE UNIVERSITY (Detroit MI)

WILLIAM MITCHELL COLLEGE OF LAW (St. Paul MN)

YMCA LAW SCHOOL (Nashville TN)

PARALEGAL DEGREES

There are many people who are interested in the law, fascinated by the law, wish to be involved working with the law, but for one reason or another absolutely cannot earn a law degree or be admitted to the Bar. A fairly satisfactory solution for some of these people is to pursue an alternative degree, entirely by correspondence, or with short residency, in a law-related subject.

For instance, many people have earned non-resident Master's or Doctorates in business law, law and society, import-export law, consumer law, law and the poor, divorce law, and so forth. The titles earned would be ones like Master of Arts in legal studies and Doctor of Philosophy in corporate law. Of course such degrees do not permit one to practice law, but for those who are involved with legal matters in the course of their business or their lives, such a degree (and the knowledge that goes with it) could well be of value. Many of the schools offering non-resident non-traditional degrees will consider such paralegal degree programs.

There are also many people with law degrees (traditional and non-traditional, residential and correspondence) who have never passed the Bar, but who are still working in the law. They have jobs with law firms, primarily doing research, preparing briefs, etc. They cannot meet with clients or appear in court, but they are most definitely lawyers working in the law.

Chapter 22

Medical Schools

There are no legitimate correspondence medical schools, of course, but there are some non-traditional approaches to earning a traditional medical degree, including one that can be done at a distance from the school itself.

The traditional approach in the United States consists of attending a regular college or university for four years to earn a Bachelor's degree (in any field), and then going on to medical school for another four years leading to the Doctor of Medicine degree (M.D.), which in turn is followed by anywhere from two to eight years of internships, residency, and training in clinical specialties (surgery, psychiatry, etc.).

The problems caused by this huge amount of time and money (tuition of $10,000 a year or more is not uncommon) are compounded by the even-greater problem of admission to a traditional medical school. The simple fact is that the great majority of applicants are not admitted. Many schools have anywhere from ten to a hundred applicants for each opening. Although schools are not allowed, by law, to have quotas by race or by sex (as they once did), they definitely have quotas based on age. Applicants over 30 have a much harder time getting in, and those over 40 have almost no chance at all. The schools argue that their precious facilities should not be taken up by persons who will have fewer years to practice and to serve humanity.

Is there a shortage of doctors?

The reason it is so hard to get into medical school is that there are not enough openings available. And the reason there are not enough openings is the subject of bitter debate between and among medical and political people. A small schism has even appeared between organized medicine's two accrediting associations, the American Medical Association and the Association of American Medical Colleges.

The Government's Council on Wage and Price Stability points out that there are fewer students per capita in medical school now than there were in 1904. But the Department of Health and Human Services has been recommending that medical schools reduce the size of their classes lest there be a critical oversupply of physicians—a position supported by the A.A.M.C. I like the comment of the Vice Chancellor of one of the Caribbean medical schools catering to Americans: "I'll believe there are too many doctors when I see they have to make house calls to make a living."

ACCELERATED PROGRAMS

One slightly non-traditional approach to the M.D. is that of compressing the total elapsed time between high school and receiving the M.D. by two or three years. Quite a few schools now offer a "3-4" program, in which you enter medical school after the junior year of college and receive the Bachelor's degree after the first year of medical school. Some combined programs are six years

(Boston University, Lehigh University of Bethlehem PA, Wilkes College of Wilkes-Barre PA) and one (Wofford College with the Medical College of South Carolina) is five. Thus the U.S. is slowly moving toward the British system, in which one enters medical school right out of high school, and earns the Bachelor of Medicine in three or four years. The Doctor of Medicine degree there is an advanced medical degree.

Ph.D. INTO M.D.

The first two years of medical school are usually spent learning the relevant academic subjects (anatomy, physiology, biology, etc.). On the assumption that a person who has already earned a Ph.D. in certain fields will have this knowledge, two schools — one in the U.S. and one in Mexico — offer a two-year M.D. to such people. Applicants must have a Ph.D. in the biological, physical, or engineering sciences, or in mathematics.

UNIVERSIDAD AUTONOMA DE CIUDAD JUAREZ
Apartado Postal No. 231, Ciudad Juarez, Chihuahua, Mexico
2-75-60

Juarez offers a special program for non-Mexicans. Since Juarez is right on the border with the U.S., some Americans choose to live in El Paso, Texas, and cross over the border to their classes each day.

UNIVERSITY OF MIAMI
Box 520875, Miami FL 33152
305/284-4323

There is theoretically no age limit to this program, but applicants under 40 have preference. The program consists of eight and a half months of preclinical study, twelve and a half months of intensive medical study, and 10 weeks of elective clinical work. The total cost is around $20,000. Only 36 students are admitted each year, and competition is strong. A few non-U.S. citizens are permitted in each class.

MEDICAL SCHOOLS IN MEXICO

Mexican medical schools have been accepting American students for many years, but only since the early 1970's has it become big business. Very big business. Until recently the medical school at Guadalajara had more American students than any medical school in the United States. And the more-than-2,000 Americans, paying more than $20,000 for the program, were financing the entire operation of the University, and subsidizing the Mexican students, who were paying a small fraction of this sum.

While the quality of Mexican medical education is generally satisfactory, there are some major problems and complications that arise with regard to language, time spent, lifestyle, and the value of the degree itself.

The typical Mexican program requires six years of study, although the final year can often be done back in the United States. All programs are in Spanish, and although the schools that recruit American students claim that intensive language study is successful, this is not always the case. Many Americans report having trouble with the highly authoritarian management style of some Mexican universities. Also, the Mexican government requires all new doctors to donate one year of social service to the people of Mexico. Not all Americans agree to this extra year, and some American licensing authorities go along with that attitude: about 60% of the states in the U.S. will allow an American who graduates from a Mexican medical school, but refuses to do the year of social service, to use the M.D. title, even if the degree has not been awarded. But 40% of the states do not do this, hence an extremely confusing situation.

In addition to Juarez, already described, these are the leading Mexican medical schools accepting American students:

UNIVERSIDAD AUTONOMA DE GUADALAJARA
U.S. office: Suite 1109, 1750 Pennsylvania Ave., Washington DC 20006

More than 2,000 Americans have helped make Guadalajara the largest medical school in the world. The facilities are said to be fair, but clinical training is poor, due to lack of hospital beds in the area.

UNIVERSIDAD DE MONTERREY
Diagonal Washington No. 2810, Pte., Monterrey, N.L., Mexico

A small, newer school (established 1969), modeled after Guadalajara. About one third of the students are non-Mexicans; these must take an admissions test not required of the Mexicans.

UNIVERSIDAD DEL NORESTE
U.S. office: 120 E. 41st St., New York NY 10017

Many foreign students attend this new (established 1970) and rapidly growing school not too far from the American border. Many students report that the attitude of the staff at Noreste is friendly and cordial, in contrast to the antagonistic or dictatorial ones elsewhere.

UNIVERSIDAD LA SALLE
U.S. office: c/o Sol Schwartz Counseling and Placement Ltd., 1279 E. 49th St., Brooklyn NY 11234

This small school requires applicants to take a seven to 16 week "pre-medical" course given in Mexico City to help weed out unqualified applicants. About one sixth of the students are non-Mexican.

MEDICAL SCHOOLS IN THE CARIBBEAN

Medical education in the Caribbean area began to mushroom first as an alternative approach for Spanish-speaking Puerto Ricans who could not get into medical school traditionally. Then businessmen, seeing a good thing, began opening new medical schools on the English-speaking island nations of the area, catering largely to Americans and other English-speaking foreigners. These five schools are the largest; the first three of them are English-speaking, but all cater to Americans:

ST. GEORGE'S UNIVERSITY SCHOOL OF MEDICINE
True Blue, Grenada, West Indies

Founded by a former medical student turned lawyer, this large new school is located on the English-speaking island nation of Grenada (pronounced "gruh-NAY-duh") and caters almost exclusively to Americans. St. George's also operates as the Kingstown Medical College on the neighboring island of St. Vincent, where hospital facilities are better. Tuition is in excess of $5,000 per year.

AMERICAN UNIVERSITY OF THE CARIBBEAN
Plymouth, Montserrat, West Indies

Founded in 1978 by Paul Tien, Ph.D. While the campus was being established, classes were held in leased quarters at Mt. St. Joseph College in Ohio, to the consternation of the U.S. medical establishment. *Medical World News,* which is not enthusiastic about Caribbean and Mexican schools, reported sarcastically that students were working under only three faculty members and using plastic "cadavers."

UNIVERSITY OF DOMINICA
Portsmouth, Dominica, West Indies

The University was established on Dominica (pronounced "doe-muh-NEE-kuh") in 1979 by two New Yorkers, in a leased beach hotel. Permanent facilities are under construction. Medical and veterinary programs are offered at a tuition approaching $10,000 a year.

UNIVERSIDAD CENTRAL DEL ESTE
Edificio Diez, Oficina 508, Conde 202-3, Santo Domingo, Dominican Republic

This school has more American students than any other medical school in the world: more than 3,000, of whom about one fourth are Puerto Ricans, one fourth expatriate Cubans, and half from mainland America. The popularity of the school is attributable to a New York lawyer, Charles Modica, who began recruiting students in the 1970's. All work is done in Spanish.

UNIVERSIDAD NORDESTANA
San Francisco de Macoris, Dominican Republic

In 1979, some disenchanted faculty of Universidad Central del Este left, taking about 300 students with them, to establish this school. Apparently one of the main disenchantments was the U.C.E. policy on clinical residence or clerkships with U.S. hospitals: students were expected to arrange their own, whereas Nordestana has arrangements with several Miami-area hospitals for this purpose. All work is done in Spanish.

OTHER FOREIGN MEDICAL SCHOOLS

The complexities of dealing with the schools just mentioned can be great, but at least they are unquestionably legal, and graduates will be able to take the Education Commission for Foreign Medical Graduates examination that is necessary for licensing in the U.S. There are a number of other schools whose legality has been challenged, although they may well be operating within the law at their location. Schools to regard with extreme caution include:

Borinquen University (Santurce, Puerto Rico)
De Hostos School of Medicine (San Juan, Puerto Rico)
Universidad del Caribe (Carey, Puerto Rico)
Universitarios Xochicalco (several locations in Mexico)
Escuela de Medicina de Saltillo Dr. Evaristo Cruz Escobedo (Saltillo, Mexico).

THE NON-RESIDENT M.D. PROGRAM

One intriguing new opportunity is being developed for a largely non-resident M.D. The Health Sciences Institute of New Jersey has reached a working agreement with the Universidad Tecnologica de Santiago (UTECA) in the Dominican Republic. Students who qualify by taking the equivalent of the first two years of basic science courses elsewhere (or who have a Doctorate in the sciences) may do their clinical work (semesters 5 to 8) under the direct supervision of a doctor and a hospital near their home, with at most a one-to-three month visit to the Dominican Republic. The pilot program will be taking a small number of students over the next few years at a cost in the vicinity of $15,000 for the entire program. The Health Sciences Institute can be contacted at P.O. Box 644, Orange, NJ 07051.

MEDICAL SCHOOL REFERRAL SERVICES

There are several services that smooth the way for Americans to deal with other foreign medical schools, in Europe and the Philippines. It used to be quite common for medical schools in Europe to accept American students, particularly for the first two years of study; then they would transfer into the third year of an American school. Foreign schools are generally making it much harder, now, for Americans to do this. These four services offer frank and realistic information and advice to potential students:

COMMITTEE FOR INTERNATIONAL MEDICAL EXCHANGE
3426 W. Coulter St., Philadelphia PA 19129
215/842-3757

They have a special arrangement with the Faculte de Medecine de L'Institute Catholique de Lille, the only private medical school in France. Students spend two years at Lille, then transfer back to one of the 46 American medical schools that will accept Lille transfers.

FOREIGN EDUCATIONAL SERVICES
Landol International Inc., Route 2, Box 388, Delano CA 93215
805/725-5536

Assistance in dealing with medical and veterinary schools in the Philippines.

INSTITUTE OF INTERNATIONAL MEDICAL EDUCATION
176 Madison Ave., New York NY 10016
212/689-9365

Assistance in dealing with medical, dental, and veterinary schools in Italy and France. They claim to have helped more Americans enter European schools than any other organization.

WORLDWIDE MEDICAL EDUCATION INSTITUTE
318 Fourth St., Union City NJ 07087
201/867-2864

Assistance is offered to Americans who wish to study medicine, dentistry or veterinary medicine in Italy or Spain.

PARAMEDICAL ALTERNATIVES

Not only are there no alternative medical schools, there are no legitimate alternative schools of near-medicine—a category including podiatry, optometry, chiropractic, osteopathy, and related fields. The good schools in this category will require three or four years of study in residence, and cannot be considered non-traditional.

However, quite a few people who have decided that it is either inappropriate or impossible to pursue a medical degree are turning to alternative Doctorates in the paramedical areas. Many schools offering short, non-residential Doctorates will accept students in areas such a holistic health, health care management, nutritional science, homeopathic medicine, rehabilitation counseling, vocational rehabilitation, medical technology, and medical engineering. The degree earned is typically the Ph.D., although the Doctor of Science, Doctor of Engineering, Doctor of Naturopathy, and Doctor of Homeopathic Medicine have been used.

Some of the relevant schools, many of them described in Chapter 17, include:

Clayton University (St. Louis)
Columbia Pacific University (California)
Donsbach University (California)
National College for the Natural Healing Arts (Star Rt. Box 311, Birchdale MN 56629)
North American Colleges of Natural Health Sciences (California)
Santa Fe College of Natural Medicine (New Mexico)
School of Natural Healing (P.O. Box 412, Springville UT 84663)
Tyler Kent School of Medicine (Arizona)
Western University (Arizona)
Wild Rose College of Natural Healing (Box 253, Station M, Calgary, Alberta T2P 2H9 Canada)

MEDICAL DEGREE MILLS

All but the boldest (and/or dumbest) degree mills avoid giving fake medical degrees because legal retribution is usually swift and sure.

There have, however, been two major efforts in recent years to establish medical degree mills. For full details on these nefarious ventures, see the listings in Chapter 24, Degree Mills, for the United American Medical College and the Keppler School of Medicine.

My cautions against having anything to do with degree mills are ten times stronger with regard to medical degree mills. Persons caught using a fake M.D. are almost certain to go to jail for a long time. In fact, in mid 1982, "Dr." L. Mitchell Weinberg, the chap who started United American and was also involved in Keppler, was sentenced to prison for a long spell, for his involvement with phony medical degrees.

Chapter 23   Bible Schools

The First Amendment to the Constitution of the United States proclaims that "Congress shall make no law respecting an establishment of religion, or prohibiting the free exercise thereof."

The various states and law enforcement agencies have generally taken this to mean that churches (and the schools they may establish) can grant any degrees they wish, with little or no regulation from any public agency.

To be sure, there are a great many church-run or church-affiliated schools that offer excellent educations and well-regarded degrees. At the other end of the spectrum, there are also quite a few churches and Bible colleges whose degrees have little or no academic value. Still, in most states and in most circumstances, the Ph.D. sold by the Universal Life Church for $100 is just as legal (if not just as useful) as the Ph.D.'s of Harvard and Yale.

The legality, however, pertains primarily to the institution issuing the degree. It is still possible to get into considerable trouble with a legally issued degree, as in the recent, highly publicized, case of a chap in New York state who was found to be running a family and sex therapy clinic with no credentials other than his Universal Life Ph.D.

Traditional Bible schools generally have graduate programs similar to any traditional school, requiring one or two years of classes and the writing of a thesis or dissertation. Such schools are accredited either by one of the six Regional Associations or by the American Association of Bible Colleges, which is the only recognized accreditor of Bible schools. There are a great many alternative Bible schools, either unaccredited or, often, accredited by unrecognized, unapproved agencies, sometimes of their own creation. Many of these offer all manner of degrees, either in exchange for a small "donation" or for completion of a small amount of work. The degree titles are usually the same as those granted by non-Bible schools, although some offer only religious titles (Bachelor of Theology, Doctor of Divinity, etc.).

There are really only two reasons to deal with such schools: either because you are associated with or have interest in the church that runs the schools, or because they offer a faster, cheaper and/or easier route to a degree than other means. (People who enroll in Southland University, for instance, presumably have no interest in the Trinitarian Church that originally established the school.)

There are 12 traditionally accredited Bible colleges offering correspondence study leading to the degree. I shall list those first, and then describe some of the unaccredited institutions.

ACCREDITED CORRESPONDENCE BIBLE SCHOOLS

APPALACHIAN BIBLE COLLEGE
Bradley WV 25818

CENTRAL BIBLE COLLEGE
3000 N. Grant St., Springfield MO

DALLAS BIBLE COLLEGE
8733 La Prada Dr., Dallas TX 75228

FORT WAYNE BIBLE COLLEGE
1025 W. Rudisill Blvd., Ft. Wayne IN 46807

GRACE BIBLE COLLEGE
1011 Aldon St. S.W., Grand Rapids MI 49509

GULF COAST BIBLE COLLEGE
911 W. 11th St., Houston TX 77008

JOHNSON BIBLE COLLEGE
Kimberlin Heights Rural Station, Knoxville TN 37920

LINCOLN CHRISTIAN COLLEGE
Box 178, Lincoln IL 62656

MOODY BIBLE INSTITUTE
820 N. La Salle St., Chicago IL 60610

PHILADELPHIA COLLEGE OF THE BIBLE
1800 Arch St., Philadelphia PA 19103

REFORMED BIBLE COLLEGE
1869 Robinson Rd. S.E., Grand Rapids MI 49506

WASHINGTON BIBLE COLLEGE
6511 Princess Garden Parkway, Lanham MD 20801

UNACCREDITED BIBLE SCHOOLS

What follows is admittedly just a sampling of what is available. I could fill the entire book with Bible school descriptions, but I fear I lack the expertise to tell a scripturally sound, doctrinally valuable institution from one that is not, especially based solely on the literature. So I present a sampling of what is offered, on the theory that people already affiliated with a church will be aware of what their own church schools are doing, and those who are not can surely find something to suit their needs from among the following array.

ACADEMY OF THE BROTHERHOOD
P.O. Box 2142, Costa Mesa CA 92626

Bachelor's, Master's and Doctorates in philosophy and theology, through the ''decentralized teaching arm'' of the Brotherhood of Peace and Tranquility. Any member ''may secure automatic appointment to the Faculty.'' Anyone may join in return for a ''minimal'' donation to the Brotherhood.

AMERICAN BIBLE COLLEGE
Pineland FL 33945

Bachelor's and Master's degrees in religious education and theology. Formerly known as the American Divinity School, and as such appearing on a list of degree mills published in 1961 by the U.S. Office of Education — a listing vigorously protested by some former students.

AMERICAN BIBLE INSTITUTE
P.O. Box 8748, Kansas City MO 64114

The cheaply-printed 16-page catalogue offers Bachelor's, Master's, and a Doctor of Divinity or Metaphysics on completion of a few correspondence courses and a ten-page thesis at a cost of about $300. This is apparently another name for the Neotarian College, which has been around for many years.

BEREAN CHRISTIAN COLLEGE
P.O. Box 2621, Wichita KS 67201

Bachelor of Theology or Sacred Literature, and a Doctor of Ministry by correspondence, for around $2,000. The catalogue lists 18 faculty and staff, only one with a traditional Doctorate. Same address as Defender's Seminary.

BERNADEAN UNIVERSITY
13615 Victory Blvd., Suite 114, Van Nuys CA 91401

A division of the Church of Universology, they offer correspondence degrees in everything from theology to agriculture to law. The headquarters is two converted motel rooms in a Los Angeles suburb. The cost is under $100 for degrees in theology and over $5,000 for all the others. Bernadean used to be in Nevada, but no longer has permission to operate in that state. Founder and President Joseph Kadans, Ps.D., N.D., Th.D., Ph.D., J.D. apparently still operates from Las Vegas himself. (Speaking of operating, Dr. Kadans vigorously denies a printed report of the American Medical Association that he has sold M.D. degrees by mail for $2,695.) There is also an affiliated Bernadean University of Florida in Fort Lauderdale whose president, Dr. Yolanda Balestra (her Ph.D. is from Bernadean of California) has written me, "I took a few Doctorats [sic] and Masters with Dr. Kadans, a notorious lecturer. Any of these can be considered as REAL."

BURTON COLLEGE AND SEMINARY
6262 E. 9th Ave., Denver CO 80220

This is a case where, despite extensive efforts, I have been unable to separate fact from fiction (or opinion). Apparently a school named the Pike's Peak Bible Seminary was chartered in Colorado in 1927. Somewhere along the line, the name became Burton College and Seminary, which was listed by the U.S. Office of Education on its official list of degree mills in 1961. The listing was protested by Burton. In 1965, according to a publication of the Evangelical College and Seminary of Colorado, Pike's Peak Bible Seminary "was obtained and reorganized by Evangelical Ministers and Churches International." Burton later claimed accreditation, in 1971, by the American Orthodox Catholic Church, but the name of this church appeared in the literature on a label glued over the name of another church (which, alas, I could not decipher). In 1977, Burton filed Articles of Dissolution in Colorado at the same time Evangelical College and Seminary was issuing a three-year catalogue, claiming to have been in continuous operation since 1927 through the Pike's Peak connection. And that's only the beginning, folks. See the listing in this chapter for Pacific Western University for more on this mystifying saga.

CALIFORNIA CHRISTIAN UNIVERSITY
P.O. Box 220, Adelanto CA 92301

They award the Bachelor's, Master's and Doctorate in many fields based on life experience or completion of correspondence Bible courses. They also award the honorary Doctorate on payment of a fee or donation of $1,000 or less. The founder and president is the Reverend Bishop Doctor Walter G. Rummersfield, B.S., Ms.D., Ps.D., GS-9, D.D., Ph.D.M. Ph.D., D.B.A., S.T.D., J.C.D., J.S.D. The school, formerly California Christian College of Los Angeles, is authorized by the state of California to grant degrees.

Comment: When I asked Dr. Dr. Dr. Dr. Dr. Dr. Dr. Dr. Dr. Rummersfield the source of his nine Doctorates, his reply was, "Well, I've really been around." He finally did identify one source as the City Temple Christian University Institute of California, whose literature says the President is Walter Rummersfield. Some California Christian diplomas have been signed by Ernest Sinclair, the notorious gent who has gone to prison several times for selling fake degrees. Dr. Rummersfield assures me there has never been any connection with Sinclair, and "he must of stole the diplomas or something." That this school is state authorized in California says more about California law than it does about California Christian University.

CHRISTIAN INTERNATIONAL COLLEGE AND GRADUATE SCHOOL
P.O. Box 27398, Phoenix AZ 85061

Bachelor's, Master's and Doctorates in theology, Biblical Studies, Divinity, and Ministry through correspondence study. Established in Texas in 1967, they moved to Phoenix in 1977 when "the Lord provided a central home." They claim their credits have been accepted by "secular colleges and universities" but have declined to tell me which ones. Tuition can range from $2,000 on up. The school is willing to establish an "extension center" in conjunction with any church that wants its own Bible school. More than 60 such centers are said to have been started. The only staff member with a Doctorate is the president, Wilford S. Hamon, whose degree is from National Christian University, a school identified by the German Office of Education as a degree mill.

CHURCH OF UNIVERSAL BROTHERHOOD
6311 Yucca St., Los Angeles CA 90028

Honorary Doctor of Divinity degree for a suggested donation of $25. The address is a mail-forwarding service.

DEFENDER'S SEMINARY
P.O. Box 886, Wichita KS 67201

Master and Doctor of Theology degrees through non-resident study for a cost of $600 to $1,200. Same address as Berean Christian College. Originally established in Eureka Springs, Arkansas, as National College in cooperation with Carry Nation. Chartered in Wichita in 1927 as the National Bible Institute and School of Music.

DIVINE SCIENCE CHURCH AND COLLEGE
1400 Williams St., Denver CO 80218

Listed as a "known degree mill" by the German Office of Education. The Director of the college, Paul M. Tyman, says this listing is "erroneous; in no way can such internal religious training be construed as questionable or providing a basis for classification as a degree or diploma mill." Mr. Tyman reports that the Divine Science Church and College has ceased to exist. What happened was that it merged into the First Divine Science Church of Denver, which in turn was renamed Divine Science College. (This seems not unlike saying that The Odyssey was not written by Homer, but by another Greek with the same name.)

EAST COAST UNIVERSITY
1919 S. Grand Blvd., St. Louis MO 63104

Master's and Doctorates in many non-religious subjects. Identical to National Graduate School. The address is an apartment hotel. When I asked for them at the desk, the man acknowledged that East Coast and National got their mail there, but would say no more. Since 1970, they have used addresses in Mobile, Alabama; Tampa, Florida; Dade City, Florida (where the name Roger Williams College is used); Brooksville, Florida; and possibly Sweet Springs, Missouri. The school is "owned and controlled by the Conservative Evangelical Baptist Church Fellowship, Inc." whose president is Andrew McAllister.

Comment: The two top officers of Western Colorado University have their Doctorates from East Coast. John Curtis says that when he attended in the early 1970's, it was a good, respectable residential school, but has "gone downhill since under new management." I can find no evidence of new management or new policies. President McAllister and many of his faculty claim degrees from schools with names like Avon, Staley, Coolidge, Iliff, Worchester, Portal, and Xavier of Bogota. I can find none of them in any reference book.

FAITH EVANGELICAL CHRISTIAN SCHOOLS
Drawer 609, Morgantown KY 42261

Bachelor's, Master's and Doctorates in Bible, theology, Christian education, and the Ph.D. in education or theology, by correspondence, either in written form or by tape cassettes. Tuition is around $2,000 for the Bachelor's and a third of that for graduate degrees. They were established in 1968, "committed to the conservative and evangelical interpretation of the Christian faith." Accreditation is claimed from the Accedition Association of Christian Colleges and Seminaries (same address), which the catalogue readily acknowledges is an unrecognized agency.

FAITH EVANGELICAL LUTHERAN SEMINARY
P.O. Box 7186, Tacoma WA 98407

Bachelor's, Master's and Doctorates by correspondence. Recommended highly by a reader, but they have never responded to my requests for further information.

FLORIDA BEACON COLLEGE AND SEMINARY
6900 142nd Ave. North, Largo FL 33540

Bible-oriented degrees at all levels through correspondence study. I have received a number of letters from disgruntled students, but my own letters to them have never been answered.

FREEDOM UNIVERSITY
Drawer 16936, Orlando FL 32811

Bachelor of Christian Education, Master in Christian Education (the school will change the "in" to an "of" after three years of satisfactory religious work), and Doctor of Christian Education, all through correspondence study. Students are encouraged to start their own Freedom Educational Centers at other locations. The "primary function of Freedom University is to teach and to train in accordance with THE HOLY BIBLE." Twenty-seven of the 46 listed faculty and staff have their own highest degree from Freedom University — a remarkably high percentage. Tuition can be as high as $4,000 depending on prior work.

FREELANDIA COLLEGE
Star Route, Cassville MO 65625

Bachelor's, Master's and Doctorates in theology by correspondence. The school is "accredited only by God." There is no tuition but students are asked to make monthly contributions to the library fund. The catalogue states that the president, C. R. Moore, attended the Dallas Theological Seminary, a well-known, traditionally accredited school. So he did — for 15 days, before withdrawing.

Comment: When an enrolled student wrote to ask Mr. Moore about the Dallas situation, in a most discreet fashion, Moore responded, "The implications are serious. You must decide for yourself what to believe. Self-defense is against my faith. . . . All relationship to Freelandia is hereby severed. We still love and pray for you." I find it hard to believe that any legitimate school would respond in this way. It is unclear whether or not God has withdrawn His accreditation.

GENEVA THEOLOGICAL COLLEGE
Maggie Valley NC 28751

Non-resident degrees, primarily for practicing ministers. Originally established in Indiana, later operating in Knoxville, Tennessee, before moving to North Carolina in 1979. Also operating in England as Geneva Theological School (U.K.) at 139-A Sloane St., London SW1X 9AY. Prior catalogues indicate involvements in Byfield, Massachusetts, and with the Curwen College of Music and with St. Columba's House of Studies, two schools I am not familiar with. The degree programs require a considerable amount of work, including the writing of six to eight lengthy papers and an examination, often given in person.

Comment: Geneva's founder and president, the Reverend R. Banks Blocher, is a sincere and hard-working clergyman. It is almost hard to take seriously a school that has been involved in so many moves and machinations, and currently operates without benefit of residential staff or telephone. Yet a number of readers have assured me of its legitimacy. The English operation has some scholars with distinguished credentials as part of the program, including at least one Lord. The English degrees are given on authority of North Carolina law, which neither licenses nor interferes with religious schools in that state.

INTERNATIONAL BIBLE INSTITUTE AND SEMINARY
P.O. Box 14025, Orlando FL 32857

Bachelor's, Master's and Doctorates in many theological fields. Five units toward the 120 required for a Bachelor's degree are given for each year of ministry, so a person with 24 years of experience would get the degree at once. The Master's requires writing ten 12-page papers, while the Doctorate requires three longer papers. The cost of each degree program is about $400, with a 10% discount for cash in advance.

Comment: The typewritten mimeographed brochure is not professional-looking. The Institute has been answering requests sent to the now-defunct Maranatha Bible Seminary.

INTERNATIONAL SPIRITUALIST UNIVERSITY
809 N. 12th St., Leavenworth, KS 66048

Bachelor's, Master's and Doctorates in esoteric subjects, by non-residential study. The graduate degrees require a dissertation plus a written and an oral examination. Tuition ranges from $200 to $500. The typewritten catalogue may not inspire confidence at first glance, but the content may have appeal for those involved in spiritualist matters who do not require an academic degree. The founder and president of this non-profit enterprise is John R. Griffin.

LUTHER RICE SEMINARY INTERNATIONAL
1050 Hendricks Ave., Jacksonville FL 32207

Bachelor's, Master's and Doctorates in divinity, ministry and theology, by correspondence. Approved by the State of Florida and endorsed by a number of fundamentalist ministers including Robert G. Lee, the "Prince of Preachers," who believes "this seminary has been chosen by the Lord as pivotal in training and equipping men of God to be prophets and leaders in . . . His kingdom."

Comment: If the Lord recommends it, who am I to say otherwise? They appear to offer a reasonable, legal, non-academic degree, and I have had some good feedback from some alumni.

MIDWESTERN UNIVERSITY
8999 St. Charles Rock Road, St. Louis MO 63114

Degrees at all levels in the social sciences, journalism, Pastral (sic) Ministry, hypnosis, religion, and business, by correspondence study. Also known as Eastern Nebraska Christian College, formerly of Valley, Nebraska. Affiliated with the Congregational Church of Practical Theology, which has "little concern for dogma, ritual, ecclesiastical garb, or other trappings of religiosity." Tuition has been reduced from over $4,000 to under $1,000.

Comment: I must confess some suspicion of a school that leaves its address off all printed materials and then rubber stamps it in. There have been other Midwestern Universities in the past in South Dakota, Oklahoma and Missouri, but I cannot determine if any or all are related.

MODULAR EDUCATION
School of External Studies, 7045 N.W. 16th, Bethany OK 73008

Bachelor of Arts in Biblical Studies awarded through one of various participating schools on completion of various "learning modules" (home study courses). The cost can be in excess of $3,000. "We enroll a student," the brochure says, "guide him, handle all transitional paper work, and transfer him to his graduation school at the end of a degree program." The claim is that more than 20 Bible schools make use of Modular Education's courses.

Comment: When I asked for the names of the participating schools (none appear in the catalogue), Modular Education replied with the names of two, saying, "These are excellent schools with good accreditation." In fact, neither one is accredited by any recognized agency.

MOTHER EARTH CHURCH
469 Pacific St., Monterey CA 93940

Established along the lines of the Universal Life Church to ordain ministers and assist them in establishing churches, as well as to award honorary religious degrees, all on payment of modest fees (under $20). Unlike the illiterate founder of Universal Life, Mother Earth was established by Bishop Theodore Swenson, former Dean of Students at the University of California's San Francisco campus. He has also published a very helpful book, *Nonprofit Can Be Profitable*, to assist people in establishing a non-profit corporation as a tax shelter. The book is sold by the Church.

Comment: I have been impressed by my interactions with Bishop Swenson, and by my reading of his book. His degrees may not be worth much, but his advice could be invaluable. The Church is also known as the American Fellowship Church, for those who may be uncomfortable with the Mother Earth name.

NEOTARIAN COLLEGE OF PHILOSOPHY
P.O. Box 8707, Kansas City MO 64114

Doctor of Philosophy and other Doctorates awarded on completion of a few correspondence courses at a cost under $350. Degrees are given in psychology, metaphysics, divinity and philosophy. Courses deal with "the WHY, and WHENCE and WHITHER of God, Man and the World." The founder is Minor C. Hutchinson, Ph.D. They have been in business for at least 20 years, and are either the same as, or affiliated with, the American Bible Institute.

OKLAHOMA INSTITUTE OF THEOLOGICAL STUDIES
1425 N. Rockwell Ave., Oklahoma City OK 73127

Degrees at all levels in Bible education, evangelism, religious education, theology and missions, through correspondence study at modest cost. Graduate degrees require a dissertation of about ten typewritten pages. They are unwilling to "compromise in these days when everything seems to be turmoiling towards socialism and liberalism." Accreditation is claimed from the American Association of Bible Colleges and Theological Schools, an unrecognized agency located at the same address as the Institute.

Comment: They appear to operate under many names, including Oklahoma Institute of Theology, Herald of His Coming Good Bible College, Evangel Bible Institute, Faith Baptist Seminary, and Fundamental Bible Seminary. They may well be operating legally under Oklahoma law, but it hardly matters to them for, as their literature says, "Did Jesus give in to the Pharisees just because they had the law on their side?" (The Pharisees are not a recognized accrediting agency.)

OTAY MESA COLLEGE
3134 Coronado Ave., San Diego CA 92154

Bachelor's and Doctorates for little work, through this college operated by the Ministry of Salvation Church. The Bachelor's requires writing some book reports, and costs $300. The Doctor of Divinity requires a donation of $66 or more. Ordination costs $11. The man in charge is Bishop Maurice Mathias.

PACIFIC WESTERN UNIVERSITY
P.O. Box 2139, Evergreen CO 80439

The saga begins earlier in this chapter under Burton College, which somehow evolved into Evangelical College and Seminary, which is also apparently known as Pacific Western University (which has nothing to do with the other Pacific Western University in California). The Most Reverend Dr. Gordon A. Da Costa, Ph.D., Ed.D., D.Sc., D.D., presiding bishop of the Anglican Church of the Americas, auxiliary bishop of the Free Protestant Episcopal Church, and president of Indiana Northern Graduate School, assures me that Pacific Western is a good, legal, and valid school. They claim accreditation from the American Association of Specialized Colleges, whose ''resident agent'' is Gordon A. Da Costa. The provost is Dr. Jacob Stauffer, who lives several states away, in La Grange, Illinois. The Newsletter of Pacific Western gives its address as 8015 Forsyth Blvd., Suite 2, Clayton, Missouri. When I visited this address I found an empty room next door to the International Institute for Advanced Studies, whose president had been doing Pacific Western a favor by collecting and forwarding their mail to (are you ready?) Bishop Da Costa in Indiana. The Pacific Western University School of Management Studies uses an address in Windsor, Ontario, Canada, but there is no telephone listing for them there. Da Costa was awarded an honorary Doctorate by Pacific Western in 1978, and I think I deserve one, too, for attempting to make sense out of all this. The story continues in the very next listing, Philathea.

PHILATHEA THEOLOGICAL SEMINARY
430 Elizabeth St., London, Ontario, Canada

The story, incredibly enough, continues. Philathea was established in 1937 by Benjamin C. Eckhardt as Philathea College. Eckhardt is the Archbishop of the Free Protestant Episcopal Church, of which Da Costa is Bishop. ''We were very poor,'' Archbishop Eckhardt told a reporter in 1973, ''so the doctorates brought in money.'' According to the *National Observer*, ''Following disclosures of Eckhardt's degree-granting operation . . . an embarrassed Ontario government told Eckhardt to stop issuing Ph.D.'s and to drop the word college.'' A brief association with Da Costa's Indiana Northern was also terminated. When Eckhardt was asked which of his various Doctorates were earned, he replied, ''Yes, ah, the one in theology from Southern something. I haven't looked at it in so long.'' When I listed Philathea as a degree mill in prior editions, I got vigorous letters of protest from its Chancellor Emeritus, a New York optometrist named L. L. Beacher, O.D., Ph.D., M.D., Sc.D., Litt.D., L.H.D. He offered a letter from a former Minister of Education for Ontario stating that the college was within its rights in granting degrees solely because ''Ontario has no general legislation concerning this matter.'' The former Minister of Colleges and Universities told the provincial parliament that Philathea was ''considered a bit of a joke.'' But as the *National Observer* points out, ''over the years, hundreds, perhaps thousands of 'students' from the United States made their academic pilgrimage to Eckhardt's little church on Elizabeth Street . . . to attend a few classes and pick up their degrees.'' For more than 20 years, the Chancellor of Philathea was Harry Cohen, M.D., Ph.D., Litt.D., etc., proprietor of the American International Academy, identified by several sources as a world-wide degree mill. And to bring things full circle, Archbishop Eckhardt was the Canadian representative of the American International Academy.

SAINT PAUL'S INSTITUTE OF BIBLICAL STUDIES
Drawer 4174, Sarasota FL 33578

Degrees at all levels in theology and divinity on completion of a thesis of at least 25,000 words and an ''unassailable Christian stance.'' The cost of around $1,000 includes all textbooks. Students are requested to stay in touch with the Director of Studies once each month. He is Dr. A. E. Longfellow,

B.A., B.D., F.R.G.S., F.Ph.S., Th.D., who has never answered any of my letters asking about the source of all those degrees.

SAVING FAITH ECUMENICAL CHURCHES
P.O. Box 251, Garden Grove CA 92642

Bachelor's degree in Pastoral Theology entirely by correspondence. The church was established as a Delaware corporation by G. S. Johnson, its International Bishop General. The claim is made that "The State of California has no power over the actions of Faith. We hold that the First Amendment gives us the right to education of our own." There is no cost to church members; a donation is asked of others. Ordination is available.

UNIVERSAL BIBLE INSTITUTE
277 S. Bells St., Box 159, Alamo TN 38001

Bachelor or Master of Bible Study, and Doctor of Divinity, offered entirely by correspondence. The cost is less than $200 per degree, and each can be completed in less than a year of home study. The only textbook is the Bible, and students are offered a 44% discount on a special edition of same. The president is Clyde C. Patrick, D.D., whose credentials apparently come from the Neotarian College of Philosophy.

UNIVERSAL LIFE CHURCH
601 Third St., Modesto CA 95351

Bishop Kirby Hensley has reportedly become one of the wealthiest men in California through the sale of ministerial credentials and academic-sounding degrees. Doctorates of all kinds are sold for "free will" offerings of $12.50 to $100 (for the Ph.D.). Bishop Hensley has won several landmark legal battles with the State of California and the Internal Revenue Service over his right to grant degrees, ordain ministers, and not pay taxes. More than eight million people have been ordained, and tens of thousands of degrees have been sold. An indeterminate number of sainthoods have been granted, as well, for a fee of $5 each.

Comment: *The National Review* found Hensley to be a "genuinely religious practitioner freed from the more foolish precepts of orthodoxy by his inability to read and write." His degrees have no academic content or value, but they are among the few that have been specifically declared legal by a state Supreme Court. Of course users of them can still get in trouble.

UNIVERSITY OF METAPHYSICS
326 S. La Brea, Los Angeles CA 90036

The Doctor of Metaphysics is offered entirely through home study, requiring completion of a substantial number of courses, and the writing of a dissertation of as much as 20 pages. The school sells its catalogue for $5, through large advertisements appearing regularly in the *National Enquirer*. The catalogue includes a guide to opportunities available in establishing a "practice" as a metaphysician. "The quality of our Doctoral studies are such as to truly merit Doctoral Degree recognition," they say. Well, perhaps, but not by me, since persons are admitted directly into the Doctoral program without having to have a Bachelor's or Master's degree or equivalent. The University is authorized to grant degrees by the State of California.

Chapter 24

Degree Mills

Degree mills have been around for hundreds of years, and they are still flourishing all over the world. One reason for this is that it is so very difficult to define legally exactly what is meant by the term "diploma mill" or "degree mill."

Surely any school that will send you a Ph.D. by return mail for payment of $100, no questions asked, is unquestionably a degree mill. But what about a school that requires a five-page "dissertation" before giving the Doctorate? 20 pages? 50 pages? 100? Who is to say? One man's degree mill is another man's alternative university.

Another large gray area is the one dealing with religious schools. Because of constitutional safeguards separating church and state, most states have been reluctant to pass any laws restricting the activities of churches—including their right to grant degrees to all who make an appropriately large donation, even if the degrees have nothing to do with religion. (An example is Southland University, run by the Trinitarian Church, awarding law degrees.)

Sometimes hiding behind a church, so to speak, doesn't work. In 1982, federal and state authorities in Oklahoma acted to shut down five degree mills operated by a Missouri religious group, the Disciples of Truth. The Church of Universal Education has been in trouble in at least five states for their dogma that everyone has the God-given right to a degree (in return for a $300 donation).

In this chapter in previous editions, I used to include all the schools that I regarded as diploma mills, religious and otherwise. The problem with this approach was that many of the schools were, in fact, operating legally, either because they were church-run, or because they were in locations with no laws regulating schools. (Arizona, for example, has no state laws covering the starting of schools or the granting of degrees, which is why Arizona has become the mecca for degree mills in the last few years.)

In this edition, I have moved a number of schools that used to be in this chapter either into Chapter 22, Bible Schools, or into the main school listings of Chapter 17 (but, of course, with detailed descriptions of why I don't think much of them).

How Can Diploma Mills Be Allowed to Operate?

The answer is that, as indicated, it is almost impossible to write a law that will discriminate clearly between legitimate schools and mills. Any law that tries to define something that is subjective, whether it is obscenity, threatening behavior, or the quality of a school, is bound to be controversial, because of differing opinions. And yet there can never be a way of holding a meter up to a school and saying, "This one scores 73; it's legitimate. That one scores 62; it's a degree mill."

Also, it is generally the case that when a degree mill only sells its degrees outside the country in which it operates, it can get away with it a lot longer. For instance, a lot of mills now operate from addresses in England, selling their degrees only to people in other countries. The British seem unwilling or unable to stop them (despite the cheapening of the formerly lofty image of British education), and the degree-buyers' countries seem unable to regulate these foreign "schools."

In California, there is a law that has actually encouraged degree mills in the past. For many years, the main requirement for being authorized by the State to grant degrees was ownership of $50,000 worth of property. The law was apparently passed to eliminate low-budget, fly-by-night degree mills. But $50,000 ain't what it used to be, and the law has served to encourage the establishment of well-financed degree mills.

In recent years, the state has added some new requirements to the law, such as a stipulation that some element of instruction be included. But how can you define that precisely? Is 1,000 pages of lessons enough? Of course. How about 132 pages? 27 pages? A page and a half? Who is to say?

When Ernest Sinclair was sent to federal prison in 1978 for selling degrees through his totally fraudulent California Pacifica University, the school was entirely legal as far as the State of California was concerned. Two years later, it was still listed in the official *Directory of California Educational Institutions*.

Another reason for the proliferation of degree mills is that the wheels of justice grind very slowly, when they grind at all. When, for instance, Dallas State College was closed down in Texas, the same people immediately bounced back with Jackson State University in California. When the Post Office shut off their mail there, they resurfaced with John Quincy Adams University in Oregon and Nevada. And the same people may well now be operating from European mail-forwarding services in England, France, The Netherlands, Belgium, and Germany. In the rare instances when diploma mill operators are convicted, they generally receive a small fine; almost never a jail sentence.

WHY DEGREE MILLS SUCCEED

The main reason—the only reason—for the success of degree mills, of course, is that people keep on buying their product. They crave the degrees, and somehow, despite much evidence to the contrary, they really believe that they are going to get away with it.

I must warn you, as emphatically as I can, that it is taking a very very big risk to buy a fake degree. **IT IS LIKE PUTTING A TIME BOMB IN YOUR RESUME.** It could go off at any time, with dire consequences. The people who sold the fake degree will probably never suffer at all—but the people who buy them often suffer mightily.

Credentials are being checked out now as never before. *Time Magazine,* in an article on fake degrees (February 5, 1979), says that "with the rate at which job candidates are now fibbing on resumes and faking sheepskins, graduate schools and companies face detective work almost every time they see an application. . . . Checking up on about 12,000 inquiries a year, U.C.L.A. finds two or three frauds a week. For its part, Yale has accumulated a file of 7,000 or so bogus Old Blues."

Often people get caught when something unexpectedly good happens to their lives, and they become the focus of the news media, which loves stories about fake degrees. A man in Kansas who was appointed to a state commission; a state agency chief in Colorado; a CBS weatherman in New York; a movie studio head in Hollywood; a sex therapist in New York; a physician in California; an elected official in Alabama—all these people, and many more, made page-one news when someone discovered that their degrees were from diploma mills, or that they didn't have the degrees they said they had.

The main consideration in most state laws is the intent of the user of a degree. If you want a Doctor of Sex Therapy diploma to hang on your bedroom wall, you're probably on pretty safe ground. But if you use such a degree to open a marriage counseling service, you'd better be sure that your lawyer has a genuine law degree, because you're going to need him or her!

Another danger of dealing with diploma mills is that you may lose your money and not even get your fake degree. Many mills use post office boxes or mail forwarding services, and they have an unfortunate tendency to take the money and run. Often, too, they are shut down, and during the long period between when the Postal Inspectors first move in and the culprits are convicted (which can be several years), all mail is held in sort of an escrow account, pending resolution of the case. If you must buy one of these things, pay by check. At least you can stop payment later on.

The final decision must, of course, be your own. Before dealing with any of the "institutions" listed in this chapter, you might wish to give serious thought to acquiring a degree from a Bible school instead. They are generally as decorative, equally without academic value, but much more likely to be legal, and usually a great deal less expensive.

WHY THIS CHAPTER IS INCLUDED

I have received some negative feedback for including this chapter in the book at all. But I continue to do so, because I believe it serves three purposes:

(1) It graphically illustrates the scope of the problem, and may open the eyes of legal authorities who have not regarded it as a problem. My guess is that hundreds of millions of dollars a year are spent in the fake degree and credential trade.

(2) It offers a sort of consumer's guide to the person who, after reading all the warnings, still wishes such a degree. Why spend $3,000 on a fake Doctorate when you get one that is just as pretty and just as useless for $10?

(3) Ultimately, I think it will help cut down on the sales of phony degrees, as more and more of these books are sold to company personnel offices and to university admissions offices. You have learned about degree mills from this chapter—but bear in mind that the company you work for probably has a copy, too.

WHAT I AM NOT INCLUDING

There are two particularly objectionable categories of organizations that I have chosen to leave out. The first are the so-called "lost diploma replacement services." A customer can go in and claim, for instance, that he had earned a Ph.D. from Harvard in 1959, but it was lost in a fire. Once he signs a disclaimer, the service will make him a new diploma with the appropriate date, using an original Harvard diploma they have somehow acquired as the model. Because of the disclaimer, the services may well be operating legally. But the buyer of such fake paper is the one who will get in big trouble. Any legitimate school will gladly replace a lost or destroyed diploma on payment of a modest fee.

I have also left out those organizations that write term papers and dissertations to order. Some of them put out huge catalogues listing the papers already written and available at so much per page. And if a customer requires a 300-page dissertation on a specific topic, that will be produced as well. A few states have passed laws requiring the two largest of these services to supply lists of their customers' names, which can be disseminated to faculty members. Big deal. The customers will start using assumed names. So if you want to go out and hire someone to do all your schoolwork for you, you're at least going to have to do the research to find such a person in the first place.

The listings that follow include every institution currently or recently operating that has been identified as a diploma mill, either by me or by one of two agencies that regularly issue reports or lists of degree mills. One is the German Office of Education, which does so on behalf of the European Economic Community (the "Common Market"); the other is *Education & Training* magazine, a respectable British publication. When I am simply passing along the designation of either of these sources, I shall put a "E&T" or a "GOE" after the school name to indicate the source. Complete addresses are given when available.

ACADEMIE BERICHONNE (E&T), France

ACADEMIE COMMERCIALES (E&T), Liege, France

ACADEMIE DES SCIENCE COMMERCIALES ET INDUSTRIELLE (GOE), Belgium

ACADEMIE EUROPE-AMERICANA (GOE), Toulouse, France

ACADEMIE INTERNATIONALE (GOE), Paris and Toulouse, France

ACADEMIE LATINE DE SCIENCE, ART ET LÉTTRES (GOE), Paris, France

ACADEMIE VICTOR HUGO (GOE), Paris and New York

ACADEMY COLLEGE OF HOLY STUDIES (E&T), Sheffield, England

ACADEMY OF ASIA (E&T), England

ACADEMY OF TECHNICAL SCIENCES (E&T), England

ACADEMY OF THE SCIENCE OF MAN: see University of the Science of man

ACCADEMIA DI STUDI SUPERIORI MINERVA (GOE), Milan, Italy. This is a case where the courts decided otherwise. In District Court of Fiorenzuola d'Arda in 1958, one Amorosa d'Aragona Francesco was brought to trial for using a degree from this school. The court apparently ruled that the school may not be great but it is legal. It moved to Milan from Bari a few years later, then went out of business.

ACCADEMIA DE STUDI SUPERIORI PHOENIX (GOE), Bari, Italy. Very likely the same as the school just listed.

ACCADEMIA INTERNAZIONALE DI ALTA CULTURA (E&T), Rome, Italy

ACCADEMIA LATINITATIS EXCALENDAE ARTIUM ET LITTERARUM (GOE), Rome, Italy

ACCADEMIA MONDIALE DEGLI ARTISTI E PROFESSIONISTI (GOE), Rome, Italy

ACCADEMIA ROMANA DI SCIENZE E ARTI JOHN F. KENNEDY (GOE), Rome, Italy

ACCADEMIA UNIVERSALE DE GOVERNO COSMO-ASTROSOFICO-LIBERO DE PSICO-BIOFISICA (GOE), Trieste, Yugoslavia. This is one of my favorite school names. Can you imagine what their school cheers sound like?

ACCADEMIA UNIVERSITARIA INTERNAZIONALE (E&T), Rome, Italy

ADAMS INSTITUTE OF TECHNOLOGY See National Certificate Company

ADDISON STATE UNIVERSITY, P.O. Box 5222, Station F, Ottawa, Canada K2C 3H5, and P.O. Box 68, Rensselaer Falls NY 13680. Sells degrees of all kinds, except medical and dental, for $29.95.

ALABAMA CHRISTIAN COLLEGE: see R/G Enterprises

ALBANY EDUCATIONAL SERVICES, 15A Collingwood Road, Northampton, England. Offers to act as an agent to obtain American Bachelor's, Master's and Doctorates for a fee of $150 to $250. Letters to the director, L. W. Carroll, asking which schools are offered, have not been answered.

ALL-INDIA VIDWAT SAMMELAN (GOE), Jaigani, Allgarh, India

AMBASSADOR COLLEGE (E&T), St. Albans, England. This presumably is a branch of a large California Bible college.

AMERICAN EXTENSION SCHOOL OF LAW (GOE), Chicago, Illinois

AMERICAN INSTITUTE OF SCIENCE (GOE), Indianapolis, Indiana

AMERICAN INSTITUTE OF TECHNOLOGY: see London Institute for Applied Research

AMERICAN INTERNATIONAL ACADEMY (GOE), New York and Washington DC

AMERICAN INTERNATIONAL UNIVERSITY, 3500 N. Central Ave., Phoenix AZ 85012 and 256 S. Robertson, Beverly Hills CA 90211. Until 1979, located in Pasadena, California, run by Edward Reddeck and Clarence Franklin. After being exposed on CBS's *60 Minutes* in an April 1978 segment on degree mills, the University apparently moved to Phoenix, while retaining the mail-forwarding service address in California. Dr. Franklin became President of American National University, at a different address on the same block, which he assures me has no connection whatsoever with American International University. He assures me that the fact that his name appears on the incorporation papers of both American National and American International is an error. Of course I believe him, which is why American International is in this chapter and American National is in Chapter 17. American International, whose catalogue is almost identical in appearance to American National, sells degrees of all kinds for a cost of $1,600 to $2,300. They do require an 8-page dissertation.

AMERICAN LEGION UNIVERSITY (E&T), U.S. location unknown

AMERICAN MEDICAL COLLEGE (GOE), Rangoon, Burma

AMERICAN SCHOOL OF METAPHYSICS (GOE), location unknown

AMERICAN UNIVERSITY, P.O. Box 65, San Ysidro CA 92173. All degrees through "home study" and payment of up to $2,500. The literature says the school is in Mexico, and the degrees are legitimate. This is doubtful.

AMERICAN WEST UNIVERSITY One of the many fake schools started by Ernest Sinclair. See California Pacifica.

AMERICAN WESTERN UNIVERSITY Operated briefly from Tulsa, Oklahoma in 1981 and 1982, heavily promoted during its short life, until closed down by the U.S. Postal Service. Operated by the same folks as Northwestern College of Allied Science, National College, and St. Paul's Seminary, listed in this chapter. See also: Southwestern University in Chapter 17.

AMRITSAR UNIVERSITY (GOE), Amritsar, India

ANGLO-AMERICAN INSTITUTE OF DRUGLESS MEDICINE See National College

ANGLO-AMERICAN UNIVERSITY COLLEGE OF MEDICINE See National College

AQUINAS UNIVERSITY OF SCHOLASTIC PHILOSOPHY (E&T), New York

ARGUS UNIVERSITY, Fairplay CO 80440. A fictitious university, formed apparently just for fun in 1977. Its stated purpose is the selling of Doctorates to dogs and humans. Founder Bill Conklin says that Argus "will confer a degree to any dog whose owner sends a check for $5 to Argus University." The fee for humans is apparently the same.

ARYA UNIVERSITY (GOE), Srinigar, India

ATLANTA SOUTHERN UNIVERSITY Another of Ernest Sinclair's degree mills. See California Pacifica University.

ATLANTIC NORTHEASTERN UNIVERSITY, 210 Fifth Ave., New York NY 10010. The address is a mail-forwarding service. They offer all degrees using well-designed and printed promotional materials which are almost identical to those used by Pacific Northwestern and Atlantic Southern universities. They also offer fake transcripts for an extra fee.

ATLANTIC SOUTHERN UNIVERSITY Operated briefly from addresses in Atlanta and in Seattle, Washington, by the same man who ran Pacific Northwestern University. Closed under an injunction from Seattle authorities in 1981.

ATLANTIC UNIVERSITY As a promotional gimmick once, *Atlantic Monthly* magazine offered a "Doctorate" from Atlantic University to new subscribers. A harmless gag, perhaps, but I am aware of one case, and would guess there are many others, where Atlantic University appeared on a job application resume.

AVATAR EPISCOPAL UNIVERSITY (E&T), London, England

AVATAR INTERNATIONAL UNIVERSITY (GOE), London, England

BELLIN MEMORIAL UNIVERSITY (GOE), Manassas VA

BENSON UNIVERSITY See Laurence University

BIBLE UNIVERSITY (GOE), Ambuhr, North Arcot, India

BONA VISTA UNIVERSITY 807 Van Buren St., Douglas WY 82663. All degrees offered for a fee of $500 to $700. Other Bona Vista literature has been mailed from Sandy, Utah, and from 1300 Market St., Wilmington, Delaware.

BOSDON ACADEMY OF MUSIC See ORB

BOSTON CITY COLLEGE See Regency Enterprises

BRADFORD UNIVERSITY Pal Mar Enterprises, P.O. Box 1796, Altadena CA 91001. All degrees except medicine or dentistry, for $300. The fake diplomas ("use at your own discretion," the literature says) may in fact be "without question the finest ones available," but you'd never know it from the cheaply-printed literature they send out. An outrageously high price for a fake degree. See also Buckner University.

BRANTRIDGE FOREST SCHOOL See Sussex College of Technology

BRETTON WOODS UNIVERSITY (E&T), England

BRITISH COLLEGE OF SOMA-THERAPY (E&T), England

BRITISH COLLEGIATE INSTITUTE See College of Applied Science London. U.S. address unknown. Mail to Dr. Charles Downs, P.O. Box 507, Inman KS 67546 is returned. They issued all degrees for a fee of $100 to $300. The provost is listed as Sir Bernard Waley, O.B.E., M.A., D.Litt.

BRITISH INSTITUTE OF ENGINEERING AND TECHNOLOGY (GOE), India

BRITISH INSTITUTE OF COMMERCE AND ACCOUNTANCY (GOE), India

BROWNELL UNIVERSITY Associated Enterprises, 6326 Autlan Drive, Jacksonville FL 32210. Degrees of this "University that does not now exist" sell for $10. An extra $5 buys a lettering kit so you can put your own name and degree title on. School rings, decals and stationery are sold as well. Also has used the address of 340 E. First St., Tustin CA 92680.

BRUNDAGE FORMS P.O. Box 9966, Atlanta GA 30319. Brundage sells blank forms for all purposes. His college degree form, which you fill in yourself, costs less than a dollar. His motto is, "No advice, just forms." My motto is, "You can get into just as much trouble with a phony fifty-cent Doctorate as with a phony $5,000 Doctorate."

BUCKNER UNIVERSITY Associated Enterprises, P.O. Box 1741, Honolulu HI 96806. All degrees, including some in medicine, for $45 each. They say there is a real Buckner in Fort Worth, Texas. There isn't. The proprietor of Buckner, Mr. John Stacy, also sells fake dgrees from Laurence University. The literature says, "We believe this modestly-priced yet extremely impressive document will give you great enjoyment, prestige, and potential profitability." It is also likely to give you the opportunity to meet some nice people from your county's District Attorney's office.

BUCKNER UNIVERSITY University Press, 8050 S. Main St., Houston TX 77025. This Buckner charges from $80 to $110 for its fake degrees, which apparently are also sold under the name of Franklin, Bradford, and Kingsley University.

CALGARY COLLEGE OF TECHNOLOGY Canada's most ambitious degree mill offered the Bachelor's, Master's, and Doctorate for fees up to $275 from its P.O. box in Calgary, Alberta. The literature included a lengthy profile of the Dean, Colonel R. Alan Munro, "Canada's premier aeronaut." Mail is now returned as undeliverable. The catalogue even included a telephone number. That phone is answered, "Spiro's Pizza Parlor." Truly. Could "Ph.D." stand for "Pizza, Home Delivery"?

CALIFORNIA CHRISTIAN COLLEGE See R/G Enterprises

CALIFORNIA INSTITUTE OF HIGHER LEARNING See London Institute for Applied Research

CALIFORNIA PACIFICA UNIVERSITY Widely advertised and promoted degree mill, operated by Ernest Sinclair, who had previously served prison time for educational fraud. He is now out on parole from his five-year sentence, and the educational world is waiting to see what he does next. California Pacifica degrees sold for as much as $3,500, and if you wanted one from another school, he would get you one from one of the "lost diploma" replacement services, marking it up 1000%. His catalogue showed photographs of his faculty (none of them really there). Sinclair was the main subject of the CBS *60 Minutes* degree mill expose in April 1978. He pleaded guilty to three of the 36 counts on which he was arrested. Even while his trial was on, he opened another degree mill, known both as Hollywood University and Hollywood Southern University. In the past he has been associated with the following fake enterprises: Atlanta Southern University, Lamp Beacon University, Lincoln-Kennedy University, and American West University, as well as with the American Education Foundation, a scholarship scheme which took money in but never gave any out. Despite his record, Sinclair's advertising was regularly accepted by many national publications, including *The New York Times*, and two years after he was arrested, California Pacifica University was still listed in the official directory of state-authorized schools published by the State of California. Mr. Sinclair once sued me for $4 million for writing certain things about him, but he went to prison, having pled guilty to those very things, before the case came to trial. An unsubstantiated report had it that he was running one of his operations at Terminal Island Federal Prison—if true, the first known instance of a University Behind Walls program.

CANADIAN TEMPLE COLLEGE OF LIFE OF THE INTERNATIONAL ACADEMY (GOE), Burnaby, British Columbia, Canada

CARDINAL PUBLISHING COMPANY P.O. Box 5200, Jacksonville FL 32207. They publish a variety of fake diploma forms and blanks.

CARLTON UNIVERSITY See Laurence University

CARNEGIE INSTITUTE OF ENGINEERING See Regency Enterprises

CAROLINA INSTITUTE OF HUMAN RELATIONS (GOE), Sumter SC

CENTRAL BOARD OF HIGHER EDUCATION (GOE), India

CENTRAL SCHOOL OF RELIGION (E&T), England, the U.S. and Australia

CENTRAL STATE RESEARCH CENTER P.O. Box 6, Port Credit Station, Mississauga, Ontario, Canada. Offers well-printed fake diplomas "in memory of famous names." The samples they send out include Christian College, the Ohio Psychological Association, Sussex College of Technology, and The Psychological Association. They also claim to have an office in Columbus, Ohio.

CENTRE INTERNATIONAL D'ETUDES PAR CORRESPONDENCE (GOE), Lieges, Belgium

CENTRO ITALIANO RICHERCHE ELLETRONICHE NUCLEARI (GOE), Rome, Italy

CHARITABLE UNIVERSITY OF DELAWARE (E&T)

CHARLESTON LINGUARUM RERUM POLITICARUM ET JOURNALISTICARUM COLLEGIUM (E&T), Lausanne, Switzerland; Australia, Hong Kong, Mexico, Morocco, and Europe

CHARTERED SOCIETY OF PSYCHIATRIC PRACTITIONERS (E&T), London, England

CHARTERED UNIVERSITY OF HURON (GOE)

CHICAGO MEDICAL COLLEGE, c/o Dr. Theodore Zinker, P.O. Box 1582, Fort Pierce FL 33454. Dr. Zinker apparently represents them, and a number of other medical degree mills. "Your beautiful 11x5 graudate (sic) diploma is printed on the finest sturdy parchtone. . . . It will add prestige and beauty to your office." Or cell. The price is a mere $450.

CHILLICOTHE BUSINESS COLLEGE (E&T), Ohio

CHIROLOGICAL COLLEGE OF CALIFORNIA (GOE), Los Angeles CA

CHRISTIAN COLLEGE See Central State Research Center

CHRISTIAN FELLOWSHIP FOUNDATION See Lawford State University

CITY MEDICAL CORRESPONDENCE COLLEGE (E&T), London, England

CLAYTON THEOLOGICAL INSTITUTE 129 Whitney Way, Clayton CA 94517. The Ph.D. is awarded on completion of a dissertation of at least 25 words, and a fee of $3. When this is done, you get a nice letter saying that you have been awarded the Doctorate, but if you want your diploma, it will cost about $50 more. The literature says that "your newly earned degree will be just as legal and equally important as one held by Billy Graham, Oral Roberts, or other great religious leaders of our time."

CLEMSON COLLEGE See R/G Enterprises

CLINTON UNIVERSITY For years, they sold fake degrees of all kinds for $25 to $35, offering "a masterpiece so perfect, it absolutely defies detection." But mail to their last known address, 11800 Merriman Road in Livonia, Michigan is returned as undeliverable. The diplomas were signed by Jackson Boyd, President.

COLGATE COLLEGE See R/G Enterprises

COLLEGE FORUM P.O. Box 32, Newburn OH 44065. Several correspondents have reported that fake degrees have been sold from this address.

COLLEGE OF APPLIED SCIENCE LONDON College House, 3 Minster Road, Kilburn, London N.W. 2, England. The President is "Commander Sir" Sidney Lawrence, whose titles are self-awarded. The College exists on paper only, but, like Brigadoon, it was real (well, almost real) for one day. As reported in an article in *Der Spiegel,* a wealthy German industrialist bought a fake Doctorate from this place, and insisted that it be presented in person. "Sir" Sidney enlisted the aid of his friend, "Archbishop" Charles Brearly, who runs several degree mills from Sheffield, England. They rented a fancy girls' school for a day, installed carpets and candelabra, and rented costumes for their friends, who dressed up as "counts hung around with medals, an abbess in a trailing robe . . . and the knights of the Holy Grail." The German arrived in a Rolls Royce and received his degree in impressive ceremony, which only cost him about $15,000. Sir Sidney, incidentally, appends a rubber stamp to his letters saying, "Hon. Attorney General U.S.A."

COLLEGE OF DIVINE METAPHYSICS (E&T), England

COLLEGE OF FRANKLIN & MARSHALL See Regency Enterprises

COLLEGE OF HOMEOPATHY (E&T), Missouri

COLLEGE OF JOURNALISM, POLITICAL SCIENCE AND LANGUAGES (E&T), Charleston WV

COLLEGE OF LIFE The Siesta Company of Siesta Key, Florida used to sell honorary Doctorates for only $2, but they have gone away.

COLLEGE OF NATURAL THERAPEUTICS See International University

COLLEGE OF NATURATRICS (E&T), Missouri

COLLEGE OF SPIRITUAL SCIENCES (E&T), England

COLLEGE OF UNIVERSAL TRUTH (E&T), Chicago

COLLEGII ROMANII See International Honorary Awards Committee

COLLEGIUM ACADEMICUM MINISTERIALE, Sheffield, England. One of several mills run by Charles Brearly, self-styled Archbishop of the Old Catholic Church of England.

COLLEGIUM TECHNOLOGICUM SUSSEXENSIS BRITANNIA See Sussex College of Technology

COLORADO CHRISTIAN UNIVERSITY Subject of a landmark court case in which the State of New York successfully sued to prevent them from selling their degrees to New Yorkers or to advertise in publications distributed in New York.

COLUMBIA SCHOOL (GOE), Unknown U.S. location

COLUMBUS ASSOCIATION (GOE), San Marino (Italy) and Trieste (Yugoslavia)

COMMERCIAL UNIVERSITY (GOE), Delhi, India

COMMONWEALTH SCHOOL OF LAW (GOE), Washington DC

CORMELL UNIVERSITY See Regency Enterprises

COVENTRY UNIVERSITY Coventry, England. Operated by Willian Duncan through his company, International Status Symbols. Degrees cost from $25 to $250. Duncan defends his activities as "harmless kidology . . . harmless bits of paper . . . just status symbols, something to hang on the wall."

CRAMWELL INSTITUTE FOR RESEARCH (GOE), Adams MA

CRANMER HALL THEOLOGICAL COLLEGE (E&T), London, England

CREATIVE UNIVERSITY OF SOUTHEAST LONDON (E&T), London, England

CROMWELL UNIVERSITY 18 St. George St., London W1R 9DE England. Degrees of all kinds on payment of fees as high as $730. The address is a mail forwarding service. Accreditation is claimed from the Western European Accrediting Society in Liederbach, West Germany, which is also a mail-forwarding service. The literature is identical to that used by half a dozen other degree mills (Lafayette, Loyola, Roosevelt, Dallas State, John Quincy Adams, and Jackson State).

DALLAS STATE COLLEGE They used to offer all degrees for $200 through the Church of Universal Education, which believed everyone should have a degree. In 1975, they were successfully sued by the Consumer Protection Division of the Attorney General's office of Texas, and enjoined from operating in that state. Now that other degree mills are using identical literature (see Cromwell, for instance), it is unclear if it is the same people, or if someone is copying their stuff.

DARTHMOUTH COLLEGE See Regency Enterprises

DELAWARE LAW SCHOOL (E&T)

DE PAUL UNIVERSITY 80 Ave. de la Grand Armee, 75017 Paris, France. Identical literature to Cromwell University, except the cost is $550. Accreditation is claimed from the Worldwide Accrediting Commission in Paris. All addresses are mail forwarding services.

DIPLOMATIC STATE UNIVERSITY See R/G Enterprises

DIPLOMATIC UNIVERSITY See National Certificate Company

EARL JAMES NATIONAL UNIVERSITY COLLEGE (GOE), Toronto, Canada

EASTERN EDUCATIONAL SYNDICATE (GOE), Parganas, India

EASTERN ORTHODOX UNIVERSITY (GOE), Ambuhr, North Arcot, India

ECOLE DENTIARE SUPERIEURE DE RADIOLOGIE ET PHYSIOTHERAPIE (GOE), Paris, France

ECOLE PROFESSIONELLE SUPERIEURE (GOE), Paris, France

ECOLE SUPERIEURE TECHNIQUE ET COMMERCIALE (GOE), Paris, France

EDINBURGH THEOLOGICAL HALL (E&T), Edinburgh and Glasgow, Scotland

EMERSON UNIVERSITY (GOE), Los Angeles CA

EMPIRE COLLEGE OF OPHTHALMOLOGY (E&T), Toronto, Canada

ENGLISH ASSOCIATION OF ACCOUNTANTS & AUDITORS (E&T)

ENGLISH ASSOCIATION OF ESTATE AGENTS AND VALUERS (E&T)

ENGLISH ASSOCIATION OF SECRETARIES (E&T)

EPISCOPAL UNIVERSITY OF LONDON (E&T), London, England

EPISCOPAL UNIVERSITY OF ST. PETER PORT (E&T), Frankfurt, Germany

ETUDES UNIVERSITAIRES INTERNATIONALES (GOE), Vaduz, Liechtenstein; also Luxembourg

EUGENIA INSTITUTE OF METAPHYSICS See ORB

EUROPEAN COLLEGE OF SCIENCE AND MAN (E&T), Sheffield, England

EVALUATION AND MANAGEMENT INTERNATIONAL P.O. Box 4277, Inglewood, CA 90309. These folks send out a 3-page, unsigned letter stating that on receipt of fees up to $2,100 they will arrange for the degree of your choice to be issued to you. They require a down payment of 50% before they will even tell you which school it is that they represent.

FACULTÉ D'ECONOMIE DE ÉTUDES UNIVERSITAIRES INTERNATIONALES (E&T), Vaduz, Liechtenstein

FACULTÉ LIBRE DE FRANCE (GOE), Paris and Bordeaux, France

FACULTY OF SCIENCE (E&T), London, England

FACULTY OF NEORELIGION (E&T), Amsterdam and Haarlem, Netherlands

FARADAY COLLEGE (E&T), England

FELIX ADLER MEMORIAL UNIVERSITY (E&T), Charlotte, NC

FIRST ACADEMY OF AFRICAN SCIENCES (E&T), Zurich, Switzerland

FLORIDA STATE CHRISTIAN COLLEGE Used to advertise nationally the sale of Bachelor's, Master's, Doctorates and honorary Doctorates from its address in Fort Lauderdale, Florida. Both the Postal Service and the State of Florida acted in the late 1970's to shut them down.

FOREST PARK UNIVERSITY (GOE), Chicago IL

FOUNDATION INSTITUTE CALIENQUE DE ROURERGUE (E&T), London, England

FOUR STATES COOPERATIVE UNIVERSITY (GOE), Jefferson, TX

FRANKLIN-INSTITUT (GOE), Lindau, West Germany

FRANKLIN UNIVERSITY See Bradford University

FREE ANGLICAN CHURCH (WORLD EVANGELICAL MISSION) (GOE), Berlin and Frankfurt, West Germany

FREE PROTESTANT EPISCOPAL ECUMENICAL CHURCH (E&T), London, England

FREE UNIVERSITY (E&T), England

GEO-METAPHYSICAL INSTITUTE 2 Park Ave., Manhasset NY 11030. They advertise a Doctor of Geo-Metaphysics diploma for $5, pointing out that it is "absolutely phoney (sic) but very impressive."

GERMAN-AMERICAN DENTAL COLLEGE (GOE), Chicago, IL

GOLDEN STATE UNIVERSITY Operated from addresses in Hollywood, California, and Denver, Colorado, in the 1950's and 1960's. Exposed as a degree mill on a Paul Coates television program in 1958. No connection with a new school of the same name that opened in 1979.

GORDON ARLEN COLLEGE (E&T), England

GOTTBOURG UNIVERSITY OF SWITZERLAND See ORB

GRADUATE COLLEGE See National Certificate Company

GREAT LAKES UNIVERSITY P.O. Box 128, Higgins Lake MI 48627. The sales letter for this mill is signed by W. (for Wiley!) Gordon Bennett, who has a Doctorate from the Northwestern College of Applied Science, another mill. The school is "under the direction of Disciples of Truth, Inc." and claims accreditation from two non-existent agencies. They have also used addresses in Chicago and Dearborn, Michigan. All degrees are sold for about $200.

GREAT SEAL OF THE STATE OF CALIFORNIA I have no idea what this means, but it appears both on a list of degree mills published by the U.S. Office of Education and on the German Office of Education list.

GULF SOUTHERN UNIVERSITY 6047 Catina St., New Orleans, LA 70124. The literature is identical to that used by several other mills, including Great Lakes, Pacific Northwestern, and Atlantic Northeastern. The degrees are sold to anyone for about $200, but the fake transcripts are not sold to people in Louisiana.

HALKYONISCHE AKADEMIE (E&T)

HAMBURGER UNIVERSITY Well yes, I know it's silly, but I am convinced that anything that can be misused will be misused. See Atlantic University, above, for instance. The employee training program of McDonald's Restaurants is known as Hamburger University, granting graduates of its training program a Doctor of Hamburgerology.

HAMILTON STATE UNIVERSITY P.O. Box 11516, Tucson, AZ 85706. Degrees of all kinds for a payment of less than $50. The fake diploma says the school is in Clinton, New York, home of the old and respectable Hamilton College. See also Regency Enterprises and R/G Enterprises.

HARLEY UNIVERSITY 31 Brook St., London W1Y 1AJ England. They offer Bachelor's through Ph.D. degrees for completion of a few trivial home study courses and a three or four page "dissertation," at a cost under $200. When I visited the "university" I found it located in a tiny room adjoining a beauty salon. The receptionist for the salon turned out to be the registrar of the university. I spoke briefly to the co-proprietor, R. Young, Ph.D. When I asked him where he got his Doctorate, he replied, "That's for me to know and for you to find out."

HARMONY COLLEGE OF APPLIED SCIENCE See International University

HARTFORD TECHNICAL INSTITUTE See Regency Enterprises

HIS MAJESTY'S UNIVERSITY OF POLYTECHNICS 2524 37th Ave., Sacramento, CA 95822. Honorary Doctorates in all subjects (but "no profanities or obscenities") for $5. The announcement says the certificates "are authentic-looking in every detail and are a real ego booster" and that they should not be construed as "an award from a so-called diploma mill." I'm afraid I must so construe.

HOLLYWOOD COLLEGE (E&T), Hollywood, CA

HOLLYWOOD SOUTHERN UNIVERSITY See California Pacifica University

HOLLYWOOD UNIVERSITY See California Pacifica University

HOLY TOLEDO UNIVERSITY c/o American Educational Publishers, P.O. Box 651, Rancho Santa Fe, CA 92067. Ph.D. in ten humorous subjects for $3 each or $10 a dozen. The degrees are offered in worrying, defrosting, adorableness, crab grass culture, and the like. They are quite realistic-looking until you get close enough to read the small type.

HONORÉ COLLEGE OF FRANCE See ORB

HUBBARD ACADEMY OF SCIENTOLOGY (E&T), England

HUMBERMAN UNIVERSITY COLLEGE (E&T), Vancouver, Canada

ILLINOIS STATE UNIVERSITY See Regency Enterprises

IMPERIAL PHILO-BYZANTINE UNIVERSITY AND ACADEMY (GOE), Madrid, Spain

INDEPENDENCE UNIVERSITY P.O. Box 1775, Independence MO 64055. The mailing service at that address forwards the mail to a man in Evanston, Illinois who, according to the Chicago *Tribune*, had been headmaster of a prestigious Chicago private school, but resigned "after disclosures that he was using his office there as a center of activity for the diploma mill." The president of a Chicago-area community college, whose Doctorate was from Independence, lost his job for falisfying his credentials. One of America's leading publishers of self-help books distributes literature showing a photo of himself with an Independence University Doctorate hanging prominently on his wall.

INDEPENDENT UNIVERSITY OF AUSTRALIA (E&T), Morwell, Victoria, Australia

INDIAN SANITARY INSTITUTE (GOE), Original Road, Delhi, India

INDIANA STATE UNIVERSITY See Regency Enterprises

INSTITUT DES HAUTES ÉTUDES COMMERCIALS (GOE), Brussels, Belgium

INSTITUT ELECTROTECHNIQUE (GOE), Brussels, Belgium

INSTITUT INTERNATIONAL DE HAUTE ÉTUDES BIBLIOGIQUES (GOE), Paris, France

INSTITUT MODERNE POLYTECHNIQUE (E&T), Liège, Belgium

INSTITUT NORMAL DE CULTURE GÉNÉRALE (E&T), Liège, Belgium

INSTITUT PATRIARCAL ST. IRENÉE Beziers, France. Established by Karl Josef Werres, now Vice President of Newport University. Apparently granted honorary Doctorates to the proprietor and some of his associates, without authority or approval of the French government. See also Inter-State University, Northwest London College, and Trinity Collegiate, this chapter.

INSTITUT SUPERIEUR TECHNIQUE ET COLONIAL DE LIÉGE (GOE), Liège, Belgium

INSTITUT TECHNIQUE SUPERIEUR (E&T), Fribourg, Switzerland

INSTITUTE ACADEMY (E&T), Burnaby, B.C., Canada

INSTITUTE OF EXCELLENCE (E&T), c/o Novelty Printing Co., 11215 N. Miami Ave., North Miami FL 33168. All degrees, including medical and dental, at $10. The fake diplomas do not look very realistic, and are intended ''for novelty purposes only.''

INSTITUTE OF GALIENNIQUE DU ROUERGUE (E&T), London, England

INSTITUTE OF HYPNOTHERAPY (GOE), U.S.

INSTITUTE OF LIFE SCIENCE (GOE), London, England

INSTITUTE OF MANAGEMENT SPECIALISTS (E&T), England

INSTITUTE OF SOCIAL ORDER (GOE), Poona, India

INSTITUTE OF THE INTERNATIONAL THYROLOGICAL ACADEMY (GOE), Brussels, Belgium

INTELLIGENT SERVICES (E&T), England

INTER-AMERICAN UNIVERSITY (GOE), Rome, Italy

INTERCOLLEGIATE UNIVERSITY (E&T), England

INTERNATION UNIVERSITY (E&T), U.S.

INTERNATIONAL ACADEMY (GOE), Vancouver, B.C. Canada and London, England

INTERNATIONAL ACADEMY FOR PLANETARY PLANNING See International Honorary Awards Committee

INTERNATIONAL AMERICAN UNIVERSITY (GOE), Rome, Italy

INTERNATIONAL ASSOCIATION OF HYPNOTISTS (GOE)

INTERNATIONAL COLLEGE OF ASSOCIATES IN MEDICINE Drawer H, Golden Acres TX 77503. Doctor of Medical Letters and Ph.D. in philanthropy on payment of moderate fees. Some correspondents report they have awarded M.D. degrees in the past.

INTERNATIONAL CORPORATION OF ENGINEERS (GOE), Delaware

INTERNATIONAL EXPORT ASSOCIATION (E&T), England

INTERNATIONAL FEDERATION OF SCIENTIFIC RESEARCH SOCIETIES (E&T) England

INTERNATIONAL FREE PROTESTANT EPISCOPAL UNIVERSITY (GOE), England

INTERNATIONAL GEISTEWISSENSCHAFTLICHES HOCHSCHULE (GOE), Haarlem, Netherlands

INTERNATIONAL HONORARY AWARDS COMMITTEE 2350 Bean Creek Road, Santa Cruz CA 95060. Wide range of Doctorates and other awards on payment of a fee of $35 to $105. Doctorates are offered from the Colegii Romanii, the International Academy for Planetary Planning, Two Dragon University, and the Siberian Institute. Diplomatic decorations, including the Grand Cross of the Imperial Order of Constantine and the Sovereign Order of Liechtenstein have also been sold, complete with rosettes, medals, and sashes. The late Francis X. Gordon, founder of all these establishments, had a good sense of humor about what he did. His widow carries on the work. The various materials are quite well designed.

INTERNATIONAL INSTITUTE OF ARTS AND LETTERS (GOE), Lindau, West Germany. Apparently the same as Franklin-Institut.

INTERNATIONAL INSTITUTE OF INFORMATION OFFICERS (E&T), England

INTERNATIONAL KNIGHTS OF GOODWILL (E&T), Chicago, IL

INTERNATIONAL PROTESTANT BIRKBEST (or BIRBEST) COLLEGE (E&T)

INTERNATIONAL UNIVERSITY P.O. Box 948, Chicago IL 60690. Degrees of all kinds on payment of fees in the vicinity of $200 and writing a "thesis" of one to five pages. Apparently unrelated to all the other International Universities described in Chapter 17. Incorporates the College of Natural Therapeutics, allegedly in Sri Lanka, and Harmony College of Applied Science, allegedly in Los Altos, California (but untraceable there). The rather crude 16-page catalogue says the school was founded as the National University and is registered under the Government of India Act XVI of 1908.

INTERNATIONAL NEORELIGISCHE FAKULTAT (GOE), Haarlem, Netherlands

INTER-STATE UNIVERSITY England, France. Established by Karl Josef Werres, granting honorary Doctorates from England. According to Dr. Ted Dalton, president of Newport University and recipient of one of the Doctorates, Inter-State's charter in England gives it the right to grant degrees. It is the case that one can say anything one wants in a corporate charter, but that doesn't make it so. The only two ways a school can legally grant degrees in England are by royal charter or by act of Parliament. Inter-State has neither, and therefore the degrees cannot be legal.

INTER-UNIVERSITY SERVICE (E&T), France

JACKSON STATE UNIVERSITY Operated from addresses in Los Angeles, Nashville, Reno and Chicago selling degrees of all kinds for about $200. "False representation orders" were issued by the Postal Service, so that mail addressed to Jackson State is returned. The materials are almost identical to those used by degree mills of many other names (Dallas State, John Quincy Adams, Lafayette, etc.). There is no connection whatever with the legitimate Jackson State University in Mississippi.

JANTA ENGINEERING COLLEGE (GOE), Karnal, India

JAPAN CHRISTIAN COLLEGE (GOE), Tokyo, Japan

JOHN QUINCY ADAMS COLLEGE Started in Portland, Oregon; later used addresses in Nevada and Illinois to sell its phony degrees for $250. Literature almost identical to Jackson State and half a dozen other mills.

JOHANN KEPPLER SCHOOL OF MEDICINE Waldmannstrasse 4, Postfach 8024, Zurich, Switzerland and P.O. Box 835, Adelaide St., Toronto, M5C 2K1 Canada. The world's only remaining non-resident medical school is, likewise, one of the few mills issuing medical degrees with some pretense of legitimacy. The M.D. program is theoretically offered only to persons who already have a Doctorate, but it can be in chiropractic, naprapathy, veterinary, herbal medicine, and so forth. They claim to be fully accredited by the American Coordinated Medical Society, a phony organization established in Norwalk, California by "Dr." L. Mitchell Weinberg, who used to run America's only active medical degree mill, United American Medical College, until he was sent to prison for selling fake M.D.'s in 1982. The Keppler catalogue is well-designed, but evasive and full of inaccuracies. While the statement is made that all degrees can be completed in one year or less, the catalogue shows five years worth of curriculum—most of which is waived, presumably, because of one's veterinary or chiropractic skills. The claim is made that Keppler medical degrees have been recognized in many countries. When I asked their representative, Dieter Luelsbach, which ones, he replied, after a long pause, "Well, Mauritius for one." The addresses in both countries are mail-forwarding services. The Canadian government has no interest in this operation (which is too bad, since it is giving Canadian education a bad name), because, they told me, the mail addressed to Kepler is actually forwarded to a chiropractor in the state of New York. Another Keppler representative says they are opening a big cancer research center in Mexico.

KINGSLEY UNIVERSITY Cape Newberry, Maine. See Bradford University.

LAFAYETTE UNIVERSITY Schipohl Airport East, Building 144, Rooms 042-043, P.O. Box 7766, Amsterdam, Netherlands. Literature identical to Dallas State and many other mills. Accreditation claimed from the non-existent West European Accrediting Association. The address is that of an air transport company in small offices in a former airport building.

LAMP BEACON UNIVERSITY See California Pacifica University

LAURENCE UNIVERSITY Associated Enterprises, P.O. Box 1741, Honolulu HI 96806. All degrees in all fields except medicine and law for a fee of $45. The literature says, "We are confident you will find the benefits you can obtain with a degree from Laurence University are very valuable indeed." The main benefit I can think of is 90 days of room and board at government expense. The same seller, John Stacy, also issues the fake degrees of Buckner University, Benson University, Carlton University and Kingsley University. There is no connection whatever with the legitimate Laurence University in California.

LAWFORD STATE UNIVERSITY They used to sell degrees of all kinds for $6.99 from Lawford, The Université de Commerce de (sic) Canada, and the Christian Fellowship Foundation. The seller, Frank Gould, operated from a P.O. Box in Baltimore, now closed.

LIBERA ACCADEMIA DI ALTO CULTURA AVIGNONE-PARIGI (GOE), Rome, Italy

LIBERA UNIVERSITA DI PSICO-BIOFISICA (E&T), Trieste, Yugoslavia

LINCOLN-JEFFERSON UNIVERSITY See California Pacifica University

LONDON COLLEGE OF APPLIED SCIENCE See College of Applied Science, London

LONDON COLLEGE OF PHYSIOLOGY (E&T), London, England

LONDON COLLEGE OF THEOLOGY (E&T), London, England

LONDON EDUCATIONAL COLLEGE (E&T), London, England

LONDON INSTITUTE FOR APPLIED RESEARCH c/o Degree Promotion Bureau, Ltd., Postbus BB-55917, Den Haag, Netherlands. A very impressive-looking certificate, awarding the honorary Doctorate of L.I.A.R. and which has been officially stamped in some manner by the Dutch government, is available for $100. Here is the curious history of this endeavor. In 1973, a group of serious academics, including faculty members from major American universities, planned to start a serious alternative school in London. To raise funds, they created a blatantly fictitious entity, known as L.I.A.R., which existed solely to sell honorary Doctorates to raise money for the legitimate school. Full-page advertisements were run in many major American magazines. L.I.A.R. upset some people for doing openly and aggressively what many traditional schools do secretly: exchanging a meaningless honorary credential for a donation. The author of this book was one of those involved in this fund-raising plan. When plans for the serious school fell through, all money on hand was donated to worthy scholarship programs in Africa, Europe, and the U.S. The L.I.A.R. business itself was traded to a gentleman in Holland for (you must believe this; I mean, who would make such a thing up?) 100 pounds of metal Ethiopian ear pickers. Said gent carries the business on, presumably for personal gain rather than worthy causes, and also offers the fake degrees of the American Institute of Technology and the California Institute of Higher Learning. And if anyone reading this would like some metal Ethiopian ear pickers, have we got a deal for you.

LONDON INSTITUTE OF BUSINESS STUDIES (E&T), London, England

LONDON SCHOOL FOR SOCIAL RESEARCH, 24 Cranbourn St., London WC2H 7AA England. The well-prepared literature offers degrees of all kinds for payment of fees as high as $2,000. From the mail I was getting, it appeared they were fooling a lot of Americans. So I made a point of visiting the campus at 24 Cranbourn St. It is a dingy little building off Leicester Square. I climbed five flights of dark stairs so narrow I had to walk sideways. At the top: a tiny one-room office of Archangel Services! The chap behind the desk assured me that this was, in fact, the London School, but that the faculty and staff were actually in Miami, Florida.

LONDON TOTTENHAM INTERNATIONAL CHRISTIAN UNIVERSITY (E&T), London, England

LOYOLA UNIVERSITY 15 Ave. Victor Hugo, 75116 Paris, France. All degrees from high school diplomas to the Ph.D., for fees up to $625. Literature identical to that of De Paul, Lafayette, and other European mills. No connection whatever with the four legitimate schools named Loyola in California, Louisiana, Illinois and Maryland. Blatantly false claims in their literature include, for instance, "Many of our successful graduates have used their transcripts to transfer to other colleges and universities in the U.S.A." (If this has happened, it is only because of confusion of name with the legitimate Loyolas). They have used agents in several U.S. cities to solicit business.

LYNE COLLEGE (E&T), England

MADISON STATE UNIVERSITY See R/G Enterprises

MARLOWE UNIVERSITY Active in New Jersey and Florida during the 1960's and 1970's, selling all kinds of degrees for $150 or less.

MARMADUKE UNIVERSITY P.O. Box 5843, South Lake Tahoe CA 95705. Degrees at all levels on sale for fees from $1,000 on up. The literature reports that "usually the student qualifies for more advanced study than he initialy (sic) expected." Mention is made of a 30-day resident course in the use of lie detectors, but the voice on the telephone said it is not being offered "because of the building program."

MARTIN COLLEGE They used to sell degrees of all kinds for $200 from a P.O. Box in Sarasota, Florida, now closed. Graduates were required to pass some tough exams. They even gave an example in their literature: "True or false—The Declaration of Independence was signed on the 4th of July 1776 by British Royalty." The president was listed as M. Alexander Welker, Ph.D.

MC KINLEY-ROOSEVELT INC. Chicago IL. Identified as a diploma mill by the U.S. Office of Education in 1961.

METROPOLITAN COLLEGIATE BCM-Collegiate, London WClV 6XX England. Sells all degrees including medical and dental degrees for $100 or less. The address is a mail-forwarding service sending the mail to Yorkshire, in the north of England. It is hard to believe that the British government could allow this to go on, but it has for years. (I have a little fantasy in which the British Minister of Education and Science becomes gravely ill on a trip to Pakistan, and the physician called in to operate got his M.D. from Metropolitan Collegiate.)

METROPOLITAN COLLEGIATE INSTITUTE Mill operating from Glendale, California, during the 1950's.

MID-WESTERN UNIVERSITY Identified as a degree mill by the U.S. Office of Education in 1961, but no longer at the address given in Arcadia, Missouri.

MILLARD FILLMORE INSTITUTE In 1966, the year the author of this book earned his legitimate Doctorate, Bob Hope was given one of his first honorary Doctorates in thanks for a large gift to a University. The Millard Fillmore Institute was thereupon established solely to poke fun at the notion of giving honorary degrees to celebrities. We named it in honor of our great 13th president, the only president ever to turn down an honorary Doctorate from Oxford. The wording on the ornate diploma stated, "By virtue of powers which we have invented...the honorary and meretricious title" was awarded "magno cum grano salis" (with a big grain of salt). Many were given away and some were sold, complete with a cheap plastic frame, for ten bucks. But people will find a way to misuse anything. When a high official of a large fundamentalist Bible school, Freedom University, was found to be claiming his Doctorate from the Institute, it seemed time to shut its fictitious gates, perhaps forever.

MILLER UNIVERSITY (E&T), Philadelphia, PA

MILTON UNIVERSITY (E&T), Maryland and New York

MINISTERIAL TRAINING COLLEGE (GOE), Ravencarr Road, Sheffield, England (also in Doncaster, England)

MONTSERRAT UNIVERSITY c/o LBSF Press, P.O. Box 4955, San Francisco, CA 94101. Degrees of all kinds for $10 to $20 from Montserrat and the equally non-existent Stanton University and Rochfort College.

MORRIS COLLEGE OF NEW JERSEY Pine Brook NJ. In 1982, the *Chronicle of Higher Education* uncovered a fraud, in which someone using the name of Dr. L. Shu, Head of Academic Affairs at this non-existent school, was ordering sample copies of textbooks from major publishing houses.

MORSTON-COLWYN UNIVERSITY (E&T), London, England and London, Ontario, Canada

MT. SINAI UNIVERSITY AND THEOLOGICAL SEMINARY (E&T), U.S.A.

NANSEN-AKADEMI (GOE), Prague, Czechoslovakia. (Also spelled Nanson.)

NASSAU STATE TEACHERS COLLEGE See Regency Enterprises

NATIONAL CERTIFICATE COMPANY 210 Fifth Ave., New York NY 10010. These people sell the degrees of eight non-existent universities at $20 to $30, and also sell a "make your own" kit consisting of a blank diploma and rub-down letters. Fake transcript kits are sold for an outrageous $50. The eight fake schools are Diplomatic University, Central University, Capital College, Adams Institute of Technology, Eastern University, Western College, Graduate University, and the Southern

Institute of Technology. Buyers of these extremely dangerous documents must sign a statement saying they will not use them for any educational purposes.

NATIONAL COLLEGE Doctorates of all kinds, including medical degrees, were sold by "Dr." Charles E. Downs from addresses in Shawnee, Oklahoma, and Inman, Kansas. Other school names used included British Collegiate Institute, the Anglo-American Institute of Drugless Medicine (with an address in Indianapolis), and the Anglo-American College of Medicine. National College claimed accreditation from a bogus accrediting association established by "Dr." Weinberg of the notorious United American Medical College. Apparently not in operation at this time.

NATIONAL COLLEGE OF ARTS AND SCIENCES A well-known mill, finally closed down by authorities in Oklahoma in 1982. Same ownership as American Western, Northwestern College of Allied Science and other mills. A most remarkable event occurred when a state official in New York innocently wrote to National College to request a transcript for a job applicant who claimed his Master's from National. By mistake, National sent the state official a fake transcript in his (the official's) name, showing that he had earned the Master of Arts, complete with a listing of all courses taken and grades received!

NATIONAL COLLEGE OF AUDIOMETRY (GOE), Chicago IL

NATIONAL ECCLESIASTICAL UNIVERSITY OF GREAT BRITAIN (E&T), Sheffield, England

NATIONAL ECLECTIC INSTITUTE (E&T), New York, Denmark, Germany, Spain

NATIONAL HOMEOPATHIC MEDICAL COLLEGE (GOE), Simla, India

NATIONAL STEVENS UNIVERSITY (E&T), California

NATIONAL RESEARCH INSTITUTE (GOE), Denver, Colorado; Huron, South Dakota; Karnal, India

NATIONAL UNIVERSITY (GOE), Nagpur, India. See also, National Research Institute.

NATIONAL UNIVERSITY—DOMINION OF CANADA (GOE), Toronto, Canada

NATIONAL UNIVERSITY OF COLORADO (GOE), Denver, Colorado

NATIONAL UNIVERSITY OF DAKOTA (E&T), Huron, South Dakota

NATIONAL UNIVERSITY OF SHEFFIELD (GOE, E&T), Sheffield, England

NAZARENE COLLEGE (or FELLOWSHIP) (E&T), England

NEBRASKA COLLEGE OF PHYSICAL MEDICINE England. News clippings report that degrees in chiropractic and osteopathy are sold to people who are said to use them to practice medicine.

NEWCASTLE UNIVERSITY (E&T), England; not to be confused with the legitimate University of Newcastle.

NEW CHRISTIAN INSTITUTE OF NEW ENGLAND See ORB

NEW YORK STATE COLLEGE See R/G Enterprises

NORTHWEST LONDON COLLEGE OF APPLIED SCIENCE 3 Minster Road, Kilburn, London N.W.2, England. Same location as the College of Applied Science, London; also known as Northwest London University. There are links with the Chicago Medical School, the Keppler School of Medicine and other medical degree mills. Do not be concerned that the name of Karl Josef Werres, Vice President of Newport University (see also Inter-State University, this chapter) appears as an officer on the poorly-designed diploma. Professor Werres assures me that he has no connection whatever with this school, and that his name is used without his permission. ''Sir'' Sidney Lawrence, President of the College, assures me that Professor Werres is his associate. Who's a fella to believe?

NORTHWEST LONDON UNIVERSITY See Northwest London College of Applied Science

NORTHWESTERN COLLEGE OF ALLIED SCIENCE Authorities in Oklahoma finally closed this mill down in 1982. Under the same management as American Western and National College, they operated under the cloak of the Disciples of Truth, a Missouri-incorporated church.

OBURA UNIVERSITY (E&T), London, England

OHIO CENTRAL COLLEGE See Regency Enterprises

OHIO CHRISTIAN COLLEGE One of the most active degree mills in the 1960's and 1970's, they sold degrees of all kinds for fees of $200 and up. The literature was identical to that of Florida State Christian College which was closed by authorities in that state. They claimed to be affiliated with the Calvary Grace Christian Churches of Faith, Inc., Alvin O. Langdon, President.

OHIO ST. MATHEW UNIVERSITY (E&T), Columbus, Ohio

ORB Box 5149, Virginia Beach, VA 23455. A supermarket of phony degrees which has, from various addresses, offered Doctorates from eight fictitious institutions for $5 to $65 each: Boston Academy of Music, Eugenia Institute of Metaphysics, Gottbourg University of Switzerland, Honoré College of France, New Christian Institute of New England, Royal Academy of Science and Art, Taylor College of England, and Weinberg University of West Germany. ORB (which stands for Occult Research Bureau) is operated by Mr. Raymond Buckland, author and former curator of the Buckland Museum of Magick.

ORIENTAL UNIVERSITY (GOE), Washington, DC

OXFORD COLLEGE OF ARTS AND SCIENCES (E&T), Ontario, Canada. May be affiliated with Sussex College of Technology

OXFORD INSTITUTE FOR APPLIED RESEARCH 30 Baker St., London W1M 2D8, England. Fake honorary Doctorates are sold for $250, apparently largely to German businessmen. The address is a mail-forwarding service which, according to one newspaper report, sends the mail to Joseph Craig in Hamburg, West Germany. The sales letter is signed by H.M. Armstrong, Ph.D.

PACIFIC COLLEGE P.O. Box 8449, Van Nuys CA 91409. They sell everything from high school diplomas to Doctorates for $75 because they believe that ''everyone has the right to live and experience life according to his or her own convictions.'' (This presumably includes convictions for fraud.) The literature claims they are a non-profit organization established in 1928, and run by Mr. William Hughes.

PACIFIC INTERNATIONAL ACADEMY (E&T), London, England

PACIFIC NORTHWESTERN UNIVERSITY Independent Career Programs, P.O. Box 36, Monterey Park CA 91754. Degrees of all kinds plus transcripts for about $200. The material is professional-looking, which is not surprising since this mill was founded by a former administrator of Seattle University, Arch Borque. The fake school in Seattle (and its counterpart, Atlantic Southern University) were closed down in 1978, but resurfaced in southern California, running ads only in foreign newspapers, presumably because they didn't think anyone would notice.

PACIFIC SOUTHERN UNIVERSITY A totally fake school of this name has operated from a variety of P.O. box addresses in the Los Angeles area, and from 205 Nassau St. in Princeton, New Jersey. The catalogue describes ''degrees you can be pround of'' (sic) for $250 each.

PALM BEACH PSYCHOTHERAPY TRAINING CENTER See Thomas A. Edison College

PENSACOLA TRADE SCHOOL See Regency Enterprises

PEOPLE'S NATIONAL UNIVERSITY (E&T), U.S.A.

PHILO-BYZANTINE UNIVERSITY AND COLLECTIVE AFFILIATION OF CONSTANTINE THE GREAT (E&T), Madrid, Spain

PHILOSOPHICAL SOCIETY OF ENGLAND (E&T), England

PHOENIX UNIVERSITY (E&T), See Accademia di Studi Superiori Phoenix

PIONEER TECHNICAL SEMINARY (E&T), Rockford IL

PONTIFICAL ATHENAEUM (GOE), Jnana Deepa, Pune (Poona) India. Claims to grant degrees "in the name and by authority of the Pope." I have been unable to confirm or dispute the papal claim. Neither Herbert Alphonso, rector of the Athenaeum, nor the Pope has answered my letters.

PROFESSIONAL INSTITUTE OF GREAT BRITAIN (E&T)

PROFESSIONAL REGISTER (E&T)

PSYCHOLOGICAL FOUNDATION OF GREAT BRITAIN (GOE), London, England

PSYCHOLOGICAL RESEARCH CLINIC FOR NERVOUS DISORDERS (E&T)

REGENCY COLLEGE See American Western; another mill under the same management, closed by authorities in Oklahoma in 1982.

REGENCY ENTERPRISES 8753 Windom Ave., St. Louis MO 63114. They sell degrees with the names of real schools, very slightly changed, with the intent of fooling many people into thinking they are the originals. Thus diplomas are offered from Stamford University, Texas University (the real one is the University of Texas), Cornell University, Indiana State University, Boston City College, the University of Pittsburg, Illinois State University, Rockford Community College, Hartford Technical Institute, Carnegie Institute of Engineering, Stetson College, Nassau State Teachers College, Darthmouth College, Ohio Central College, College of Franklin and Marshall, Buchanan High School, and Pensacola Trade School. Blank diplomas (the buyer fills in the name and degree with a lettering kit provided) cost about $20 each. Buyers must sign a statement that they will not use these phony documents for any fraudulent purposes. It is hard to imagine any other purpose to which they could be put, but the disclaimer may be enough to keep Regency out of trouble.

R/G ENTERPRISES P.O. Box 16067, Tampa FL 33687. They sell degrees from ten almost-real schools (e.g. Colgate College instead of Colgate University) at prices up to $37.50. The other schools offered are Clemson College, Tulsa College, New York State College, California Christian College, Alabama Christian College, Hamilton Institute of Technology, Hamilton State University, Madison State University and Diplomatic State University. The literature says, "This offer not valid in states where prohibited by law." That probably includes all 50 of them.

RHODE ISLAND SCHOOL OF LAW, INC. (E&T), Located in Wyoming, they say.

ROCHFORT COLLEGE See Montserrat University

ROCKFORD COMMUNITY COLLEGE See Regency Enterprises

ROOSEVELT UNIVERSITY Rue de la Presse 5, 1000 Brussels, Belgium. Degrees of any kind for a "tuition" of $400 to $600. Literature identical to De Paul, Dallas State, and many other mills. They also use an address in Zurich, and agents at various U.S. addresses, and advertise a great deal in

American classified sections. Accreditation is claimed from an equally phony German agency. No connection, of course, with the legitimate Roosevelt University in Chicago.

ROYAL ACADEMY OF SCIENCE AND ART See ORB

ROYAL COLLEGE OF SCIENCE (E&T), Toronto, Canada. Apparently affiliated with (or the same as) Empire College of Opthalmology.

SACRORUM STUDIORUM COLLEGIUM ACADEMICUM (E&T), Sheffield, England

ST. ANDREWS CORRESPONDENCE COLLEGE (E&T)

ST. ANDREWS ECUMENICAL CORRESPONDENCE COLLEGE (E&T)

ST. ANDREWS ECUMENICAL FOUNDATION UNIVERSITY INTERCOLLEGIATE (E&T, GOE) London, England

ST. JOHN CHRYSOSTOM COLLEGE (GOE), London, England

ST. JOHN'S UNIVERSITY (GOE), Ambuhr, North Arcot, India

ST. JOSEPH UNIVERSITY 1370 St. Nicholas Ave., Suite 3OR, P.O. Box 44, New York, NY 10033. They have offered Bachelor's, Master's, Doctorates and Law degrees (which they say qualify people to take the California Bar), using some impressively produced literature—and some ludicrously unimpressive literature, in which the name "St. Joseph" has been inserted in gaps where some other school name once appeared. One brochure says the Academic Office is in Donaldson, Louisiana; another says Canon City, Colorado; a third, New York. Degrees cost from $2,000 to $3,000. The only name on any of the literature is Sabih Ali, Director of Admissions.

ST. OLAF'S (or OLAV's) CATHEDRAL ACADEMY OF RELIGIOUS SCIENCE (GOE), London, England; Norway, Denmark, Lebanon, U.S.A.

ST. PAUL'S SEMINARY See American Western University.

SCHOLA POPULARIS BOTANICAE (E&T), Madrid, Spain

SCHOOL OF APPLIED SCIENCES (E&T), London, England, and New York

SCHOOL OF PSYCHOLOGY AND PSYCHOTHERAPY (E&T), England

SELF-CULTURE UNIVERSITY (GOE), Kizhanattam, India

SIBERIAN INSTITUTE See International Honorary Awards Committee

SIR EDWARD HEYZER'S FREE TECHNICAL COLLEGE (GOE), Hong Kong. Also known as the Institution of Technology for the Underprivileged Refugees; apparently associated with the National University of Canada.

SOCIETÉ SAVANTES (GOE), Paris and Bordeaux, France. Apparently the same as Faculté Libre de France.

SOCIETY OF PHYSIATRICIANS LTD. (E&T), England

SOUTHERN INSTITUTE OF TECHNOLOGY See National Certificate Company

SOUTH CHINA UNIVERSITY (E&T), Hong Kong, formerly Macau

SPECIAL FACULTY FOR NEORELIGIE (GOE), Haarlem, Netherlands

SPICER MEMORIAL COLLEGE (GOE), Poona, India

STAMFORD UNIVERSITY See Regency Enterprises

STANTON UNIVERSITY University Novelty and Engraving Co., P.O. Box 5172, Tampa FL 33675. All kinds of fake degrees for $39.50. They "feel sure that your friends and associates will recognize the superior quality of such items. . . ." Also available are fake marriage licenses for those who wish to appear both married and educated when in fact they are neither.

STATON UNIVERSITY In 1982, music teachers in America and Canada received an invitation to join the American Guild of Teachers of Singing, upon which they would be awarded an honorary Doctorate by Staton University. I can find no evidence of the existence of either the American Guild or Staton University (which was supposed to be in Ohio).

STETSON COLLEGE See Regency Enterprises

SUSSEX COLLEGE OF TECHNOLOGY Highfield, Dane Hill, Hayward's Heath, Sussex RH17 7EX, England. Bachelor's, Master's, and Doctorates in almost any field. Sussex is run by "Dr." Bruce Copen from his large home south of London. At the same address, and with similar catalogues, are the Brantridge Forest School and the University of the Science of Man. They all offer "earned" degrees for which a few correspondence courses are required, and "extension awards" which are the same degrees and diplomas for no work at all. Honorary Doctorates are awarded free, but there is a $100 engraving and processing charge. Other programs cost from $100 to $500. One may be declared a "Professor Emeritas" (sic) for $100, and a like amount gets you a listing in a sort of vanity "Who's Who" that lists anyone willing to buy his or her way in. "Dr." Copen has been the subject of intense interest by the British press for at least 15 years. But he sells no degrees in Britain, thus is apparently beyond the reach of the law. Not so the people who buy them. Many have lost good jobs, suffered public humiliation, and even gone to prison or (in the case of a foreign-born high state official in Colorado) been deported. Sussex advertises extensively in U.S. newspapers and magazines.

TAURUS INTERNATIONAL UNIVERSITY Creative Book Company, P.O. Box 214998, Sacramento CA 95821. The Ph.D. sells for $2 and a Doctor of Whimsey for $1. The claim is made that the Taurus International Society was established in 1764 by James Boswell.

TAYLOR COLLEGE OF ENGLAND See ORB

TEMPLE BAR COLLEGE (E&T), Missoula MT

TENNESSEE CHRISTIAN UNIVERSITY Affiliated with Ohio Christian and Florida State Christian Universities in the sale of fake degrees. Mail is no longer delivered to the Chattanooga address.

TEXAS THEOLOGICAL UNIVERSITY (E&T), E&T places them in "Fort Worth, California." We all make mistakes.

TEXAS UNIVERSITY See Regency Enterprises

THOMAS A. EDISON COLLEGE 707 Chillingworth Drive, West Palm Beach FL 33409. One of America's most notorious degree-mill operators, the Right Reverend Doctor George C. Lyon, M.D., Ph.D., LL.D., D.D., having been fined heavily and sentenced to prison twice for running phony schools in Florida, may be attempting to move his operations to Arkansas. According to a Little Rock newspaper, Lyon arrived in Benton, Arkansas, with a green Rolls Royce and a red Mercedes, paid $140,000 cash for a vacant church, and announced his intentions of setting up shop there. In Florida, Thomas Edison College fooled a great many people, including *Lovejoy's College Guide*. Following five years of legal actions, Lyon was found guilty of contempt of court for selling fake degrees after being ordered to stop. As soon as he got out of prison, he picked up where he left off. Following a few more years of legal maneuvers, he was again fined and sentenced to prison, and headed for Arkansas. Lyon's enterprises have also included the Palm Beach Psychotherapy Training Center, the Florida Analytic Institute, the Order of St. John of Jerusalem, and the Holy Episcopal Church of America. He has also been associated with purveyors of phony medical degrees, including the United American Medical College and the Keppler School of Medicine. No connection whatever with the excellent Thomas Edison State College of New Jersey.

THOMAS UNIVERSITY They used to sell their fake degrees for up to $1,000 from an address in Willow Grove, Pennsylvania, but mail is now returned stamped, "Moved, Left No Address." They claimed accreditation from the fake Middle States Accrediting Board. The letters were signed by Norman Renner, Vice President.

TRINITY COLLEGE Identified as a degree mill by the U.S. Office of Education, but no longer in business in Indianapolis.

TRINITY COLLEGIATE INSTITUTE Stockerstrasse 21, Zurich, Switzerland. They have operated from a mail-forwarding service in London, which sent the mail to Carl Bleisch in Zurich. Bleisch had told the forwarding service that he was running a language school and "there was no question of awarding degrees." According to an exposé in the London *Times*, within two months, Trinity was handing out degrees in subjects ranging from beer marketing to scientific massage. Among the holders of the degree is Karl Josef Werres, Vice President of Newport University.

TUIT UNIVERSITY 18 Perimeter Park, Suite 100, Atlanta GA 30341. Humorously-worded degrees (when you read the small print). The small print says that the recipient "has not had the time to do the necessary work leading to the degree" of such-and-such. The cost is $5 for a blank diploma and $10 if they fill it in. Certainly more harmless than most. Proprietor Steven Caudill has his tongue well in his cheek.

TULSA COLLEGE See R/G Enterprises

TWO DRAGON UNIVERSITY See International Honorary Awards Committee

UNITED AMERICAN MEDICAL COLLEGE A Medical degree mill which had been operated from the apartment of its founder, "Dr." L. Mitchell Weinberg in Metairie, Louisiana, and from a mail-forwarding service in Canada. The approach was almost identical to that of the Johann Keppler School of Medicine, described earlier. At the time Weinberg was first arrested (1977) for violating Louisiana school laws, he claimed his school was fully accredited by the American Coordinated Medical Society of Norwalk, California. Said society indeed wrote that "we of the accreditation committee feel that U.A.M.C. has the highest admission requirements of any medical college in the world . . . due to the great leadership of it's (sic) president L. Mitchell Weinberg . . . Dr. Weinberg and U.A.M.C. we Salute you." The only problem with this is that the founder of the American Coordinated Medical Society is L. Mitchell Weinberg. In 1982, Dr. Weinberg pleaded guilty to charges of selling medical degrees, and was sentenced to three years in Federal Prison.

UNITED FREE UNIVERSITY OF ENGLAND (E&T), England

UNITED NATIONS UNIVERSITY (GOE), Delhi, India. Not to be confused with the legitimate United Nations University in Japan.

UNIVERSAL CORRESPONDENCE SCHOOL (E&T), England

UNIVERSAL ECCLESIASTICAL UNIVERSITY Offered their Doctorates in all fields except law and medicine for a 10-page dissertation, and honorary Doctorates to anyone with "good moral character" and $200 to spend. My last letter to Professor Cecil Gilbert at the University's address in Manchester, England, was returned with the word "Demolished" written in big blue crayon letters across the front. I do hope they were referring to the building and not the professor.

UNIVERSAL EXTENSION CONSERVATORY 2000 S. Michigan Ave., Chicago IL 60616. Identified as a degree mill by the U.S. Office of Education.

UNIVERSIDAD BRASILEIRA (GOE), Rio de Janeiro, Brazil

UNIVERSIDAD INDIGENISTA MOCTEZUMA (GOE), Andorra

UNIVERSIDAD LATINO-AMERICANA DE LA HABANA (GOE), Havana, Cuba

UNIVERSIDAD SINTETICA LATINA Y AMERICANA (GOE), El Salvador

UNIVERSIDAD TECNOLÓGICA NACIONAL (GOE), Havana, Cuba

UNIVERSITAIRES INTERNATIONALES (E&T), Vaduz, Liechtenstein; also India, Sudan, Morocco, Japan, Australia, Hong Kong, Europe

UNIVERSITAS ILTIENSIS (E&T), Kusnacht, Switzerland, and London, England

UNIVERSITATES SHEFFIELDENSIS, Sheffield, England. According to the London *Times,* they offer "academic degrees for money." It is run by Charles Brearley, a car mechanic who calls himself Archbishop of the Old Catholic Church of England and Rector Magnificus of the University.

UNIVERSITÉ DE COMMERCE DE CANADA See Lawford State University

UNIVERSITÉ DES SCIENCE DE L'HÔMME Bordeaux, France. Same as the University of the Science of Man; see Sussex College of Technology.

UNIVERSITÉ INTERNATIONAL DE PARIS (GOE), Paris, France. Same as École Professionelle Supérieure.

UNIVERSITÉ NOUVELLE DE PARIS (GOE), Paris, France

UNIVERSITÉ PHILOTECHNIQUE (GOE), Brussels, Belgium and Paris, France

UNIVERSITÉ VOLTAIRE DE FRANCE (GOE), Marseilles, France

UNIVERSITY EXTENSION CONSERVATORY Same as Universal Extension Conservatory

UNIVERSITY IN LONDON Same as Obura University

UNIVERSITY OF CAPE COD Fictitious university whose paraphernalia (tee shirts, etc.) are sold in eastern Massachusetts.

UNIVERSITY OF CORPUS CHRISTI (E&T), Reno, Nevada; affiliated with the Society of Academic Recognition.

UNIVERSITY OF COVENTRY (E&T), Coventry, England

UNIVERSITY OF EASTERN FLORIDA P.O. Box 948, Chicago IL 60690. Degrees of all kinds, except medicine and law, sold for $40 each. They claim to be a "state chartered university" in Florida (not true), whose purpose is "to grant degrees to persons with actual experience." No new-born babies need apply.

UNIVERSITY OF EAST GEORGIA P.O. Box 14592, Savannah, GA 31406. Degrees in all fields including medicine, psychiatry, surgery and neurology for completion of a thesis on "a subject and length of your own choosing." I was duped by the first literature I received from John Blazer in 1975. At that time, he said he would administer standard examinations and award degrees based on test performance, as is done in Europe. That sounded O.K. But soon after, they began selling degrees in Europe for $500, and offering to backdate the diplomas to any date. Then they began offering medical degrees, and generally went downhill from there. They may also operate the University of the Bahama Islands.

UNIVERSITY OF PITTSBURG See Regency Enterprises

UNIVERSITY OF ENGLAND or UNIVERSITY OF ENGLAND AT OXFORD Suite 66, Kent House, 87 Regent Street, London W1R 7HF England. When I visited the address in 1982, I found a mail receiving service who told me that "an American" comes by every so often to pick up the mail. The literature is almost identical to that of De Paul, Loyola, and other mills using European addresses.

UNIVERSITY OF MAN'S BEST FRIEND See Holy Toledo University. The same people offer a Ph.D. in love and loyalty for $3, with paw prints instead of signatures on the diplomas.

UNIVERSITY OF THE BAHAMA ISLANDS P.O. Box 24576, Fort Lauderdale FL 33302. Similar literature and offer to that of the University of East Georgia, with material mailed from Savannah. Has also used an address in Hilton Head Island, South Carolina.

UNIVERSITY OF THE EASTERN UNITED STATES OF AMERICA (E&T)

UNIVERSITY OF THE NEW WORLD (E&T), Phoenix, Arizona; also Austria, Germany, Italy, Norway, Switzerland

UNIVERSITY OF THE OLD CATHOLIC CHURCH OF THE NORTH OF ENGLAND (E&T), Sheffield, England. Presumably the same "Archbishop" Brearly who runs the University of Sheffield and other mills.

UNIVERSITY OF THE PRESIDENT P.O. Box 20241, Salt Lake City UT 84120. Sells honorary degrees in iridology, psionics, macrobiotics, endogenous endocrinotherapy, and dozens more, for a $25 "donation."

UNIVERSITY OF THE SCIENCE OF MAN See Sussex College of Technology

UNIVERSITY OF SEALAND (E&T), England

UNIVERSITY OF SHEFFIELD Sheffield, England. Identified by the London *Times* as a degree mill operated by Charles Brearly, a car mechanic who calls himself Ignatius Carelus, successor to Cardinal Barberini of Rheims. He is a friend and associate of "Sir" Sidney Lawrence, proprietor of the College of Applied Science, London.

UNIVERSITY OF SULGRAVE (E&T), England

UNIVERSITY OF WALLA WALLA c/o S.J. Enterprises, P.O. Box 15625, San Diego CA 92115. Advertised in *Woman's Day* magazine a Doctor of anything ending in "ologist" for $18.90.

UNIVERSITY OF WINCHESTER 24 Cranbourn St., London WC2H 7AA, England. Same address as the London School of Social Research, described earlier in this chapter. Their diplomas are widely advertised as "completely spurious, nonetheless as impressive as genuine," for $15.

VOCATIONAL UNIVERSITY (GOE), Amritsar, Delhi, India

WASHINGTON INTERNATIONAL ACADEMY (E&T), New York

WASHINGTON NATIONAL UNIVERSITY Chicago IL. Identified as a degree mill by the U.S. Office of Education in 1961. No connection with the legitimate school of this name in Washington DC.

WEBSTER UNIVERSITY (E&T), Atlanta, Georgia.

WEINBERG UNIVERSITY OF WEST GERMANY See ORB

WESTERN CASCADE UNIVERSITY 681 Ellis St., San Francisco CA 94109. Bachelor's, Master's and Doctorates in any field for $45. The address is that of a mail receiving and forwarding service. In an apparent effort to avoid prosecution, the proprietors will not sell degrees or transcripts to California residents. The sales literature is similar to that used by Pacific Northwestern University.

WESTERN COLLEGE See National Certificate Co.

WESTERN ORTHODOX UNIVERSITY (or ACADEMY) (E&T), Glastonbury, England

WESTERN RESERVE EDUCATIONAL SERVICES For years, they sold diplomas that they claimed to have ''salvaged'' from ''genuine schools that have gone out of business'' from a P.O. Box in Shaker Heights, Ohio, now closed. The proprietor was Robert Kim Walton, who claimed to have been commended by the Sacred Congregation in Rome—not, one hopes, for selling fake degrees.

WESTERN UNIVERSITY One of the old-time degree mills, operating from San Diego and Jacumba, California, in the 1940's and 1950's.

WESTERN UNIVERSITY (E&T), Atlanta, Georgia and Delaware

WESTERN UNIVERSITY OF COLORADO (E&T)

WESTERN UNIVERSITY OF KAPURTHALA (GOE), Kapurthala, India

WESTERN UNIVERSITY OF MONTANA Identified as a degree mill by the U.S. Office of Education in 1961.

WILLIAMS COLLEGE 1310 State St., Boise ID 83702. When Lane Williams left Santa Fe, New Mexico, to move his ''college'' to Mexico, he changed its name from Williams to Elysion. But his Williams College was presumably left in other hands, and is now operating from Idaho, selling Bachelor of Arts and Bachelor of Laws degrees for about $300 each.

WORDSWORTH MEMORIAL UNIVERSITY (GOE, E&T) London, England, and Odhi, India

WORLD JNANA SADHAK SOCIETY (GOE), Jalpaiguri, India.

Chapter 25

Honorary Doctorates

The probable origin of the honorary Doctorate is discussed in Chapter 3. The persistence of this "degree" — indeed, its usage has grown tremendously during the twentieth century — is one of the mysteries of the academic world, for there is nothing whatever educational about the honorary Doctorate. It is, purely and simply, a title that some institutions have chosen for a variety of reasons to bestow upon certain people (and animals!) from time to time.

That the title given is "Doctor" — the same word used for academic degrees — is what has caused all the confusion, not to mention most of the desirability of the honorary Doctorate. It is exactly as if the government were to honor people by giving them the title of Senator or Judge.

Whatever the reason, honorary Doctorates have become highly valuable, and even negotiable, commodities.

Not everyone takes them seriously, however. When a German university handed its Doctor of Music diploma to the composer Handel, he rolled it into a dunce cap, placed it on the head of his servant, and said, "There! Now you're a Doctor, too."

Poet Robert Frost expressed particular delight at the announcement of his 50th honorary Doctorate (from Oxford), because he confessed that he had been having the decorative hoods given with each award made into a patchwork quilt, and now it would all come out even.

When artist Thomas Hart Benton accepted an honorary degree from Rockhurst College, he gestured to the graduating class and said, "I know how those boys behind me feel. They're thinking 'I worked four years for this, and that bum gets it free.'"

One of the curiosities of honorary Doctorates is that the titles given rarely have much relevance to the qualifications of the recipient. Hence we have actor Fess Parker getting a Doctor of Letters (after portraying Davey Crockett), actress Rosalind Russell a Doctor of Humane Letters, ballerina Margot Fonteyn a Doctor of Laws, and the late head of the Postal Telegraph, Clarence Mackay, a Doctor of Music (but it must be admitted that in this case there was a logical reason: his daughter had married Irving Berlin!).

As Mark Twain wrote:

> "I rejoiced when Missouri made me a Doctor of Laws because it was all clear profit, I not knowing anything about laws except how to evade them and not get caught. And now at Oxford I am to be made a Doctor of Letters — all clear profit, because what I don't know about letters would make me a millionaire if I could turn it into cash."

Not all titles have been inappropriate, of course. Charlie McCarthy, the impertinent ventriloquist's dummy, received a Master of Innuendo from Northwestern University. Admiral Byrd received a Doctor of Faith and Fortitude. Antioch University gave a Master of Communication to a campus switchboard operator, and Brooklyn College, which averages only one honorary degree every four years, gave a Doctor of Delectables degree to a long-time campus hot dog vendor. A heroic seeing eye dog, Bonzo, received a Doctor of Canine Fidelity from Newark University. And so it goes.

These humorous (or, some say, ludicrous) situations illuminate one of the four major reasons that honorary Doctorates are given: to bring publicity to the graduation ceremonies of the school. If a small college can lure a baseball star, a movie or television personality, or even the wife of a famous politician to the campus, the commencement is more likely to make the evening news and the next morning's papers, which may help student or faculty recruiting, fund raising, or memberships in the alumni association, or it may increase the chances that that top high school quarterback will come to the school next year. Indeed, when John Carroll University awarded an honorary Doctorate to Miami Dolphins coach Don Shula, it almost certainly was not for his academic achievements. And that is why we have Dr. Marlon Brando, Dr. Henry Fonda, Dr. Stan Musial, Dr. Bob Hope (at least 20 times over), Dr. Captain Kangaroo, and hundreds of similar Doctors.

Sometimes the publicity is not the kind the school had in mind. St. Joseph's College (a Catholic school) offered its honorary Doctorate to columnist Ann Landers, then created a big flap by withdrawing it after Landers wrote a pro-abortion column. And as Louisiana Tech was presenting its honorary Doctorate to Pittsburgh quarterback Terry Bradshaw, outraged alumni flew over the ceremony and dropped a cascade of leaflets protesting the award.

The second major reason honorary Doctorates are given is, perhaps, the most academically defensible one: to honor distinguished faculty and administrators at the donating school or at other schools. In American society, there is nothing equivalent to the national honors of many European countries (e.g., the Queen's Honours List, in which hundreds of people each year become knights, Members of the British Empire, etc.). The honorary Doctorate remains one of the few honors we have to bestow. And so, each June, from 40% to 60% of all honorary degrees go to usually unknown academics, often, it is said, in the hope that their school will honor someone from our school next year.

This practice has resulted in a new world record, established in June 1982. The previous record for receiving honorary Doctorates—Herbert Hoover's 89—was eclipsed by Notre Dame University's president, Father Theodore Hesburgh, as he collected his 90th honorary title.

The third major reason is to honor and provide a platform for world-famous persons. American presidents, British prime ministers, and other statesmen, are regularly so honored, and often take the opportunity to make major speeches on the occasion. General George Marshall announced the Marshall Plan while receiving an honorary Doctorate, and Winston Churchill used the occasion of his reception of an honorary degree from Westminster College in Missouri to deliver his famous "iron curtain" speech.

Although every single American president has collected some honorary Doctorates (George Washington had seven), none caused quite the furor of Harvard's award of an honorary Doctor of Laws to President Andrew Jackson. The Sons of Harvard erupted in anger. John Quincy Adams wrote about how his alma mater had degraded herself, "conferring her highest literary honors on a barbarian who could not write a sentence of grammar and could hardly spell his own name." Harvard's president Josiah Quincy defended the action: "As the people have twice decided that this man knows enough law to be their ruler, it is not for Harvard College to maintain they are mistaken."

(The ceremony itself must have been quite extraordinary. After Jackson had been given the sheepskin and expressed his thanks in a few short and perfunctory remarks, an aide reminded him that he was expected to make some remarks in Latin. Thereupon, according to biographer Robert Rayback, he bellowed out, in tones of thunder, all the Latin he knew: "E pluribus unum, sine qua non, multum in parvo, quid pro quo, ne plus ultra." So much for Dr. Andrew Jackson.)

The fourth major reason, the one that has brought the most criticism of honorary Doctorates, and the one that offers some hope to the common man, is the practice of awarding honorary degrees to people who perform certain services for the school, the most common (but by no means the only one) of which is donating a lot of money.

Although schools publicly deny there is any connection whatsoever, they have regularly, for centuries, awarded Doctorates to academically undistinguished folk who "just happened" to donate a bundle of money. In *A Distant Mirror,* Barbara Tuchman writes that in the 14th century, the University of Paris "had taken to selling degrees in theology to candidates unwilling to undertake its long and difficult studies or fearful of failing the examination."

A few centuries later, George Baker gave Harvard millions for a new business school. Harvard gave George Baker a Doctor of Laws along with their hearty thanks. John Archbold contributed a new football field to Syracuse University. Soon after, he was doctored by Syracuse University. William Randolph Hearst "traded" $100,000 and 400 acres of land to Oglethorpe University for an honorary Doctorate.

A British drygoods merchant named Isaac Wolfson gave about $10 million to Cambridge University a few years ago, and they not only gave him an honorary Doctorate, they named a college of the university for him. A couple of years later, he repeated the performance for another $10 million with Oxford. Oxford, too, both doctored him and named a college for him. Thus, as one London newspaper wrote in a caustic editorial, only two men in all history have had a college named for them at both Oxford and Cambridge: Isaac Wolfson and Jesus Christ.

John Hope Franklin of the National Humanities Center worries about "the delicate matter of honorary degrees. One cannot help wondering in how many ways some institutions sell their souls in conferring them. . . . Better that a university cease to exist altogether than sell its soul."

Another approach is to award the honorary Doctorate first, in the hopes that the recipient will give the school his blessing in the form of money or other favors. This approach made big news a while back when the *Washington Post* uncovered the "Koreagate" scandal, in which eleven U.S. congressmen had accepted (among other favors) honorary Doctorates from Korean universities, complete with all-expense luxury trips to Korea to collect them, in an apparent effort to win Congressional approval by the Korean regime.

To their credit, at least three congressmen rejected these honorary Doctorates. Such degrees are rarely turned down. Oxford University used to have a policy, before Richard Nixon came along, of offering an honorary Doctorate to every outgoing U.S. president. Of all those to whom it was offered, only good old Millard Fillmore turned it down, saying that he felt he had done nothing to merit it, and besides, the diploma was in Latin and he never accepted anything he couldn't read.

HOW TO GET AN HONORARY DOCTORATE

How, then, does the ordinary person, who is not a movie star, an athlete, or a millionaire, acquire an honorary Doctorate? There is no simple way, other than buying one from a less-than-respectable institution; more on that shortly. Here are some possibilities:

1. Donate money

Not necessarily big money. If a school is small and/or has urgent financial needs, as little as $10,000 has been said to turn the trick. In 1982, a major university, whose building fund was in trouble, exchanged an honorary Doctorate for a "mere" $50,000 donation. The donation need not be in cash, but can be in securities, property, even an assigned life insurance policy.

A Los Angeles businessman once ran small ads in the *New Republic* and other intellectual magazines saying, "Will donate $10,000 in return for honorary doctorate from accredited school anywhere." When I contacted him, he told me he had gotten the degree, but refused to disclose the name of the school.

2. Perform a valuable service.

Honorary Doctorates have gone to heads of fundraising committees who never gave a dime themselves; to real estate brokers who "put together" a big deal to acquire more land or to refinance a mortgage for the school; to friends of friends of celebrities who managed to get the Senator or the Star or the Second Baseman to speak at commencement; to a nurseryman who wangled the donation of hundreds of trees and supervised their planting on campus; to a golf pro who donated his time to the college golf team; and so on.

Finding a cash donor is perhaps the most valuable service. Remember that $50,000 honorary Doctorate previously described. The man who found that donor for the University in question also got an honorary Doctorate, for so finding.

3. Capitalize on trends.

Honorary Doctorates are often very trendy things. Trends seem to run for three to five years. For instance, in the late 1950's, space science was in vogue, and people ranging from Wernher von Braun to the founder of a local rocketry society were being honored. In the early 1960s, it was the Peace Corps. Sargent Shriver, its first Director, set a record that still stands by accepting seven Doctorates in one month (June, 1964), and a lot of other Peace Corps people and other youth workers were in demand on commencement platforms.

Time Magazine, sadly, no longer runs its "Kudos" columns during the month of June, listing many of the honorary Doctorates being dispensed, but they still generally run one article a year on the subject.

Some people have reported success by directly contacting (or, more often, indirectly contacting) a school that has given a certain honorary degree this year, suggesting they may wish to consider a similar one next year.

So far in the 1980's, it looks as if there are trends toward both jazz and classical musicians, medical researchers, people who work with handicapped or retarded children, the very elderly (several people over 100 have gotten them for no apparent reason other than survival), Vietnam veterans, economists, and public interest lawyers.

4. Buy one.

If all you really want is a fancy but meaningless document to hang on the wall (actually, all honorary Doctorates fit that description, but some may be perceived as more meaningless than others), many of the schools described in Chapters 23 and 24 dispense honorary Doctorates on payment of their fee for so doing, which can range from $5 to more than $1,000.

5. Wait.

In an earlier edition of this book, I wrote, "Wait. I think it is inevitable that one or more well-known, respectable, fully-accredited colleges, faced by the cash crunch that is upon so many worthy institutions, will face reality and openly put their honorary doctorates up for sale, or, possibly, for bids." One school did so soon after. A small, accredited college took out a national ad and suggested a donation of $25,000. I am confident that others will follow. In a similar vein, the well respected Embry-Riddle University advertised in the *Wall Street Journal* in 1982 a Trusteeship of the University, in exchange for a one million dollar donation. Things are moving. Wait and see.

THE ETIQUETTE OF SOLICITING DEGREES

Here's one Emily Post never had to deal with. How straightforward should one be in letting it be known that one would like an honorary Doctorate? There is no way to know. My feeling is that in the majority of situations, the direct approach is inappropriate. One must work through intermediaries — friends of school officials or trustees, who drop hints. But there are also some schools and awards committees who find the blunt approach refreshing. These are the ones who realize and admit that what they are really doing, anyway, is selling honorary degrees, so why not be up front? The president of a small eastern college told me that he was once approached by a second-rate actor who really wanted an honorary Doctorate, just like Marlon Brando and Henry Fonda. They negotiated terms, and the degree was awarded the following June.

On the other hand, a high Air Force official in Europe got a lot of unfavorable publicity when *Stars and Stripes* revealed that he had solicited honorary Doctorates for himself and some associates, from universities that were doing contractual work for the Air Force. Two of the universities (University of Southern California and University of Maryland) turned him down. "It wasn't appropriate to ask for it, and it wasn't appropriate to give it," one school official said. But the third school, Ball State University, gave it. (The Army's counterpart in Europe, when asked if he would solicit honorary Doctorates replied, "You've got to be out of your tree.")

Part Five
Reference Section

Chapter 26

Glossary of Important Terms

ACADEMIC YEAR: The period of formal academic instruction, usually from September or October to May or June, and divided into Semesters, Quarters, or Trimesters.

ACCREDITATION: Recognition of a school by an independent private organization. Not a governmental function. There are more than 100 accrediting agencies, some recognized by the Department of Education or by COPA, some not.

A.C.T.: American College Testing program, administrators of aptitude and achievement tests.

ADJUNCT FACULTY: Part-time faculty member, often at a non-traditional school, and often with a full-time teaching job at another school.

ADVANCED PLACEMENT: Admission to a school at a higher level than one would normally enter, because of getting credit for prior learning experiences.

ALMA MATER: The school from which one has graduated, as in "My alma mater is Michigan State University."

ALTERNATIVE: Offering an alternate, or a different means of pursuing learning or degrees, or both.

ALUMNI: Graduates of a school, as in "This school has some distinguished alumni." (The word is technically for males only; females are "alumnae.") The singular is "alumnus" (male) or "alumna" (female).

ALUMNI ASSOCIATION: A confederation of alumni, who have joined together to support their alma mater in various ways, generally by donating money.

APPROVED: In California, a level of state recognition of one or more specific programs or departments within a school. Generally regarded as one step above "authorized" and one step below "accredited."

ARBITRATION: A means of settling disputes, as between a student and a school, in which an independent arbitrator, or judge (or team of them), listens to both sides, and makes a decision. A means of avoiding a legal trial. Many learning contracts have a binding arbitration clause.

ASSISTANTSHIP: A means of assisting students (usually graduate students) financially by offering them part-time academic employment, usually in the form of a Teaching Assistantship or a Research Assistantship.

ASSOCIATE'S DEGREE: A "two-year" degree, traditionally awarded by community or junior colleges after two years of residential study, or completion of 60 to 64 semester hours.

AUDITING: Sitting in on a class, with no intention of earning credit for the course.

AUTHORIZED: In California, a form of state recognition of schools, authorizing them to exist, to accept students, and to grant degrees.

BACHELOR'S DEGREE: Awarded after four years of full-time residential study, or earning from 120 to 124 semester units by non-traditional means.

BINDING ARBITRATION: Arbitration in which both parties have agreed in advance that they will abide by the result and take no further legal action.

BRANCH CAMPUS: A satellite facility, run by officers of the main campus of a college or university, at another location. Can range from a small office to a full-fledged university center.

CAMPUS: The main facility of a college or university, usually comprising buildings, grounds, dormitories, cafeterias and dining halls, sports stadia, etc. The campus of a non-traditional school may consist solely of offices.

C.L.E.P.: The College-Level Examination Program, a series of equivalency examinations given nationally each month.

COEDUCATIONAL: Education of men and women on the same campus or in the same program. (Female students are sometimes called coeds.)

COLLEGE: In the U.S., an institution offering programs leading to the Associate's, Bachelor's, and possibly higher degrees. Often used interchangeably with "university" although traditionally a university is a collection of colleges. In England and elsewhere, "college" may denote part of a university (Kings College, Cambridge), or a private high school (Eton College).

COLLOQUIUM: A gathering of scholars to discuss a given topic, often over a period of a few hours to a few days. ("The university is sponsoring a colloquium on marine biology.")

COMMUNITY COLLEGE: A two-year traditional school, offering programs leading to the Associate's degree and, typically, many non-credit courses in arts, crafts, and vocational fields for community members not interested in a degree.

COMPETENCY: The philosophy and practice of awarding credit and degrees based on learning skills, rather than time spent in courses.

C.O.P.A.: The Council on Postsecondary Accreditation, one of the two organizations that officially recognize accrediting agencies.

CORRESPONDENCE COURSE: A course offered by mail, completed entirely by home study, often with a single proctored examination at the end.

COURSE: A specific unit of instruction, such as a course in microeconomics, or a course in abnormal psychology. Residential courses last for one or more semesters (or quarters); correspondence courses often have no time requirements.

CRAMMING: Intensive preparation for an examination.

CREDIT: Units used to record courses taken. Each credit typically represents the number of hours spent in class each week. Hence a 3-credit or 3-unit course might represent a class that met three hours a week for a quarter or a semester.

CURRICULUM: A program or series of courses to be taken in pursuit of a degree or other objective.

DEGREE: A title conferred by a school to show that a certain course of study has been completed.

DEPARTMENT OF EDUCATION: The national agency concerned with all educational matters not handled by the 50 state Departments of Education.

DIPLOMA: The certificate that shows that a certain course of study has been completed. Diplomas are awarded for completing degree studies or other, shorter courses of study.

DISSERTATION: The major research project normally required as part of the work for a Doctorate. Dissertations are expected to make a new, creative contribution to the field of study, or to demonstrate one's excellence in the field.

DOCTORATE: The highest degree one can earn. Includes Doctor of Philosophy, Education, and many other titles. (Most people with degrees from professional schools do not speak of "having a Doctorate" but rather of "having a medical degree, a law degree, etc.")

DORMITORY: Student living quarters on residential campuses. May include dining halls and classrooms.

EARLY DECISION: Making a decision on whether to admit a student sooner than decisions are usually made. Offered by some schools primarily as a service either to students applying to several schools, or those who are especially anxious to know the outcome of their application.

E.C.F.M.G.: The Education Commission for Foreign Medical Graduates, which administers an examination to physicians who have gone to medical school outside the United States, and wish to practice in the U.S.

ELECTIVES: Courses one does not have to take, but may elect to take, as part of a degree program.

ESSAY TEST: An examination in which the student writes narrative sentences as answers to questions, instead of the short answers required by a multiple choice test. Also called a "subjective test."

EQUIVALENCY EXAMINATION: An examination designed to demonstrate knowledge in a subject where the learning was acquired outside a traditional classroom. A person who learned nursing skills while working in a hospital, for instance, could take an equivalency exam to earn credit in obstetrical nursing.

FEES: Money paid to a school for purposes other than academic tuition. Fees might pay for parking, library services, use of the gymnasium, binding of dissertations, etc.

FELLOWSHIP: A study grant, usually awarded to a graduate student, and usually requiring no work other than usual academic work (as contrasted with an assistantship).

FINANCIAL AID: A catch-all term, including scholarships, loans, fellowships, assistantships, tuition reductions, etc. Many schools have a financial aid officer.

FRATERNITIES: Men's fraternal and social organizations that exist on many larger university campuses, often with their own living accommodations. Often they are identified by Greek letters, such as Zeta Beta Tau. Also, there are professional and scholastic fraternities that are societies open to men and women who meet the requirements, such as Beta Alpha Psi, the national society for students of accounting.

FRESHMAN: The name for the class in its first of four years of traditional study for the Bachelor's degree, and its individual members ("She is a freshman.")

GRADE POINT AVERAGE: The average score a student has made in all his or her classes weighted by the number of credits or units for each class.

GRADES: Evaluative scores provided for each course, and often for individual examinations or papers written for that course. There are letter grades (usually A, B, C, D, F) and number grades (usually expressed as percentages from 0% to 100%, or on a scale of 0 to 4). Some schools use a pass/fail system with no grades.

GRADUATE: One who has earned a degree from a school. ("He is a graduate of Yale University.")

GRADUATE SCHOOL: A school or a division of a university offering work at the Master's or Doctoral degree level.

GRADUATE STUDENT: One attending graduate school.

G.R.E.: The Graduate Record Examination, which many traditional schools and a few non-traditional schools require for admission to graduate programs.

HONOR SOCIETIES: Organizations for persons with high grade point averages or other evidence of outstanding performance. There are local societies on many campuses, and several national ones, the most prestigious of which is called Phi Beta Kappa.

HONOR SYSTEM: A system in which students are trusted not to cheat on examinations, and to obey other rules, without proctors or others monitoring their performance.

HONORARY DOCTORATE: A non-academic award, given regularly by more than 1,000 colleges and universities to honor distinguised scholars, celebrities, and donors of large sums of money. Holders of the award may (and often do) call themselves "Doctor."

JUNIOR: The name for the class in its third year of a four-year traditional Bachelor's degree program or any member of that class ("He is a junior this year.")

JUNIOR COLLEGE: Another name for community college.

LANGUAGE LABORATORY: A room with special audio equipment to facilitate learning languages. Many students can be learning different languages at different skill levels at the same time.

LEARNING CONTRACT: A formal agreement between a student and a school, specifying independent work to be done by the student, and the amount of credit the school will award on successful completion of the work.

LECTURE CLASS: A faculty member lecturing to a class of anywhere from a few dozen to more than 1,000 students. Often lecture classes are followed by small group discussion sessions led by student assistants or junior faculty. The most common method of instruction at most larger and many smaller universities.

LIBERAL ARTS: A term with many complex meanings, but generally referring to the non-scientific curriculum of a university: humanities, the arts, social sciences, history, and so forth.

LICENSED: Holding a permit to operate. This can range from a difficult-to-obtain state school license to a simple local business license.

LIFE EXPERIENCE PORTFOLIO: A comprehensive presentation listing and describing all learning experiences in a person's life, with appropriate documentation. The basic document used in assigning academic credit for life experience learning.

L.S.A.T.: The Law School Admission Test, required by most law schools of all applicants.

MAINTENANCE COSTS: The expenses incurred while attending school, other than tuition and fees. Includes room and board (food), clothing, laundry, postage, travel, etc.

MAJOR: The subject or academic department in which a student takes concentrated coursework leading to a specialty. ("Her major is literature; he is majoring in chemistry.")

MASTER'S DEGREE: The degree earned after the Bachelor's, typically in one or two more years of study.

MENTOR: Faculty member assigned to supervise independent study work at a non-traditional university.

MINOR: The secondary subject or academic department in which a student takes concentrated coursework. ("She has a major in art and a minor in biology.")

M.S.A.T.: The Medical School Admission Test, required by most medical schools of all applicants.

MULTIPLE CHOICE TEST: An examination in which the student chooses the best of several alternative answers provided for each question. ("The capital city of England is (a) London, (b) Ostrogotz-Plakatz, (c) Tokyo, (d) none of the above.")

MULTIUNIVERSITY: A university system with two or more separate campuses, each a major university in its own right, such as the University of California or University of Wisconsin system.

NARRATIVE TRANSCRIPT: A transcript issued by a non-traditional school in which, instead of simply listing the courses completed and grades received, there is a narrative description of the work done and the school's rationale for awarding credit for that work.

N.M.S.Q.T.: National Merit Scholarship Qualifying Test, given annually to high school juniors.

NON-TRADITIONAL: Something done in other than the usual or traditional way. In education, refers to learning and degrees completed by methods other than spending many hours in a classroom and lecture hall.

NON-RESIDENT: (1) A means of instruction in which the student does not need to visit the school; all work is done by correspondence, telephone, or exchange of tape or video cassettes.

(2) A person who does not meet residency requirements of a given school and, as a result, often has to pay a higher tuition or fees. Often out-of-state residents pay two to five times as much tuition as residents of the state in which a school is located.

OBJECTIVE TEST: An examination in which questions requiring a very short answer are posed. It can be multiple choice, true/false, fill-in-the-blank, etc. The questions are related to facts (thus objective) rather than to opinion (or subjective).

OPEN ADMISSIONS: An admissions policy in which everyone who applies is admitted, on the theory that the ones who are unable to do university work will drop out before long. (Advice from the author, who once did so: Never accept a teaching job in a first semester course in a school with open admissions!)

OUT-OF-STATE STUDENT: One from a state other than that in which the school is located. Because of much higher tuition rates for such students, many people attempt to establish legal residence in the same state as their school.

PARALLEL INSTRUCTION: A method in which non-resident students do exactly the same work as resident students, during the same general time periods, doing everything except actually attending classes.

PASS/FAIL OPTION: Instead of getting a letter or number grade in a course, the student may elect, at the start of the course, a pass/fail option in which the only possible "grades" are either "pass" or "fail." Most schools say that a student may take only one or two pass-fail classes at one time.

P.E.P.: Proficiency Examination Program, a series of equivalency exams given nationally every few months.

PLAN OF STUDY: A detailed description of the program an applicant to a school plans to pursue. Many traditional schools ask for this as part of the admissions procedure. The plan of study should be designed to meet the objectives of the Statement of Purpose.

PORTFOLIO: See Life Experience Portfolio.

PREREQUISITES: Courses that must be taken before certain other courses may be taken. For instance, a course in algebra is often a prerequisite for a course in geometry.

PRIVATE SCHOOL: A school that is privately owned, rather than operated by a government department.

PROCTOR: A person who supervises the taking of an examination to be certain there is no cheating and that other rules are followed. Many non-traditional schools permit unproctored examinations.

PROFESSIONAL SCHOOL: School in which one studies for the various professions, including medical and dental school, law school, nursing school, veterinary school, optometry school, etc.

P.S.A.T.: Preliminary Scholastic Aptitude Test, given annually to high school juniors.

PUBLIC SCHOOL: A school operated by the government of a city, county, district, state, or the federal government.

QUARTER: An academic term at a school on the "quarter system," in which the calendar year is divided into four equal quarters. New courses begin each quarter.

QUARTER HOUR: An amount of credit earned for each classroom hour spent in a given course during a given quarter. A course that meets four hours each week for a quarter would probably be worth four quarter hours. Same as quarter units.

RECOGNIZED: A term used by some schools to indicate approval from some other organization or governmental body. The term usually does not have a precise meaning, and may mean different things in different states.

REGISTRAR: The official at most universities who is responsible for maintaining student records and, in many cases, for verifying and validating applications for admission.

ROLLING ADMISSIONS: A year-round admissions procedure. Many schools only admit students once or twice a year. A school with rolling admissions considers each application when received and notifies the student as quickly as possible. Many non-traditional schools, especially non-resident ones, permit students to begin work as soon as they are admitted.

S.A.T.: Scholastic Aptitude Test, one of the standard tests given to qualify for admission to colleges and universities.

SCHOLARSHIP: A study grant, either in cash or in the form of tuition or fee reduction.

SCORES: Numerical ratings of performance on various tests. ("His score on the Graduate Record Exam was not so good.")

SEMESTER: A school term, generally four to five months. Schools on the semester system will have two semesters a year, often with a shorter summer session.

SEMESTER HOUR: An amount of credit earned in a course representing one classroom hour per week for a semester. A class that meets three days a week for one hour would be worth three semester hours. Also called Semester Units.

SEMINAR: A form of instruction combining independent research with meetings of small groups of students and a faculty member, generally to report on reading or research the students have done.

SENIOR: The fourth year of study of a four-year traditional Bachelor's degree program, or a member of the senior class.

SOPHOMORE: The second year of study of a four-year traditional Bachelor's degree program, or a member of that class. ("Corinna is a sophomore this year, and was elected president of the sophomore class.")

SORORITY: A women's social organization, often with its own living quarters on or near a campus, and usually identified with two or three Greek letters, such as Sigma Chi.

SPECIAL STUDENT: A student who is not studying for a degree either because he or she is ineligible, or does not wish the degree.

STATEMENT OF PURPOSE: A detailed description of the career the applicant intends to pursue after graduation. A statement of purpose is often requested as part of the admissions procedure at a university.

SUBJECT: An area of study or learning covering a single topic, such as the subject of chemistry, or economics, or French literature.

SUBJECTIVE TEST: An examination in which the answers are in the form of narrative sentences or long or short essays, often expressing opinions rather than reporting facts.

SYLLABUS: A detailed description of a course of study, often including the books to be read, papers to be written, and examinations to be given.

THESIS: The major piece of research that is completed by many Master's degree candidates. A thesis is expected to show a detailed knowledge of one's field and ability to do reserach and integrate knowledge of the field.

T.O.E.F.L.: Test of English as a Foreign Language, required by many schools of persons for whom English is not the native language.

TRADITIONAL EDUCATION: Education at a residential school in which the Bachelor's degree is completed through four years of classroom study, the Master's in one or two years, and the Doctorate in two to four years.

TRANSCRIPT: A certified copy of the student's academic record showing courses taken, examinations passed, and grades or scores received.

TRANSFER STUDENT: A student who has earned credit in one school, and then transfers to another school.

TRIMESTER: A term consisting of one third of an academic year. A few schools have three equal trimesters per year.

TUITION: The money charged for formal instruction. In some non-traditional schools, tuition is the only expense other than postage. In other schools there may be additional fees covering non-instructional matters such as books, insurance, library charges, etc.

TUITION WAIVER: A form of financial assistance in which the school charges little or no tuition.

TUTOR: see Mentor. A tutor can also be a hired assistant who helps a student prepare for a given class or examination.

UNDERGRADUATE: Pertaining to the period of study from the end of high school to the earning of the Bachelor's degree; also to a person in such a course of study. ("Barry is an undergraduate at Reed College, one of the leading undergraduate schools.")

UNIVERSITY: An institution that usually comprises one or more undergraduate colleges, one or more graduate schools, and, often, one or more professional schools.

Chapter 27

Bibliography

Most of these books are available in bookstores and libraries. Some are sold only by mail; in those cases, I have provided the address of the publisher or distributor.

DIRECTORIES

Accredited Institutions of Postsecondary Education, published by the American Council on Education, One Dupont Circle, Washington DC 20036. The standard reference book for accredited schools, issued each year (about mid-year), listing every accredited institution and candidates for accreditation. This is the book most people use to determine conclusively whether or not a given school is accredited.

Comparative Guide to American Colleges, by James Cass and Max Birnbaum (Harper and Row). One of the three ''standard'' directories of traditional schools. Unlike Lovejoy's and Barron's, however, it is both factual and opinionated, a good feature. More than 700 pages of school descriptions and statistical information.

Barron's Profiles of American Colleges (Barron's Educational Series), a massive, two-volume, 1300-page description of every accredited college and university in America, with lists of majors offered by each school.

Lovejoy's College Guide, by the late Clarence E. Lovejoy (Simon and Schuster). Unfortunately, the usefulness of this 400-page directory is marred by the listing of some very poor schools or degree mills, without identifying them as such (e.g., Thomas Edison College of Florida, Bernadean University).

Peterson's Annual Guide to Undergraduate Study (Peterson's Guides). Another massive directory (over 2,000 pages), unique in that most schools prepare their own entries, covering up to two pages of small type. It is interesting to see how they present themselves.

Peterson's Annual Guides to Graduate Study (Peterson's Guides). Five large books, each describing in detail opportunities for residential graduate study in the U.S. in various fields. There is a volume covering social science and humanities, biological and agricultural sciences, physical sciences, engineering, and a summary volume.

Guide to Independent Study through Correspondence Instruction, by Joan Hunter (Peterson's Guides). In effect a master catalogue, listing all courses offered by all 69 American universities that offer correspondence courses. Only the course titles are given, so it is still necessary to write to the individual schools for detailed information and prices. This guide is helpful in deciding which schools to write to, in spite of an extremely hard-to-use index.

Who Offers Part-time Degrees, by Patricia Consolloy (Peterson's Guides). Very brief descriptions of

248

more than 2,000 colleges (including junior colleges) where degree programs for part-time students are available.

CREDIT FOR LIFE EXPERIENCE LEARNING

Assessing Prior Learning — a CAEL Student Guide, by Aubrey Forrest (Council for the Advancement of Experiential Learning, Lakefront North, Suite 300, Columbia MD 21004). A most useful and valuable guidebook, whch helps the student or prospective student identify and describe his or her experiential learning experiences. It includes sections on how to document and measure amounts of learning that can lead to earning credits. Includes samples of relevant documents and worksheets to use in preparing one's own materials.

Portfolio Development Guide, and *Sample Portfolio* (Marylhurst College for Lifelong Learning, Prior Learning Experience Program, Marylhurst OR 97036). One of the very good non-traditional programs has issued a very useful handbook on how to prepare a life experience portfolio; the *Sample Portfolio* is an outstanding example for you to use as a model. Both are sold by mail at modest prices.

The National Guide to Educational Credit for Training Programs (American Council on Education, One Dupont Circle, Washington DC 20036). Most non-traditional schools use this large volume, and the military volume described next, to assess credit for non-school learning. It describes hundreds of corporate training programs offered by large and medium-sized companies, and suggests the number of semester units to assign for each program (e.g., the Sheraton Hotel food and beverage seminar is worth two semester units).

Guide to the Evaluation of Educational Experiences in the Armed Forces (American Council on Education). This three-volume set, issued annually, recommends college credit to be assigned for military learning experiences. It is used by most college admissions officers. Example: a 301-hour Army course in map reading is recommended for three semester hours.

FINANCIAL AID

Your Own Financial Aid Factory: the guide to locating college money, by Robert Leider (Octameron Associates, P.O. Box 3437, Alexandria VA 22302). Contains an immense amount of useful information and good advice in 140 pages. Highly recommended.

How to Get the Money to Pay for College, by Gene R. Hawes and David M. Brownstone (David McKay Company). Covers much of the same material as the first book listed, with worksheets and samples of various forms. Recommended if there is an up-to-date edition; the one I bought was four years old, and things have changed mightily in that time.

After Scholarships, What?: Creative ways to lower your college costs and the colleges that offer them, edited by Patricia Consolloy (Peterson's Guides). Three pages of text, followed by nearly 400 pages of charts and tables, giving information on nearly 2,000 schools: tuition costs, average scholarship size, whether loans are available, if part time or accelerated studies are offered, etc. Only accredited schools are covered.

"HOW TO" BOOKS

Barron's Guides
Barron's is a major educational publisher, with a good many books on post-secondary education: getting admitted to colleges, preparing for exams, how to study, and so on. Among the most useful are the following.

   How to Prepare for College Entrance Examinations (series of large volumes for various exams, including SAT and ACT series)

How to Prepare for... series: books covering many specific tests, ranging from freshman equivalency exams to the TOEFL (Test of English as a Foreign Language), to the Graduate Record Exam to law and medical school admission tests.
    Getting Into Medical School
    How to Succeed in Law School
    How to Write Better Resumes

College Degrees for Adults, by Wayne Blaze and John Nero (Beacon Press). Detailed descriptions of 120 college and university programs offering non-resident or, mostly, short residency degrees. More detailed than my book, but many fewer programs described, and (unless there has been a new edition) badly out of date in the 1979 printing. 140 pages.

College Learning Anytime Anywhere, by Ewald B. Nyquist and others (Harcourt Brace Jovanovich). Although the book describes a few programs in great detail, its main value is inspirational. It includes case histories and reports from dozens of people who have earned or are earning non-resident degrees. Nyquist was President of the University of the State of New York, America's largest non-resident accredited university.

Getting College Course Credits by Examination, by Gene R. Hawes (McGraw-Hill). Describes in detail virtually all the various equivalency examinations that can be taken for college credit. Describes each test and suggests best means of studying for them. Some sample questions are given. 180 pages.

College on Your Own, by Gail Parker and Gene R. Hawes (Bantam Books). This remarkable book, which unfortunately may be out of print, serves as a syllabus for a huge variety of fields, for people who want to do college-level work at home, with or without the guidance of a college. Contains a brief overview of each field (anthropology, biology, chemistry, history, etc.), and a detailed reading list to learn more about that field. Should be most valuable in preparing learning contracts. About 400 pages.

This Way Out: a guide to alternatives to traditional college education in the U.S., by John Coyne and Tom Herbert (E.P. Dutton). A delightful, if out-of-date, book that describes a small number of alternatives in detail, with inspirational interviews with participants. Includes an intriguing essay on self-education by hiring tutors, and sections as diverse as how to study, how to hitchhike successfully, and how to deal with large universities worldwide.

MEDICAL SCHOOLS

World Directory of Medical Schools (World Health Organization of the United Nations). This directory is issued every five to seven years, and includes a chapter on each country of the world, listing the approved medical schools and offering much statistical information on medical education in that country. There are companion volumes covering veterinary, dental, and pharmacy education.

The Rejected Medical School Applicant: options and alternatives, by Dr. Carlos Pestana (P.O. Box 32617, San Antonio, TX 32617). This outstanding volume covers, in 360 well-written pages, every conceivable alternative to getting a medical education, from ''buying your way in'' to using political pressure to dealing with foreign medical schools that accept large numbers of American students. There are detailed descriptions of the author's visits to many ''alternative'' schools in Mexico and the Caribbean. If only there were an index!

FOREIGN SCHOOLS

International Handbook of Universities (International Association of Universities, 1 Rue Miollis, 75732 Paris Cedex 15, France). This is the ultimate directory of the world's universities: Along with the book described next, 1,200 pages describe virtually every university in the world, with names of officers, departments, department heads, fees, etc. Extremely useful, and absurdly expensive (over $100 in the most recent edition).

Commonwealth Universities (Association of Commonwealth Universities, 36 Gordon Square, London WC1H OPF, England). Companion volume to the one just described, for the British Commonwealth. Also very expensive.

World Guide to Higher Education (UNESCO; available through Unipub, Box 433, New York NY 10016). Describes in detail the educational systems of every nation on earth, including the degrees and degree titles offered, how long it takes to earn degrees, and a glossary of educational terms used to that country. Three hundred pages, at the remarkable cost of about twenty cents a page.

World-Wide Inventory of Non-Traditional Degree Programs (UNESCO, Paris; available through Unipub, Box 433, New York NY 10016). A generally useful report on what many of the world's nations are doing in the way of non-traditional education. Some useful school descriptions, and lots of detailed descriptions of evening courses offered by workers' cooperatives in Bulgaria, etc., etc.

World Education Series: guides to the academic placement of students from foreign countries in educational institutions in the U.S. (ACCRAO, One Dupont Circle, Suite 330, Washington DC 20036). The American Association of Collegiate Registrars and Admissions Officers has issued a series of many volumes as a guide to understanding the systems in other countries. Recommendations are given for how much credit to give for learning experiences in each country. The books range from 150 to 200 pages, and are available for dozens of countries.

How to Earn an American University Degree Without Ever Going to America, by John Bear (Mendocino Book Company, P.O. Box 646, Mendocino, CA 95460). A companion to the book you are now reading, this one contains much of the same information in abridged form, plus a great deal of information specifically for people living outside North America, ranging from student visas to language exams, and from currency exchange problems to transfer of foreign academic credit.

Chapter 28

State Laws and Regulations

There are two totally different kinds of laws relevant to the subject of college degrees: those regulating the use of degrees, and those regulating the awarding of degrees. Please bear in mind that I am not a lawyer, and cannot give legal advice. If you have concerns or questions with regard either to awarding or using degrees in your state, I urge you to seek qualified legal counsel.

USING DEGREES

In every state of the union, misuse of degree or credential comes under the statutes governing fraud. In almost all cases, the intent of the law is that if one uses a degree or title he or she does not have with the intent of deceiving another, then the law has been broken. "Deceiving another" can be interpreted very broadly to include not just fake lawyers and doctors, but people who put phony degrees on their resumes for a job application, and people who use their degree in business or professional life. For instance, a court in New York ruled that a garage owner who listed a fake Bachelor of Technology degree on his business card was deceiving the public, some of whom might come to him because of the degree, and therefore he had violated the law. Using a fake degree, or claiming a degree from a real school that was not earned is grounds for dismissal from a job, and probably grounds for prosecution in every state.

AWARDING DEGREES

46 of the 50 states of the union have laws of one kind or another regulating private (non-government-run) degree-granting schools in that state. Many such laws undergo regular review and revision, and the general direction of change has been to make the laws tougher. Even Arizona, which has become a haven for degree mills in recent years, as they are forced to leave other states, may be changing. At this writing, here is what the states have to say about non-public colleges and universities. The extent to which any state can regulate the operation of out-of-state schools in that state is a very murky area of the law.

ALABAMA
All degree-granting schools except those operating for more than 20 years must be licensed by the Commission on Higher Education.

ALASKA
All private colleges and universities must be given authority to grant degrees by the Commission on Postsecondary Education.

ARIZONA
No laws whatsoever, although the Board of Regents tries each year to get one passed by the state legislature, to no avail.

ARKANSAS
Schools must be both certified and incorporated to operate in the state.

CALIFORNIA
The state authorizes universities to operate if they own $50,000 worth of property, offer some element of instruction, and file an annual disclosure statement. The state approves specific degree programs within schools, which permits holders of such degrees to take state licensing examinations without further qualification. Religious schools are exempted.

COLORADO
Degree-granting schools must be regionally accredited or otherwise specifically approved by the state.

CONNECTICUT
State license required to grant degrees or use the words "college" or "university." Schools operating before 1965 are excluded.

DELAWARE
All institutions chartered after 1945 must be state-approved.

DISTRICT OF COLUMBIA
All schools must be licensed by the Educational Institution Licensure Commission.

FLORIDA
All degree-granting schools must be licensed by the State Board of Independent Colleges and Universities.

GEORGIA
All schools must be state-licensed.

HAWAII
There are no laws requiring the licensing of degree-granting institutions, nor any regulation of private or out-of-state schools.

IDAHO
State law requires registration and certification by the State Board of Education of "courses" offered in the state.

ILLINOIS
State approval is required to operate and to grant degrees.

INDIANA
All private colleges must be licensed by the State.

IOWA
The State Board of Education must approve private colleges that grant degrees.

KANSAS
Institutions must be state authorized to confer degrees.

KENTUCKY
Private degree-granting institutions must be licensed by the state.

LOUISIANA
Proprietary institutions must register with the state, but there is no element of evaluation or approval.

MAINE
All schools not exempted by the state legislature must be licensed by the state.

MARYLAND
The law sets minimum standards by which a school can qualify to be licensed to grant degrees.

MICHIGAN
The law sets standards for curriculum, faculty, and financial stability, and requires annual reports.

MINNESOTA
All institutions except those educating for the ministry or other religious duties must be approved by the state.

MISSISSIPPI
State approval is required for all proprietary institutions.

MISSOURI
There are no laws regulating private postsecondary education, although, as in Arizona, the educational establishment has been trying for years to get some passed.

MONTANA
The state must approve ''course adequacy'' before degree-granting permission is given.

NEBRASKA
State approval is required in order to grant degrees.

NEVADA
All degree-granting institutions must be licensed by the state.

NEW HAMPSHIRE
Approval by the state legislature is required before degrees can be granted.

NEW JERSEY
Schools must be licensed and courses must be approved before degrees can be granted.

NEW MEXICO
Degree-granting schools must secure a permit and post a surety bond before granting degrees.

NEW YORK
All schools must have the approval of the Board of Regents before offering courses or degrees.

NORTH CAROLINA
Private degree-granting colleges must be licensed by the state.

NORTH DAKOTA
Schools must be authorized to operate by the state, and be granted a license to do so.

OHIO
Authorization from the state is required for all schools established after 1966.

OKLAHOMA
Private colleges must be both licensed and accredited by the state.

OREGON
Approval of the Educational Coordinating Commission is required before granting any degrees.

PENNSYLVANIA
Schools must receive permission of the state before incorporating as a degree-granting institution.

PUERTO RICO
All schools must be licensed by the Council on Higher Education.

RHODE ISLAND
State authorization is required to grant degrees.

SOUTH CAROLINA
All institutions formed after 1952 must be licensed by the state before confering degrees.

SOUTH DAKOTA

The law sets minimum standards schools must meet before getting the license necessary to grant degrees.

TENNESSEE

Institutions must meet minimum standards to obtain authorization to grant degrees.

TEXAS

A Certificate of Authority is required to enroll students or grant degrees. Private schools whose credits are accepted by the University of Texas are exempt.

UTAH

Apparently has no laws governing granting of degrees.

VERMONT

State approval is required before awarding degrees.

VIRGINIA

State approval is required before awarding degrees.

WASHINGTON

Degree-granting institutions must register with the state and agree to comply with certain minimum standards. "Hardship cases" may be excluded from compliance.

WEST VIRGINIA

State approval is required before degrees can be granted.

WISCONSIN

State law sets minimum standards for the approval necessary to operate as a school, and requires a $25,000 surety bond.

WYOMING

Private schools must be licensed by the State Board of Education.

The "Hello/Goodbye" Index

The "Hello" index is a list of those schools that are appearing in this edition of the book for the first time. The "Goodbye" index is a list of those schools that were listed in the 7th edition of the book, but do not appear in this edition, along with the reasons for their departure.

HELLO

Aalborg University Centre
Acadia University
Adams Institute of Technology
Allama Iqbal Open University
American Institute of Technology
American National University
American Technological University
American Western University
Andrew Jackson College
Andrew Jackson University
Anna Maria College
Appalachian Bible College
Atlantic University
Biscayne College
Brandon University
Burlington College
California Coast University
California Graduate School of Marital and
    Family Therapy
California Institute of Integral Studies
California Institute of Higher Learning
Cambridge College
Capital University
Central Bible College
Centre de Tele-Enseignement Universitaire
Charter Oak College
Chicago Medical College
Clayton Theological Institute

College of Clinical Hypnosis
College of Life Science
Cooley School of Law
Cromwell University
Deakin University
De La Salle University
De Paul University (France)
Dominion Herbal College
Duarte Costa University
Eastern University
Emerson College of Herbology
European University Institute
Everyman's University
Fort Wayne Bible College
Geo-Metaphysical Institute
Graduate School of Human Behavior
Graduate School of Patent Resources Institute
Graduate University
Gulf Coast Bible College
Hamburger University
Harley University
Hawthorne University
Headlands University
Holistic Life University
Holy Names College
Illinois School of Professional Psychology
Instituto Politecnico Nacional
International Graduate School

International University (California)
International University (Greece)
International University (New York)
International University (Philippines)
International University (Switzerland)
Inter-State University
John F. Kennedy University
Johnson Bible College
Karma University
Kingsley University
Lafayette University
La Jolla University
Lincoln Christian College
London School for Social Research
Martin Center College
Maryville College
Massey University
Metropolitan State College
Moody Bible Institute
Morris College
National College for the Natural Healing Arts
National Institute for Higher Education
North American Colleges of Natural
    Health Science
North Continental University
Northern Utah Management Institute
Northwest London College of Applied Science
Northwest London University
Norwich University
Open University of the Netherlands
People's Law School
Philadelphia College of the Bible
Prachathipok University
Professional Studies Institute
Ramkamhaeng University
Rangoon Arts and Sciences University
Reformed Bible College
Rockwell University
Roskilde University Center
Sacred Heart University
St. John's University (Louisiana)
St. Joseph University
Santa Fe College of Natural Medicine
Saybrook Institute

School of Natural Healing
Sonoma Institute
Southern Institute of Technology
Southeast Asia Interdisciplinary
    Development Institute
Southwest University
Southwestern University
Staton University
Swinburne College of Technology
Tennessee Southern University
Tennessee Wesleyan College
Thomas Jefferson University (Missouri)
Trinity College of Medicine
Tyler Kent College of Medicine
Universidad de Monterrey
Universidad Estatal a Distancia
Universidad Iberoamericana
Universidad La Salle
Universidad Mexicana del Noreste
Universidad Nacional Autonoma de Mexico
Universidad Nacional Abierta
Universidad Nacional de Educacion a Distancia
Universidad Nacional de Educacion Enrique
    Guzman y Valle
Universidad Tecnologica de Santiago
Universite de Paris
Universiti Sains Malaysia
University of Delhi
University of England
University of Man's Best Friend
University of New England
University of New South Wales
University of Quebec
University of the President
Uppsala University
Vermont College
Vermont State College System
Washington Bible College
Wentworth Institute of Technology
Western Australian Institute of Technology
Western College
Western University
Wild Rose College of Natural Healing
World University of America

GOODBYE

American Floating University: no longer in business

Atlantic Institute of Education: public funds cut off, and went out of business in 1982

California Institute of Asian Studies: name changed to California Institute of Integral Studies

California Western University: name changed to California Coast University

Carthage College: no non-traditional programs

Centro de Estudios Universitarios Xochicalco: letters to both competing schools of this name returned as undeliverable

Colegio Jacinto Trevino: letters returned as undeliverable

Connecticut Board for State Academic Awards: name changed to Charter Oak College

Escuela de Medicina de Saltillo: letters returned as undeliverable

Graduate School of Suggestive Sciences: letters returned as undeliverable

Humanistic Psychology Institute: name changed to Saybrook Institute

International Graduate School of Behavioral Science: absorbed into the Florida Institute of Technology

International Studies in Humanistic Psychology: program no longer offered

Juarez-Lincoln Bilingual University: letters returned as undeliverable

La Salle Extension University: out of business. La Salle lost its accreditation in 1981 after years of continuing problems with the Federal Trade Commission, struggled on for a while, and finally closed its doors in 1982.

Morgan State College: no longer offers non-traditional program

Prometheus College: out of business

Open University of America: see University of Mid-America, this section

Southeastern University (South Carolina): following an F.B.I. investigation, which clearly established the school as a degree mill, owner Alfred Q. Jarrette committed suicide, and the school went out of business

Synthesis Graduate School for the Study of Man: apparently no longer in business. Letters not returned, but no telephone listing any more

University of Canterbury: apparently no longer in business. Letters not returned, but no telephone listing any more

University of Central Arizona: closed following a consent judgment by the State of Arizona on 14 counts of consumer fraud. This school was far more legitimate than a number of the out-and-out fradulent degree mills that have been operating in Arizona before, during, and after the closing of U.C.A.

University of Mid-America: this heavily funded (millions of dollars) attempt to establish a nationwide non-resident university, eventually to be called the Open University of America, was abandoned in 1982. The University claimed that they were cut loose by the foundations just when things were about to get going. Critics suggested that both the rate of progress and the nature of the work undertaken left things to be desired.

Vermont Institute of Community Involvement: name changed to Burlington College

Washington International College: went out of business in 1982

Windsor University: letters returned as undeliverable

Index to Subjects

Index to Schools

This index lists every school mentioned in the book. "U" stands for "university" and "C" stands for "college."

261

Indiana Northern Graduate
School, 111
Indiana State U, 60, 177, 219
Indiana U, (Indiana), 49, 60,
112, 177, 190
Indiana U (Pennsylvania), 112,
180
Institut des Hautes Etudes
Commercials, 219
Institut Electrotechnique, 219
Institut International de Haute
Etudes, 219
Institut Moderne Polytechnique,
219
Institut Normal de Culture
Generale, 219
Institut of Management
Specialists, 219
Institut Patriarcal St. Irenee, 219
Institut Superieur Technique et
Colonial, 219
Institut Technique Superieur,
219
Institute Academy, 219
Institute for the Advanced Study
of Human Sexuality, 112
Institute of Excellence, 219
Institute of Galiennique du
Rouergue, 219
Institute of Hypnotherapy, 219
Institute of Life Science, 219
Institute of Social Order, 219
Institute of the International
Thyrological Academy,
219
Instituto de Estudios
Iberoamericanos, 113
Instituto Politecnico Nacional,
113
Intelligent Services, 219
Inter-American U, 219
Inter-State, U, 220
Inter-University Service, 220
Interamerican U, 190
Intercollegiate U, 219
Internation U, 219
International Academy, 219
International Academy for
Planetary Planning, 219
International American U, 219
International Association of
Hypnotists, 219
International Bible Institute &
Seminary, 203
International C, 50, 51, 113

International C of Associates in
Medicine, 219
International Corporation of
Engineers, 219
International Federation of
Scientific Research
Societies, 220
International Free Protestant
Episcopal U, 220
International
Geistewissenschaftliches
Hochschule, 220
International Graduate School,
50, 113
International Graduate School of
Behavior, 258
International Honorary Awards
Committee, 220
International Institute for
Advanced Studies, 51,
114
International Institute of Arts,
220
International Institute of
Information, 220
International Knights of
Goodwill, 220
International Neoreligische
Fakultat, 220
International Protestant Birkbest
C, 220
International Spiritualist U, 203
International Studies in
Humanistic Psychology,
258
International U (California), 114
International U (Greece), 114
International U (Illinois), 220
International U (Missouri), 114
International U (New York), 115
International U (Philippines),
115
International U (Switzerland),
115
Iona C, 115
Iowa State U, 115
Iowa State U, 177
Iowa Wesleyan C, 177
Ithaca C, 179

Jackson State C, 178
Jackson State U, 220
Jacksonville State U, 176
Jacksonville U, 177

James Madison U, 181
Jamestown C, 180
Janta Engineering C, 220
Japan Christian C, 220
Jarvis Christian C, 181
Jefferson U, 149
Jersey City State C, 179
Johann Keppler School of
Medicine, 221
John Brown U, 176
John F. Kennedy U, 116, 190
John Quincy Adams C, 220
Johns Hopkins U, 116
Johnson Bible C, 199
Johnson C. Smith C, 179
Johnson State C, 181
Johnston State C, 116
Juarez-Lincoln Bilingual U
Judson C, 176
Julliard School, 179
Juniata C, 180

Kansas State Teachers C, 178
Kansas State U, 116, 178
Kansas Wesleyan U, 178
Karma U, 116
Kean C, 116
Kearney State C, 179
Keene State C, 179
Kennedy U, 116
Kensington U, 50, 51, 116
Kent State U, 180
Kentucky State C, 178
Kentucky Wesleyan C, 178
Keppler School of Medicine,
221
King C, 181
Kings C, 117
Kingsley U, 221
Klempner Institute, 179
Knoxville State C, 180

La Jolla U, 117
La Salle C, 180
La Salle Extension U, 258
Lafayette U, 221
Lake Erie C, 117, 180, 182
Lakeland C, 181
Lamar State C, 181
Lamar U, 117
Lambuth C, 181
Lamp Beacon U, 221
Lander C, 180

About the Personal Counseling Services Available

If you would like personal advice and recommendations, based on your own specific situation, a personal counseling service is available, by mail. I started this service in 1977, at the request of many readers. The actual personal evaluations and consulting are done by two friends and colleagues of mine, who are leading experts in the field of non-traditional education, under my own close supervision and direction.

For the modest consulting fee of $35 ($40 for persons outside the United States), these three things are done:

1. You will get a long personal letter (usually three or four typewritten pages), evaluating your situation, recommending the best schools, and estimating how long it will take and what it will cost to complete your degree.

2. You will get answers to any specific questions you may have, with regard to any schools you may now be considering, schools you have already dealt with, or other relevant matters.

3. You will get detailed, up-to-the-minute information sheets on schools and degree programs, equivalency examinations, and other relevant topics, in the form of one to ten-page handouts.

If you are interested in this personal consulting service, please write for free detailed information on the service. We will send you descriptive literature, and a counseling Questionnaire, without obligation.

Once you have these materials, if you wish counseling, simply fill out the Questionnaire and return it, along with the fee, and your personal reply and report will be prepared and sent to you.

For free information on this service, write or telephone:

Degree Consulting Services
P.O. Box 2146
Santa Monica, California 90406
(213) 395-2896

NOTE: Use this address only for matters related to the counseling service. For all other matters, write to me at Ten Speed Press, PO Box 7123, Berkeley, CA 94707.

—John Bear, Ph.D.